Faith in Democracy

Why have some churches in Africa engaged in advocacy for stronger liberal democratic institutions while others have not? *Faith in Democracy* explores this question, emphasizing the benefits of liberal democratic protections for some churches. The book explains how churches' historic investments create different autocratic risk exposure, as states can more easily regulate certain activities – including social service provision – than others. In situations where churches have invested in schools as part of their evangelization activities, which create high autocratic risk, churches have incentives to defend liberal democratic institutions to protect their control over them. This theory also explains how church fiscal dependence on the state interacts with education provision to change incentives for advocacy. Empirically, the book demonstrates when churches engage in democratic activism, drawing on church-level data from across the continent, and the effects of church activism, drawing on microlevel evidence from Zambia, Tanzania, and Ghana.

Kate Baldwin is Associate Professor of Political Science and Global Affairs at Yale University. She is the author of *The Paradox of Traditional Chiefs in Democratic Africa* (2016), which was awarded the Gaddis Smith International Book Prize.

Cambridge Studies in Comparative Politics

General Editors

Anna Grzymala-Busse, *Stanford University*
Dan Slater, *University of Michigan*

Associate Editors

Lisa Blaydes, *Stanford University*
Catherine Boone, *London School of Economics and Political Science*
Thad Dunning, *University of California, Berkeley*
Anna Grzymala-Busse, *Stanford University*
Torben Iversen, *Harvard University*
Stathis Kalyvas, *University of Oxford*
Melanie Manion, *Duke University*
Prerna Singh, *Brown University*
Dan Slater, *University of Michigan*
Susan Stokes, *University of Chicago*
Tariq Thachil, *University of Pennsylvania*
Erik Wibbels, *University of Pennsylvania*

Series Founder

Peter Lange, *Duke University*

Editors Emeritus

Margaret Levi, *Stanford University*
Kathleen Thelen, *Massachusetts Institute of Technology*

Other Books in the Series

Killian Clarke *Return of Tyranny: Why Counterrevolutions Emerge and Succeed*
Tanu Kumar, *Building Social Mobility: How Subsidized Homeownership Creates Wealth, Dignity, and Voice in India*
Luis Schiumerini, *Incumbency Bias: Why Political Office is a Blessing* and *a Curse in Latin America*
Alexander Reisenbichler, *Through the Roof: Housing, Capitalism, and the State in America and Germany*
Raúl L. Madrid, *The Birth of Democracy in South America*
Nicholas Kuipers, *States against Nations: Meritocracy, Patronage, and the Challenges of Bureaucratic Selection*
Nicholas Barnes, *Inside Criminalized Governance: How and Why Gangs Rule the Streets of Rio de Janeiro*

(Continued after the Index)

Faith in Democracy

The Logic of Church Advocacy for Liberal Democratic Institutions in Africa

KATE BALDWIN
Yale University

CAMBRIDGE
UNIVERSITY PRESS

Shaftesbury Road, Cambridge CB2 8EA, United Kingdom

One Liberty Plaza, 20th Floor, New York, NY 10006, USA

477 Williamstown Road, Port Melbourne, VIC 3207, Australia

314–321, 3rd Floor, Plot 3, Splendor Forum, Jasola District Centre,
New Delhi – 110025, India

103 Penang Road, #05–06/07, Visioncrest Commercial, Singapore 238467

Cambridge University Press is part of Cambridge University Press & Assessment,
a department of the University of Cambridge.

We share the University's mission to contribute to society through the pursuit of
education, learning and research at the highest international levels of excellence.

www.cambridge.org
Information on this title: www.cambridge.org/9781009391627
DOI: 10.1017/9781009391634

© Kate Baldwin 2026

This publication is in copyright. Subject to statutory exception and to the provisions
of relevant collective licensing agreements, no reproduction of any part may take
place without the written permission of Cambridge University Press & Assessment.

When citing this work, please include a reference to the
DOI 10.1017/9781009391634

First published 2026

Cover image: School kids on break at Sacred Heart Cathedral of the Catholic
Diocese of Kericho, Kericho, Kenya. Architect: John McAslan & Partners, 2016.
(Photo by: Edmund Sumner/View Pictures/Universal Images Group via Getty Images)

A catalogue record for this publication is available from the British Library

*A Cataloging-in-Publication data record for this book is available from the
Library of Congress*

ISBN 978-1-009-39165-8 Hardback
ISBN 978-1-009-39162-7 Paperback

Cambridge University Press & Assessment has no responsibility for the persistence
or accuracy of URLs for external or third-party internet websites referred to in this
publication and does not guarantee that any content on such websites is, or will
remain, accurate or appropriate.

For EU product safety concerns, contact us at Calle de José Abascal,
56, 1°, 28003 Madrid, Spain, or email eugpsr@cambridge.org

For my parents Kristin and Richard and my daughter Anna

Contents

List of Figures	*page* ix
List of Tables	xi
Acknowledgments	xv

PART I THEORY

1. Church Interests in Liberal Democracy — 3
2. Liberal Democracy as an Institutional Guarantee of Church Interests — 29
3. The Politics of Church Education in Sub-Saharan Africa — 46

PART II TESTING THE MAIN HYPOTHESES

4. Evidence on Church Democratic Activism in Africa: The Effect of Church Schools and Autocratic Risk Exposure — 73
5. Evidence on Catholic Democratic Activism in Africa: The Effect of Church School Dependence on State Subsidies — 100

PART III TESTING UNDERLYING ASSUMPTIONS

6. Church Activism and Support for Liberal Democratic Institutions: Evidence from Zambia and Tanzania — 121
7. Tracing Liberal Democracy's Influence on Educational Policy: Evidence from Zambia, Ghana, and Beyond — 157

PART IV EXTENSIONS AND IMPLICATIONS

8. Church School Legacies for Citizenship: Evidence from Zambia and Tanzania — 201

9 Reconsidering Churches, Education, and Democracy in the Contemporary World   233

Appendices   245
Bibliography   269
Index   283

Figures

1.1	Proportion of countries with union or church activism for liberal democracy	page 11
1.2	Proportion of countries with church activism for aspects of liberal democracy	13
2.1	Predictions of the theory for church democratic activism	42
3.1	Christian mission-school students per 1,000 people circa 1925	60
3.2	Percentage of students at church-affiliated schools (average across primary and secondary schools) circa 2008	65
4.1	Amount of state financing of church education against amount of church education provision (church-level observations) circa 2008	85
5.1	Proportion of country years in which at least one collective pastoral letter was issued with content indicated	110
5.2	Catholic democratic activism by time to public school fee removal	114
6.1	Timeline of opposition leader's arrest and church statements in Zambia	136
6.2	Average marginal component effects on likelihood of voting for candidate by endorsement condition	142
6.3	Average marginal component effect of antidemocratic position by endorsement condition and respondent religion	144
6.4	Timeline of opposition leader assassination attempt and church activism in Tanzania	147

6.5 Levels of support for candidate proposing legal changes to workers' rights by endorsement conditions for (a) all respondents, (b) Catholic respondents, (c) Protestant respondents, (d) Muslim respondents ... 155
7.1 Timeline of events expanding and contracting church educational control ... 192
8.1 Catholic primary school access by birth year ... 208

Tables

1.1	Mapping the book's theoretical claims to evidence	page 26
3.1	Significant religious parties in the thirty-four country sample, 1970–2020	51
3.2	Classifying church school finances	68
4.1	Measuring church democratic activism	81
4.2	Testing the effects of religious denomination and co-religious identity on church democratic activism	87
4.3	Testing the effects of ethnic and class identity on church democratic activism	88
4.4	Testing the effects of civil society capacity and religious competition on church democratic activism	90
4.5	Testing effect of autocratic risk exposure on church democratic activism: church education provision	93
4.6	Testing effect of autocratic risk exposure on church democratic activism: extensions	95
5.1	Comparing countries that removed school fees by the status of church primary schools	106
5.2	Effect of fee removal on church primary school enrollment	107
5.3	Effect of fee removal on critical pastoral letters	113
5.4	Effect of fee removal on other outcomes	115
6.1	Percentage of respondents reporting the organization to be in favor of or against democratic government	132
6.2	Effect of church statements on assessments of democracy	138
6.3	Support for candidates by endorsement conditions and candidate's political attributes	144

6.4	Key passages from pastoral letters issued during Easter season, 2018	149
6.5	Candidate pair conditions in the Tanzanian survey	153
7.1	Episodes of analysis in Zambia	161
7.2	Episodes of analysis in Ghana	163
7.3	Relationship between liberal democracy and policy changes to church educational control	194
8.1	Comparison of (former) Catholic primary schools, pre- and post-government handover	209
8.2	Effects of Catholic schools on conversion and primary school completion	214
8.3	Effects of Catholic school attendance on socioeconomic status and political attitudes – men	216
8.4	Effects of Catholic school attendance on socioeconomic status and political attitudes – women	217
8.5	Comparison of mission and government schools in colonial Tanzania	223
8.6	Effects of father's religious school attendance on socioeconomic, religious, linguistic, and political outcomes (Christians only)	228
8.7	Effects of mother's religious school attendance on socioeconomic, religious, linguistic, and political outcomes (Christians only)	230
A.1	List of interviews	245
B.1	Summary statistics for country-level data set on church and union democratic activism (1988–1998 and 2009–2018)	248
B.2	Summary statistics for church-level democratic activism data set (2009–2018)	250
B.3	Summary statistics for Catholic democratic activism data set (1980–2018)	255
B.4	Summary statistics for church educational control data set (independence–2018)	257
B.5	Variables in Zambia opinion survey data set (summary statistics for birth years 1958–1973)	258
B.6	Variables in Tanzania household survey data set (summary statistics for Christian families in sample)	260
C.1	Relationship between liberal democratic checks index and policy changes to church educational control	262

D.1	Effects of Catholic schools on conversion and primary school completion (1958–1976 birth years)	263
D.2	Effects of Catholic school attendance on socioeconomic status and political attitudes – men (1958–1976 birth years)	264
D.3	Effects of Catholic school attendance on socioeconomic status and political attitudes – women (1958–1976 birth years)	265
D.4	Catholic schools, conversion, and primary school completion – dichotomous measure of access	266
D.5	Effects of Catholic school attendance on socioeconomic status and political attitudes – men – dichotomous measure of access	267
D.6	Effects of Catholic school attendance on socioeconomic status and political attitudes – women – dichotomous measure of access	268

Acknowledgments

The writing of this book has been a long journey. I initially approached the topic through an interest in the implications of church social service provision for political accountability in fledgling democracies in sub-Saharan Africa. But as I watched creeping authoritarianism in many of my cases of interest, my focus quickly turned to understanding why some churches spoke out forcefully in defense of democratic institutions, including in Burundi, the Democratic Republic of the Congo, and Zambia, while many others did not. These observations reoriented my research around explaining the causes and effects of varied church activism for liberal democratic institutions.

My thanks go first to the numerous people in Ghana, Tanzania, and Zambia who spoke with me and answered my survey questions. Thank you for helping me understand the complexity of the relationship between churches, education, and democratic institutions in your communities.

I was lucky to complete the work on this book as part of the vibrant academic community at Yale. I am thankful for exceptional feedback from Dawn Brancati, Maria Jose Hierro, Egor Lazarev, Daniel Mattingly, Isabela Mares, Gerard Padro-i-Miguel, Didac Queralt, Joan Ricart-Huguet, Jeremy Seekings, Emily Sellars, Milan Svolik, Steven Wilkinson, and Elisabeth Wood in the Department of Political Science. Special thanks to Ana de la O for all her advice and friendship. I also thank Eran Rubenstein for his insights and ongoing collaboration in studying religious education systems in and beyond sub-Saharan Africa. The subject of this book is inherently interdisciplinary, and I am grateful to Michael Glerup at Yale's Project on Religious Freedom and Society in Africa, and John Azumah, a visiting professor at Yale's Divinity School and director of the Lamin Sanneh Institute at the University of Ghana, for opening doors to other disciplines. I thank Mira Debs and her Education Studies class for providing detailed comments on two chapters of the manuscript.

Beyond Yale, I thank the following scholars for sharing their expertise with me: Ellen Lust for data collection opportunities through the Governance and Local Development Institute (GLD), Elizabeth Sperber for her knowledge of pastoral letters, T. J. D'Agostino and Nicole Garnett for their systematic information on Catholic school systems around the world, Cati Coe for her understanding of education in Ghana, and David Owusu-Ansah for his research on religious education in West Africa.

I could not have completed this book without the support and companionship of Dawn Teele and Alisha Holland, who suggested the virtual writing group that ensured this project continued to move forward during the COVID-19 pandemic. I also thank Dawn Teele's Frontiers of Empirical Political Science class at John Hopkins University for its detailed feedback on the first half of the book. I am grateful to Alexandra Scacco, Rebecca Weitz-Shapiro, and Matthew Winters for providing an incredible support network and always being available to weigh in on issues, no matter how big or small.

The book benefited enormously from a book conference organized through the Yale Junior Faculty Manuscript and Research Colloquium and the Yale Macmillan Center. Thanks to Melani Cammett for her insight on how to articulate key claims, Kimuli Kasara for her ability to point out empirical and logical gaps, Gwyneth McClendon for her clarity of vision in suggesting how to streamline my theory and empirical sections, Daniel Posner for his insight into the relationship between churches and democratic institutions, David Stasavage for his elucidation of the book's contribution to the study of democracy, and Jeremy Weinstein for his advice on tightening the argument and presentation of evidence. Ken Scheve deserves special mention for chairing the conference as does Shikhar Singh for helping to organize it. I am also grateful for constructive feedback from seminar participants at Columbia University, Harvard University, the London School of Economics, Princeton University, and the University of Pennsylvania.

I would like to thank the dozens of research assistants who worked on the project including Sepo Lemba in Zambia and Ansila Kweka and Febronia Massawe in Tanzania. Many thanks to Innovations for Poverty Action (IPA) for assistance with survey data collection in Tanzania and to Maxim Fison Mujenja's team at Ubuntu Research and Rural Development Company Ltd. for overseeing survey data collection in

Zambia. At Yale, I am thankful to Charlotte Bednarski, Dermot Byrne, Enoch Osei Koduah, Gerardo Manrique de Lara Ruiz, Laila Delpuppo Messari, Sam Weber, and Jiayi Zhang for their significant contributions to the data collection. Thanks also to Kat Berman, Ritik Chamola, James Casemore, Olivia Canie, Steven Dykstra, Sakshi Hallan, Chaste Niwe, Helen Qi, Morgan Ross, Gall Sigler, Eliana Singer, Teigist Taye, Shawn Thacker, and Alissa Wong for research assistance.

Many thanks to the Global Religion Research Initiative at the University of Notre Dame, the Jackson School of Global Affairs at Yale University, the Yale Macmillan Center, the Yale Institution for Social and Policy Studies, and the Yale Junior Faculty Manuscript and Research Colloquium for funding support. At Cambridge University Press, I am grateful to Rachel Blaifeder for her encouragement at key stages and to the series editors Anna Grzymala-Busse and Dan Slater for supporting the project. Thanks also to Joy Scharfstein for her excellent copy editing and to Jessica Hickle for editorial assistance.

My final thanks go to my family. Thank you to my husband Kiran for his endless support, including knowing whether either a laugh or a practical suggestion is most needed at any given time. Thank you to my son Alden for his cheerful encouragement, to my in-laws Gayatri and Keshav for providing extra help with a smile at key points, and to my sisters Juliet and Jane for their lifelong confidence. This book is dedicated to my parents Kristin and Richard and my daughter Anna. Thank you for providing me with love and optimism.

PART I

THEORY

I

Church Interests in Liberal Democracy

Core liberal democratic institutions have been under attack by politicians around the world since the beginning of the twenty-first century. Many rulers seek to avoid the constraints of strong legislatures, autonomous judiciaries, independent media, and well-established opposition parties.[1] Scholars and policymakers often project fatalism in describing the unchecked rise of illiberal regimes.[2]

But liberal democracy has some brave advocates. Consider the case of one Zambian organization that repeatedly stood up to President Edgar Lungu's attacks on liberal democratic institutions between 2015 and 2021. When the government introduced a bill to reduce the power of the legislature, this organization educated members of parliament about the bill's implications. When the administration shuttered independent newspapers and TV and radio stations, it spoke out against the closures. When the police arrested the main opposition leader on charges of treason and threw him in jail for four months, it mobilized popular opinion against the arrest and facilitated talks between the president and the opposition leader that led to the latter's release. This organization did not mince words in its advocacy against the attacks on liberal democracy, pointing out to Zambians, "Our country is now all, except in designation, a dictatorship and if it is not yet, then we are not far from it."[3]

---

[1] Bermeo 2016; Graham and Svolik 2020; Slater 2013.
[2] Plattner 2019; Zakaria 1997.
[3] Zambia Conference of Catholic Bishops, "If You Want Justice Work for Peace: Statement on the Current Political Situation in Zambia," April 23, 2017.

Which organization took this bold stance? Popular accounts often emphasize the role of young activists and novel social movements in defending democracy.[4] Scholars of democracy tend to give special attention either to representatives of the working class, such as trade unions, or capitalist interest groups, including business associations.[5] But the organization that spoke up so forcefully in response to the attacks on liberal institutions was none of these. Interestingly, it was the Zambia Conference of Catholic Bishops that did this work, sometimes acting alone and sometimes acting in partnership with other church groups.

From many perspectives, this activism by the Zambian Catholic bishops is puzzling. Why would an organization that is primarily focused on saving souls stick its neck out in defense of liberal democratic institutions? Why would a religious group support democratic processes that empower men to decide laws when their own religious texts are believed to provide the foundation of governance? Church leaders may seem more likely to align with autocrats who promise them religious monopolies than to embrace liberal democratic institutions that promote the individuals' right to oppose authority.

And certainly, for every example of a church standing up for liberal democratic institutions in the contemporary period, as in Zambia, there are multiple examples of churches remaining silent or even explicitly supporting rulers' attacks on liberal democracy. For instance, on the same continent, the Catholic Church in Benin failed to speak out forcefully in the face of democratic backsliding after President Patrice Talon took power in 2016. The Catholic bishops there did not comment on the political manipulations that prevented any opposition party from contesting the 2019 legislative elections and only issued calls to stop the violence and find a peaceful solution when angry citizens took to the streets after the elections to protest their illegitimacy.[6] Similarly, the historically influential Lutheran churches in Namibia have not spoken up in support of liberal democratic checks on the ruling party's power in the postindependence period. They were notably silent when the country's constitution

---

[4] For example, Senegal's Y'en a Marre, South Africa's #FeesMustFall, and the Occupy Nigeria and End SARS movements in Nigeria have all been hailed as youth movements that can potentially advance democracy in sub-Saharan Africa.

[5] Acemoglu and Robinson 2006; Ansell and Samuels 2014; Arriola 2013; Boix 2003; Rueschemeyer, Stephens, and Stephens 1992.

[6] *Crux*, "Benin Bishops Accused of Supporting Government after Controversial Election," May 11, 2019, https://cruxnow.com/church-in-africa/2019/05/benin-bishops-accused-of-supporting-government-after-controversial-election.

was changed to allow President Sam Nujoma a third term in 1997.[7] The leaders of the largest Lutheran church even released a pastoral letter in 2007 attacking local human rights organizations for their efforts to hold Nujoma accountable for past actions against opponents.[8]

As a result, an adequate explanation for why some churches engage in advocacy for liberal democratic institutions must also explain why other churches do not. Churches are contingent, rather than inherent, activists for liberal democracy.[9] This book explains the logic of why some churches decide it is in their interest to engage in activism for these institutions.

Many existing theories of religious politics cannot explain this variation since they start from the premise that any political engagement by churches is a detriment to democracy. As a result of their presumed prioritization of religious teachings as a basis for law, churches are often viewed as inherent opponents of democratic institutions, which instead empower citizens to make laws.[10] Church political engagement is thought to make democratic compromise on issues more difficult.[11] Indeed, in nineteenth-century Europe and Latin America, the Catholic Church was one of the main opponents of the introduction of liberal democracy, with Pope Pius IX declaring it an error to think "that the Roman Pontiff can and ought to reconcile himself to, and agree with, progress, liberalism and modern civilization."[12]

Some recent scholarship indicates that the tension between church goals and liberal democratic institutions may no longer be as stark. Groundbreaking new work documents the importance of internal institutional innovation within the medieval Catholic Church in creating the foundations for the rule of law and representative assemblies.[13] And church views on religious liberty and human rights have evolved in the past century, particularly in the Catholic Church since the Second Vatican Council in the 1960s.[14] Research demonstrates that liberal democracy does not as an empirical matter require full separation of

---

[7] Botha 2016; Groop 2012.
[8] Oswald Shivute, "NSHR Meets Church Critics," *Namibian*, September 17, 2007, www.namibian.com.na/nshr-meets-church-critics/.
[9] The phrase "contingent democrats" is from Bellin 2000, who described labor and capital in these terms.
[10] Hook 1940.
[11] Rawls 1993.
[12] Pope Pius IX, Syllabus of Errors, 1864.
[13] Grzymała-Busse 2023.
[14] Huntington 1991; Philpott 2004.

church from politics and governance.[15] Scholars show that some church leaders have both theological and material motivations for engaging in political activism for human rights, with examples of Catholic or Protestant churches supporting opponents of autocratic regimes in the late twentieth century in settings as diverse as Chile, the Philippines, Poland, and South Korea.[16]

But existing scholarship generally stops short of offering a positive explanation for varied church advocacy for liberal democracy as opposed to its advocacy for human rights more broadly. Likewise, Christian scriptures contain teachings relevant to human rights but do not contain explicit tenets about the value of democracy as a form of government. As a Nigerian Catholic bishop reminded the audience in a lecture series on the relationship between the church and multiparty democracy in Africa, Jesus did not live in a time or place of democracy.[17]

We lack an adequate explanation for why some churches engage in advocacy for liberal democratic institutions specifically. Why do some church leaders mobilize around the quality of elections, rulers' violations of the constitutional limits on their power, and the rights of political opposition, while other church leaders remain silent on these issues or even support these power grabs? With this book, I seek to explain why churches may pursue activism for liberal democracy as a strategy for advancing their more fundamental interest in spreading the teaching of the gospel.

AFRICAN CHURCHES AS MAJORS ACTORS IN ADVOCACY FOR LIBERAL DEMOCRATIC INSTITUTIONS

The Zambian bishops' campaign described in the opening pages of this chapter is not exceptional. However, to date, we have not had a clear sense of how frequently churches engage in activism for liberal democratic institutions due to an absence of data. Among the tasks I undertake in this book is to show that churches are significant actors in advocacy for liberal democratic institutions and that there are significant differences among them in whether they choose to engage in this kind of activism, with considerable variation both within and across countries. I present

---

[15] Fox 2020; Stepan 2001.
[16] Gill 1998; McClendon and Riedl 2019; Toft, Philpott, and Shah 2011.
[17] Presentation by Most Rev. Matthew Hassan Kukah, Bishop of Sokoto, Sanneh Institute Virtual Lecture Series, June 2021.

new evidence from original data collected across sub-Saharan Africa to highlight the degree to which churches engage in activism for various aspects of liberal democracy. But before turning to the data, I offer some examples that highlight the range of activities in which African churches engaged when they chose to participate in democratic activism in the late twentieth and early twenty-first centuries.

Numerous Catholic and Protestant church leaders in Africa participated in democratization campaigns at the end of the Cold War. For example, high-ranking Kenyan clergymen opposed President Daniel arap Moi's efforts to further centralize power and spearheaded efforts to protect the secret ballot in elections in the 1980s.[18] Leaders within the Kenyan Presbyterian and Anglican churches were the first public voices calling for the introduction of a multiparty system in early 1990, with politicians only subsequently taking this position.[19] Similarly, churches in Malawi set off that country's transition from one-party rule when the Catholic Church released a critical Lenten letter – read in all parishes in the country – in March 1992, breaking the silence around the country's political institutions.[20] Catholic and Presbyterian churches subsequently supported the country's democratic transition through a coordinated dialogue with opposition groups and the government.[21]

Further, and less widely recognized, a considerable number of African churches continue to advocate for liberal democracy in the twenty-first century as elected rulers have sought to eliminate checks on their power. For example, the Burundian Catholic bishops raised early opposition to President Pierre Nkurunziza's circumvention of the country's constitutional two-term limit in 2015, releasing a statement in all churches that clarified that the constitution limited the presidency to two terms.[22] Following the subsequent crackdown on opposition supporters and the independent media, the bishops withdrew church representatives from the electoral commission in protest of the unfair conditions under which

---

[18] Sabar-Friedman 1997; Widner 1992.
[19] Widner 1992, 192. Reverend Timothy Njoya was the first to draw the parallels between the situation in Eastern Europe and Kenya in a New Year's sermon to mark the start of 1990, while Bishop Henry Okullu openly called for a multiparty system in early May 1990. Two former KANU cabinet ministers, Kenneth Matiba and Charles Rubia, only subsequently took up this claim in a prominent press conference.
[20] Catholic Bishops of Malawi, "Living Our Faith," March 10, 1992.
[21] Ross 1995, 105.
[22] Conference Des Eveques Catholiques du Burundi, "Deuxieme Message de La Conference des Eveques Catholiques du Burundi en Vue des Elections de 2015," March 6, 2015.

the 2015 election was being held.[23] In the run-up to the 2018 constitutional referendum that further eliminated checks on the president's power, the bishops publicly opposed these changes.[24]

Similarly, in the Democratic Republic of the Congo, Catholic bishops played a key role in protecting checks on the power of the executive as President Joseph Kabila's second term came to a close. The bishops released multiple public statements opposing constitutional changes that would permit Kabila a third term.[25] In addition, the bishops convened and mediated a conference to agree on rules that would limit Kabila's power when the country lapsed into an extra-constitutional period in December 2016, hammering out a deal that stipulated that the existing constitution and electoral laws would govern this period, that a prime minister from the opposition would be appointed during the transitional period, and that numerous political detainees would be released.[26] When Kabila continued to drag his feet in implementing the details of the accords, the bishops issued a powerful pastoral letter that called on people "to stand up" for their rights "in public spaces" and then legitimated a series of Sunday protests organized by a Catholic association, the Comité Laïc de Coordination (CLC), demanding that elections be held.[27]

---

[23] *News 24*, "Catholic Church Says Withdrawing Support for Burundi Polls," May 28, 2015, www.news24.com/news24/catholic-church-says-withdrawing-support-for-burundi-polls-20150528. See also Conference Des Eveques Catholiques du Burundi, "Communique de La Conference des Eveques Catholiques du Burundi Concernant La Periode Actuelle De Preparation Des Elections de 2015," May 5, 2015.

[24] *Iwacu*, "CECAB: The Current Context Is Not Propitious for an Amendment to the Constitution," May 7, 2018, www.iwacu-burundi.org/englishnews/referendum-campaign-kick-off/.

[25] *Le Potential*, "Congo-Kinshasa: Révision constitutionnelle – la CENCO dit non," March 5, 2013; Conference Episcopale Nationale du Congo, "Protegéons notre nation : pour un processus électoral apaisé et porteur d'un avenir meilleur : message de la 51ème Assemblée plénière des evêques membres de la Conférence épiscopale nationale du Congo," June 27, 2014; Conference Episcopale Nationale du Congo, "Lettre des eveques de la conference episcopale national du Congo aux fideles catholiques et aux hommes et femmes de bonne volonte de la Republique Democratique du Congo," September 14, 2014.

[26] Weber 2020; United States Conference of Catholic Bishops, "Backgrounder on the Democratic Republic of the Congo," 2018.

[27] Conference Episcopal Nationale du Congo, "Le Pays Va Tres Mal. Debout, Congolais! Decembre 2017 Approche," June 23, 2017. Weber 2020 notes that although attitudes toward the CLC varied among Congolese bishops and levels of support for the protests varied across diocese, the bishops collectively signed off on key documents permitting the activities of the CLC.

In another example, Catholic and Lutheran bishops in Tanzania spoke out against the stifling of liberal democratic rights under President John Magufuli. When numerous opposition party members and political activists in Tanzania were attacked or disappeared, individual church leaders spoke out during Christmas sermons in December 2017. During the Lent and Easter seasons of 2018, Catholic and Lutheran churches alike issued collective pastoral letters against this suppression of democratic principles.[28]

Turning again to Zambia, Catholic and Protestant churches there successfully helped to defend that country's democratic institutions multiple times in the twenty-first century. When President Frederick Chiluba announced that he would consider a bid for a third term in 2001, the umbrella bodies of the major churches, including the Zambia Episcopal Conference (representing the Catholic Church), the Christian Council of Zambia (CCZ, representing mainline Protestant churches), and the Evangelical Fellowship of Zambia (EFZ, representing many evangelical churches), joined forces through the Oasis Forum to provide public education in support of term limits, organize peaceful demonstrations against a third term, and coordinate with anti-third term politicians inside the governing party.[29] When President Edgar Lungu introduced a constitutional amendment in 2019 that proposed reducing the power of the legislature and the judiciary to check the president, these organizations again engaged in civic education against the bill and participated in lobbying efforts directed at parliamentarians, helping to ensure enough votes to defeat the bill.[30]

The success of these church campaigns for liberal democratic institutions varied from case to case but in all instances, rulers viewed the threat as sufficiently large to merit venomous responses. Ruling party leaders accused the Zambian bishops of spreading misinformation, Tanzanian authorities threatened Catholic and Lutheran religious leaders with travel bans and legal action if they did not walk back their criticism, violent

---

[28] Tanzania Episcopal Conference, "Lenten Letter," February 11, 2018; Evangelical Lutheran Church in Tanzania, "Our Nation, Our Peace," March 15, 2018.

[29] This alliance of churches and civil society organizations in support of presidential term limits was called the Oasis Forum because it was founded in the Oasis Restaurant in Lusaka. Gould 2006, 933, 935; Anthony Kunda, "Zambian Churches and Lawyers Oppose Presidential Plan for Third Term," *Christianity Today*, March 1, 2001, www.christianitytoday.com/2001/03/zambian-churches-and-lawyers-oppose-presidential-plan-for-t/.

[30] *Lusaka Times*, "The Controversial Constitution Amendment Bill 10 Fails by 6 Votes in Parliament," October 29, 2020, www.lusakatimes.com/2020/10/29/the-controversial-constitution-amendment-bill-10-fails-by-6-votes-in-parliament/.

mobs attacked Catholic clergy and property in the wake of the Catholic bishop's mediation efforts in the Democratic Republic of the Congo, and the ruling party in Burundi called for bishops to be defrocked following their statements in support of opposition rights.[31]

Of course, for every example of a church speaking out in favor of political liberties and democratic institutions, there are multiple instances of them failing to act. The anecdotes above provide examples of how churches have mobilized in support of liberal democratic institutions, but they do not provide a full assessment of the extent to which churches are major actors in advocacy for liberal democracy in sub-Saharan Africa. To consider this, I collected original data on activism for liberal democratic institutions by churches as compared to other civil society advocates in sub-Saharan Africa, including though a systematic review of newspaper reports. My data collection effort is described in detail in Chapter 4.

In Figure 1.1, I use this original data set to compare church activism to trade union activism given the acknowledged importance of trade unions in democratic mobilization in existing cross-national and regional literature.[32] I collected this data from two distinct periods for the thirty-four countries on the continent with significant Christian populations.[33] The first is from 1988 to 1998, which represents the wave in which multiparty elections were introduced across sub-Saharan Africa around the end of the Cold War. The second is from 2009 to 2018, which was a period of presidential power grabs and executive aggrandizement.[34]

---

[31] *Lusaka Times*, "Some Comments by Catholic Bishops on Bill 10 Were a Product of Misinformation," June 16, 2020; *France 24*, "Burundi Govt Accuses Catholic Bishops of Spreading 'Hatred,'" September 22, 2019, www.aljazeera.com/news/2019/9/22/burundi-accuses-catholic-bishops-of-spreading-hatred; Jonathan Luxmoore, "Congo Bishops Fault Politicians for Failed Mediation," *National Catholic Reporter*, April 22, 2017, www.ncronline.org/congo-bishops-fault-politicians-failed-mediation; Interview with Tanzanian leader of Christian advocacy group, May 2018; Interview with leader of international church group in Tanzania, April 2019; Interview with Zambian Catholic religious leader, April 2022; Interview with Zambian Anglican religious leader, April 2022.

[32] Acemoglu and Robinson 2006; Bratton and van de Walle 1992; Collier 1999; Haggard and Kaufman 2017; Kraus 2007; Rueschemeyer, Stephens, and Stephens 1992.

[33] These countries are Angola, Benin, Botswana, Burkina Faso, Burundi, Cameroon, the Central African Republic, Chad, Cote D'Ivoire, the Democratic Republic of the Congo, Ethiopia, Equatorial Guinea, Eritrea, Gabon, Ghana, Guinea-Bissau, Kenya, Lesotho, Liberia, Madagascar, Malawi, Mozambique, Namibia, Nigeria, the Republic of the Congo, Rwanda, Senegal, South Africa, South Sudan, Tanzania, Togo, Uganda, Zambia, and Zimbabwe.

[34] The coding for the period from 1988 to 1998 is based on earlier data collection efforts by Bratton and van de Walle 1992, Haggard and Kaufman 2017, and Toft, Philpott, and

African Churches as Majors Actors

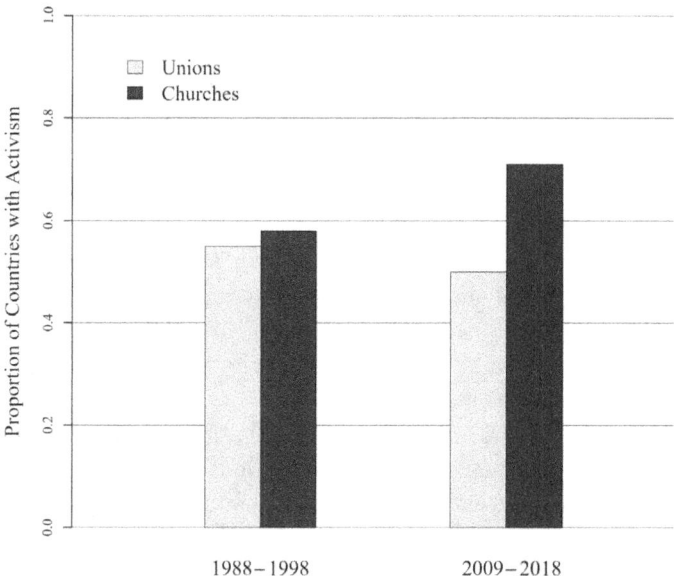

FIGURE 1.1 Proportion of countries with union or church activism for liberal democracy
Source: Baldwin 2025a.
Note: Bar graphs indicate proportion of countries in which at least one union or church in the country advocated for liberal democracy in each decade.

The data codes churches and trade union federations as engaging in advocacy for liberal democratic institutions if they made a public statement demanding improvements in the quality of elections, checks on the power of the executive, or the rights of the political opposition. I then aggregated the data to the country level to account for the varied number of trade union federations and churches in each country; the data in the graph measures whether each country experienced any activism by trade union federations or churches in the decades under consideration.

As Figure 1.1 illustrates, trade unions have often been involved in advocacy for liberal democratic institutions, with at least one trade union

Shah 2011. I adopt a generous coding scheme, indicating that either unions or churches were involved if at least one of the sources codes them this way, and consider the same set of countries analyzed above for comparability. The coding for the period from 2009 to 2018 is based on original data collection described in detail in Chapter 4 for churches. The data in Figure 1.1 is based on an equivalent effort for each trade union federation in the country associated with the International Trade Union Confederation. Figure 1.1 and 1.2 include instances of church advocacy by church councils, which are ecumenical bodies that unite multiple churches. See also Appendix B for details on the data set.

federation engaging in democratic advocacy in 55 percent of countries between 1988 and 1998 and in 50 percent of countries between 2009 and 2018. Churches have been even more frequent advocates for liberal democracy, with at least one church engaging in democratic activism in 59 percent of countries in the earlier period and in 71 percent of countries in the later one. In the earlier decade, countries were about equally likely to experience church versus union activism for democracy, but in the later period, they were almost 50 percent more likely to experience church activism. The figure also demonstrates variation across countries in whether churches engaged in activism for liberal democracy; there is no church advocacy in 41 percent of countries in the first period and in 29 percent of countries in the second.

In this book, I focus on advocacy for liberal democratic institutions, which is a more demanding concept than electoral or majoritarian democracy because it encompasses both quality elections and institutions that limit the power of elected rulers. In the past four decades, most countries in sub-Saharan Africa have institutionalized elections that formally permit political competition as a means of selecting leaders. Far fewer have established institutional checks and legal limits on the power of executive rulers.[35] Elected rulers frequently wield unchecked power due to weak legislatures, captured judiciaries, censored media, and hobbled opposition parties. The issue is not primarily one of presidential versus parliamentary constitutional designs, but rather one of weak institutional and legal restraints on presidents and prime ministers alike. Liberal democratic institutions remain weak across sub-Saharan Africa.

Figure 1.2 breaks down church advocacy between 2009 and 2018 by whether it was for free and fair elections (including the independence of the electoral commission and the fairness of election rules); checks on the ruler's power (including the existence of presidential term limits, the protection of legislative powers, and the independence of the judiciary); or the right to express nonviolent opposition to the ruler (including the right to peaceful protest, freedom of the media, and the issue of political prisoners). Church advocacy for free and fair elections is the most common form of democratic advocacy, occurring in 59 percent of countries. But churches also frequently advocate for checks on the power of the president, occurring in 32 percent of countries, and for the rights of opponents of the ruler to express and organize dissent, occurring in

---

[35] Levitsky and Way 2010; Little and Meng 2024.

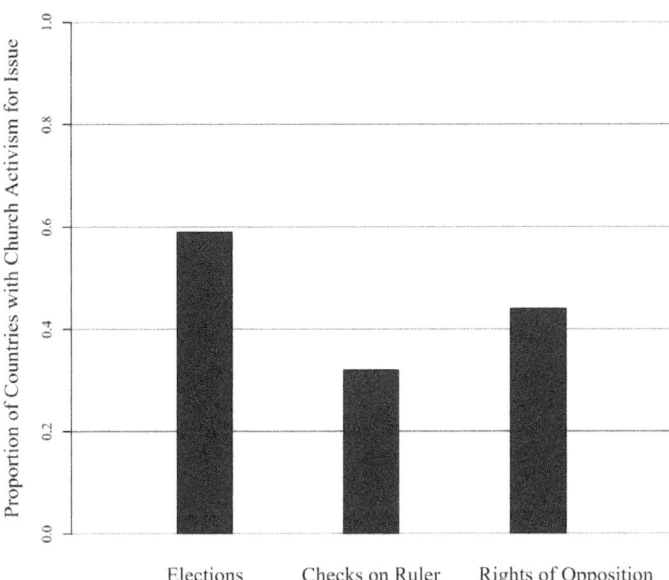

FIGURE 1.2 Proportion of countries with church activism for aspects of liberal democracy
Source: Baldwin 2025a.
Note: Bar graphs indicate proportion of countries in which at least one church in the country advocated for aspect of liberal democracy between 2009 and 2018.

44 percent of countries. Thus, some churches in sub-Saharan Africa have advocated for both free and fair elections and liberal democratic institutions that restrain the power of elected rulers.

In conceptualizing liberal democracy, I focus narrowly on its core political institutions. In my usage, liberal democratic political institutions are not synonymous with American presidential democracy, capitalist market systems, or a philosophical commitment to individual choice in the pursuit of happiness.[36] A political system is more liberal democratic to the extent that the ruler's power is limited by elections, institutions, and legally enforceable rights for political opponents.

Similarly, I describe churches as engaging in liberal democratic advocacy when they engage in activism for free and fair elections, institutional limits on the power of rulers, or the legal rights of the ruler's opponents. In measuring advocacy for liberal democracy, I exclude activism for closely associated liberal ideas that some churches have a more direct

[36] Galston 2020; Plattner 1999.

interest in promoting, such as religious freedom and property rights.[37] I also exclude activism for individual liberties that churches frequently oppose, including those related to sexual orientation and gender equality. When I say that a church is an advocate for liberal democracy, I mean only that it has engaged in activism for institutions that ensure limits on elected rulers' power, not that it espouses liberal views that promote individual liberty in all spheres of life. Indeed, church advocacy for liberal democratic institutions in sub-Saharan Africa is a puzzle worth explaining precisely because most of the churches that have become advocates for them are not otherwise liberal in their views.

LIBERAL DEMOCRACY AS AN INSTITUTIONAL GUARANTEE OF CHURCH AUTONOMY

Why do some churches engage in activism for liberal democratic institutions? The existing literature on democracy provides limited guidance in explaining this phenomenon. Scholars of democracy have extensively debated which group is more important in driving democratization – the lower class, the middle class, or regime insiders – providing theoretical explanations for these actors' positions on expanding the franchise and increasing political competition.[38] But even if the involvement of churches in democratic movements is sometimes descriptively acknowledged by this literature, it is rarely explained.[39] In contrast, scholars of religion have provided insight into when churches are more likely to advocate for human rights and to seek changes in government but rarely explain church advocacy for liberal democracy specifically.[40]

In seeking to understand the decision to advocate for liberal democracy, I build on the literature on the determinants of liberal democratic political institutions, which is scant compared to the ample literature on the conditions that favor a minimalist version of electoral democracy.[41]

---

[37] Locke 1689.
[38] Acemoglu and Robinson 2006; Ansell and Samuels 2014; Arriola 2013; Boix 2003; Haggard and Kaufman 2017; O'Donnell, Schmitter, and Whitehead 1986; Przeworski 1991; Rosenfeld 2017; Rosenfeld 2021; Rueschemeyer, Stephens, and Stephens 1992.
[39] See, for example, Bratton and van de Walle 1992 and Haggard and Kaufman 2021.
[40] See, for example, Gill 1998 on advocacy for human rights and Toft, Philpott, and Shah 2011 on regime change. Partial exceptions are Chapter 4 of Toft, Philpott, and Shah 2011, which emphasizes the importance of theology and religious groups' relationship to the state in explaining democratic activism broadly conceived, and Hoffman 2021, which emphasizes how group demographics condition support for majority rule.
[41] North and Weingast 1989; Stasavage 2002; Rovny 2023; Weingast 1997.

The potential of liberal democratic institutions is that they provide reinforcing mechanisms for limiting the power of the ruler. Historically, liberal democracy's limits on the power of rulers were viewed as a means of securing property rights for the economic activities of the industrial class. As a result, it was the rising industrial class that had incentives to advocate for liberal democratic institutions as a means of restraining the grabbing hand of the state.

But unchecked rulers pose threats beyond property expropriation.[42] They can quash a wide variety of activities in pursuit of their political goals. All-powerful rulers are particularly likely to curtail activities that spread dissenting ideas within society, given the threat such ideas present to their political control.[43]

In that way, unchecked rulers pose a threat to churches, which are defined by their commitment to their specific theologies. Religious groups differ from most other organizations in that their boundaries are defined in significant part by members' beliefs; consequently, their primary goal is to disseminate their associated worldviews. A church of unbelievers is not nearly as desirable as a church of believers. Thus, churches have a core interest in spreading their own ideas and unchecked rulers pose a threat to them insofar as they may restrict churches from disseminating their beliefs.[44]

Historically, churches around the world have tried to spread their worldviews through alliances with rulers committed to the same religious views, which I call a coalitional strategy.[45] Under this strategy, churches offer political support for a party in return for policy concessions. For example, in nineteenth-century Europe, the Catholic Church sought conservative allies who opposed the secularization of the state that had been proposed by liberal parties.[46] In the mid twentieth century, European churches sought alliances with various Christian democratic parties that supported key policy goals.[47] In the United States, evangelical leaders have had a coalitional alliance with the Republican Party

---

[42] Indeed, in the contemporary period, the risk of property expropriation may be lower given the increasing mobility of capital. See Boix 2003; Eichengreen 1996.
[43] On the importance of information control to autocrats, see Baggott Carter and Carter 2023; Guriev and Treisman 2022; Wallace 2022; Roberts 2018; Rosenfeld and Wallace 2024.
[44] For a similar conception of church interests, see Hagopian 2008.
[45] For similar terminology, see Grzymala-Busse 2015.
[46] Gould 1999 shows the diverse types of coalitions formed in support of church goals during this period.
[47] Warner 2000.

since the 1970s with goals including securing tax breaks for Christian institutions and rolling back abortion rights.[48] This type of alliance is not risk free, as politicians may defect on promises to churches in their efforts to win the popular vote and church reputations may be muddied by their involvement in politics.[49] But a coalitional strategy is a conceivable option where potential partisan allies exist.

Nevertheless, these sorts of alliances are difficult to find in the contemporary world and in postindependence Africa in particular. This book moves beyond the scope conditions of previous scholarship by illuminating the strategies churches employ when they cannot count on partisan allies. Specific historical legacies have limited the incentives of rulers to tie themselves to specific denominational churches in sub-Saharan Africa, even if these rulers sometimes invoke religious imagery to legitimize their personal power. Countries with significant Christian populations are all denominationally or religiously diverse so that an alliance with one specific church could easily alienate a majority of voters. In addition, most churches were headed by foreign leaders at the moment of national independence, which made political alliances with them unpalatable to politicians at the time.

As a result, postindependence politicians in sub-Saharan Africa generally avoid founding religiously oriented parties and African churches do not enjoy credible partisan allies. Church interests cannot be secured by bolstering the power of one political faction over another. The major risk to churches is that autocratic institutions will allow unchecked rulers to use state power to impinge on the spread of ideas within society, including church efforts to teach their worldviews.

In this context, liberal democracy offers a means of protection for churches. Churches can use institutional and legal restraints on the power of rulers to ensure that all-powerful rulers do not use the state apparatus to limit the dissemination of church beliefs. Independent-minded legislators, autonomous judges, and legal limits on the power of rulers provide churches with protection against excessive state intervention, even in the absence of partisan coalition partners. Liberal democracy is a means of preventing state suppression of their freedom to share the messages of the gospel. Counter to conventional wisdom that churches are a threat to democracy due to their strong commitment to specific beliefs, the

---

[48] Balmer 2007; Gorski 2020.
[49] Grzymala-Busse 2015; Kalyvas 2000. Tunón 2017 also demonstrates that changes in church leadership can make churches unreliable allies of particular parties.

protection liberal democracy affords can give churches the motivation to defend it. The importance of ideas to the fundamental mission of churches provides an interest-based explanation for their activism.[50]

Thus, churches may become advocates for liberal democracy as a means of securing limited governmental intervention in the activities they undertake to spread their worldviews.[51] Why do they need to accept liberal democracy as a means of securing limited government interference? There are inherent analytic and contingent historic reasons for doing so. Analytically, limited government is difficult to achieve without democracy because the lack of turnover in autocratic regimes makes it easier for rulers to centralize power and eliminate dissent.[52] In contrast, liberal democracy can be self-enforcing because it gives multiple actors the ability to criticize and restrain the centralization of power.[53] Historically, liberal democracy has come to denote a specific bundle of institutions in the twentieth and twenty-first centuries, with international advocacy networks forming in support of this type of government over the past fifty years.[54] As a result, churches can mobilize broader groups in support of liberal democracy than they can for other forms of limited government.

Of course, there is great variation in whether churches speak out in defense of liberal democracy. Although most churches could be said to have an interest in freedom of expression insofar as they are in the business of advancing their worldviews, church gospel-spreading activities are differently at risk of crackdown by autocrats based on the spheres in which these activities take place. Depending on the activities through which churches spread the gospel, they are more or less likely to have their instruction impinged on by autocrats intent on centralizing power and eliminating dissent. As a result, churches are exposed to different

---

[50] In contrast, ideational explanations usually emphasize the compatibility of religious actors' theological commitments to democracy in explaining their activism. For an example, see Toft, Philpott, and Shah 2011.
[51] Locke 1689; Mill 1859.
[52] Scholars who analyze the minimum conditions for electoral democracy generally acknowledge that competitive elections cannot be maintained without some respect for civil liberties, including freedom of information and the press. As a result, a political system must have some liberal checks in order to be considered a full electoral democracy. Dahl 1971; Przeworski 1999. Equally important is the fact that multiparty democracies tend to protect liberalism by making it harder for regimes to accumulate power that restrict citizens' freedom. Plattner 1999.
[53] North and Weingast 1989; Stasavage 2002.
[54] Bush 2015; Carothers 2020; Dunning 2004; Hyde 2011; Levitsky and Way 2010.

levels of autocratic risk, defined as the risk that an institutionally uninhibited ruler could shut down the dissemination channels in which a church has invested.

For example, even under highly illiberal regimes, Sunday worship within congregations is rarely at risk of being shut down. Catholic and mainline Protestant churches that rely on services in houses of worship to spread their worldviews have limited risk of having that mode of instruction suppressed under an illiberal regime.[55] Such regimes are much more likely to assert control over church social service activities; rulers have the regulatory tools to do so and greater incentive to take control of these activities because they are also considered state responsibilities. As such, church-run media, health care clinics, and charity work are all subject to greater autocratic risk than congregational worship. Church education systems are particularly at risk of having their autonomy quashed by unchecked rulers, as I elaborate in the next section.

My argument emphasizes the historic investment of churches in different modes of disseminating their worldviews to explain variation in church democratic activism. In making this claim, I emphasize path dependencies in investments in activities that give their historic decisions influence over contemporary outcomes. There is institutional stickiness in the types of activities in which churches are interested in engaging. Over time, churches develop specialized staff, bureaucracies, and clientele around particular activities, entrenching their interests in them. As a result, churches that have historically invested in activities that are subject to higher autocratic risk cannot quickly shift away from them; to protect them, they may advocate for liberal democracy.

My argument highlights the varied regulatory power of the state over different church activities and how this variation explains church activism for liberal democratic institutions. But states can also exert financial influence over church activities, and this plays a secondary role in helping to explain church activism for liberal democracy. Churches may depend on the state to provide operational financing for activities. In some contexts, states provide direct transfers to churches that can be used to support all their operational activities. In a wider range of contexts, states subsidize particular activities, such as church-provided

---

[55] The term mainline Protestant church refers to non-evangelical Protestant churches, including Anglican churches, Lutheran churches, Presbyterian churches, and Baptist churches. Mainline Protestant churches in sub-Saharan Africa are on average older, more institutionalized, less literal in their interpretation of the bible, and place less emphasis on born-again experiences than evangelical Protestant churches.

social services and education. Churches whose activities depend on government subsidies will weigh the cost of reduced financial support against any benefits gained from mobilizing in defense of liberal democracy in deciding whether to speak out. For example, there is little benefit in advocating for democracy in an effort to defend the medium-term autonomy of an activity if that activity can be shut down instantly through withdrawal of the state subsidies on which it depends.[56]

Thus, the theory's main hypothesis is that churches that have historically invested in dissemination modes over which the state has greater regulatory power have greater autocratic risk exposure. These churches are more likely to engage in liberal democratic activism to protect these activities from overreach by an unchecked ruler. A second hypothesis is that state financing of activities can mitigate the incentive to speak out in support of liberal democratic institutions.

OPERATIONALIZING THE THEORETICAL VARIATION: CHURCH EDUCATION SYSTEMS IN SUB-SAHARAN AFRICA

In the context of sub-Saharan Africa, I gain traction on church autocratic risk exposure and dependence on state subsidies by narrowing my focus to one important sphere of activity: church education systems. Historically, education has been the main point of contestation between church and state.[57] Churches provided a huge portion of formal education in colonial Africa, as Chapter 3 details. In the newly independent, economically poor, and administratively weak states of postcolonial Africa, most rulers had a great deal of interest in and some capacity to control the formal education system, but limited interest in and low capacity to regulate church congregations.

Church education systems are at particular risk of having their autonomy stifled by unchecked rulers. Many churches place high value on providing formal education to young people because they want to shape the worldviews of the next generation. Political rulers are also interested in the content of education for young people for overlapping reasons. For

---

[56] As Chapter 2 explains, liberal democratic institutions are conceived to be less effective in guaranteeing fiscal transfers from the state so that fiscal dependence does not provide similar incentives for activism.

[57] Conflict over education systems has obviously been salient in other contexts as well but, in periods of anticlericalism in Europe and Latin America, regimes simultaneously attacked other privileges of churches, which had more wealth and landholdings than their counterparts in postindependence Africa.

at least the past 100 years, state authorities have viewed education as legitimately within their purview due to both the economic salience of it and its capacity to inculcate particular belief and value systems.[58] As a result, church education systems have often been the focus of conflict between church and state.[59] Rulers have greater interest in and more tools for controlling church education than most of the other activities undertaken by churches. As a result, churches that are more engaged in running schools have greater exposure to autocratic risk than those that have smaller educational investments. Without institutional constraints, rulers will typically try to increase their control over instruction in church schools for reasons I elaborate in Chapters 2 and 3.

In addition, in sub-Saharan Africa, state subsidies for church educational systems are the most consistent financial transfer between the state and churches. States in sub-Saharan Africa provide minimal financial support for church operational activities outside of social services.[60] As a result, in this context, I can capture the greatest sources of variation in autocratic risk exposure and dependence on state subsidies by narrowing my focus to church educational activities.

It is well known that early missionaries in Africa used "the school as the nucleus to church planting."[61] What is less appreciated is the high level of their continued involvement in education in many countries. For example, in the Democratic Republic of the Congo, Kenya, Lesotho, Rwanda, and Uganda, the majority of primary schools are still church affiliated. Even in countries such as Tanzania and Zambia, where governments fully nationalized most former mission schools, churches still run a sizable portion of the country's secondary schools due to gaps in the government's ability to fulfill the demand for them. Furthermore, in countries where older churches founded schools in the colonial era, newer churches sometimes establish education wings because of local expectations that education provision is a church matter.[62] As Chapter 3

---

[58] Ansell and Lindvall 2013; Darden and Grzymala-Busse 2006; King 2013; Paglayan 2021.
[59] For historical examples, see Kalyvas 1996; Lipset and Rokkan 1967; Wittenberg 2006.
[60] *Pew Research Center*, "In Western European Countries with Church Taxes, Support for the Tradition Remains Strong," April 30, 2019, www.pewresearch.org/religion/2019/04/30/in-western-european-countries-with-church-taxes-support-for-the-tradition-remains-strong/. In contrast, in a number of European countries, churches continue to receive large operational subsidies from the state through church taxes.
[61] Interview with Ghanaian Pentecostal religious leader, September 2021.
[62] Ibid.

demonstrates, there is considerable variation across countries and within denominations in how much education churches provide.

Applying my theoretical argument to the educational sphere leads to the following predictions. Other things being equal, education provision tends to increase the benefits of liberal democracy to churches. Churches with higher numbers of schools are more exposed to autocratic risk because rulers introduce regulations that restrict church school autonomy more frequently than they do regulations that restrict worship in congregations. Liberal democratic institutions support mission-critical activities for education-providing churches.

But there is another aspect of church educational systems that also influences the likelihood of a church engaging in democratic activism: financing. In some cases, parents are the main source of church school operational financing while in other cases, it is the state. Church school financing varies by country and within countries over time due to strategic and exogenous factors. Churches whose schools depend on state subsidies will weigh the cost of reduced financial support against any benefits of mobilizing to oppose autocracy in deciding whether to speak out. As a result, churches with fiscally independent schools are the most likely to speak out against autocracy as a means of protecting their autonomy over the education they provide, while churches without significant involvement in schooling and churches with schools that are fiscally dependent on the state are less likely to do so.

In providing evidence for this argument, I show that these two aspects of church education systems explain variation in church leaders' democratic activism across countries in sub-Saharan Africa. They explain cross-national variation in activism across churches that have similar political theologies or that may even belong to the same global church, as in the case of Catholic churches. It is true that Catholic churches tend to provide more education and to advocate for democracy more frequently than other churches, but the characteristics of church education systems explain variation in democratic activism by Catholic churches across countries that is otherwise difficult to explicate.[63] Differences in church education systems also explain differences in democratic activism between churches that otherwise have similar membership sizes and organizational capacity.

My argument applies most directly to older, institutionalized churches. Institutionalized churches have historic commitments to

---

[63] On Catholic advocacy for democracy, see Huntington 1991; Philpott 2004.

sets of teachings and governance structures that set church direction. As a result, they can be seen as having institutional goals beyond the personal aspirations of founding leaders. This is an important scope condition because my theory implies that churches act on institutional interests distinct from the interests of individual church leaders. In contrast, in newer, less institutionalized churches, church leaders are less constrained in bending church teachings to serve the interests of political rulers and as such, they are more likely to be co-opted. The theory thus explains the behavior of Catholic and mainline Protestant churches, as well as some older independent and Pentecostal churches, but does not as easily apply to new (mainly neo-Pentecostal) churches that have been founded in recent decades.

My argument is also temporally bounded in that it assumes an environment in which churches can mobilize broader coalitions in support of liberal democratic institutions than in support of policy positions that are important to them. As a result, my findings apply most easily to the past four or five decades, a time in which key international actors and networks have supported liberal democracy.[64]

Throughout this book, I focus on variation in Christian church involvement in formal education provision in sub-Saharan Africa. Islamic educational centers have also historically played a significant role in many countries but have had distinct relationships with the state. Islamic schools were rarely subsidized by colonial administrations. States have only very recently begun to formally incorporate them into their education systems in large numbers, and there is little variation across countries in their dependence on state subsidies.[65] As a result, although pioneering research on these schools suggests that their founders share the concerns I elaborate about defending educational autonomy, Islamic education systems do not vary on the same dimensions as Christian church education systems.[66] In addition, the lack of hierarchy within many Islamic communities in sub-Saharan Africa hinders national-level advocacy and allows for state-imposed and co-opted national-level Islamic organizations.[67] Importantly, the exclusion of Islamic communities from the scope of this study is not the result of presumptions about the theological compatibility of Islam with liberal democracy; on the

---

[64] Bush 2015; Dunning 2004; Hyde 2011; Levitsky and Way 2010.
[65] Bleck 2015; Owusu-Ansah, Iddrisu, and Sey 2013.
[66] Owusu-Ansah, Iddrisu, and Sey 2013.
[67] Elischer 2021.

contrary, existing empirical research demonstrates high levels of support for democratic institutions among Muslims in sub-Saharan Africa.[68]

CONTRIBUTIONS

With this book, I aspire to bring the study of church democratic activism into conversation with the broader comparative literature on the forces behind democratic and autocratic transitions. The literature on democratization fiercely debates whether regime insiders, the middle class, or the lower class are the main forces behind it. Only rarely do comparative scholars of democratization note that churches have become advocates for democracy in some recent contexts, emphasizing the change in Catholic political theology after the Second Vatican Council as crucial.[69] This book provides a framework for understanding the contexts in which religious versus economic actors are likely to play leading roles.

In a largely separate literature on religion and politics, scholars seek to explain instances in which churches engage in broader forms of human rights activism, often emphasizing theology or religious competition as the key explanatory factor, but they do not theorize why churches engage in activism for liberal democratic institutions as a distinct outcome.[70] Liberal democracy is different from other human rights, which often have clearer links to Christian theology and the messages of the gospel.[71] As a result, church positions on liberal democracy are likely to be highly instrumental and potentially driven by different considerations than its advocacy for other human rights. I provide a positive explanation for why churches may engage in activism for liberal democracy distinct from activism for human rights more broadly. This explanation emphasizes that the various activities of churches expose them to

---

[68] Bratton 2003.
[69] Huntington 1991; Philpott 2004. On religious actors and advocacy for majoritarian democracy in the Middle East, see Hoffman 2021.
[70] Gill 1998; Huntington 1991; Philpott 2004; Trejo 2012. On the religious marketplace approach to the study of religion, see Iannaccone, Finke, and Stark 1997. Dowd provides an alternative explanation for the relationship between religious diversity and religious actors' greater support for liberal democratic political culture. In diverse settings, he argues that religious leaders eventually come to adopt a "live and let live" ethic due to the necessity of social tolerance. Dowd 2015, 3.
[71] On this point, see also Pope John Paul II's statement in Chile in 1987: "I am not the evangelizer of democracy; I am the evangelizer of the Gospel. To the Gospel message, of course, belong all the problems of human rights; and, if democracy means human rights, it also belongs to the message of the Church," quoted in Huntington 1991, 84.

different levels of autocratic risk, thereby accounting for differences in activism among churches with the same theological commitments.

This book contributes to a growing literature that focuses on understanding the political consequences of service provision by nonstate actors, including churches and other religious actors.[72] Recent research demonstrates the implications of nonstate service provision for how citizens evaluate different political parties, candidates, and the government more generally.[73] My work focuses instead on how nonstate service provision affects democracy and political institutions. Churches with educational investments care more about liberal democratic institutions and engage more in democratic activism because their activities are more exposed to autocratic risk.

This book also advances the understanding of religious politics in sub-Saharan Africa, demonstrating how religion in sub-Saharan Africa has political implications even if political parties rarely base their appeals on religious ideologies or win support from religious coalitions. Interestingly, social scientists have engaged very little in thinking about religious politics on the continent.[74] The limited study of this phenomena is remarkable, especially when juxtaposed with the extraordinarily vast literature on ethnic politics in sub-Saharan Africa. My work demonstrates that many religious actors in sub-Saharan Africa do engage in political debates at critical moments and that their actions have political consequences. Precisely because they lack coalitional allies, some churches in sub-Saharan Africa advocate for liberal democratic institutions to guarantee their interests.

PLAN OF THE BOOK

Empirically, the book is an example of mixed methods research, with different methods and research designs employed to understand different components of the relationship between church education systems and democratic activism. The main predictions about the relationship between education provision and democratic activism are best tested at the mesolevel and as such, I examine patterns across all significant-sized churches in sub-Saharan Africa.[75]

---

[72] See Cammett 2014; MacLean and Cammett 2014.
[73] Brass 2016; MacLean 2010; Thachil 2014.
[74] For important exceptions, see Longman 2010; McCauley 2017; McClendon and Riedl 2019; Sperber, McClendon, and Kaaba 2024.
[75] I define a church as significant-sized if its membership constitutes at least 5 percent of the population of a country.

But many of the claims underpinning the theory are more naturally examined using within-case evidence, including process tracing of church influence on policymaking over time within countries, experimental analysis of the effects of church statements about democracy on citizens' behavior, and cohort analysis of the effects of church education systems on citizens' beliefs. For this analysis, I employ within-country studies, drawing on evidence from Ghana, Tanzania, and Zambia. In each of the empirical chapters, I pair the main case of Zambia with a more religiously diverse second country to understand the scope conditions of the theory, with Christians making up 85 percent of the population in Zambia, 71 percent of the population in Ghana, and 55 percent of the population in Tanzania.[76]

In all three countries, churches ran the majority of schools at the time of independence, but their subsequent educational provision varies, with the highest contribution across time and churches in Ghana, varied contribution across both aspects in Zambia, and the lowest contribution in Tanzania. The cases of Zambia and Ghana offer possibilities for understanding how within-country changes in political institutions influence church policy given the significant over-time variation in the level of liberal democracy within each country. The cases of Zambia and Tanzania provide unique opportunities to trace whether and how church democratic advocacy mobilizes other actors given recent examples of churches speaking out in defense of liberal democratic institutions.

To understand all facets of the relationship between church democratic activism and education systems, I draw on an extremely wide variety of evidence. The research for this book involved more than seventy-five interviews; the implementation of original public opinion surveys in Zambia and Tanzania, including endorsement experiments designed to measure the efficacy of church democratic activism; and the construction of three original data sets on church education systems and church activism for liberal democracy covering up to thirty-four countries in sub-Saharan Africa over time.[77] Additionally, I have reviewed hundreds of historical educational documents, read more than 150 pastoral letters from church leaders, reviewed thousands of news articles,

---

[76] Throughout the manuscript, I rely on statistics on the size of churches and other religious communities from the Christian World Database. See Zurlo and Johnson 2025. The year of the statistic is 2015 unless otherwise indicated.

[77] A full list of interviews is included in Appendix A. A description of data sets and data sources is included in Appendix B.

tracked down obscure publications related to education policy and church schools, and analyzed a variety of existing data sources.

The book is divided into four parts. Part I provides the theoretical claims and the historical background regarding church educational systems and church advocacy for liberal democracy. Parts II and III empirically test my theoretical claims (see Table 1.1). Using data sets at the country-church–year level, Part II tests the core hypotheses about when churches engage in democratic activism. Drawing on within-country analysis from Ghana, Tanzania, and Zambia, Part III considers additional assumptions behind and implications of the theory. Part IV considers the broader implications of church education systems and the beliefs they foster for democracy.

Breaking down the chapters that constitute each part of the book, Chapter 2 provides a deeper explication of the theory. It explains how liberal democratic institutions provide a solution to the problem that rulers cannot otherwise credibly commit to preserving church control of their schools. As a result, churches with significant education systems have an incentive to speak out in support of liberal democratic

TABLE 1.1 *Mapping the book's theoretical claims to evidence*

Theoretical claim	Empirical evidence
Hypothesis 1: Churches with more schools engage in greater advocacy for liberal democracy	Chapter 4: Quantitative comparison of advocacy by churches across sub-Saharan Africa with different educational investments
Hypothesis 2: Churches with higher dependence on state subsidies to operate their schools engage in less advocacy for liberal democracy	Chapter 5: Difference-in-difference analysis of effects of increasing church schools' dependence on state financing on advocacy by Catholic churches in thirteen countries
Underlying assumption 1: Churches have the potential to mobilize broad constituencies – including the public and international actors – in support of liberal democracy	Chapter 6: Qualitative interviews, survey data, and endorsement experiments from Zambia and Tanzania
Underlying assumption 2: Churches can better guarantee the autonomy of their schools when liberal democratic institutions are stronger	Chapter 7: Within-country comparison and process-tracing evidence from Zambia and Ghana; comparison of educational policies toward church schools by regime type across sub-Saharan Africa

institutions, although this incentive is mitigated when their schools are fiscally dependent on the government to operate. Chapter 3 concludes Part I by providing a brief history of church–state relations and church education provision in sub-Saharan Africa.

Part II empirically tests the main theoretical predictions about the effects of church education systems on church democratic activism. Chapter 4 draws on original data on church activism for liberal democracy and church education systems to demonstrate that churches with more schools are more likely to speak out in support of liberal democratic institutions across sub-Saharan Africa, independent of country-level or denominational trends, but the effects are mitigated when churches receive large public subsidies for their schools. Chapter 5 shows that the decisions of Catholic churches to speak out against autocracy depend on their reliance on state fiscal transfers. This chapter draws on a novel data set that measures the annual pro-democracy activism of churches through an examination of their public pastoral letters. An exogenous policy intervention – the introduction of universal primary education policies across sub-Saharan Africa between 1994 and 2008 – shows that churches reduce public advocacy for liberal democratic institutions when their schools become increasingly dependent on government transfers.

Part III draws on within-country evidence to empirically examine underlying assumptions behind the theory's main predictions. Chapter 6 considers the political effects of church pro-democracy stances, contrasting the effects of church activism in Zambia and Tanzania between 2016 and 2021. Drawing on interviews, survey data, and combined endorsement/conjoint candidate experiments in both countries, I show how churches in Zambia have galvanized international actors, domestic elites, and public opinion in support of liberal democratic institutions while churches in Tanzania have had more limited success. Chapter 7 examines the policy influence of churches when liberal democratic institutions are stronger and weaker. The main analysis focuses on Zambia and Ghana, both of which have undergone numerous periods of democratization and autocratization. It shows how stronger liberal democratic institutions improve the ability of churches to accomplish their educational policy goals in these two countries and, suggestively, across sub-Saharan Africa more generally by giving churches greater influence over policymaking and protecting their agreements with the state.

Part IV considers the broad implications of church education systems and the book's theoretical claims for democracy. Chapter 8 considers whether church education itself makes a difference to citizens' democratic attitudes. Parochial schools are often thought to be inferior to public schools in inculcating democratic citizenship. But drawing on evidence from the handover of Catholic primary schools to the Zambian government in the early 1970s, I find limited effects of the handover on students' political attitudes except that Catholic schools foster more conservative gender norms. In Tanzania, Protestant school attendance improves women's citizenship on many dimensions compared to secular school attendance, but Catholic school attendance does not. Chapter 9 concludes by discussing the implications of the book for understanding democracy and democratic activism beyond churches in sub-Saharan Africa. It emphasizes that some churches in other regions of the world employ coalitional strategies to advance their interests and, in such cases, their attitudes toward liberal democracy are contingent on whether doing so will advance or hinder the power of their preferred parties. It also shows that some churches rely on liberal democracy as an institutional guarantee of their interests, suggesting that my argument applies to some churches beyond Africa. Last, it explains how the theory can be applied to other types of actors in other regions of the world.

2

Liberal Democracy as an Institutional Guarantee of Church Interests

What explains why some churches engage in activism for liberal democratic institutions? From many perspectives, such activism is puzzling. Why would an organization that is primarily focused on saving souls stick its neck out in defense of political rights and liberal democratic institutions? Why would churches support democratic institutions as a means of lawmaking if they believe their religious laws and codes provide the foundations of governance? It would seem to make more sense for churches to either keep out of politics or to throw in their lot with autocrats. And yet there are numerous examples of churches publicly advocating for liberal democratic institutions in sub-Saharan Africa and beyond.

This chapter provides an explanation for why some churches engage in liberal democratic activism and others do not. It begins by examining the circumstances under which churches are likely to seek institutional versus coalitional guarantees of their interests. It then outlines the cost–benefit calculations behind church decisions to engage in democratic activism rather than remain silent, describing how autocratic risk exposure and financial dependence on the state jointly determine those decisions. It next explains the mechanisms that churches have for advancing democratic political institutions and why churches may need to defend democracy to uphold their policy interests. The penultimate section describes the critical role of church education systems in determining church autocratic risk exposure and state financial dependence in many settings. It concludes by describing how this theory departs from existing explanations of democratic activism by churches and its distinct empirical implications.

INSTITUTIONAL VERSUS COALITIONAL GUARANTEES OF CHURCH INTERESTS

This book provides a theory of democratic activism by the leadership of older, institutionalized churches. These churches have commitments to particular teachings and governance structures that set their direction beyond pronouncements from the founding leader. Catholic and mainline Protestant churches fall in this category, as do some older African Independent and Pentecostal churches, but new churches are outside of it because their leaders are less institutionally constrained. Because institutionalized churches have organizational interests and capacity beyond the goals and abilities of individual leaders, it is possible to conceive of them as unitary actors in some strategic settings, and in my exposition, I often use the term church as shorthand for church leadership.

My theoretical framework starts with the observation that churches have strong commitments to teaching their worldviews. Religious groups are distinct from many other groups in that the boundaries of their membership are defined in significant part by members' beliefs.[1] As a result, a primary goal of churches is to spread their worldviews according to their interpretation of the gospel. Their goal is a church of believers and as a result, they care not only about their nominal market share vis-à-vis other religious groups but also about their ability to disseminate their teachings unrestricted by state regulations.

Prior scholarship tends to view churches' commitments to their particular teachings as inclining them toward the obstruction rather than the embrace of liberal democracy. If church members believe that their religious teachings rather than the laws passed by democratic majorities should form the basis of government, it creates intrinsic tension between the church and democratic institutions. But as I outline below, churches are neither inherently democratic nor undemocratic actors. Instead, they favor more liberal democratic rule when it is the best way to protect and advance their interest in spreading their worldviews.[2]

Historically, church leaders have sought to advance church interests by seeking coalitions with politicians with whom they share commitments. In cases in which some political factions and parties are closely aligned with one church, that church may seek a favored position in society by throwing its support behind these political groups. In cases in

---

[1] Laitin 1986; McCauley 2014; Toft, Philpott, and Shah 2011, 21.
[2] Bellin 2000.

which one political group is deeply committed to a church, that church may be able to win special privileges or even a religious monopoly if that group comes to power. In these instances, the church has an interest in maximizing its political partner's power, possibly to the detriment of liberal democratic institutions, which explains the Catholic Church's opposition to liberal democracy in nineteenth-century Europe and Latin America.[3]

Yet in many, more recent settings, there are no political groups with deep commitments to church interests. Even in cases of church-founded parties like the Christian Democrats, the primacy of the party's electoral goals may give church leaders limited control over their political platforms and policy actions in office. In highly secular societies, such as contemporary Western Europe, these parties are especially likely to be weak agents of church interests.[4] In other contexts, church-affiliated parties have never formed. For a variety of historical reasons, including the size of churches, the political cleavage structure in the country, or the limited political legitimacy of the church at critical junctures, there are many highly religious societies without church-affiliated parties.[5] This includes much of sub-Saharan Africa, as I elaborate in Chapter 3.

In cases in which churches lack deeply committed coalition partners, politicians may try to curry favor by promising advantageous treatment. But these promises will rarely be credible insofar as rulers will be interested in advancing their own political power above all else once in office. They are likely to renege on promises to provide policy favors to churches if such favors reduce their own resources or control over society. In other words, politicians may promise to promote church activities, including social service and educational work, but once in office, they have incentives to take more direct control of those activities.

Where churches do not have credible coalitional partners through which to advance their interests, the institutional solution of liberal democracy presents an attractive alternative: They can seek the institutional guarantees of liberal democracy to ensure that an all-powerful ruler does not use the state's regulatory power to infringe on their core activities. Specifically, liberal democracy is distinct from electoral democracy in the limits it places on the power of elected rulers. In the conceptualization of this book, liberal democracy is conceived as a set

---

[3] Gill 1998; Gould 1999.
[4] Kalyvas 1996.
[5] Lipset and Rokkan 1967; Smith 2019.

of core political institutions that restrain rulers' power through institutional checks, including term limits, independent legislatures, autonomous judiciaries, and legal codes that protect civil rights.

Limited government is difficult to achieve without democracy because autocrats can centralize power over time. In contrast, liberal democracy can be self-enforcing within a country as it empowers individuals who have incentives to resist the centralization of power.[6] By the late twentieth century, a broad network of donors and civil society actors had come to accept and promote that particular configuration of institutions under the term liberal democracy, creating international support for this type of limited government. Although liberal democracy is often used as a binary classification, it is possible to rank all regimes in terms of the degree to which they constrain the power of elected rulers.[7] In this book, liberal democraticness is conceived as a continuous variable with countries considered more liberal democratic to the extent that there are greater institutional and legal restraints on the power of elected presidents or prime ministers.

Stronger liberal democratic institutions create better opportunities to protect and advance church interests than weaker ones. First, they create more openings in the policymaking process, giving church leaders opportunities to insert themselves even in the absence of strong coalitional allies. The church can use legislative, judicial, and other opportunities for public input into policymaking to promote its positions. Second, liberal democratic institutions limit the power of the state to overstep existing law, offering legal protection for any agreements negotiated by the church. This protection provides assurances that rulers cannot quickly stifle church core activities.

Under liberal democratic institutions, all churches receive protections from state regulatory power. In return, they give up the possibility of maximizing their privileges vis-à-vis other churches. Insofar as churches are particularly concerned with securing autonomy from state regulation rather than maximizing their status vis-à-vis other religious groups, liberal democracy is a good bet for securing their interests.[8]

---

[6] North and Weingast 1989; Stasavage 2002.
[7] See also Coppedge et al. 2016 and Meng 2020 on the Varieties of Democracy data set, which provides the continuous coding used throughout this book.
[8] On the relationship between liberal democracy and discrimination against religious minorities, see Fox 2020. Importantly, liberal democracy cannot fully guarantee that religious minorities will not face discrimination in any sphere.

This protection from state power explains why liberal democracy may be attractive to churches, but it does not explain why they risk speaking out in support of it rather than remaining silent. For churches to engage in prodemocratic activism to secure better policy outcomes, two additional conditions must be met. First, the benefits secured from liberal democracy must outweigh the costs of advocacy. Second, their activism for liberal democracy must be effective in a way that direct policy advocacy under partially autocratic conditions is not. The next two sections address these points in turn.

EXPLAINING VARIATION IN CHURCH ADVOCACY: AUTOCRATIC RISK EXPOSURE AND STATE SUBSIDIES

Not all churches judge it worthwhile to engage in activism for liberal democracy as a means of guaranteeing protection from state regulations. In this section, I argue that whether churches decide to mobilize for liberal democracy depends on the value of the regulatory protection they will achieve under more liberal democratic institutions and the costs the state can inflict on them for prodemocratic activism. I describe how the cost–benefit calculation varies for churches depending on their autocratic risk exposure and their dependence on state subsidies for operation.

Churches experience different benefits from liberal democracy depending on their autocratic risk exposure, defined as the risk that a core activity through which they teach the gospel could be stifled by state regulation imposed by an unchecked ruler. States have more tools and capacity for restricting certain types of church activities than others. They have ample tools for regulating goods and services, such as education and health care, that they themselves supply.[9] They have fewer tools for restricting other activities, including worship within congregations of well-established churches.

Churches also vary in the types of activities they engage in to spread the gospel. Some churches have historically invested in education and charity work as a means of spreading their teachings, while others have focused mainly on evangelization through traditional worship services. Church activity profiles vary across denominations and within churches across different countries and contexts. Furthermore, historical investments driven by past opportunities in specific countries tend to be self-propagating over time. There are path dependencies in church

---

[9] Ansell and Lindvall 2020.

activity profiles within countries because historic investments in particular activities create constituencies – including administrators and beneficiaries – who have a contingent interest in maintaining them. As a result, churches cannot quickly pivot away from these activities and their different historical investments give them distinctive interests over the medium term.

As such, the varied activity profiles of churches generate different autocratic risk exposure. Churches that have historically invested in activities that states have numerous regulatory tools for restricting are at high risk of an unchecked autocrat seizing control of those activities. Most autocrats cannot credibly commit to respecting church autonomy over these activities. For these churches, the policy benefits achieved under liberal democracy as compared to autocracy are large. In contrast, churches that have historically focused mainly on worship services within congregations have a low risk of an autocrat shutting down their core activities. For these churches, the policy benefits from liberal democracy are much smaller.

In addition to churches having different policy benefits under liberal democracy, autocratic rulers can inflict different costs on them for prodemocratic activism. Churches that depend on state financing to run core activities face greater costs for activism and they are unlikely to bite the hand that feeds them. Democratic activism to defend key activities from state regulation is not worthwhile if those activities cease to exist due to the withdrawal of state funding. Churches expect liberal democratic institutions to offer protection against anti-church regulations but understand they cannot guarantee public financing flows to churches.

In contrast, churches that are independent of state funding, relying instead on donations from members or international religious communities to finance core activities, are not as easily incentivized by the promise of potential future funding from the state. There is an asymmetry because vested institutional interests and loss aversion make it more costly for churches to eliminate existing programming through budget cuts, for example, than to give up an opportunity to expand programs through new state financing. As a result, fiscally independent churches are more likely to engage in democratic activism to defend their ongoing activities from state regulation.

Thus, churches engage in a cost–benefit calculation about whether liberal democratic activism is worth it. The results of this calculation are contingent on the specific operations of churches in particular countries. The activities they engage in to spread the gospel and their dependence on the state to finance those activities jointly determine the likelihood of their speaking out in defense of democracy. Churches are most likely to advocate for liberal democracy to the extent that they depend on independent financing for evangelization activities that the state has high capacity to regulate.

MECHANISMS OF CHURCH INFLUENCE: WHY CHURCHES PROTECT POLITICAL INSTITUTIONS FOR POLICY INTERESTS

Church advocacy for liberal democracy only makes sense if it has some chance of success and, indeed, a greater chance of success than direct advocacy for its preferred policy positions. Why can churches defend liberal democratic institutions better than they can directly lobby for policy under conditions of autocracy?

The answer is that there is a wider constituency with an interest in democracy who can be mobilized by church democratic activism than can be mobilized by most church policy positions. Church prodemocratic advocacy is powerful because of its unique capacity to mobilize a range of other actors in support of democratic institutions. Specifically, church advocacy is powerful to the extent that it has the potential to mobilize three groups that have both an interest in and the capacity to act in support of liberal democratic institutions: political elites, citizens, and the international community.

First, political elites within the regime collectively have an interest in preserving their power vis-à-vis the ruler and can potentially maneuver within the state to preserve and augment checks and balances, for example, by voting against legislation that eliminates presidential term limits or reduces the power of the judiciary.[10] Second, citizens collectively have an interest in democratic institutions that give them political power and they can mobilize against the autocratic actions of rulers either by protesting in the streets or, in cases of democratic backsliding, by voting against those rulers in elections.[11] Third, many members of the international community – including Western powers and numerous international organizations – have a stated interest in advancing democratic institutions and a variety of symbolic and material tools for punishing autocratic actions by rulers.[12]

---

[10] Haggard and Kaufman 2021; Posner and Young 2007.
[11] Brancati 2016; Svolik 2019.
[12] Bush 2015; Dunning 2004; Hyde 2011; Levitsky and Way 2010.

Yet despite these actors' collective interests in democracy and the actions available to them to support liberal democratic institutions, they often fail to act due to information and coordination problems. The international community, citizens, and to some extent, political elites can face information problems in identifying specific actions by rulers as antidemocratic. The challenge is that violations of democratic norms are not always easily identifiable, especially for citizens and international actors who have only a peripheral interest in the intricacies of a country's domestic politics. Rulers find ways to justify violations of the constitution and political rights, for example, political opponents are arrested for corruption or inciting violence rather than for criticizing the government, or political rallies are banned for public safety reasons rather than to prevent mobilization against the regime.[13]

In addition, citizens and political elites face coordination problems in acting collectively in support of democratic institutions. Even if they have private preferences for liberal democratic institutions, they are only willing to act in support of these preferences if they are confident others will join them so that there is a greater probability of success.[14] Citizens are only likely to turn up at protests if they believe numerous others will too, and parliamentarians are more willing to vote down illiberal laws if they believe a majority of colleagues will join them.

As a result of these information and coordination problems, church advocacy can play a critical role in mobilizing action by political elites, citizens, and the international community. Churches are often considered credible sources of information about autocratic acts. Many political actors are closely aligned with specific political coalitions and are perceived as politically biased. As such, it is difficult for receivers of their messages to assess whether their statements about the democratic appropriateness of specific actions are credible or self-serving. In contrast, churches can be credible sources of information about autocratic acts especially when they have a material interest in liberal democracy over autocracy. As broadly trusted and well-known institutions, churches have the capacity to coordinate diverse groups in support of pro-democracy actions. Church statements can potentially coordinate action by political elites and citizens across partisan lines. In addition, interchurch coordinating bodies can help to organize citizens across denominations. In

---

[13] Bermeo 2016 refers to this as the "vexing ambiguity" in determining whether any particular legal change poses sufficient threat to democracy to mobilize against it.

[14] On the coordination problem, see Kuran 1991; Weingast 1997.

highly religious Christian-majority societies, the church is likely to have unique coordinating capacity due to its prominence.

Thus, churches advocate for liberal democracy when their actions have the possibility of mobilizing some combination of political elites, citizens, and international actors to effectively preserve or advance liberal democratic institutions. Strengthening liberal democracy is a positive outcome for the church in circumstances in which church policy interests are better guaranteed under its institutions. Furthermore, churches need to defend democratic political institutions before they can defend their own policy interests because they cannot rely on the same broad coalition to mobilize in support of those narrower interests. A wider range of political elites, citizens, and international actors share an interest in liberal democracy than share an interest in policies that further the ability of a church to advance its worldview.

Why don't autocratic rulers concede to church policy interests to avoid confrontations over political institutions? Why doesn't the shadow of church activism for liberal democracy permit rulers to credibly commit to policy concessions under more autocratic institutions? The answers to these puzzles lie in the monitoring and enforcement of policy agreements under autocratic institutions. Under such institutions, rulers monopolize information, making it difficult for churches to even assess whether agreements are being kept. In addition, insofar as church policy interests often involve restraining the power of the state in particular sectors, rulers cannot adequately guarantee the enforcement of these agreements by lower-level bureaucrats – each with individual incentives to demonstrate regime loyalty above all else. As a result, even if autocratic rulers would like to make policy guarantees to churches to stave off any church democratic activism, their promises are not credible.

CHURCH EDUCATION SYSTEMS AS SITE OF CONTESTATION

Although numerous activities can potentially increase church autocratic risk exposure and dependence on state subsidies, in many countries, a key source of variation in both autocratic risk and financial dependence on the state is the size and structure of church education systems. Just as some scholars have emphasized the centrality of education to church-state coalitional conflict, the structure of the education system helps to explain church decisions about whether to engage in democratic activism.[15]

---

[15] Kalyvas 1996; Lipset and Rokkan 1967.

Churches vary in the amount of education they provide; the more they provide, the greater their autocratic risk exposure and, therefore, the greater the benefits from liberal democratic institutions. But they also vary in the extent to which they depend on the state to finance their schools; the greater the extent, the greater the cost of democratic activism.

Most churches have an interest in educating young people as a means of evangelizing and nurturing the next generation, but there is considerable range among churches in their investment in formal schools. This variation is due partly to denominational differences in the value placed on formal education and partly to country- and church-specific path dependencies. Some churches made investments in formal education as the result of opportunities in particular countries at key historical moments, setting off a self-propagating dynamic that created enduring interests in church-controlled schools. Church-run schools create within-church constituencies – whether school administrators, teachers, parents, or former students – who have a vested interest in the church maintaining control of the schools. Importantly, these constituencies do not immediately dissolve if church schools are shuttered.

Churches with significant educational wings typically become dependent on their schools as an important mechanism for spreading the gospel. They rely on the education of students, networks of teachers, and broader school communities to propagate their worldviews. For their schools to serve this goal, churches must be able to appoint teachers of their choosing who will teach church beliefs through the school's formal and informal curricula. Thus, education-providing churches have a vested interest in continued church control of their education systems. In running their schools, they want significant autonomy from the state.

Political rulers also have an interest in the control of education, and they have at their disposal significant regulatory tools for controlling the management of schools. Rulers determine whether church schools are permitted to exist in a country. Beyond that, they have two particularly important regulatory powers over such schools – regulation of the education curriculum, including and especially the role of religion in it, and regulation of the role of churches in teacher selection for church-affiliated schools, including head teachers. If churches are to be able to teach their religious beliefs, they need to include religious studies as part of the curriculum and have it taught by teachers of their choosing. Church autonomy in these two areas is influenced by the level of de facto regulation by the state, which is determined not only by official regulations but also by the bureaucracy's inclinations toward enforcement, and state administration may be either more lax or more aggressive than the law in constraining the autonomy of church schools.

Under an autocratic system, rulers are likely to use the state's regulatory power to curtail church autonomy over education systems. Unrestrained rulers have an incentive to maximize state power in general. More specifically, the ruler may have educational goals that are poorly served by church schools, whether these involve developing stronger regime loyalty, promoting national identity, or improving workforce training. Insofar as church-state agreements are not enforceable via courts under autocracy, churches are concerned that the state will implement policies that curtail church influence over schools. The highly centralized policymaking processes in illiberal autocracies mean that churches are not guaranteed policymaking input once their interests clash with those of the ruler, as they typically do over education systems.

In contrast, democracy offers some protection for church-run schools from the regulatory state. Electoral democracy by itself may mobilize voting blocs in support of church schools in some contexts, but liberal democracy offers particular promise of guaranteeing churches' educational interests. To begin, the checks and balances within liberal democratic political systems generate opportunities for policymaking input that well-established churches can use to their advantage. Liberal democratic institutions offer opportunities for input via the legislature, judiciary, and bureaucracy that churches can use even when they lack committed partnerships with political parties. The openness of the policymaking process creates opportunities for church policy advocates – individual legislators, judges, or bureaucrats from diverse parties – to lobby for positions that advance the autonomy of church schools, even in the absence of partisan coalition partners.[16] Equally important, liberal democratic institutions offer the possibility of enforcing church-state educational agreements. Under liberal democracy, churches can challenge the expansion of state power vis-à-vis church schools through the legal system. If bureaucrats expand state power beyond existing policy agreements, churches can challenge this enforcement.

As a result, education-providing churches receive greater benefits from liberal democracy than churches without such an investment. For

---

[16] Smith 2019 observes a similar dynamic in the Brazilian case, where, she notes, churches are not aligned with parties but do have significant connections to and influence over particular legislators.

this reason, churches with large education systems should be more likely to advocate for liberal democracy as a means of constraining the regulatory power of the state.

But rulers may also wield a second distinct power over church schools – financial subsidies. States often provide financial subsidies to church schools, although whether and the extent to which they do so varies across countries and time periods. This provision depends partly on historical legacies and partly on budget constraints, in addition to strategic considerations. Aside from state transfers, parents are the main source of funding through payment of tuition and fees for the operation of church schools. Churches often provide the buildings for their schools, but they do not typically provide inputs into the operating budget.[17]

Importantly, the ruler's influence over church school finances and over instruction in church schools are conceptually and empirically distinct. Rulers can regulate schools regardless of whether they finance them, and they may finance them without significant regulation of the curriculum. Financial and regulatory powers over church schools are both important. A school's budget determines whether it can exist, and a school's autonomy determines what it can teach.

Rulers are often willing to finance church schools because these schools present a cost-effective way to provide a particular standard of education. Their ideal would be for church schools to exist but to be so heavily regulated by the state that there is no church autonomy over the instruction. In this way, rulers could ensure their preferred curricula are taught to the maximum number of students at the minimum possible cost.[18]

In cases in which churches depend on the state for funding, they must consider the likelihood of losing it and needing to close schools as a result; these concerns may cause them to remain silent in terms of prodemocratic activism. In contrast, when churches rely on fees from parents, they cannot as easily be silenced by the promise of educational funding from the state. This asymmetry is because vested institutional interests and loss aversion make it more costly for churches to close existing schools than, for example, to forgo expansion of their school systems.

---

[17] Schools may receive small subsidies from religious congregations and missionaries, but these are generally minimal and cover few recurring costs.

[18] Rulers are conceived as having sufficient control over state financing that they can credibly threaten to withdraw it from church schools.

Furthermore, although liberal democratic institutions can protect churches from the state's regulatory power, they are less effective in protecting funding from the state because the level of financial support that the state can offer church schools is constrained by many other factors. For instance, budget constraints may prevent states from offering an otherwise strategically optimal level of financing to church schools. As a result, liberal democratic institutions have a stronger positive effect on church regulatory autonomy from the state than on its financial support from the state. Hence, church advocacy for liberal democracy is more likely to improve its regulatory autonomy than its financial support.

Pulling the argument together, under what conditions do churches become public advocates for liberal democracy? Churches that run schools are more exposed to autocratic risk than churches that do not because illiberal autocratic regimes are more likely to impose regulations that restrict church autonomy to teach their beliefs in schools than to regulate what is taught via church services. As a result, all things equal, churches with more schools should be more vocal in their support of liberal democracy.

But church incentives to speak out in support of liberal democracy are also influenced by the second factor, the extent to which they depend on parents' payment of school fees rather than state transfers to fund their schools. In cases in which churches are highly dependent on state transfers to run their schools, they are less likely to speak out in support of liberal democracy, which does little to protect those financial flows. For churches, it is not worth mobilizing to protect the autonomy of schools that will be shut down if state funding is withdrawn. In contrast, in cases in which churches depend more on school fees paid by parents, they are more likely to speak out in defense of liberal democracy.

The predictions of the theory are summarized in Figure 2.1. At critical moments, churches decide whether to speak out in support of liberal democracy, potentially mobilizing sufficient citizen and politician activism to influence the country's political institutions. Churches are unlikely to speak out when their autonomy is at low risk (due to having few schools) or when the withdrawal of state transfers could undermine their education system. They are most likely to speak out when their autonomy is at high risk and their schools operate independently of state transfers.[19]

---

[19] For the purposes of the figure, risk and transfers are displayed as dichotomous rather than continuous variables.

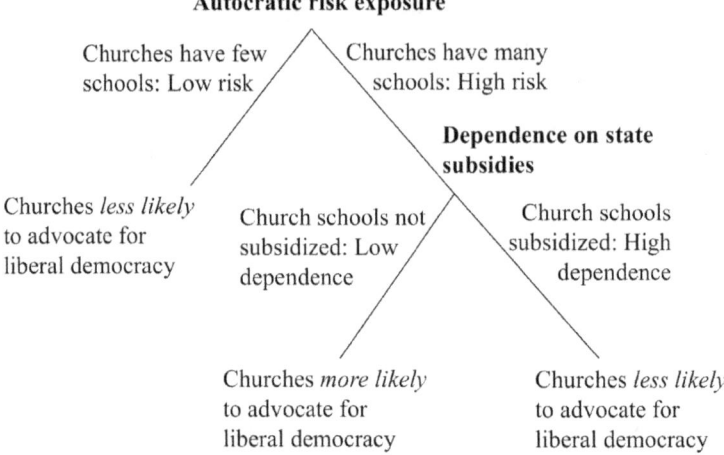

FIGURE 2.1 Predictions of the theory for church democratic activism

DISTINGUISHING THEORY FROM ALTERNATIVE EXPLANATIONS

My theory offers a novel explanation of varied church activism for liberal democracy, making distinct predictions about the circumstances under which churches engage in activism. In this section, I compare the theory to existing explanations for church democratic activism and draw out the empirical implications that differentiate it from those theories.

A first set of existing explanations for church democratic activism emphasizes denominational shifts in political theology. In particular, the Catholic Church's new commitment to religious liberty and human rights following Vatican II in the 1960s is often used to explain the emergence of Catholic democratic activism in subsequent decades.[20] These explanations provide insight into the increased embrace of human rights by churches as part of Christian teaching, but provide less understanding of why they specifically advocate for liberal democratic political institutions. In addition, explanations that emphasize changes in political theology have difficulty interpreting variation in democratic activism by church leaders from the same denomination across countries. In contrast, this book explains the diverse commitments of church leaders across countries, emphasizing how variation in

---

[20] Huntington 1991; Philpott 2004.

their country-specific activities create distinct levels of autocratic risk exposure and distinct levels of dependence on state financing. In doing so, it provides an explanation for variation in democratic activism by Catholic bishops and Protestant church leaders across countries.

A second set of explanations emphasizes the role of religious competition in driving church democratic activism.[21] These arguments build on the religious marketplace framework, arguing that church leaders will only be responsive to congregant interests where they face competitors. For these scholars, church democratic activism is a response to popular interests under conditions of competition for congregants, and churches should engage in higher levels of activism when they face higher levels of competition from other religious groups. In contrast, I argue that church leaders advocate for liberal democracy not when they are forced to make concessions to popular interests, but when doing so will protect the institutional interests of the church in disseminating their teachings with minimal obstruction by the state. Churches coordinate, rather than follow, their congregants' democratic activism in my explanation, and their level of activism is not expected to increase with religious fractionalization.

A third set of explanations emphasizes the alignment of church leaders with the ruling class to explain their varied commitment to democracy. Some scholars argue that leaders of Catholic and mainline Protestant churches are part of the dominant class and that they often personally benefit from patronage from the ruling regime.[22] From this perspective, upper-class church leaders are rarely expected to confront regimes and will only embrace democracy in exceptional circumstances. Other scholars argue that the varied alignment of church leaders with the ruling class depends on whether they share the same ethnic or religious identity.[23] In this view, church leaders are more likely to engage in democratic activism when they do not share the same ethnic or religious identity as the ruler. These theories treat church leaders as individuals whose likelihood of personal cooptation is a function of class, ethnic, or religious identities. In contrast, my theory focuses on well-established churches that are presumed to have institutional mechanisms for ensuring that church leadership act not only in their personal best interest but also in the best interest of the organization. This is not to say that

---

[21] Gill 1998; Iannaccone, Finke, and Stark 1997; Trejo 2012.
[22] Haynes 2004.
[23] Longman 2010.

individual leaders within these churches are never personally coopted by regimes, but church leadership is conceived as existing beyond any one individual. As a result, the theory predicts church institutional interests play a critical role in explaining church activism beyond any role of class, ethnic, or religious cleavages.

The framework of this book is most closely related to interest group approaches to the study of churches. In this vein, Stathis Kalyvas, Carolyn Warner, and Anna Grzymala-Busse explain the decision of the Catholic Church to ally itself with specific political coalitions rather than take alternative actions by conceptualizing it as an interest group seeking to advance its institutional interests, with all three books focusing mainly on European cases.[24] The innovation of my work is conceiving church activism for liberal democratic political institutions, rather than the decision to ally with a particular political coalition, as the type of political engagement to be explained. In contexts where churches do not have credible coalition partners, they can instead seek the institutional solution of liberal democracy to protect their policy interests. In such cases, churches decide whether to engage in liberal democratic activism or to remain silent, weighing the costs and benefits of these options against one another. The book follows Grzymala-Busse in emphasizing the benefits to churches of openings in the policymaking process that allow them direct influence instead of relying on coalition partners, but it moves beyond previous work by showing how liberal democratic institutions help guarantee institutional access for churches when comparing across countries and a wider range of political regimes.[25]

*****

This chapter outlines the book's theory and explicates its main theoretical predictions. The theory predicts that churches with higher autocratic risk exposure are more likely to engage in activism for liberal democracy but that this incentive is mitigated when they are highly dependent on state subsidies to run core activities. The chapter also explains that in the context of sub-Saharan Africa, churches' autocratic risk exposure and dependence on state subsidies are well captured through a focus on church education systems. The main predictions of this theoretical

---

[24] See Grzymala-Busse 2015; Kalyvas 1996; Warner 2000.
[25] Grzymala-Busse 2015.

framework are tested in Part II, Chapters 4 and 5. Subsequently, in Part III, Chapters 6 and 7, I test the underpinning assumptions that churches have a positive probability of success when they engage in activism for liberal democracy and that they enjoy higher levels of policy influence when liberal democratic institutions are strong. But first, in Chapter 3, I do the important background work of describing the situation of churches in postindependence sub-Saharan Africa, further explaining why the variables of interest can be operationalized through a focus on church education systems in this context.

3

The Politics of Church Education in Sub-Saharan Africa

This chapter provides background on the position of churches in post-independence sub-Saharan Africa (1957 to the present), describing how historical context shapes their interests and the strategies available to them for defending those interests. Although citizens of sub-Saharan Africa are, on some measures, the most religious in the world, the relationship between church and the state has been more arm's length than in other global regions. I show that in the context of sub-Saharan Africa, churches have lacked strong coalitional allies who can represent their positions in government. The lack of these allies helps to explain why churches there have frequently turned to liberal democratic institutions to guarantee their interests. The chapter also demonstrates the centrality of church education systems to church–state relations on the continent. I describe how states have neither provided subsidies for church ecclesiastical activities nor had the regulatory capacity to shut down the preaching activities of well-established churches.[1] As a result, church education systems, which sometimes receive state funding and which are generally subject to state regulation, are central to church–state relations. In this context, I can home in on differences in church education systems to analyze the two key variables in my explanation for church democratic activism: autocratic risk exposure and dependence on state resources.

This context helps to explain why churches sometimes turn to liberal democratic institutions to guarantee their educational interests, and it

---

[1] This contrasts with situations in which states provide general subsidies for the church, as in some countries in Europe and Latin America. On church–state relationships in Europe, see Stepan 2001 and Wittenberg 2006. On Latin America, see Gill 1998.

sets the stage for subsequent chapters that test my theoretical predictions about when Christian churches will engage in democratic activism. I focus on the history of church–state relations in sub-Saharan countries with significant Christian populations, defined as countries where the largest church made up at least 5 percent of the population in 2015. These countries also make up the sample of cases in subsequent chapters.[2]

THE ABSENCE OF CHURCH COALITIONAL ALLIES IN POSTINDEPENDENCE AFRICA

To understand the position of churches in sub-Saharan Africa in the postindependence period, some historical background is necessary. Christian churches only established themselves firmly in most of sub-Saharan Africa during the colonial period. Aside from the Ethiopian Orthodox Church, Christian churches had limited footholds on the continent prior to the late nineteenth century. In contrast, Islam spread across the northern half of the continent between the eighth and thirteenth centuries, so that in 1900, less than 10 percent of Africans were Christian, just over 30 percent were Muslim, and approximately 60 percent practiced traditional religions.[3] The colonization of Africa by European powers between 1870 and 1910 – with Belgium, Britain, France, Germany, and Portugal as the major players – undoubtedly created opportunities for Christian missionaries to spread the gospel across the continent.[4] But missionary societies were not simply arms of colonial administrations; in most instances, they operated with some autonomy.

Most colonies in Africa did not recognize one established church. In the British colonies, for example, diverse churches were allowed to compete for converts in the spirit of increased religious tolerance in Britain itself. In the French Empire, anticlericalism in the French Third Republic prohibited close association between colonial administrators and churches.[5] The exceptions were the Catholic Church in Portuguese colonies post-1940 when agreements between the Vatican and Portugal

---

[2] Zurlo and Johnson 2025 provide religious group statistics for 2015 in the World Christian Database, which is also the relevant time period for the analysis in Chapter 4. Muslim-majority countries that meet this threshold are included, such as Burkina Faso, Chad, Guinea-Bissau, and Senegal.

[3] Iliffe 1995; Zurlo and Johnson 2025.

[4] German colonies were subsequently transferred to France, Belgium, Britain, and South Africa after World War I. The Portuguese colony of Mozambique also gained a small portion of southern Tanzania at this time.

[5] Hastings 1979, 20.

resulted in the colonial administration paying many church expenses in return for significant state oversight, including a veto over the appointment of non-Portuguese bishops, and the Catholic Church in the Belgian Congo between 1906 and 1946 when a similar agreement provided preferential subsidies to Catholic missionaries who were required to be mainly Belgian.[6]

Otherwise, colonial administrations did not generally financially support church evangelization efforts, which depended instead on local volunteers and funding from international missionary societies. They were much more likely to support church educational work, as I elaborate in the next section.[7] In most colonies, churches were eligible for educational subsidies from the colonial administration if the education provided by their schools met certain standards.

National independence movements emerged across sub-Saharan Africa after World War II.[8] Ghana led the way in 1957, gaining independence from Britain, followed by French, Belgian, and other British colonies within the course of a decade. Nationalist movements quickly transformed into ruling political parties in these countries. Portuguese colonies were an exception and the last to achieve independence – only doing so in the mid-1970s after long wars.

Churches in sub-Saharan Africa entered the postindependence period in an incongruous position. Their members were dramatically increasing in the decades after World War II; the number of Christians in Africa is estimated to have increased sixfold between 1950 and 1990, from 34 million to 200 million.[9] But despite their evangelical success during this period, churches were in a difficult situation in two ways.

First, churches had low political legitimacy at independence. Despite their relative autonomy in Africa and their role in educating nationalist leaders, church leadership had been slow to support nationalist movements and nascent political parties. A related problem was that mission churches remained – in fact and in popular perception – foreign-led in the 1950s. There were still a significant number of foreign leaders at

---

[6] Hastings 1979, 18–19; McKenna 1997, 82. Even in these exceptional cases, political rulers probably had less control over the church than in the "royal patronage systems" in colonial Latin America where the Vatican gave the Spanish and Portuguese crown the right to make all ecclesiastical appointments and to collect all tithes on its behalf in exchange for a monopoly over evangelization. See Gill 1998, 20.

[7] Hastings 1979, 97, 142.

[8] Cooper 2002.

[9] Iliffe 1995, 265.

the highest levels in mainline Protestant and Catholic churches, and the Catholic Church was particularly dependent on foreign missionaries, with only about 800 African priests and 1 African bishop across the continent in 1950.[10]

Second, each church's membership was small as a portion of the country's population. Even as churches grew dramatically in their number of congregants, each church's membership typically made up only a small fraction of the population of the country in which it operated; no one church monopolized the religious landscape. Interdenominational missionary competition during the colonial period resulted in high levels of denominational diversity in virtually all majority-Christian countries at independence. Some churches also operated in contexts with significant Muslim populations. As a result, except for the Catholic Church in Burundi and Equatorial Guinea, no church's membership made up even a bare majority of their country's population by 1970.[11]

Thus, the limited size and political legitimacy of churches at independence posed challenges for them in advancing their interests in the postindependence period. The newly independent governments were supposed to represent the African majorities; indeed, even following coup d'etats, unelected rulers typically took pains to present themselves in that light. As a result, it was awkward for foreign-led groups that made up a minority of the population to present themselves as core constituents of the political parties and movements founded in this period and difficult for churches to build strong political alliances with parties and political rulers.

Church leaders and politicians alike understood the challenges of building political coalitions with churches as key constituents. There are three notable instances in sub-Saharan Africa where the idea of forming Christian Democratic parties was explicitly floated as a means of protecting church interests in the 1950s and early 1960s. The reactions of church leaders, politicians, and citizens in these cases underscore the challenges posed by their limited demographic bases and foreign leadership.

In Lesotho, Catholic politicians Chief Leabua Jonathan and Gabriel Manyeli began drafting a manifesto for a Christian Democratic Party

---

[10] Hastings 1979, 61; Iliffe 1995, 225.
[11] According to Zurlo and Johnson 2025, Catholics made up two-thirds of the population in Burundi and three-quarters of the population in Equatorial Guinea in 1970. The proportion Catholic is lower in both countries in 2000 and 2015 but still a comfortable majority.

in late 1957 but changed the party's name to the more religiously inclusive Basotho Nationalist Party by the time the party officially launched in early 1959.[12] One of the country's Catholic bishops similarly expressed that he did not "think it desirable for a Catholic party to be formed in Basutoland. All Christians should join forces in the fight against Communism."[13]

In Uganda, some politicians floated the idea of forming an interdenominational Christian Democratic Party in the 1950s, but Anglican Archbishop Leslie Brown opposed it, stating, "The Church should not support any political party."[14] Catholic politicians, including Benedicto Kiwanuka (the country's prime minister during the period of self-governance before independence), led the Democratic Party, and many of the party's opponents attempted to limit its political appeal by branding it *Dini ya Papa* (religion of the pope). But the party itself downplayed any Catholic identity, emphasizing an inclusive anticolonial nationalist platform.[15]

The inability of the church to advance its interests through explicit coalitions with political parties is perhaps best illustrated by Malawi, the one case in sub-Saharan Africa in which some Catholic leaders and opposition politicians miscalculated and formed a (short-lived) Christian Democratic Party. The nationalist movement immediately branded the party an act of "Vatican Imperialism By Archbishop Theunissen," the Dutch archbishop of Blantyre.[16] The Catholic Church was described as trying "to control the governments of [countries around the world] from Rome," and the archbishop was accused of "rank opportunism" in seeking to enjoy "the fruits of independence" despite having failed to participate in the "desperate war against the injustices of his fellow-whites" during the colonial period.[17] Supporters

---

[12] Khaketla 1971, 20–22.
[13] Bishop Joseph-Delphis Des Rosiers, according to a report of the South African newspaper *The Friend* on January 6, 1959, quoted in Khaketla 1971, 22.
[14] Carney 2020, 219.
[15] Carney 2020, 220–23. Kiwanuka extended "an open invitation to all [Africans] to join our camp ... Come ye Muslims, Protestants, pagans, Catholics" in 1958, while working to diversify its leadership. See also Lwanga-Lunyiigo 2015, 10–12; 35–43.
[16] Schoffeleers 1999, 34, 40. The degree to which the archbishop actively supported the formation of a new party was emphasized by the party's opponents and denied by the Catholic Church, including in a pastoral letter, read in all churches on October 20, 1960, denying that the archbishop had started a political party.
[17] Schoffeleers 1999, 36; Henry Chipembere, *Malawi News*, November 12, 1960, quoted in Schoffeleers 1999, 48.

of the largest nationalist group, the Malawi Congress Party, burned the homes of the party's leaders and more than fifty prominent Catholics disowned the political actions of the archbishop as a "foreigner" with "no right to meddle in the politics of this country ... While acknowledging his spiritual leadership over us, we refuse to be influenced by him as far as our Malawi affiliations are concerned."[18] Just six months after its launch, the Christian Democratic Party joined the Congress Liberation Party as a junior partner, but the merger failed to produce any seats in the August 1961 elections, which effectively spelled the end of the only explicit Christian Democratic experiment on the continent.

The limited viability of religiously affiliated parties in sub-Saharan Africa continued beyond the moment of independence. The Varieties of Democracy (V-DEM) project's political party data set shows a small number of religious parties in the thirty-four sub-Saharan African countries that had significant Christian populations in the period between 1970 and 2020. Table 3.1 lists all significant parties that used religious

TABLE 3.1 *Significant religious parties in the thirty-four country sample, 1970–2020*

Islamic	Catholic or Mainline Protestant church	Nondenominational or independent Christian church
Civic United Front (Tanzania)	Democratic Party (Uganda) I Love Madagascar[a] (Madagascar)	Zimbabwe African National Union-Patriotic Front[a] (Zimbabwe) Central African Democratic Rally[a] (the Central African Republic) Movement for the Liberation of the Central African People (the Central African Republic) Convergence Nationale "Kwa Na Kwa"[a] (the Central African Republic)

Note: The table includes all significant religious parties, defined as parties that used religion to justify their positions more than "rarely" and whose core support came from a particular religious group (as indicated by a majority of V-DEM coders) in at least one election. The parties also needed to win at least 10 percent of the vote or 10 percent of the parliamentary seats in one election for inclusion. In total, there are 183 parties or political coalitions in the V-DEM data set that are significant-sized and that have valid data on these attributes.
[a] Indicates party held national power at some point.

[18] *Malawi News*, November 19, 1970, quoted in Schoffeleers 1999, 53.

appeals to mobilize religious support bases according to this data set. Specifically, I coded parties as religious if they used religion to justify their positions more than rarely and their core support came from a particular religious group. I then categorized these parties by the religious group providing support to it, which is not described in the published V-DEM data and required original research. Across the thirty-four countries and the fifty-year period, only the Democratic Party in Uganda and the I Love Madagascar Party are coded as religious parties affiliated with Catholic or mainline Protestant churches (the Catholic Church and the Reformed Protestant Church, respectively), and only the Civic United Front in Tanzania is regarded as an Islamic party. In addition, the Zimbabwe African National Union-Patriotic Front is considered to have an affiliation with Independent Apostolic churches, and three parties in the Central African Republic are considered to have a broadly Christian base of support. In contrast, there are 176 significant-sized parties in these countries that are not religiously affiliated by this definition.

Thus, most churches in sub-Saharan Africa have not had natural partisan allies through whom they could advance their interests. Indeed, twenty-seven of the thirty-four countries in this study had laws banning religious parties as of 2010, but because there are some instances of religious parties occurring in countries with bans, this by itself does not fully explain the limited number of religious parties on the continent.[19] A more insightful explanation is the reluctance of politicians and parties to align themselves with particular denominational churches even if they often drew on religious language and symbols in their campaigns.[20] The diverse denominational landscape and the perceptional problem of church foreign ties hindered the development of church-affiliated parties. Instead, churches have needed to find alternative ways of advancing their institutional interests.

CHURCH INTERESTS AND STATE POWER IN SUB-SAHARAN AFRICA

What are the main concerns of churches vis-à-vis the state in sub-Saharan Africa? In conceptualizing church institutional interests, it is important to distinguish between the individual interests of church

---

[19] Moroff 2010.
[20] Sanneh 1996, 95.

leaders and the organizational interests of the church. Political rulers have had considerable carrots and sticks with which to co-opt or repress individual church leaders in the decades since independence. In terms of carrots, they can provide individual bishops with gifts like mansions and fancy cars, as happened in Cote D'Ivoire and the Democratic Republic of the Congo.[21] In terms of sticks, they can deny church leaders visas to remain in the country or find pretenses for jailing them, among other things. Indeed, senior church leaders have been executed or found dead under mysterious circumstances in Ethiopia, Equatorial Guinea, the Republic of the Congo, and Uganda.[22]

Nevertheless, well-established churches have interests beyond those of their individual leaders and institutional mechanisms for ensuring that those interests are pursued beyond the lifetime and impulses of any one leader. The primary institutional interest of a church, then, is ensuring that it can spread the word of God according to its interpretation of the gospel through preaching and other activities.

For well-established churches, there has been little reason to worry that states in postindependence Africa may limit their capacity to preach. African states do not provide budget transfers to churches to support their ecclesiastical activities, and so churches are not concerned about financial support for these activities being withdrawn. African states can typically enforce some regulations, such as whether churches receive tax exemptions or personnel receive entry visas, making church activities easier or more difficult at the margins. But these states lack the capacity to implement stronger regulations that could genuinely suppress the preaching activities of well-established mainline churches. For example, some rulers have restricted the number of officially recognized churches in their country to the detriment of newly established or fringe churches, as happened in the Republic of the Congo, Togo, Uganda, and the Democratic Republic of the Congo in the 1970s. But in pairing down the number of recognized churches, these efforts did not suppress the activities of the well-established ones.[23] There are only

---

[21] Bayart 1989; MacGaffey 1990.
[22] Barrett 1982, 247, 282, 688; Sanneh 1996, 94; Sundkler and Steed 2000, 930.
[23] In the Republic of the Congo, only five churches were recognized in February 1978: the Roman Catholic Church, the Evangelical Church of Congo, the Salvation Army, the Kimbanguist Church, and the Church of Zepherin Lassy. In Togo, many Pentecostal churches and the Jehovah Witnesses were banned in 1978. In Uganda, all churches except the Anglican Church of Uganda, the Roman Catholic Church, and the Orthodox Church were banned in decrees passed in 1973 and 1977. In the Democratic Republic

two examples of rulers trying to suppress the preaching activities of a well-established church, and they provide warnings about the difficulty of this task. President Macías Nguema attempted to ban all activities of the Catholic Church in Equatorial Guinea in the 1970s, and President Jean-Baptiste Bagaza severely restricted even the most basic Catholic parish activities in Burundi in the 1980s. Both efforts were short-lived, as each of the two leaders was overthrown shortly thereafter and the regulations were overturned.[24]

My point is that postcolonial rulers have not been able to impose persistent limits on the preaching activities of well-established churches. They have better capacity to take control of church social services and educational activities, as the next section details. Indeed, the exploration of the possibility of forming Christian Democratic alternatives to nationalist parties in Lesotho and Malawi was motivated in significant part by concerns that the leading parties planned to nationalize church schools.[25] Given that coalitional allies with strong commitments to church schools did not emerge in any country, church leaders needed to find alternative ways to protect and advance their educational interests.

CHURCH–STATE EDUCATIONAL RELATIONSHIPS AND THEIR PATH DEPENDENCIES

Churches have a long-standing interest in education and value it as a means of evangelizing and nurturing the minds of young people. Although most churches perceive instruction of young people as a vehicle for disseminating their worldviews, there is considerable variation

---

of the Congo, only four churches were recognized in legislation passed in the early 1970s: the Catholic Church, the Church of Christ in Zaire, the Kimbanguist Church, and the Greek Orthodox Church. In the last two cases, the larger effect was not to force other mainline Protestant churches underground but to induce their affiliation with the Anglican church (in Uganda) and the Church of Christ in Zaire (in the Democratic Republic of the Congo). See Barrett 1982, 247, 670, 688, 760; Knighton 2015.

[24] In Equatorial Guinea, most church activities were prohibited in February 1976, and all Catholic Church services were banned in June 1978; Macías Nguema was overthrown in August 1979. In Burundi, rural prayer meetings were banned in May 1979, weekday worship services were banned in March 1984, and most parish activities were curtailed by abolishing Catholic parish councils and disempowering lay catechists in April 1987; Bugaza was overthrown in September 1987. Barrett 1982, 282; Fegley 1981, 39; Lemarchand 1996, 113–14; James Brooke, "Rule By Minority Persists in Burundi," *New York Times*, June 4, 1987, A12; *Associated Press*, "John Paul II Notes that there are Religious Restrictions in Burundi" August 18, 1985.

[25] Hincks 2009, 551; Schoffeleers 1999, 24.

among churches in the priority placed on church-affiliated schools. These differences are partly attributed to denominational differences in theology, but they are also influenced by country-specific path dependencies that reinforce historical patterns of education provision by churches.[26]

Differences in church interest in schooling are partly attributable to theological differences that variably emphasize the importance of formal church-run education in deepening spirituality and connection to God. For the Catholic Church, formal Catholic education is a central pillar of its work. The Second Vatican Council's Declaration on Education in 1965 emphasizes the church's "most serious obligation to see to it that all the faithful, but especially the youth who are the hope of the Church, enjoy this Christian education" and reminds Catholic parents of "the duty of entrusting their children to Catholic schools wherever and whenever possible ..."[27] These ideas are further developed in the 1977 document, *The Catholic School*, which emphasizes "The absence of the Catholic school would be a great loss for civilization ... In the light of her mission of salvation, the Church considers that the Catholic school provides a privileged environment for the complete formation of her members, and that it also provides a highly important service to mankind."[28]

Among Protestant churches worldwide, there are more varied views on the importance of church-run schools to their mission. Mainline Protestant churches emphasize the importance of being able to read for bible study, and missionaries from these churches made early investments in mission schools as agents of conversion in sub-Saharan Africa. The historical involvement of early churches in formal education in many countries effectively diffused the idea that education should be an integral part of church activities. For example, Protestant educationalists, including those associated with the Anglican, Assemblies of God, Baptist, Brethren, Evangelical, Lutheran, Methodist, Presbyterian, Reformed, and Salvation Army churches in twenty-six countries and territories, held a conference on Christian Education in Africa in the early

---

[26] Following Pierson 2000, path dependencies are self-reinforcing processes within institutions that make them difficult to change once established.

[27] Paul VI, *Gravissimum Educationis* [Declaration on Christian Education], The Holy See, October 28, 1965, www.vatican.va/archive/hist_councils/ii_vatican_council/documents/vat-ii_decl_19651028_gravissimum-educationis_en.html.

[28] Congregation for Catholic Education, *The Catholic School*, March 19, 1977, www.vatican.va/roman_curia/congregations/ccatheduc/documents/rc_con_ccatheduc_doc_19770319_catholic-school_en.html.

1960s. The principles issued at the end of the conference affirm that "the spread of education is not therefore a secondary consideration of the Church, but stands at the very core and center of the Christian message, bidding the Christian ... to see that the young are truly nurtured in His way through the family, the schools and the other institutions that society has created for their nurture."[29]

Even evangelical and Pentecostal churches, which have sometimes derogated formal education as an instrument of salvation in other contexts, frequently embraced schools as central to their mission in sub-Saharan Africa. This action was in large part due to the legacy of involvement of other churches in the education sector, which created local demands from members of evangelical and Pentecostal churches that their churches also provide schools. As a former leader of Ghana's largest Pentecostal church puts it, "The mainline churches helped Africans by providing education. Our members said 'if they have started schools, why can't we?'"[30] Scholars note a similar dynamic in East Africa, where against the objections of foreign missionaries, evangelical churches developed educational systems as a result of local pressure, with African church members insisting that schools be an important part of the church's mission.[31] By the early 1980s, a number of evangelical and Pentecostal churches in Africa had significant educational systems.[32] Some evangelical and Pentecostal church leaders have come to view schools as central to their mission "to train disciples of Christ," appreciating that "if you are able to inculcate these kinds of beliefs from the very beginning, students are able to accept Christian values."[33]

Historical investments in church schools also generated path dependencies in church interest in education, and in this, there were differences among churches in sub-Saharan Africa. The extent to which churches established mission schools in sub-Saharan Africa was significantly

---

[29] All Africa Churches Conference, *Christian Education in Africa: Report of a Conference held at Salisbury, Southern Rhodesia 29 December 1962 to 10 January 1963* (Oxford University Press, 1963), 31–32.

[30] Interview with Ghanaian Pentecostal religious leader, September 2021.

[31] Stambach 2009, 48–49.

[32] According to Hollenweger 1972, African Pentecostal churches were already building schools in significant numbers in the 1970s. In Ghana, the Church of Pentecost formed its social services wing, PENTSOS, in 1982. Stambach also dates the development of educational activities among Evangelical Churches in East Africa to the 1980s. See Hollenweger 1972, 472–473 and Stambach 2009, 50.

[33] Interview with Ghanaian Pentecostal religious leader, September 2021.

a function of the regulatory and financial policies of colonial governments.[34] Although "bush schools" were an important aspect of church planting across the continent, missionary societies could not run official schools without permission from the colonial government, and they could rarely support a large number of formal schools without some state funding.[35] Foreign missionary societies were rarely willing or able to support the expenses associated with large numbers of schools.[36] Instead, the size of a school network depended on support from colonial governments along with contributions by African parents and teachers.

There were significant differences between empires in the choice to recognize and subsidize mission schools within their colonies.[37] For most of the colonial period, missionaries did not receive subsidies to run schools in French colonies, while mission schools were subsidized in British, Belgian, German, and Portuguese colonies with variations as described in the following paragraphs.

British colonial education policy depended on churches to establish and maintain schools. Across most of its colonies, the British offered grants-in-aid to assist mission schools with teacher salaries and the costs of school buildings. The document, *Educational Policy in British Tropical Africa*, published in 1925, encouraged codification of the system of grants-in-aid across much of British Africa, and these grants were in principle available to missionaries from all denominations.[38] There were

---

[34] As the Christian Education in Africa Report described the situation at the end of the colonial period, "Although, in capital expenditure on educational buildings the Churches' record is not unimpressive, actual expenditure by the Churches in running their educational undertakings is a small percentage of national educational budgets." All Africa Churches Conference, *Christian Education in Africa: Report of a Conference held at Salisbury, Southern Rhodesia 29 December 1962 to 10 January 1963* (Oxford University Press, 1963), 72.

[35] Bush schools were remote teaching outposts, usually staffed by evangelists without training in teaching who focused on spreading the gospel in their classrooms. See Sundkler and Steed 2000, 638–39.

[36] Frankema 2012, 341–42; Iliffe 1979, 223–25.

[37] Frankema 2012 emphasizes that even if the British administration had an official policy of subsidizing mission schools, there was great variation in the amount that the colonial government subsidized education across colonies. Frankema estimates that the Nyasaland government contributed only 8 percent of the cost of running mission primary schools in 1938, while the Gold Coast government contributed two-thirds of this cost in 1938. This variation is explained largely by the greater finances of the colonial government in successful export colonies.

[38] Berman 1975; Brown 1964; Oliver 1952; Whitehead 2007. Although these grants were available to all missionaries in principle, Becker and Schmitt 2023 provide evidence consistent with a bias toward financing British missionary societies due to network effects.

a few exceptions to this rule, especially in Muslim areas like Northern Nigeria where Governor Frederick Lugard prohibited the establishment of Christian missions and their schools.[39]

Belgian, German, and Portuguese colonial administrations also offered significant subsidies to missionaries for running schools, with preferential treatment given to missionaries from certain missionary societies at different points in time.[40] For example, the colonial administration in the Belgian Congo (now the Democratic Republic of the Congo) exclusively funded national Catholic missions from 1905 until 1948 when Protestant missions became eligible for educational subsidies.[41] The German state encouraged the formation of German Catholic and Protestant missionary societies that could act as "national missions" in the colonies it held until World War I.[42] The Portuguese colonial administration strongly favored Portuguese Catholic missions after Prime Minister António de Oliveira Salazar signed a missionary agreement with the Vatican in 1941.[43]

In contrast, the French colonial administration viewed the government as the correct provider of education. This stance combined with an explicitly anticlerical position made it reluctant to subsidize missionary activities. After 1905, the French administration cut support to mission schools entirely in French West Africa and reduced funding to minuscule levels in French Equatorial Africa.[44] Although the French administration began to again provide some support to mission schools across its empire after World War II, the number of mission schools in Francophone Africa was low compared to elsewhere on the continent, although mission schools still educated a majority of students in Gabon and the Republic of the Congo at independence.[45]

The former German colonies that were transferred to France – French Cameroon (now part of Cameroon) and French Togoland (now Togo) – are also intermediate cases. Large numbers of mission schools in these colonies had already been established with the help of German subsidies

---

[39] See Sutton 1965 on the policy in Nigeria and Sundkler and Steed 2000 on the policy more generally. Bauer, Platas, and Weinstein 2022 demonstrate that missionary investments were generally lower in areas ruled by Islamic states, whether the result of explicit colonial policy or decentralized missionary decisions.
[40] Bondo 2015; Fonkeng 2007; Gabudisa 1997.
[41] Sundkler and Steed 2000, 638.
[42] Iliffe 1979, 217.
[43] McKenna 1997, 83; Silva 2017.
[44] Gardinier 1980.
[45] Ibid. See also Gardinier 1974, 530.

by the end of World War I, and the League of Nations mandate agreements gave missionaries from member states the right to open schools.[46] The French administration dramatically reduced, but did not eliminate, subsidies to schools in the mandate territories, and these schools benefited from the administration's increased educational investment after World War II.[47]

Figure 3.1 shows the number of mission-school students per 1,000 people across various colonies circa 1925. The data on students come from the World Missionary Atlas and the Manuel des missions Catholiques, both published in 1925, and the population data come from Patrick Manning's estimates of each country's population total in 1920.[48] This was the period before the dramatic expansion of state subsidies to mission schools by British colonial administrations, but even so, the cross-empire differences in mission education provision are clear, with considerably higher numbers of mission students in the British colonies.[49] Within the British Empire, Lesotho, Malawi, and Uganda stand out for having particularly high numbers of students per capita.

The number of students in mission schools continued to grow after 1925, with most colonial administrations increasing their support for these schools post-1940 in belated recognition of the demand for education on the continent. It is estimated that mission schools educated 97 percent of Nigeria's students in 1942, 97 percent of Ghana's students in 1950, and 95 percent of students in the (future) Democratic Republic of the Congo in 1958.[50] At the end of the colonial period, a majority of students were being educated in mission schools in Angola, Botswana, Burundi, Cameroon, the Democratic Republic of the Congo, Equatorial Guinea, Gabon, Ghana, Guinea-Bissau, Kenya, Lesotho, Liberia, Madagascar, Malawi, Mozambique, Namibia, Nigeria, the Republic of the Congo, Rwanda, South Africa, Tanzania, Togo, Uganda, Zambia, and Zimbabwe.[51]

---

[46] Gardinier 1980.
[47] Ibid. See Cogneau and Moradi 2014 on the case of Togo.
[48] Arens 1925; Beach, Fahs, and Bartholomew 1925; Manning 2014.
[49] Brown 1964; Oliver 1952. In the British Empire, the principle of educational cooperation between the colonial government and missions through grants-in-aid was established following the recommendations of the British Advisory Committee, which met in 1923.
[50] Berman 1975, xi, 42.
[51] For Liberia and South Africa, I consider the proportion in 1950.

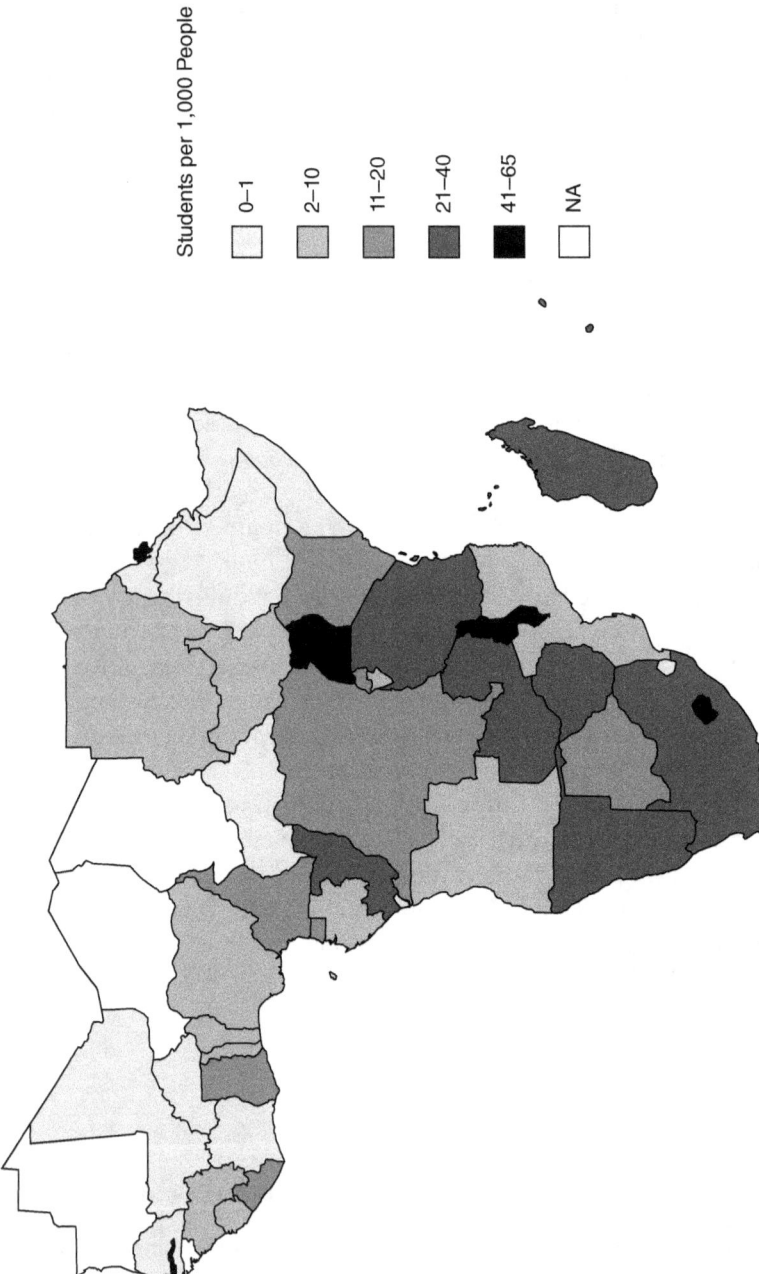

FIGURE 3.1 Christian mission-school students per 1,000 people circa 1925
Source: Author's calculations based on data in Arens 1925, Beach, Fahs, and Bartholomew 1925, and Manning 2014.

Once a church makes an investment in providing schools, it sets off a self-propagating dynamic. Church schools create constituencies – school administrators, teachers, parents, and students – who have a personal stake in the continuation of those schools. School administrators and teachers may have bureaucratic interests and identities tied up in church-affiliated schools, while parents and students may view other schools as inadequate substitutes. For example, it proved impossible for the Catholic bishops to hand over their schools to the apartheid regime in Southern Rhodesia (now Zimbabwe) in the 1970s – a move they had discussed making to protest the territory's racially segregated education system – due to pressures from Catholic school administrators and powerful former students.[52] In addition, churches with significant educational investments typically become reliant on their schools as mechanisms of evangelization. When schools are handed over to the government, pivoting from that strategy is not easy. For example, the Jesuits had difficulty engaging with communities in Zambia in the 1970s after their primary schools were transferred to the government because they depended on their teachers to lead evangelization efforts.[53] In Burkina Faso, the Catholic Church began developing Christian Base Communities in 1970 in direct response to the handover of its schools to the government in 1969, but these communities were described as still being in an "embryonic state" more than twenty years later.[54]

The difficulties in developing alternatives make church interest in education very sticky, as it takes considerable time for pro-school constituencies to disband and for churches to develop substitute instruments for disseminating their worldviews. Even if states fully nationalize church educational systems, it may take decades for church interest in recapturing their former schools to wane.

In postindependence Africa, political rulers have also been interested in the content of education for young people. For at least the past 150 years, governments around the world have viewed education as legitimately within their purview due to its economic importance and its capacity to inculcate beliefs relevant to nation-building and political legitimacy.[55] And they have a variety of regulatory tools with which to accomplish these goals, including setting the criteria for selecting teachers

---

[52] Linden 1980.
[53] Hinfelaar 2004, 258.
[54] Somé 2001, 301.
[55] Ansell and Lindvall 2013; Darden and Grzymala-Busse 2006; Paglayan 2021.

and designing curricular standards. Although it has been hard for rulers to shut down churches, they have been able to exert power over church schools as they centralize their control of the education sector as a means of economic, social, and political development.

Specifically, postindependence rulers have aimed to use their countries' education systems to accomplish three types of goals. The first is workforce training for the purposes of staffing the state administration and economic growth. At independence, many sub-Saharan African countries had only a handful of university graduates, which made skill-building a key priority for most leaders.[56] The second is promoting national identity, including through instruction in local languages, promotion of national culture, and the propagation of new national ideologies. In Africa's new nations, many rulers appreciated the possibility of using their countries' education systems to develop common identities.[57] The third is maximizing political support for the regime by providing jobs and economic opportunities to supporters and through a curriculum that lauds the regime's accomplishments.[58] Educational reforms to achieve these three goals are often homegrown, but interventions to achieve the first two are sometimes pushed by donors as required conditions for receiving international financing.

Many postindependence African political leaders have felt that church-school education is not well designed to meet their own educational priorities. Some criticized mission schools as "not designed to prepare young people for the service of their own country";[59] as creating "contrasting cultures exist[ing] side by side in a state of uneasy balance";[60] or as separating "our students from the community, from their traditions, from the authority of the elders, from African culture as opposed to western culture, from African religion as opposed to christianity (sic)."[61] Even in cases in which African leaders initially collaborated with church educational systems, their economic, nationalist, and political goals for education could potentially bring them into conflict with the church. And church and state interests are frequently at odds insofar as there are only so many hours in the day for instruction in

---

[56] Iliffe 1995.
[57] Coe 2005.
[58] Harber 1985; Kramon and Posner 2016; N'Gambwa 1997.
[59] Nyerere 1967.
[60] Kwame Nkrumah Ideological Institute, *The African Intellectual in the African Revolution*, September 1965, 12–13.
[61] Banana 1982, 53.

moral versus academic subjects, and each school has only one set of teachers who can be appointed, with churches preferring individuals committed to church beliefs and the regime preferring those with different credentials, including support for the regime.

Historians commonly refer to mission schools as having been nationalized across sub-Saharan Africa during this period, essentially ending the era of church–state conflict over education, but there are two problems with this perspective.[62] First, the broad use of the term nationalization to refer to any state centralization of control misses critical variation in the extent to which churches maintained affiliation with schools and influence over the educational instruction in them. In most cases, churches were not entirely pushed out of their schools in the decades after independence. Second, nationalization itself is not irreversible. In many cases, churches have had previously nationalized schools returned to them, sometimes only a few years after attempted nationalization (as in the Democratic Republic of the Congo in the 1970s and Burundi in the 1980s), and sometimes more than a decade later (as in the Republic of the Congo, Burkina Faso, and Benin, where Catholic primary schools were nationalized in 1965, 1969, and 1974, respectively, and then returned in the 1990s). As a result, church and state have continued to contest control of church-affiliated schools well into the twenty-first century.

Two sets of issues remain particularly contentious in the management of church schools. The first is the appointment and discipline of teachers, including head teachers, with both church and state wishing to appoint teachers based on distinct characteristics and loyalties. The second is the curricular framework for education, with church and state often differing on the content and amount of moral instruction that should be included during the school day.

On the first point, churches are typically opposed to reforms that increase the state's ability to select and discipline teachers, arguing that doing so would make it impossible for them to ensure the religious ethos and culture of their schools. They have been vocal opponents of legislation that centralizes management of their schools and control of the teachers in them, including laws and decrees passed in Burundi, Kenya, Rwanda, and Uganda in the 1960s; Cameroon in the 1970s; Zimbabwe in the 1980s; Lesotho in the 1990s; and Madagascar in the 2000s. In many countries, including the cases of Ghana and Zambia detailed in

[62] Berman 1975, 213; Hastings 1979.

Chapter 7, conflicts over the control of teachers have persisted through the decades since independence.

On the second point, churches often take issue with reforms to religious and civic education that reduce the amount of time devoted to confessional education. Ruling parties sometimes introduce a new moral curriculum with greater interreligious content that eulogizes the political ruler of the day or propounds antireligious ideologies like scientific socialism. Churches mobilized against these types of reforms in Uganda in the 1990s and in the Democratic Republic of the Congo and Zambia in the 1970s. In addition, churches often raise concerns about curricular reforms that propose greater emphasis on technical subjects at the expense of moral instruction. For example, in Ghana, Catholic and Protestant churches coordinated with Islamic groups in 2007 and 2017 to protest government curricular reforms that removed religious and moral education from syllabi so that more time could be spent on academic subjects (discussed further in Chapter 7). In South Africa, churches also contested a curriculum proposal by the government in 1997 that indicated that religious education would not be offered as a distinct subject.

Thus, in contexts in which churches have a vested interest in education, church–state conflict over educational policy is pervasive. Churches and political rulers have different preferences over the amount of time devoted to academic, political, and religious education and different preferences over the teachers appointed and promoted within the school system, putting them in direct conflict on these issues.

CHURCH EDUCATION SYSTEMS, AUTOCRATIC RISK, AND STATE SUBSIDIES IN CONTEMPORARY SUB-SAHARAN AFRICA

The importance of church education systems to church–state relations in sub-Saharan Africa allows me to home in on them to measure the autocratic risk of churches and their dependence on state subsidies. The continued importance of church schools in many countries is illustrated in Figure 3.2, which displays estimates of the contributions of church-affiliated schools to each country's educational system in 2008. This figure is based on an original data set constructed for this book that compiles data from dozens of different sources to estimate the proportion of the population attending church-affiliated primary and secondary schools. The data was collected for the year 2008 in order to capture

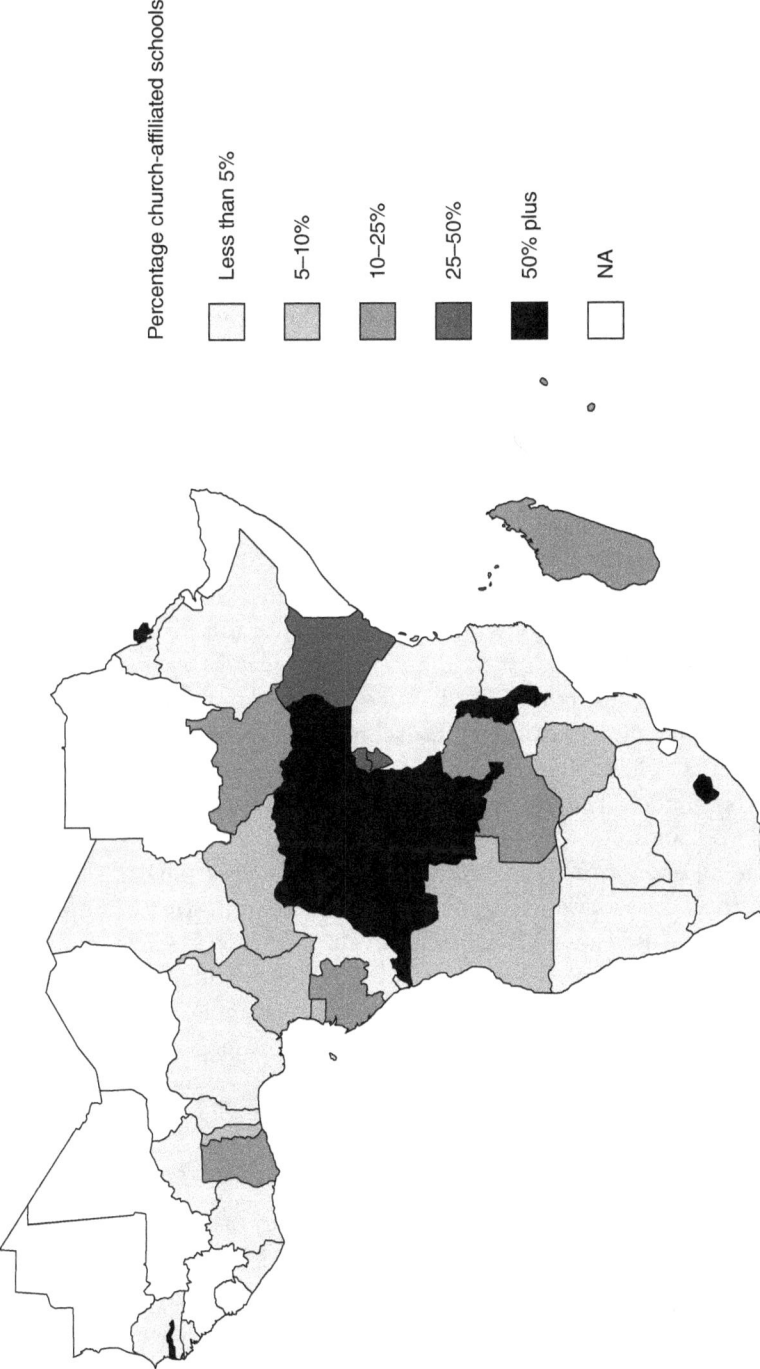

FIGURE 3.2 Percentage of students at church-affiliated schools (average across primary and secondary schools) circa 2008
Source: Baldwin 2025b.

educational investment prior to the decade of church activism that is the focus of analysis in Chapter 4. In the figure, I aggregate the data from all churches within specific countries to determine the total church contribution to primary and secondary education and then average these two numbers to calculate one summary measure for each country.[63] Countries in which no church makes up at least 5 percent of the population are excluded from the map.

The numbers are striking. In many countries, church-affiliated schools continued to provide a considerable proportion of education in 2008, and in four countries – the Democratic Republic of the Congo, Lesotho, Malawi, and Uganda – most students attended schools that were church affiliated. Importantly, this does not mean that most students in these schools belong to these churches. Contemporary church schools are typically religiously (or at least denominationally) diverse, with only a slight overrepresentation of students belonging to the affiliated church. For example, at the beginning of the twenty-first century, the percentage of Catholic school students who are Catholic in Ghana is estimated at only 20 percent, and in Zambia, it is estimated to be 40 percent – numbers that are only slightly higher than the overall proportion of the country's population that is Catholic (approximately 15 percent and 30 percent, respectively).[64] Equally importantly, church affiliation does not mean that churches can run these schools as they wish – among these cases, churches have significantly different levels of autonomy from the state – but it does mean that education is a significant church concern in numerous countries.

Contemporary church education systems differ not only in size but also in their classifications as public or private and in sources of funding. As Ben Ansell and Johannes Lindvall point out in their analysis of primary education systems elsewhere in the world, these are distinct concepts. States may finance church-run schools as part of the public school system, but they may also provide public subsidies to

---

[63] The data set includes only churches whose population makes up at least 5 percent of the population, as described in the preceding chapter, but this introduces minimal aggregation error since smaller churches do not educate significant proportions of the population. Alternatively, one could weigh primary and secondary education by the number of students at each level, which would give greater weight to churches' contribution to primary education. However, churches and states often attach particular weight to secondary education, motivating the decision to take the unweighted average.

[64] Interview with Ghanaian Catholic religious leader, August 2021; Private email from Zambian Catholic educationalist, December 2021.

church-run schools that are classified as private.[65] At independence, former mission schools were considered to be public (or quasi-public) in most former Belgian, British, and Portuguese colonies, where they had formed the backbone of the colonial education system. Only with state centralization of control of the church-affiliated public schools (including complete nationalization in some cases) did churches begin to establish private schools in these countries. In contrast, at independence, mission schools were generally considered to be private schools in former French colonies, where, in the colonial period, they had operated alongside state-run public schools.

Levels of state support for church schools are distinct from their classification as public or private and have varied over time. In many former French colonies, private church schools have received significant support through transfers from the state. In some countries and time periods, states have fully financed teachers' salaries, which represents a vast portion of school operating costs. In countries where church-affiliated schools are part of the public school system, the levels of public support also varied over time. In some time periods, the level of state support for ostensibly public church-affiliated schools dropped to such minuscule levels that those schools depended almost entirely on school fees for their operating costs.[66]

For each of the countries included in Figure 3.2, I coded the amount of state support for church schools in the late 2000s. This coding was accomplished using a wide variety of sources, most of them country specific, to analyze the funding mechanisms provided to church primary and secondary schools in each country in each period. Based on these funding mechanisms, I classified each church primary and secondary schools' financial situation into one of four categories: no state transfers, which means that most church-affiliated schools received no financial transfers from the state; some state transfers, which means that less than half of church schools received significant transfers from the state or that most church schools received small transfers from the state, representing less-than-full salaries for teachers; significant state transfers, which means that most church schools received large transfers from the state, sufficient to cover most teacher salaries, but they also charged fees; and mainly state transfers, which means that most

---

[65] Ansell and Lindvall 2013.
[66] Mehrotra and Delamonica 1998. For example, at public schools in Uganda in the early 1990s, parents paid more than two-thirds of the total costs of education.

TABLE 3.2 *Classifying church school finances*

School finance category	Definition	Examples	Cases (circa 2008)
No state transfers	Most church schools receive no financial transfers from the state	Schools rely on fees and do not receive financial transfers from the state	Benin, the Central African Republic, Mozambique, Nigeria, the Republic of the Congo, South Sudan (secondary), and Tanzania
Some state transfers	Some church schools receive significant financial transfers from the state or many church schools receive small transfers from the state	Small proportion of schools are grant-aided	Angola, Uganda (Catholic secondary), and Zambia (primary)
		Small proportion of confessional schools receive state support for serving underprivileged students	Namibia
		Small state transfers to religious education systems or limited state support for teacher salaries	Burkina Faso (Catholic schools), Cote D'Ivoire, the Democratic Republic of the Congo, Liberia, Madagascar (secondary schools), Togo, and Senegal
Significant state transfers	Most church schools receive significant financial transfers from the state; these schools also charge school fees	Majority of schools are grant-aided (public) but also charge fees	Burundi (secondary), Ghana (secondary), Lesotho (secondary), Malawi (secondary), South Africa, and Zambia (secondary)
		Significant state transfers to private confessional schools or full state support for teacher salaries	Cameroon, Chad, Equatorial Guinea, Gabon, Guinea-Bissau, South Africa, Zimbabwe, Madagascar (primary), and South Sudan (primary)
Mainly state transfers	Most church schools receive close to 100 percent of their budget from the state; these schools do not charge schools fees	Majority of schools are grant-aided and do not charge fees	Botswana, Kenya, Rwanda, Burundi (primary), Ghana (primary), Lesotho (primary), Malawi (primary), and Uganda (primary, Church of Uganda secondary)

Source: Baldwin 2025b.

church schools depended only on transfers from the state, as they did not charge fees. Table 3.2 summarizes these categories and provides examples of cases falling into each category circa 2008. As the table indicates, the funding mechanisms available for primary and secondary schools often differ within countries.

As Chapter 4 demonstrates, the number of students in church schools and the degree of state support for church schools are correlated but distinct. Some churches provide a large amount of education that is almost entirely state subsidized (as in Kenya), some provide a limited amount of education that is almost entirely state subsidized (as in Botswana), some provide high amounts of education with minimal support from the state (as in the Democratic Republic of the Congo), and some provide a small amount of education with minimal support from the state (as in Mozambique). This variation permits me to separately analyze how the size of church education systems (as a measure of autocratic risk exposure) and the amount of funding they receive from the state (as a measure of state fiscal dependence) influence church leaders' political strategies.

*****

The first section of this chapter describes how churches in sub-Saharan Africa lack coalitional allies who can help protect their educational interests. Instead, liberal democratic institutions fulfill that role and offer a potential way to guarantee church interests. First, the checks and balances within liberal democratic political systems generate opportunities for individual church policy advocates – legislators, bureaucrats, and judges from diverse parties – to lobby for positions that protect the power of a church over its schools. Second, liberal democratic institutions increase the likelihood of enforcement of church-state educational agreements. Absent the policy openings and enforcement mechanisms offered by liberal democratic institutions, I argue that it is very difficult for church leaders to secure their educational interests vis-à-vis political rulers and test this claim fully in Chapter 7. Thus, whether churches engage in activism for liberal democracy depends on their educational investments and their schools' dependence on state financing.

This chapter provides important background on churches in sub-Saharan Africa. It explains why they seek institutional versus coalitional guarantees of their interests and why a focus on church education systems can capture their autocratic risk exposure and dependence on state subsidies. It also introduces the data sets measuring church education systems that will be employed in Part II, which tests my main theoretical predictions. In Chapter 4, I test the prediction that church autocratic risk exposure, as proxied by educational investments, increases church democratic activism. In Chapter 5, I test whether increased church school dependence on state financing reduces church activism.

PART II

TESTING THE MAIN HYPOTHESES

4

Evidence on Church Democratic Activism in Africa

The Effect of Church Schools and Autocratic Risk Exposure

What can explain patterns of activism for liberal democracy by churches in sub-Saharan Africa? As the opening chapter describes, some churches organize workshops, engage in intensive advocacy of members of parliament, and organize street protests in defense of democratic institutions. But many others keep their heads down, instead focusing on their evangelization efforts and staying out of politics. Still others even endorse autocratic leaders. These choices do not fall neatly along denominational lines, and there is considerable variation in advocacy by churches belonging to the same denomination across countries.

Existing scholarship suggests a number of possible frameworks for understanding these decisions. Most frequently, religious politics in sub-Saharan Africa is seen through the lens of intergroup conflict. There are multiple ways this framework can be applied to understand church activism. In the most obvious application, churches are predicted to criticize rulers who belong to different religions or denominations as they seek to maximize political power for members of their own group.[1] Alternatively, churches are sometimes described as simply another type of organization through which ethnic politics is pursued, with church interests determined by the ethnic group that has captured the institution.[2] Another variant conceives churches as a forum for class politics, with church leaders – especially those of affluent

---

[1] On religious identity as a form of ethnic identity, see Chandra 2005; Montalvo and Reynal-Querol 2005; Posner 2005.
[2] Longman 2010.

churches – forming part of the ruling class and therefore avoiding the criticism of political rulers.³

A distinct starting point for understanding church activism is through the lens of civil society. In this view, churches can best be understood as one among many types of civil society organizations that could, in theory, engage in democratic activism. If they are more likely than trade unions, women's groups, or other civic associations to engage in democratic activism at particular times, it is because they have more resources and political opportunities than other civil society groups.⁴ In the specific context of sub-Saharan Africa, it is sometimes argued that churches have greater protection from autocrats than other civil society organizations and engage in democratic activism only when there is no one else in civil society to do it.⁵

Another framework for understanding church advocacy is the religious marketplace. According to this perspective, churches that face higher levels of competition have greater incentives to provide attractive products to their consumers.⁶ Initially developed to explain the responsiveness of churches to consumer demand for religious products, the theory has been adopted to explain political activism by churches, especially in Latin America.⁷ In instances in which civilians value democratic activism from church leaders, churches are more likely to make the effort to provide this activism if they face stiff competition from other churches and religious groups for members.

In this chapter, I test the explanatory power of each of these frameworks because their utility in understanding patterns of church democratic activism is ultimately an empirical matter. Importantly, none of these frameworks start from the position that churches, by virtue of their religious mission, are distinct from other organizations. Churches are conceived as venues for communal or class conflict, as generic (if particularly well-resourced) civil society organizations, or as economic actors seeking to maximize market share. Furthermore, while these broad theoretical frameworks can be applied to understand why churches may engage in criticism of the government of the day, they do not provide guidance for considering why churches may engage in liberal democratic activism specifically.

---

³ Haynes 2004; Longman 2010.
⁴ Gifford 1995.
⁵ Sabar-Friedman 1997; Phiri 2001.
⁶ Iannaccone, Finke, and Stark 1997.
⁷ Gill 1998; Trejo 2012.

In contrast, the theory I develop takes seriously the specific institutional goal of churches to spread their teachings within society and how this aim influences their position on liberal democracy. All churches have an institutional interest in defending the core activities in which they have invested to spread their interpretation of the gospel. But some church activities are at greater risk of expropriation by an unchecked autocratic ruler than others. Although it is almost impossible for rulers to shut down worship services in older churches, they have considerable regulatory powers over church activities, such as education provision, for which modern states share responsibility. As a result, churches with large educational investments have more to lose if an unchecked autocrat expropriates this core evangelization activity and have a greater institutional interest in liberal democracy as a check on the power of rulers. For these reasons, churches with large educational investments are more likely to defend liberal democracy as a means of protecting their core institutional interests.

Evidence on how countries with stronger liberal democratic institutions provide greater openings for church advocates to advance church educational interests in sub-Saharan Africa is presented in Chapter 7. Here, I simply note that many church leaders are aware that elections, strong parliaments, and legal restrictions on the power of presidents can protect their educational interests. For example, during campaigns in support of free and fair elections in Ghana in the late 1960s and in Kenya in the late 1980s, Catholic bishops in both countries released pastoral letters recommending the election of parliamentarians who would advocate for increased church influence over the management of their schools.[8] In the interviews I conducted for this book, contemporary church leaders in Ghana and Zambia emphasized the benefits of their country's movement toward independent legal systems in ensuring that the state respects church–state agreements regarding their role in running their schools.[9] This demonstrates that religious leaders often understand how liberal democratic institutions can protect church schools from the regulatory impulses of an unchecked executive.

This understanding underpins my hypothesis that churches with greater investments in education are more likely to engage in liberal

---

[8] Catholic Bishops of Ghana, *Message from the Catholic Hierarchy of Ghana to All Christians on Civic Responsibilities*, October 6, 1968; Catholic Bishops of Kenya, *Pastoral Letter on the Occasion of the 1988 Elections*, January 1988.

[9] Interview with Zambian Catholic educationalist, June 2021; Interview with Ghanaian Pentecostal religious leader, September 2021.

democratic advocacy. Churches with larger education systems are, on average, more likely to advocate for liberal democracy as a means of protecting their investments from regulatory encroachment by unchecked rulers. But rulers have two distinct powers over church schools, regulatory and financial, although the latter varies less with the degree of democracy and more with the fiscal well-being of the country. As a result, if churches are sufficiently dependent on state transfers to run their schools, they may hold back criticism of the country's political institutions for fear of having funding withdrawn and their schools consequently closed due to financial constraints. Democratic political institutions can protect the autonomy of church schools but are less effective in securing financial transfers from the state because these are limited and subject to competing priorities. As a result, churches that have a large number of schools and that are dependent on state financial transfers to fund them face trade-offs in speaking out to defend those schools. In contrast, churches for which a sizable portion of school funding comes from fees paid by parents can criticize the ruling authorities without fear of their schools collapsing financially as a result.

This chapter and Chapter 5 systematically test these two sets of claims drawing on cross-national evidence from sub-Saharan Africa. As emphasized in Chapter 3, specific historical legacies have made the education system the main point of interaction between church and state in sub-Saharan Africa. As a result, I operationalize church autocratic risk exposure and dependence on state resources through a focus on this sector. In this chapter, I draw on the measures of church education systems introduced in Chapter 3 and a novel data set on church democratic activism to test my predictions. The resulting data set includes eighty-one churches in thirty-four countries across sub-Saharan Africa, representing every church whose membership made up at least 5 percent of the country's population in 2015.[10] The main analysis in this chapter focuses on church democratic activism in the period 2009–18 when elections had been established across most of the continent but liberal democracy was not consolidated in any country. I also consider patterns of activism between 1988 and 1998 in the discussion of the robustness of the findings.

---

[10] This sample includes thirty-two Catholic churches, nine Anglican churches, seven Assemblies of God churches, five Lutheran churches, three Seventh Day Adventist churches, and two Orthodox churches, among others. A full list of the eighty-one churches is included in Table B2 in the appendices.

MEASURING CHURCH ACTIVISM IN SUPPORT OF DEMOCRATIC POLITICAL INSTITUTIONS

My analysis draws on an original data set on the extent of church activism in support of democratic political institutions in sub-Saharan Africa. This data set focuses on the amount of public activism by church leadership in support of liberal democracy. Church leaders are coded as engaging in advocacy for liberal democracy in a particular year if I found evidence that they directly challenged the regime to improve any of the three aspects of liberal democracy: the quality of elections for the ruler, the strength of institutional checks on the rulers' power, and the civil liberties of political opponents. Although churches may prefer behind-the-scenes lobbying when engaging in other forms of policy advocacy, especially those that do not have majority support, activism for democracy has the biggest effect when it is widely visible, and therefore, it is more likely to be done in the public eye.[11] Public statements have the capacity to inform and coordinate political elites and citizens in support of liberal democratic institutions. As a result, public activism is both empirically measurable and of theoretical relevance for this study.

I focus on official statements made by the highest church leadership on behalf of each country-level church as a collective. Inevitably, churches contain individuals who have their own opinions about the country's government and its political institutions. I am not interested in democratic activism by individual church leaders, which can be found in most churches if one looks hard enough, but rather in activism by the church's institutional leaders at the country level. The church leadership in each country is formally responsible for the well-being of their church in that country, and these leaders should be most attentive to autocratic risk and resource dependence on the state.

I focus on church advocacy for liberal democracy in 2009–18, the most recent decade at the time I collected data for this book. No country in sub-Saharan Africa can be considered a fully consolidated liberal democracy in this period.[12] As a result, all country years are contexts with an objective basis for advocacy to improve elections, institutional checks, or civil liberties. If churches remained silent in a particular year, it was not because there was absolutely no reason for advocacy.

---

[11] Grzymala-Busse 2015.
[12] This is true regardless of the metric used to measure consolidation. For different approaches, see Linz and Stepan 1996; Svolik 2008.

In focusing on church democratic activism in the twenty-first century, I bring attention to advocacy efforts that have received scant attention from scholars. Although many scholars of African political history acknowledge the role of churches in democratic activism in the 1980s and 1990s, limited attention has been paid to such activism in more recent decades. And even when countries experienced a degree of democratization in the 1990s, liberal democracy was never fully consolidated. Not only has there been room to improve liberal democratic institutions, but there has also been considerable advocacy on the ground that has not been systematically measured or studied.

As a result, a major contribution of this book is the creation of a new data set on church activism for democracy in the early twenty-first century. I accomplished this by conducting a newspaper analysis of thirty-four countries in sub-Saharan Africa. The measures were constructed by a team of research assistants who comprehensively reviewed newspaper articles found via the Factiva news database that mentioned any one of the eighty-one churches in the study between 2009 and 2018.[13] English, French, Spanish, and Portuguese news sources were searched, depending on the official language of the country under study.

A measure of activism based on reports in a news aggregator can only capture activism that is reported in local news and then included in a global news aggregator. At the time of my research, Factiva included information from about 441 Africa-specific sources, including 180 newspapers, 97 newswires (including AllAfrica.com), and 82 news websites. In addition, many international news sources include coverage of the African content. Factiva's coverage obviously represents only a fraction of all news articles published on the continent, but it is likely to provide good coverage of prominent events.[14]

A larger challenge is that a substantial number of these newspapers and press agencies are government-owned and practice various degrees of self-censorship. A related problem is the nuanced language that churches often use when engaging in democratic activism. As a result, I expected most incidents of major democratic activism to be reflected in the content of Factiva's articles but not necessarily in obvious ways. Church statements that criticize a country's political institutions are

---

[13] For some churches, this involved reviewing more than 1,000 articles over the ten-year period.
[14] At the time of research, Factiva included at least two newspapers for every country in the data set, except Eritrea, Guinea-Bissau, and Equatorial Guinea, and I triangulated the results for these three countries with additional sources.

considered newsworthy in sub-Saharan Africa, and when churches make these types of public statements, they often issue press releases that are picked up by national newspapers. Even pro-government newspapers that may prefer not to disclose these statements often end up acknowledging them as they try to diffuse their impact. Coders needed considerable background knowledge on a country to be able to interpret whether a particular statement was critical of its democracy. Each member of the coding team reviewed all *Economist Intelligence Unit* and *Africa Confidential* reports on a country from 2009 to 2018 before reviewing the Factiva articles. Due to the nuanced language often used to describe church democratic activism, I chose not to narrow the searches ex ante but to have the coders review all articles on the Factiva platform that mentioned the churches in the data set. The coders were also trained to read between the lines of the newspaper articles. The instruction was to use the articles to deduce whether the church had made a statement that was critical of the government's democratic practices, even if the criticism was only indirectly acknowledged in the article. In cases in which the article itself was ambiguous, coders were instructed to conduct further research on the event. For each article that mentioned a church member taking a stance on the country's democratic institutions, the coders recorded whether the statement was made by the church as a collective or by a particular individual within the church, whether the stance was critical or supportive of the government's position, and the specific aspect of democratic practices on which the church was taking a position.

I subsequently reviewed all the article codes to generate a measure of church activism in support of democratic institutions in each year. I coded a church as making a pro-democracy statement if it issued a formal statement by its highest country-level leaders or leadership council criticizing either the quality of elections or the government's democratic practices, including its respect for the rights of political opponents and government institutions to check the power of the president. I did not include nonspecific statements in support of the idea of democracy that did not also contain suggestions about the government needing to change its laws, policies, or democratic practices to further this ideal.

Among pro-democracy statements, I further distinguished between statements that represent narrow or strong democratic activism. Narrow statements criticize and recommend changes in the government's democratic practices without including wording that fundamentally questions the democratic legitimacy of the regime. This encompasses statements that are critical of electoral management practices (i.e., concerns about the composition of the electoral commission or about the use of state resources during election campaigns); statements against the government's policies toward public opposition (i.e., the media, civil society, or opposition parties); and statements that criticize changes to the balance of power between branches of government without explicitly suggesting that the country is becoming undemocratic. In contrast, statements of strong democratic activism criticize government policies and actions while including wording that makes a direct link between those behaviors and the country's democratic legitimacy.

I provide examples of both narrow and strong democratic activism in Table 4.1. The distinction between the two is theoretically important. In the case of narrow activism, the church is throwing its support behind a specific policy or legal change without using the language of democratic legitimacy to activate public support for its position. In the case of stronger activism, the church is making public appeals that include language that activates citizens' concerns about protecting democratic institutions.

In the data set, examples of narrow democratic activism include calls to change the leadership of the electoral management body (Cote D'Ivoire 2014 and Kenya 2017–18); calls to improve the transparency of the election count (Zambia 2011 and Gabon 2016); criticism of laws restricting media freedom or freedom of association (South Africa 2012); criticism of state-orchestrated violence against political opponents (Madagascar 2009 and South Sudan 2013); concerns about disrespect for judicial checks and balances on the executive (Kenya 2017); and activism in support of (prodemocratic) constitutional changes (Zambia 2013 and Togo 2014). Examples of strong democratic activism include withdrawing support for elections under the current legal framework (Burundi 2015); mounting a public campaign to hold elections (the Democratic Republic of the Congo 2011–18); explicitly condemning a coup d'etat (Guinea-Bissau 2012); and labeling persecution of political opponents as undermining a country's democratic legitimacy (Tanzania 2018 and Zambia 2017). I am very confident that the newspaper reports allow us to identify all cases of strong democratic activism, but there may be some cases of narrow democratic activism that the newspaper reports failed to capture.

There is considerable variation in democratic activism across churches in sub-Saharan Africa. Among the eighty-one churches in our data set, 38 percent engaged in at least narrow democratic activism at

TABLE 4.1 *Measuring church democratic activism*

Democratic activism category	Definition	Examples	Illustrative cases
None	No critical statements about democracy or elections		
Narrow	Statements regarding specific democratic practices (without explicitly challenging country's democratic legitimacy)	Concerns about the use of state resources during the election campaign	Benin (2016): Catholic Church called for the prime minister to resign and the president to avoid using public resources during the campaign
		Concerns about the composition of the electoral commission	Cote D'Ivoire (2014): Catholic Church resigned from the electoral commission when a presidential loyalist was appointed to lead it
		Calls for an election recount	Gabon (2016): Catholic Church and Eglise Evangelique de Gabon called for a transparent recount of votes
		Concerns about disrespect for institutional checks and balances	Kenya (2017): Catholic and Anglican churches called for respect of the Supreme Court's independence
		Concerns about media or anti-terrorism laws	Malawi (2014): Church of Central Africa Presbyterian requested that the public broadcaster give opposition more air time
		Concerns about the persecution of political opposition	Madagascar (2009): Catholic and Lutheran churches condemned the killing of opposition protestors
		Concerns about changes to the constitution or rule of law	Togo (2014): Catholic Church and Eglise Evangelique du Togo supported prodemocratic constitutional reforms

(*continued*)

TABLE 4.1 (*continued*)

Democratic activism category	Definition	Examples	Illustrative cases
Strong	Strong statements including language regarding the country's democratic legitimacy	Statements calling into doubt the results of elections Statements criticizing coup d'etat against elected leaders Statements questioning whether the country qualifies as a democracy following a political crackdown or legal changes Sustained actions or campaigns to improve democratic practices	Burundi (2015): Catholic Church withdrew support for elections following the president's decision to stand for a third term Guinea-Bissau (2012): Catholic Church criticized coup d'etat Tanzania (2018): Evangelical Lutheran Church of Tanzania criticized the government's adherence to democratic laws and values in view of political abductions and reduced freedom of expression, assembly, and information The Democratic Republic of the Congo: (2011–18): Catholic Church challenged the results of the 2011 elections, opposed revision of the constitution to allow the president to run for another term, and organized pressure to hold an (overdue) election

some point between 2009 and 2018, while 62 percent did not. Only 9 percent of churches ever engaged in strong democratic activism.

A DATA SET ON CHURCH ATTRIBUTES IN SUB-SAHARAN AFRICA

The analysis also required data on the attributes of the eighty-one churches in the data set. For information on the size of churches at different times and their denominational affiliations, I relied on the World Christian Database.[15] I complemented that data source with measures of church members' ethnic composition and educational attainment from the Afrobarometer survey, combining ethnicity data with Kristen Harkness' ethnic stacking data set to measure whether the plurality ethnicity in any church matched the ethnicity of the political leader.[16] Additional church attributes were coded based on original research using country-specific sources, as described below.

I constructed measures of whether the country's political leader belonged to a particular church each year in the data set based on consultation of historical and news sources. The first co-denominational measure codes rulers' church affiliation narrowly, indicating a co-denominational match only if the leader belongs to the specific church. The second co-denominational measure codes rulers' religious affiliations more broadly, indicating a co-denominational match if the leader belongs to the same denominational family (e.g., Catholic, mainline Protestant, evangelical/Pentecostal, or African Independent).[17]

To test the book's central hypotheses about how autocratic risk and fiscal dependence affect church democratic activism, I used the original data set on church education systems introduced in Chapter 3. For each church, I coded the amount of education provided circa 2008 and at independence, drawing on a wide variety of data sources and historical articles.

To measure the amount of education provided by each church, I separately coded the proportion of primary and secondary school students in the country attending church-run schools, where 0 indicates none (less than 1 percent of all students), 1 indicates a little (1–2.5 percent

---

[15] Zurlo and Johnson 2025.
[16] *Afrobarometer* 2025; Harkness 2022.
[17] Numerous rulers in these countries are Muslim, so they do not match any church or its denominational family.

of all students), 2 indicates some (2.5–7.5 percent of all students), 3 indicates a significant number (7.5–20 percent of all students), and 4 indicates a lot (more than 20 percent of all students). To create an aggregate measure of church education provision, I sum the amount of primary and secondary education provided and then rescale the variable so that it runs between 0 and 1.[18]

To measure the extent to which churches depend on financial support from the state to fund their educational empires, I classified church primary and secondary schools' financial situations according to the scheme introduced in Table 3.2. Each primary and secondary education system is coded on a 4-point scale, where 0 indicates no state transfers; 1 indicates some state transfers (less than 50 percent of operating expenses); 2 indicates significant state transfers (more than 50 percent of operating expenses but also charge fees); and 3 indicates mainly state transfers (mainly dependent on state funds and do not charge fees), and then rescaled this variable so it runs between 0 and 1. Financial dependence on the state often differs between primary and secondary church schools. I multiply the amount of state transfers churches receive at the primary and secondary level by the amount of education they provide at those levels, respectively, summing the two products to create an aggregate measure of state financing of church education.

Figure 4.1 plots the amount of state financing of churches for their schools against the amount of education they provide. Each data point represents a Catholic or Protestant church within a country.[19] The figure shows that the amount of education provided and the amount of state support for church schools are correlated but distinct; some churches provide significant amounts of education with high levels of state support, for example, the Catholic Church in Rwanda, but some provide very high amounts with limited state support, for example, the Church of Christ in the Democratic Republic of the Congo.

In addition to these core measures, the data set includes other country- and church-level attributes. Civil society strength in a country in a given year is measured using FHI 360's Civil Society Organization

---

[18] I adopt this simple rule due to complexities in deciding how churches and states value primary versus secondary education. Although more students attend primary compared to secondary school, both churches and states may place greater value on educating students in secondary school due to their presumed greater societal, economic, and political influence.

[19] The two Orthodox churches are excluded from the figure, neither of which provides education above the minimum level on this scale.

A Data Set on Church Attributes in Sub-Saharan Africa 85

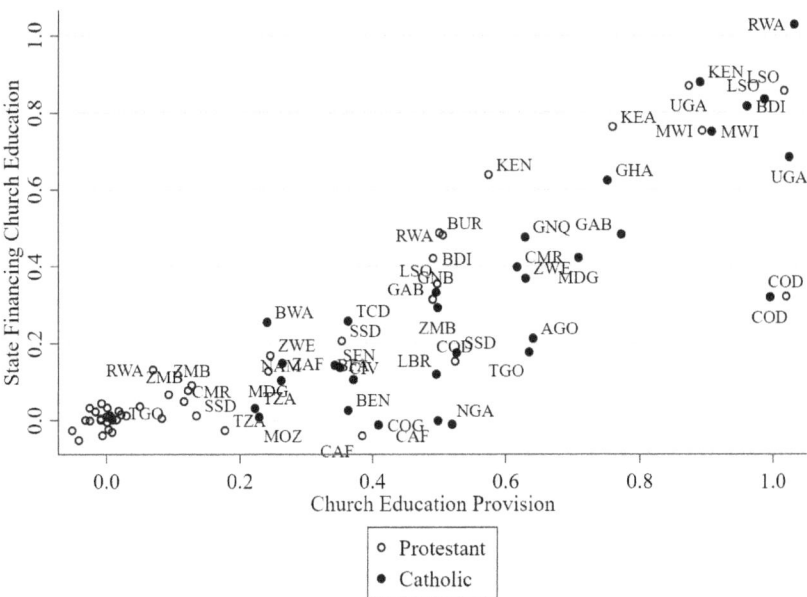

FIGURE 4.1 Amount of state financing of church education against amount of church education provision (church-level observations) circa 2008
Source: Baldwin 2025b.
Note: Figure plots the amount of state financing of church education, scaled to between 0 and 1, against the amount of church education provision, scaled to between 0 and 1, for all Catholic and Protestant churches in the sample. Churches are labeled by alpha-3 country codes from the International Organization for Standardization.

Sustainability Index, and the country's Muslim population is measured using information from the World Christian Database.[20] I coded variation in theology within the Catholic Church using data on the location of mission stations run by Catholic orders with commitments to social activism. Specifically, I created a measure of Catholic social activism by matching data on the location of Jesuit and Order of Friars Minor Capuchin mission stations in Africa in the 1920s to country boundaries in 2015.[21]

As alternative measures of church autocratic risk exposure, I collected data on whether each of the churches in the data set owned a bank or an insurance company and the proportion of the country's hospitals that it

---

[20] FHI 360 2025; Zurlo and Johnson 2025.
[21] For the location of Catholic mission stations, see Arens 1925 and Streit 1929. On the social activism of different Catholic orders, see Burdick 1994 and Stamatov 2010.

operated between 2009 and 2018. Churches that own businesses have high levels of economic risk exposure because unchecked leaders may expropriate these businesses, but business activities are different from school systems to the degree that they only indirectly support evangelization; as a result, church leaders may be more willing to trade off those assets against other costs and benefits. Hospitals are a common form of church social service provision in Africa and are also sometimes a core part of evangelization strategies. They are subject to state regulatory risk, but they likely play a more limited role in disseminating worldviews than formal education. The data was collected by research assistants who scoured church websites and news articles for evidence of these types of institutions. Appendix B contains full descriptions of all the variables in the data set and their sources.

CHURCH DEMOCRATIC ACTIVISM IN TWENTY-FIRST-CENTURY AFRICA: TESTS OF EXISTING FRAMEWORKS

The new data set allows me to examine how well various theories of church activism explain the patterns observed in sub-Saharan Africa between 2009 and 2018. As described above, the main measure of church activism is a 3-point scale, where 0 indicates no activism, 1 indicates narrow activism, and 2 indicates strong activism. I am particularly interested in intradenominational variation in activism, with the theories described in the first section of this chapter seeking to explain how country-specific contexts affect variation in activism by churches belonging to the same denominational families. As a result, all models are ordinary least squares (OLS) regressions with denomination fixed effects along with year fixed effects. Most explanatory variables are time invariant within the church decade, and for those models, the standard errors are clustered at the church level. For instances in which the explanatory variable differs over time with changes in political leadership, I run models with and without country fixed effects; standard errors are clustered at the church-political leader level in these models.

I begin by running a basic model that shows how well denominational families predict democratic activism by churches (see Table 4.2, model 1). This model separately compares Catholics and mainline Protestants to all other denominations (evangelical/Pentecostal and African Independent churches), showing that Catholic churches, on average, score 0.21 points higher than the comparison churches and that mainline Protestant churches score 0.07 points higher (both statistically significant at the

TABLE 4.2 *Testing the effects of religious denomination and co-religious identity on church democratic activism*

	(1)	(2)	(3)	(4)	(5)
Catholic	0.21**	0.21**	0.28**	0.21**	0.27**
	(0.06)	(0.07)	(0.08)	(0.07)	(0.07)
Mainline Protestant	0.07**	0.07**	0.07	0.07**	0.07
	(0.02)	(0.02)	(0.06)	(0.02)	(0.06)
Co-denomination president (narrow)		−0.01	−0.06		
		(0.07)	(0.06)		
Co-denomination president (wide)				−0.02	−0.04
				(0.05)	(0.05)
Year FEs	Yes	Yes	Yes	Yes	Yes
Country FEs	No	No	Yes	No	Yes
N	804	758	758	758	758
R^2	0.08	0.07	0.26	0.07	0.26

$^+p < 0.10$, $^*p < 0.05$, and $^{**}p < 0.01$; coefficients with standard errors are given in parentheses; standard errors are clustered by church in model 1 and clustered by church-political leader in models 2–5.

99 percent confidence level). Thus, Catholics engage in the most democratic activism, followed by mainline Protestants, which is consistent with observations about church activism during earlier periods of democratization as well.[22]

The remaining models in Table 4.2 test the evidence in support of the theory that church democratic activism is based largely on religious identity politics, with churches publicly criticizing leaders from other denominations but staying quiet when someone from their own church is in power because of their preference for a coreligionist.[23] Model 2 measures co-denominational leaders narrowly (leaders who belong to the same church) and considers variation within and across countries, finding no evidence that churches refrain from criticizing co-denominational leaders. Model 3 considers only within-country variation by adding country fixed effects to the model and again finds that churches do not significantly change their criticism over time if a co-denominational leader leaves or comes to office. Models 4 and 5 run the same specifications but employ a wider definition of co-denominational leader (leaders belonging to the

---

[22] Huntington 1991; Philpott 2004.
[23] A different explanation that yields the same empirical prediction is that churches have more backdoor access to leaders from their denomination, so they do not need to criticize them in public.

same denominational family, whether Catholic, mainline Protestant, evangelical/Pentecostal, or African Independent) and find no evidence of a co-denominational effect. Overall, the evidence suggests that preferences for co-denominational leaders cannot explain patterns of church democratic activism.

Table 4.3 considers whether churches may instead make decisions about whether to criticize democratic institutions based on whether their members share an ethnic or class identity with the country's political leader. I only have data on membership characteristics for churches that are included in the Afrobarometer survey, and so the sample sizes in these models are lower than in Table 4.2.

Considering first the ethnic politics lens, it is important to note a major empirical challenge to this framework before looking at how well it correlates with democratic activism: there is considerable ethnic diversity in virtually all the churches in this analysis. The average ethnolinguistic fractionalization within the churches is 0.75, and in only 31 percent of churches does any one ethnic group make up a majority. As a result, although ethnic politics is sometimes invoked to explain religious politics in sub-Saharan Africa, there are major conceptual difficulties in describing churches as agents of ethnic groups. The first two models of Table 4.3 show whether churches are less likely to engage in democratic

TABLE 4.3 *Testing the effects of ethnic and class identity on church democratic activism*

	(1)	(2)	(3)
Catholic	0.19**	0.24**	0.19**
	(0.04)	(0.04)	(0.04)
Mainline Protestant	0.07**	0.02	0.08**
	(0.02)	(0.04)	(0.02)
Co-ethnic president (church plurality ethnicity)	0.01	0.00	
	(0.04)	(0.05)	
Economic advantage (church members)			−0.00
			(0.03)
Year FEs	Yes	Yes	Yes
Country FEs	No	Yes	No
N	517	517	510
R^2	0.09	0.18	0.08

$^+p < 0.10$, $^*p < 0.05$, and $^{**}p < 0.01$; coefficients with standard errors are given in parentheses; standard errors are clustered by church-political leader in models 1 and 2 and by church in model 3.

activism when the country's political leader shares the same ethnicity as the plurality ethnic group within each church, finding no evidence of this in either the specification considering variation within and across countries (model 1) or the specification considering only variation within countries (model 2). Democratic activism by church leaders is not easily explained through the lens of ethnic politics.

Next, I consider whether the class identity and educational attainment of church members influence their democratic activism. Some Marxist scholars argue that churches that share the same upper-class identity as state leaders will avoid criticizing them, including by avoiding democratic activism. According to this perspective, socioeconomically advantaged churches should refrain from democratic activism. Alternatively, modernization theorists predict that citizens become concerned with democratic rights only at higher levels of socioeconomic development. From this perspective, more socioeconomically advantaged and educated church members should be more likely to value democratic activism from church leaders. My measure of church socioeconomic advantage is a 3-point scale that considers whether the percentage of church members who graduated from secondary school is 15 percent higher than, within plus-or-minus 15 percent of, or 15 percent lower than the percentage of citizens in the country who graduated from secondary school. Model 3 of Table 4.3 shows that there is no evidence that socioeconomic advantage or disadvantage influences church democratic activism. This is important evidence against the class-politics lens for understanding church activism. It also helps to rule out a modernization-based explanation for why church schools influence church democratic activism. It isn't the case that churches with more educated members engage in greater democratic activism, and so it cannot explain any correlation between church schools and democratic activism.

Table 4.4 illustrates how well civil society and religious marketplace frameworks explain patterns of church democratic activism. The civil society framework suggests that churches will engage in democratic activism when they are particularly well resourced to do so. One variant of this hypothesis suggests that churches only get involved in democratic activism when there is no one else in civil society left to do so. To test this hypothesis, I examine whether church activism is higher when civil society capacity, measured at the country-year level, is lower, finding no evidence that this is the case (model 1). Another implication of this theory is that churches are particularly likely to engage in activism when they are better resourced and larger in size. The evidence in model 3 of

TABLE 4.4 *Testing the effects of civil society capacity and religious competition on church democratic activism*

	(1)	(2)	(3)
Catholic	0.25**	0.14**	0.12**
	(0.09)	(0.04)	(0.04)
Mainline Protestant	0.09*	0.06*	0.05+
	(0.04)	(0.03)	(0.03)
Civil society capacity (country year)	0.04		
	(0.05)		
Size of the church		0.39	0.86
		(0.30)	(0.56)
Size of the church squared			−0.73
			(1.09)
Year FEs	Yes	Yes	Yes
Country FEs	No	No	No
N	550	804	804
R^2	0.09	0.10	0.10

+$p < 0.10$, *$p < 0.05$, and **$p < 0.01$; coefficients with standard errors are given in parentheses; standard errors are clustered by church.

Table 4.3 already speaks against the hypothesis that better resourced churches engage in more activism. In model 2 of Table 4.4, I consider how the proportion of the population belonging to a church influences the likelihood of democratic activism. An increase in church size from the minimum proportion (0.05) to the maximum proportion (0.71) is associated with a 0.26-point increase in democratic activism, but the effect is measured with considerable error and is not statistically significant.[24] Churches do not appear particularly likely to engage in activism when other civil society organizations are weak, nor can we be statistically confident that they engage more when their membership is large.[25]

---

[24] Another potential measure of church capacity for collective action is the size of congregations, with collective action more difficult for churches with a greater number of smaller congregations. But the average size of congregations does not significantly affect activism if included in the model, either alongside membership size or independently (results not shown).

[25] Hoffman 2021 provides an argument for why majority religious groups should prefer democracy. Very few of the churches in this data set are so large that their membership constitutes a majority of the country's population, and there is not a significant relationship between majority-sized churches and democratic activism (results not shown in tables).

The religious marketplace framework is sometimes applied to understand political activism by churches, especially in Latin America. One challenge in applying this framework to sub-Saharan Africa is that, by most measures of religious competition, all churches in contemporary sub-Saharan Africa face significant levels of competition for parishioners. No country in the data set recognized one official church during the period studied here, and only one – Zambia – recognized Christianity as its official religion.[26] Similarly, no church monopolized religious beliefs in any country, with the Catholic Church in Equatorial Guinea having the largest membership share at 71 percent of the population in 2015. Still, models 2 and 3 of Table 4.4 test the argument that upstart churches seeking new followers are more likely to take on activist positions than larger churches. These models test whether there is a negative relationship between church size and democratic activism by looking at the linear relationship (model 2) or the quadratic relationship (model 3). The coefficient on the size of the church is positive but insignificant in model 2, which is inconsistent with the religious marketplace framework, and there is no clear evidence that activism taps out above a certain size either, with the quadratic term negative but measured with considerable error in model 3.

Thus, existing theoretical frameworks perform poorly in explaining church democratic activism in sub-Saharan Africa. Church activism for liberal democracy is not easily explained as a form of communal politics, a manifestation of class politics, a symptom of civil society weakness, or a function of a strong religious marketplace. Scholars need to move beyond these frameworks to understand why churches choose to engage in activism for liberal democratic institutions.

TESTING THE EFFECT OF CHURCH EDUCATION SYSTEMS AND AUTOCRATIC RISK EXPOSURE ON DEMOCRATIC ACTIVISM

The theoretical framework of this book predicts that church autocratic risk exposure increases democratic activism and that church education systems are major determinants of church autocratic risk in sub-Saharan Africa. This conceptualization suggests that churches that provide more education should be more likely to engage in democratic activism. How well can this hypothesis explain patterns of democratic activism? This

---

[26] Pew Research Center, *Many Countries Favor Specific Religions, Officially or Unofficially*, October 3, 2017, www.pewresearch.org/religion/2017/10/03/many-countries-favor-specific-religions-officially-or-unofficially.

section tests this hypothesis by considering whether the amount of church education provided in 2008 affects the amount of democratic activism by the church in the subsequent decade. As in the preceding section, I am mainly interested in how country-specific contexts affect variation in activism by churches belonging to the same denominational families, and so all models are OLS regressions with denomination fixed effects and year fixed effects. The amount of church education provision is measured on a 0–1 scale, as shown in Figure 4.1. In addition, all models control for the size of churches in 2015 to account for the fact that larger churches tend to have larger school systems.

As a barebones model, model 1 of Table 4.5 provides a first test of the effect of church education provision on democratic activism. It finds that education provision has a strong positive effect on church democratic activism. An increase in educational provision from the empirical minimum to the empirical maximum is associated with a 0.22-point increase in democratic activism. This is a substantively large effect, and it is statistically significance at the 95 percent confidence level.[27] Furthermore, neither the Catholic nor mainline Protestant indicator variables are still statistically significant in this model, suggesting that Catholic and mainline Protestant churches are no more likely than Pentecostal and African Independent churches to engage in democratic activism when they do not have educational empires.

The remaining models in Table 4.5 test the robustness of this relationship when additional variables that may correlate with both church education provision and democratic activism are added to the regression models. In model 2, I add a variable measuring whether the country's Catholic Church was founded in part by Jesuits and Capuchins, orders known for their commitment to education and social activism. The coefficient on the Catholic activist variable is positive but statistically insignificant, and it does not alter the measured relationship between church education provision and democratic activism. In model 3, I add a measure of whether in each year the country's leader is from the church. The co-denomination variable has a negative, insignificant effect, and it does not weaken the relationship between church education provision and democratic activism. In model 4, I add controls for two variables known to have influenced the amount of church education in the colonial

---

[27] The coefficient on size is larger, but since the range of the size variable is narrower, an increase from the empirical minimum to the empirical maximum results in a smaller increase in democratic activism (0.18 points).

TABLE 4.5 *Testing effect of autocratic risk exposure on church democratic activism: church education provision*

	(1)	(2)	(3)	(4)	(5)
Church education provision	0.22*	0.22*	0.23*	0.21+	0.17+
	(0.10)	(0.10)	(0.11)	(0.11)	(0.09)
Catholic	0.05	0.03	0.05	0.05	
	(0.05)	(0.05)	(0.05)	(0.06)	
Mainline Protestant	0.01	0.01	0.01	0.01	
	(0.03)	(0.03)	(0.03)	(0.04)	
Size of the church	0.25	0.27	0.35	0.27	0.62*
	(0.25)	(0.25)	(0.31)	(0.24)	(0.26)
Activist Catholic missionaries		0.13			
		(0.11)			
Co-denomination president (narrow)			−0.08		
			(0.09)		
Former British colony				0.02	
				(0.04)	
Muslim population				−0.00	
				(0.08)	
Year FEs	Yes	Yes	Yes	Yes	Yes
Country FEs	No	No	No	No	Yes
N	804	804	758	804	804
R^2	0.12	0.12	0.13	0.12	0.26

+$p < 0.10$, *$p < 0.05$, and **$p < 0.01$; coefficients with standard errors are given in parentheses; standard errors are clustered by church.

period – whether the country was colonized by Britain and the size of the Muslim population in the country (measured in 1970, which is the closest date to the colonial period for which data is available). Neither of these variables has a statistically significant effect on church democratic activism, and the relationship between church education provision and church democratic activism remains large and statistically significant at the 90 percent confidence level. In model 5, I consider how well variation in education provision across churches in the same country can explain variation in democratic activism. This model does not include denominational fixed effects but instead includes country fixed effects. The strength of the relationship between church education provision and democratic activism remains similar in size to the other models in the table and is statistically significant at the 90 percent confidence level. Thus, overall, the relationship between church education provision and democratic activism is strong and statistically robust.

The models in Table 4.6 consider various extensions to these main findings. I begin by considering how alternative operationalizations of church autocratic risk influence the models. In model 1, I add a dichotomous variable measuring whether the church owned any banks or insurance companies. This measure captures church organizational capacity to engage in commerce as well as a more conventional view of economic expropriation risk. But banks and insurance companies are not directly part of church evangelization strategies and only indirectly support those efforts. As a result, this measure captures something distinct from autocratic risk exposure as conceived in my theory. The coefficient on the commercial activities variable is positive and statistically significant at the 90 percent confidence level, but it does not substantively alter the relationship between church education provision and democratic activism. In model 2, I add a variable measuring hospital provision by the church. Church-run health care is sometimes a core part of church evangelization strategies. It is also subject to regulations from unchecked rulers who often view health care as a state responsibility and may have competing goals regarding its provision. As a result, this measure can be conceived as an alternative conceptualization of church autocratic risk exposure. Indeed, I find that church hospital provision has an effect on democratic activism (0.16 points, statistically significant at the 95 percent confidence level), but the effect of church education provision is equally large (0.16 points, statistically significant at the 90 percent confidence level). This finding underscores the importance of diverse evangelization activities that are subject to state regulatory power in creating autocratic risk exposure.

Model 3 of Table 4.6 moves toward disentangling the endogenous relationship between church education provision and church democratic activism. An implication of my theoretical framework is that churches engage in democratic activism precisely because it is protective of their degree of power in running their education systems. As a result, it is conceivable that historical democratic activism by churches is driving both church education provision in 2008 and their contemporary levels of democratic activism. To rule out this endogenous relationship, model 3 uses church education provision at independence as an instrument for church education provision in 2008 in a two-stage least squares model. Church education provision at independence is a useful instrument because it cannot have been caused by previous democratic activism by churches and captures churches' historic interest in education, which is likely to persist to some degree over time even if rulers subsequently nationalized schools. Model 3 shows that the relationship between church education

TABLE 4.6 *Testing effect of autocratic risk exposure on church democratic activism: extensions*

	(1) OLS	(2) OLS	(3) IV 2SLS	(4) OLS 1988–98	(5) OLS 1988–98	(6) OLS
Church education provision	0.19* (0.09)	0.16+ (0.09)	0.24+ (0.14)			0.65+ (0.35)
Church education provision independence				0.46 (0.40)		
Autocratic exposure index independence					1.09* (0.50)	
State financing of church education						−0.51 (0.35)
Catholic	0.06 (0.05)	−0.02 (0.07)	0.06 (0.06)	0.76* (0.32)	0.56+ (0.31)	−0.02 (0.08)
Mainline Protestant	0.01 (0.04)	−0.02 (0.04)	0.00 (0.04)	0.38+ (0.22)	0.23 (0.23)	−0.00 (0.04)
Size of the church	0.23 (0.22)	0.28 (0.24)				0.20 (0.21)
Church bank or insurance company	0.17+ (0.09)					
Church hospital provision		0.16* (0.08)				
Church size 1970			0.22 (0.27)	−0.00 (0.62)	0.03 (0.52)	
Year FEs	Yes	Yes	Yes	No	No	Yes
Country FEs	No	No	No	No	No	No
N	804	804	780	75	75	804
R^2	0.15	0.13	0.12	0.31	0.35	0.15

+$p < 0.10$, *$p < 0.05$, and **$p < 0.01$; models 1, 2 and 4–6 are OLS models; model 3 is an instrumental variable (IV) model implemented using the two-stage least squares (2SLS) method; coefficients with standard errors are given in parentheses; standard errors are clustered by church in models 1, 2, 3, and 6, with robust standard errors in models 4 and 5.

provision and democratic activism is estimated to be slightly higher in this instrumental variable model, although the coefficient is estimated with more error, so the statistical significance of the relationship falls to the 90 percent confidence level.

How well does church autocratic risk exposure explain church democratic activism during the period of democratic activism that began in the late 1980s? For this period, I do not have annual data on church democratic activism, only an aggregate measure of whether a particular church engaged in democratic activism at any point between 1988 and 1998 constructed from existing data compilation efforts and secondary sources. I include only countries that were independent in 1985 in the analysis, reducing the sample of churches to seventy-five. This measure uses a 3-point scale to distinguish between churches engaging in no democratic activism during this period (scored as 0), limited democratic activism (scored as 1), and strong democratic activism (scored as 2), which is consistent with the previous analysis and also with other scholars' empirical approaches to church activism during this period.[28]

As emphasized above, church educational interests are theorized to be sticky. If the state nationalizes church-run schools, church interest in education does not evaporate overnight. In the analysis so far, I have used data on church education systems circa 2008 to consider how church educational interests affect their democratic activism in the subsequent decade. Because church educational interests are thought to be sticky, I could also have used a measure of church education provision from a slightly earlier decade. But as a practical matter, these numbers would be highly correlated, as there were no instances of states fully nationalizing schools during recent decades and only a few incidents of states returning significant numbers of previously nationalized schools to churches.[29] In contrast, in the late 1980s, a number of churches had recently had their schools nationalized. As a result, church educational interests at that moment would be poorly captured by the number of schools they ran circa 1988. Instead, I measure the number of church-run schools at independence to proxy church educational interests.

Model 4 shows that there is a positive correlation between church education provision at independence and the amount of democratic

[28] In particular, Bratton and van de Walle 1992 and Toft, Philpott, and Shah 2011 make similar distinctions between medium and high levels of activism in their own coding schemes.

[29] In particular, in Nigeria, some former mission schools were returned to churches in some states between 1999 and 2008.

activism in which a church engaged in the 1980s, but the relationship is estimated with considerable error. Moving from the minimum to the maximum amount of education provided is associated with a 0.46 increase in activism on the 3-point scale, a large but statistically insignificant relationship. Notably, the coefficient on Catholic is larger and statistically significant in this model, supporting the idea that the third wave of democracy (1974–2000) was, in significant part, a Catholic wave.[30] Thus, there is possibly a relationship between church education provision and democratic activism in earlier periods, but due to data limitations, the evidence is weaker than in the contemporary period.

In model 5, I maximize my ability to detect changes caused by institutional risk in this earlier period by creating an index of autocratic risk exposure that averages both church education provision at independence and church hospital provision in the 1970s. The coefficient on this variable is very large (1.09) and achieves statistical significance at the 95 percent confidence level. This finding suggests that concerns about autocratic risk exposure were important to democratic activism decisions in the earlier period, with both education and health care investments creating autocratic risk.

I conclude the analysis by testing the prediction that state educational financing depresses democratic activism. As described in Chapter 2 and at the beginning of this chapter, not all education is expected to be equal in providing incentives for democratic activism. The effect of education on democratic activism is predicted to be conditional on education financing. The larger the component of education that is financed by parent fees and other nongovernment sources, the larger the incentive to engage in democratic activism. The larger the component of education that is financed by the government, the weaker the incentive to engage in democratic activism.

This prediction is tested at length in Chapter 5. In model 6 of Table 4.6, I take a first step toward testing it by adding a measure of the amount of financing churches received from the state to support their education in 2008 (scaled to fall between 0 and 1). The coefficients on church education and state financing of church education provide suggestive evidence that the degree to which church education provision influences democratic activism depends on how it is financed, with the positive coefficient on church education provision (0.65 points, statistically significant at the 90 percent confidence level) offset by the negative coefficient on state financing of church education (–0.51 points,

---

[30] Huntington 1991; Philpott 2004.

though not statistically significant at conventional levels). Considering only churches that fall within the empirical range of outcomes observed in the data (as displayed in Figure 4.1), a shift from providing no education to providing the highest level of education is associated with a 0.14-point increase in activism for churches that are most highly dependent on state funding (total state financing = 1) and with a 0.48-point increase in activism for churches that are least dependent on state funding (total state financing = 0.33). In other words, high levels of state support for church schools appear to attenuate the positive effect of church schools on democratic activism.

Collectively, these results provide considerable support for my theoretical hypotheses. Churches with higher education provision engage in higher levels of democratic activism. These results are not explained by other dimensions of church organizational capacity, such as size or commercial ventures. They are also not explained by theological differences, including different commitments to social activism within the Catholic Church. The relationship does not appear to be driven by reverse causality, as it holds even when instrumenting contemporary education provision with a measure of historical education provision prior to any church activism.

The evidence also supports the broader claim that education provision translates into democratic activism insofar as it creates autocratic risk exposure, rather than through alternative mechanisms like changing the socioeconomic and political composition of the church. Church education provision correlates only weakly with the education level of church members, and as the evidence shows, churches with highly educated memberships are not more likely to engage in democratic activism. Church education provision correlates positively with having a co-denominational president, but churches are not particularly likely (or unlikely) to engage in democratic activism when someone from their church is in power. Instead, the evidence is most consistent with the claim that churches with historic investments in education have higher autocratic risk exposure and therefore are more concerned with the risks that an unchecked autocrat poses to their activities. Church health care provision, which creates similar types of risk, has a similar positive effect on church democratic activism. In both instances, churches need to be concerned with an unchecked ruler using the state's regulatory power to weaken their ability to spread their teachings through their social service provision.

* * * * *

This chapter demonstrates that church autocratic risk exposure helps to explain church democratic activism in contemporary sub-Saharan Africa and that alternative theoretical frameworks do a poor job in explaining the varied propensities of churches to engage in democratic activism. Churches with larger education systems engage in higher levels of democratic activism, consistent with my claim that these historic investments create greater exposure to the state's regulatory power.

Of course, states do not have only regulatory power over church schools; they also have financial power over them when they subsidize their budgets. As the last evidence presented in this chapter suggests, the financing of church schools may complicate the relationship between church education provision and democratic activism, with churches engaging in reduced levels of activism when they depend on state funding to run their schools. Chapter 5 further investigates whether changes in state financing alter levels of democratic activism by churches.

5

Evidence on Catholic Democratic Activism in Africa

The Effect of Church School Dependence on State Subsidies

This chapter examines the effects of church school financing on church activism. Do state subsidies to religious schools reduce church advocacy for liberal democratic institutions? Churches that provide education to greater numbers of students are more likely to speak out in defense of democracy due to their greater exposure to autocratic risk, as Chapter 4 demonstrated. Yet this tendency may be mitigated if the education they provide is financed largely through state subsidies. Churches care about protecting the autonomy of their schools, attaching very little value to running schools in which they cannot also teach their ideas and values. But if a school system will entirely collapse if state transfers are withdrawn, then issues of autonomy are moot. Thus, the effect of education on church activism is hypothesized as being contingent on how their school systems are financed.

There are significant challenges in measuring the effects of church school financing on church activism using observational data. Building on the book's central argument, one may expect it to be empirically difficult to observe any effect of subsidies on church advocacy because rulers could strategically offer funding to buy church silence only when the risk of church activism is high. But in practice, state subsidies provided to church schools are subject to many constraints; rulers can rarely fund them at the level they would choose if quashing church activism were their only (or main) consideration. Ruling authorities in sub-Saharan Africa face limited budgets and competing priorities.[1] In economic downturns, rulers can typically provide only limited transfers to church schools. In countries and time periods in which state education budgets receive

---

[1] Stasavage 2005; van de Walle 2001.

significant support from donors, their preferences also factor into state decisions about financing schools, including church schools. As a result, there are often shifts in state support for church schools that are exogenous in the sense that they are not driven by the dynamics of church–state conflict over the education system.

The analysis in this chapter takes advantage of one such shift that affected some church schools' financial dependence on the state – the removal of primary school fees as part of the global push for universal primary education. This major policy initiative differentially affected church financing depending on how churches were integrated into the country's education system, which allows me to identify the effects of state subsidization independent of the attributes and behaviors of churches that make them targets of subsidies and the societal effects of increasing access to primary education. Drawing on the introduction of fee-removal policies across sub-Saharan Africa between 1994 and 2008, I use a difference-in-difference analysis to show that these policies decrease church democratic activism only in contexts in which church schools were classified as public schools prior to the policy initiative and therefore forced to eliminate fees because of the policy.

This chapter focuses on the effects of increased financial dependence on the state for Catholic churches with significant educational empires in countries that eliminated school fees in the late twentieth and early twenty-first centuries. I focus on Catholic churches for two reasons. First, across countries, they are the largest provider of education. Second, I can construct an annual measure of their public activism for liberal democratic institutions from 1980 until 2018 due to their tradition of producing pastoral letters – open missives in which bishops provide counsel on various issues. I draw on these letters to construct a novel data set on Catholic advocacy for liberal democracy.

CHURCH SCHOOL SYSTEMS AND THE DIFFERENTIAL EFFECTS OF SCHOOL FEE REMOVAL

The analysis in this chapter examines the effects of increasing church school financial dependence on the state on church advocacy for liberal democracy. As Chapter 2 elaborates, the effects of church schools on church advocacy are expected to be contingent on the financing of these schools. Church schools with significant financing from parents are expected to be stronger advocates for liberal democracy than church schools that depend entirely on state financing. I test these predictions by analyzing the effects of increased dependence on state financial support as a result of primary school fee removal in many countries in sub-Saharan Africa.

School fee removal was widely adopted in primary public schools in sub-Saharan Africa post-1990 as part of a global campaign toward achieving universal primary education. In the roughly two decades between 1994 and 2013, eighteen countries in sub-Saharan Africa abolished primary school fees. Existing studies of the effects of school fee removal have focused on the broad societal effects on educational attainment and female empowerment resulting from the elimination of parental fiscal constraints to sending children to school.[2] In my analysis, I am able to parse the effects of school fee-removal policies on church financial dependence from those other societal effects by comparing the effects across two sets of countries. School fee-removal policies made church-run public primary schools newly dependent on central government transfers but left church-run private primary schools and secondary schools financially independent of the state. Only in countries where the Catholic Church runs large numbers of primary schools that are classified as public should fee-removal policies make Catholic schools more financially dependent on the state.

As a result, the analysis focuses on countries in which churches provide a significant amount of education, further distinguishing between countries in which church primary education systems are largely classified as public and those in which they are considered private. As discussed in Chapter 3, in some sub-Saharan African countries, many or all church primary schools are considered public, while in others, all church primary schools are considered private, despite the fact that many of the latter schools receive significant support from the state, and their curriculum and instruction can be considerably regulated by the state.

The classification of church schools as public or private schools is largely a colonial legacy, with former mission schools considered public or quasi-public in former Belgian, British, and Portuguese colonies and private in former French colonies. Among non-Francophone colonies, mission schools were only partially or temporarily nationalized in most cases during the postindependence period, and as a result, churches continue to play a role in running schools that are officially designated as public schools. The exceptions are Angola, Guinea-Bissau, Mozambique, and Tanzania, where primary and secondary schools were fully nationalized, and Zambia, where only primary schools were fully nationalized.

---

[2] World Bank 2009; Koski et al. 2018.

In these countries, the primary schools of existing churches were established fairly recently, and these small numbers of schools are usually classified as private.[3]

As discussed in Chapter 3, church education systems in sub-Saharan Africa have two main sources of operating funds: fees from parents and transfers from the state. As a group, they receive only nominal financial support from local congregations or international donors, although local church communities may help with the upkeep of school buildings and school oversight. In general, parent fees must cover costs that are not borne by the state.

In Africa, during the period of fiscal crisis that began in 1980, most church schools in sub-Saharan Africa were relatively financially independent from the state. Regardless of whether church-run schools were public or private, by the mid-1980s, almost all were substantially dependent on parent payment of school fees and community contributions for their financing due to low levels of state support for primary education.[4] For example, across all public primary schools in Uganda in the early 1990s, parents covered 81 percent of the recurrent costs of public primary education; in Burkina Faso, the equivalent figure was 41 percent.[5] For church-affiliated public schools, the state's contribution was probably even lower than these averages insofar as infrastructure upkeep was subsidized by the church.

The formula of parents bearing a large portion of the costs of public primary education changed with the push toward universal primary education at the close of the twentieth century, with eighteen countries in sub-Saharan Africa abolishing primary school fees between 1994 and 2013. The decision to remove fees was driven partly by donor support for the initiative, including through the UN's Millennium Development Goals, and partly by domestic pressures, with school fee removal becoming a common manifesto promise in elections, even in countries with poor democratic credentials, such as Rwanda and Uganda.[6]

---

[3] In Zambia at the time of primary school fee removal, about half of Catholic primary schools were community schools and about half were grant-aided schools, but the church provided limited primary education compared to secondary education. Carmody 2007, 543.

[4] Stasavage 2005; van de Walle 2001.

[5] Mehrotra and Delamonica 1998; Jimenez 1987.

[6] The UN established eight Millennium Development Goals in 2000 as social and economic development targets for all member states by 2015, including the goal of universal primary education. On domestic pressure for universal primary education, see Harding and Stasavage 2014.

Importantly, countries with stronger liberal democratic institutions were not more likely to adopt the reform. In addition, the decision to remove fees was not made regarding churches, and neither incumbent politicians nor churches seem to have fully anticipated its effects. No exemptions were made for church-run public schools, and although individual church schools may have formally had the option of privatizing entirely if they did not want to remove school fees, this did not happen in any country on any scale.[7]

Thus, school fee removal made church-run public primary schools newly dependent on central government transfers but left church-run private primary schools and church-run secondary schools financially independent of the state. In countries with church-run public primary schools, the removal of primary school fees as part of government policies aimed at universal primary education changed the financial dependence of these schools on the government. Church-run public primary schools became newly dependent on capitation grants from the central government for their finances, and although these grants were supposed to be formula based, bureaucratic discretion could conceivably result in church schools receiving less financial support than dictated by the formula. In contrast, in countries in which the church ran mainly private primary schools or mainly secondary schools, the removal of primary school fees had little impact on church school financing; private schools and public secondary schools were not required to remove fees as part of these policies and maintained their levels of independence from the government.

As a result, I expect the policy intervention to have differential effects on advocacy for liberal democracy in countries where churches run public primary schools compared to countries where churches are involved in schooling but do not run public primary schools. I use the removal of school fees to identify the effect of church school financial dependence on democratic activism using a difference-in-difference approach. I compare the effect of school fee removal on the willingness of churches to criticize nondemocratic practices in countries with church-run public schools and in those without them, allowing separation of the effects of

---

[7] In particular, this was discussed but did not happen on any scale in Lesotho. In two countries with large numbers of public church schools – Malawi and Kenya – private schools could also choose to remove fees and receive state capitation grants as part of the reform. As far as I am aware, this did not happen in any of the cases in which churches mainly ran private schools or secondary schools (Cameroon, Liberia, Mozambique, Tanzania, Togo, and Zambia). See World Bank 2009.

dependence on state transfers from the other societal effects of school fee removals. The identification strategy hinges on the assumption that the effect of school fee removal would otherwise have been the same in countries with church-run public schools and in those without them.

This chapter focuses on advocacy for liberal democratic institutions by the Catholic Church, which has the widest presence and is the largest religious provider of primary and secondary education across sub-Saharan Africa. As a result, it should have been particularly influenced by the policy change. Narrowing the empirical analysis to the Catholic Church also removes any denominational differences in theology and organization. I only include countries in which the Catholic Church provided significant primary or secondary schooling in the 1990s, defined as providing more than 5 percent of either primary or secondary education.

Table 5.1 compares the set of countries with church-run public primary schools that removed school fees during this period to the set of countries without church-run public primary schools that removed school fees during the same period. Only countries in which the Catholic Church has a significant ecclesiastical and educational presence are included, totaling seven countries with church-run public primary schools and six without significant numbers of church-run public primary schools.[8] As the table indicates, the sets of countries that have church-run public primary schools are not notably different from those that do not on other dimensions. As one may expect, the Catholic Church has many more church-affiliated primary schools in countries where their public schools are classified as public as opposed to private. The Catholic Church is also typically more involved in secondary education in these countries, but the difference in the percentage of students at Catholic secondary schools is smaller than the difference at the primary school level and may partly reflect that Catholics make up slightly larger percentages of the population in this set of countries. Considering the economic and political developments in these countries between 1980 and 2000, the two sets look very similar in terms of levels and trajectories. Both sets of countries experienced little economic development but significant improvements in democracy during these two decades, and

---

[8] Two countries that removed school fees have very small Catholic populations (less than 5 percent of the population in 2000): Ethiopia and Sierra Leone. Three countries that removed school fees have Catholic churches that did not provide significant levels of education in the sense that their schools had less than 5 percent of all primary *and* less than 5 percent of all secondary school students in 2000: Benin, Namibia, and the Republic of the Congo.

TABLE 5.1 *Comparing countries that removed school fees by the status of church primary schools*[a]

Country	Primary school status	Nationalization	Percent of primary students at Catholic schools (2000)	Percent of secondary students at Catholic schools (2000)	Catholic percent of country (2000)	GDP per capita, constant 2015 US $ (1980)	GDP per Capita, constant 2015 US $ (2000)	Liberal democracy score (1980)	Liberal democracy score (2000)	Civil conflict (1980s–1990s)	Church pro-dem (1988–98)
Burundi	Public	Coercive to incomplete	30	18	62	277	229	0.09	0.17	Yes	Yes
Ghana	Public	Incomplete	15	14	12	881	953	0.45	0.55	No	Yes
Kenya	Public	Incomplete	32	24	23	890	820	0.12	0.26	No	Yes
Lesotho	Public	Incomplete	35	36	48	547	810	0.13	0.27	No	Yes
Malawi	Public	Incomplete	36	6	24	401	393	0.08	0.40	No	Yes
Rwanda	Public	Incomplete	44	30	46	439	351	0.13	0.13	Yes	Yes
Uganda	Public	Incomplete	27	51	42	402	551	0.04	0.25	Yes	No
Public average			31	26	37	548	587	0.15	0.29	43%	86%
Cameroon	Not public	None	14	8	26	1323	1147	0.08	0.17	No	Yes
Liberia	Not public	None	4	8	5	n/a	614	0.05	0.17	Yes	Yes
Mozambique	Not public	Coercive	1	6	21	238	290	0.05	0.29	Yes	Yes
Tanzania	Not public	Cooperative	0	6	28	n/a	522	0.24	0.41	No	Yes
Togo	Not public	None	14	5	25	733	559	0.07	0.16	No	No
Zambia	Not public	Cooperative	1	17	29	1292	949	0.15	0.39	No	Yes
Not public average			6	8	22	n/a	680	0.11	0.27	33%	83%

[a] See Appendix B for full details on the sources of these measures. Secondary enrolment figures are not available for Zambia, so this figure reflects the percentage of the country's secondary schools run by the Catholic Church in 2001; Carmody 2007. The measure of GDP per capita, constant 2015 US $ is missing for Uganda in 1980, so this cell of the table instead indicates the measure for 1982.

both were equally exposed to civil conflict. Perhaps most importantly, the two sets of countries did not have different histories of democratic activism prior to school fee removal. The Catholic Church was equally (and highly involved) in the democratic transitions between 1988 and 1998 in both sets of countries.

In addition, school fee removal did not differentially affect the proportion of primary school students attending Catholic schools across the two sets of countries. In cases in which the church runs mainly private primary schools, these proportions may be expected to drop post-fee abolition as the public school sector is flooded with new students. Table 5.2 presents an OLS regression model that measures the effects of school fee abolition on the proportion of primary students attending Catholic schools, including an interaction term to examine whether the effect differs by status as public or not public. The model estimates a drop in market share across all countries (about 5 percent, statistically significant at the 90 percent confidence levels), consistent with Catholic schools taking a smaller share of the new students than other schools. Interestingly, we do not observe significantly larger drop-offs in the market share of Catholic primary schools in the set of countries where these schools are not public and thus maintained school fees.[9]

TABLE 5.2 *Effect of fee removal on church primary school enrollment*

	Proportion of primary school students in Catholic schools
Fee removal × public	0.037
	(0.030)
Fee removal	−0.049[+]
	(0.024)
N	474
Country FEs	Yes
Year FEs	Yes

[+]$p < 0.10$, *$p < 0.05$, and **$p < 0.01$; coefficients are from OLS regression models; standard errors are clustered at the country level in parentheses.

[9] This is consistent with existing research that shows growth in demand for private schools in Africa following school fee abolition as public schools became overcrowded and the quality of education provided in them declined. See World Bank 2009; İşcan, Rosenblum, and Tinker 2015.

To the extent that we observe differences in democratic activism by churches with and without public primary schools after the removal of primary school fees, differential changes in market share cannot explain the results. But it remains possible that the student composition of Catholic schools changed differentially across these two sets of countries because of fee abolition; Catholic public primary schools are likely to increase the proportion of children from poorer families who could not previously afford fees, while Catholic private primary schools are likely to increase the proportion of students from wealthier families who can afford to leave overcrowded public primary schools. I return to this point below in a discussion of why I don't think differential school composition by itself, rather than the differential dependence on government financing that it reflects, is the main driver of the observed effects.

A NOVEL MEASURE OF DEMOCRATIC ADVOCACY: PASTORAL LETTERS

I focus on the effect of school financing on the Catholic Church's advocacy for liberal democratic institutions at the national level. In countries in sub-Saharan Africa with significant Catholic populations, bishops are organized into episcopal conferences at the national level (often simply called bishops' conferences). These conferences coordinate the national-level activities of the bishops, including those related to liturgy, pastoral care, training, church media, charity, and social services, such as health care and education. The conferences coordinate bishops, rather than having authority over them, with one bishop elected as the president for a particular term.

To create a measure of churches' willingness to speak out in support of liberal democracy that is sensitive to changes over time, I consider the content of the pastoral letters issued collectively by the country's Catholic bishops in every year from 1980 to 2018. Pastoral letters are open letters in which bishops provide counsel, including instructions on how to act in various ecclesiastical, social, or political situations.[10] I am especially interested in letters that are addressed to the laity or the public. These are typically sent out during liturgical seasons, with many bishops issuing letters to mark Advent, Lent, or the Pentecost, but they are also issued in response to social and political developments within countries.

---

[10] On the importance of pastoral letters in measuring church democratic activism, see also Sperber and Wietzel 2024.

Bishops' conferences issue a wide variety of statements, including press releases, memoranda, and communiques. But pastoral letters are particularly powerful because they are messages to the laity and the public that provide instruction on how to interpret particular situations. Furthermore, they are distinguished from other statements in that they are usually read publicly in churches, in addition to being publicized by church media. As a result, these messages have a wide platform and can reach a broad audience. Bishops in other churches also issue pastoral letters, but Catholic bishops issue them most frequently.

I compiled a list of more than 250 pastoral letters from 1980 by searching library sources (including worldcat.org and hathitrust.org), web sources (including websites of episcopal conferences), and news sources. In deciding what constitutes a pastoral letter versus another kind of communication, I tried to follow each national church's conventions regarding the documents they recognize as pastoral letters. Some episcopal conferences have published comprehensive compilations of their letters as books covering particular periods, and a few even have full lists of their letters on their websites. I tried to obtain as much of the text of these letters as possible. One particularly useful source was *Weltkirche*, a publication of the German Catholic Church that ran until 2004, which contained excerpts of important letters from episcopal conferences in Africa, Asia, and Latin America. In 66 percent of cases, I was able to obtain most of the original text of a letter; for the remaining cases, I had to rely on news coverage of letters to assess their commentary.

Pastoral letters can be issued on a variety of topics, including liturgical issues, social issues (abortion, the family, and education), economic issues (inequality and economic corruption), and political issues (elections, constitutions, and political rights). They are released with differential frequency by different churches, but bishops' councils in all the countries included in Table 5.1 issued some pastoral letters between 1980 and 2018. This activity ranged from the Lesotho Catholic Bishops' Conference, which issued only a few pastoral letters over the four decades, to the Conférence des Evêques Catholiques du Burundi, which issued more than seventy in the same period.

The varying frequency of issuance is one of the challenges in dealing with pastoral letters. I attenuate this problem by collapsing the data set to country-year observations, so that for each year I coded whether the church issued any pastoral letters, whether these letters discussed the country's political institutions, and whether they were critical of the degree of liberal democracy in the country. The data is summarized in Figure 5.1, showing that Catholic bishops in Africa frequently released pastoral letters.

How frequently do bishops comment on the degree to which the country respects key liberal democratic institutions? I consider a letter as addressing these institutions if it comments on elections in the country, how political institutions allocate power, or the rights of the political opposition and civil society, including the media. Importantly, these letters do not need to use the term liberal democracy directly if they address these core components. Across the thirteen countries included in the analysis, churches issued letters addressing topics related to core liberal democratic institutions in 23 percent of the years.

I distinguish between letters that are strongly critical of the country's respect for liberal democratic institutions and those that are mildly critical of it. An example of mild criticism is a Malawian pastoral letter that, in remarking on the importance of a free press, pointed to the problem

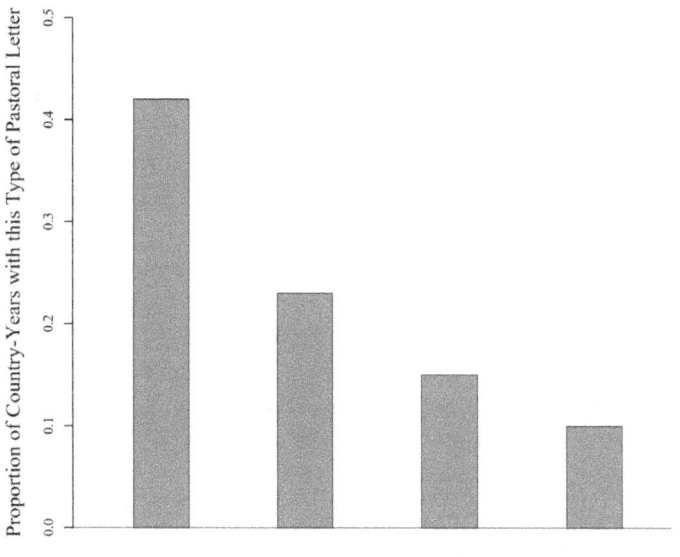

FIGURE 5.1 Proportion of country years in which at least one collective pastoral letter was issued with content indicated
Source: Baldwin 2023c.
Note: Bar graphs indicate the proportion of country years in which Catholic bishops' conference released at least one collective pastoral letter containing the indicated content.

of a radio monopoly in the country without noting that the government was the one with the monopoly or expanding on its criticism.[11] In contrast, letters that are strongly critical make major criticism more central to their letters and use language that is more critical of the government. Strongly critical letters don't simply note a controversy; they take a position on it. Such letters may be polite in tone or use the sandwich method of feedback, but they take a clear position on the government's actions or failures to act. An example is a Kenyan pastoral letter that called for greater rights of opposition parties, noting that the absence of a healthy opposition can lead to a "constitutional totalitarianism of the winner."[12] Letters that criticize society without noting the need for changes by the ruling authorities or government officials are not considered critical.

Critical pastoral letters can be extremely influential in informing and mobilizing citizens against autocracy. For example, many people have credited the 1992 Lenten letter of the Catholic bishops of Malawi, "The Truth Will Set You Free," with instigating the reintroduction of multi-party politics in that country.[13] In about 15 percent of the country years in the data set, Catholic bishops issued letters that offered at least some mild criticism of political institutions, but in only 10 percent of years were they truly critical.

THE EFFECTS OF EDUCATIONAL FINANCING ON CATHOLIC ADVOCACY FOR LIBERAL DEMOCRACY

My estimation strategy examines the differential effect of the removal of school fees on Catholic churches' annual criticism of the extent to which their country's political institutions approximate liberal democratic ideals in countries with Catholic public primary schools compared to countries without them. I examine political criticism by the Catholic Church in each country from 1980 to 2018. I chose 1980 as the year in which to begin the analysis because it marks the beginning of the period of economic downturn and reduced support for public education.[14] The year 2018 was the most recent at the time of data collection.

The outcome variable, Catholic criticism, is measured by country year. In some models, it is a dichotomous measure that captures whether the

---

[11] Episcopal Conference of Malawi, "Come Back to Me and Live," March 1998.
[12] Catholic Bishops of Kenya, "God is Lord of All Choices," November 7, 1997. Quote translated from German translation of original letter.
[13] Englund 2000; Ross 1995.
[14] van de Walle 2001.

church issued a pastoral letter that was strongly critical of a country's degree of liberal democracy in a particular year (with 0 indicating that the church did not issue any pastoral letters, that they issued pastoral letters only on other topics, or that they issued uncritical or mildly critical pastoral letters on liberal democratic institutions, and 1 indicating that the church issued a truly critical letter). In other models, it is measured on a 3-point scale, with 0 indicating that the Catholic Church did not issue any critical pastoral letters in a particular year (either because they issued no pastoral letters or the ones that they issued were not critical), 1 indicating that the Catholic Church issued at least one pastoral letter that offered mild criticism of political institutions, and 2 indicating that the Catholic Church issued at least one pastoral letter that was strongly critical of the country's respect for liberal democratic institutions. Countries removed school fees in different years, with the first incidence in 1994 (Malawi) and the last incidence in 2008 (Togo).

The analysis in this chapter identifies the effect of increased church school dependence on state financing by taking advantage of the logic that fee removal should have a distinct effect on church schools in two sets of countries. In countries where church schools are classified as part of the public school system, they are directly affected by fee-removal mandates; in contrast, in countries where they are not classified as part of the public school system, they are not mandated to remove fees. I measure the differential effect of fee removal in countries where Catholic schools are classified as public primary schools as compared to countries where they are not through an interaction term between fee removal (measured at the country-year level) and whether Catholic schools are classified as public (measured at the country level). To isolate the effects within countries over time, the models always include country fixed effects, with standard errors clustered at the country level. I present the results with and without year fixed effects and year trends to show the robustness of the results.

The main coefficient of interest is the interaction term, fee removal × public, which captures the differential effect of fee removal in countries with Catholic public primary schools. In these countries only, the removal of school fees makes church schools more financially dependent on the government, allowing me to estimate the effects of this dependency on their willingness to criticize the country's political institutions independent of any other possible consequences of school fee removal. As in Chapter 4, I do not include controls for either the level of liberal democracy or change in the level of liberal democracy in the country in the main specifications. My view is that all countries in the sample have imperfect democratic institutions, and so there are few periods in which churches could not criticize liberal democratic institutions for lack of material.

Table 5.3 presents the main results from this analysis. The first three models consider the effects of fee removal on a dichotomous measure of whether the Catholic Church issued a pastoral letter that was strongly critical of a country's political institutions in the previous year. Model 1 shows that there is a significant interaction effect between primary school fee removal and the existence of Catholic public primary schools in a country. In these countries, the removal of primary school fees reduces the likelihood of a critical letter from the Catholic bishops by about 16 percentage points more than in countries without Catholic public primary schools, and the effect is statistically significant at the 95 percent confidence level. In contrast, the coefficient on fee removal by itself is smaller and statistically insignificant in model 1, suggesting that primary school fee removal does not significantly impact criticism by Catholic bishops in countries without Catholic public primary schools. Only in instances in which school fee removal reduces the ability of Catholic schools to raise funds from parents to support their schools do they become less critical of the government. Models 2 and 3 show that this result is robust to including either year fixed effects or a year trend.

In models 4–6, I replace the dichotomous measure of criticism with a 3-point measure of criticism, where 0 indicates that the church did not issue a pastoral letter that was even mildly critical of political institutions

TABLE 5.3 *Effect of fee removal on critical pastoral letters*

	Critical (0/1)			Degree of criticism (0–2)		
	(1)	(2)	(3)	(4)	(5)	(6)
Fee removal × public	−0.161*	−0.156+	−0.157*	−0.302+	−0.288+	−0.295+
	(0.068)	(0.074)	(0.069)	(0.144)	(0.158)	(0.144)
Fee removal	0.074	−0.045	−0.092	0.149	−0.033	−0.140
	(0.048)	(0.041)	(0.063)	(0.104)	(0.073)	(0.111)
N	499	499	499	499	499	499
Country effects	FEs	FEs	FEs	FEs	FEs	FEs
Year effects	None	FEs	Trend	None	FEs	Trend

+$p < 0.10$, *$p < 0.05$, and **$p < 0.01$; coefficients are from OLS regression models; standard errors are clustered at the country level in parentheses.

(either because they issued a noncritical letter or because they did not issue any letters on this topic), 1 indicates the church issued a pastoral letter that was mildly critical of political institutions, and 2 indicates the church issued a pastoral letter that was strongly critical of political institutions. The interaction effect remains substantively large (around a 0.3-point drop), and the effect is statistically significant at the 90 percent confidence level in all models. Together, the results in Table 5.3 suggest that increased church dependence on state funding has a negative causal effect on church criticism of the government.

Figure 5.2 presents the results using the 3-point measure graphically, plotting the average level of criticism of the country's democratic institutions by the country's Catholic bishops in pastoral letters in three-year periods before and after the country's removal of public school fees. The average for the six countries without Catholic public primary

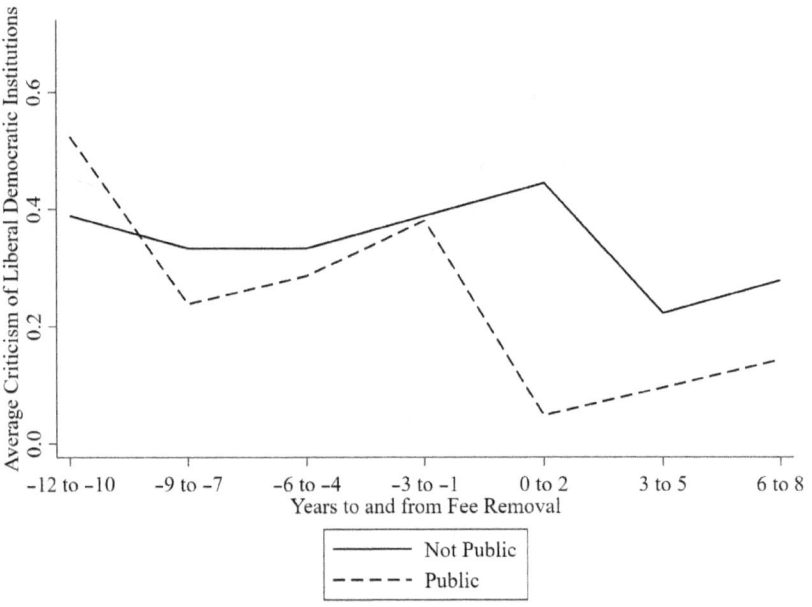

FIGURE 5.2 Catholic democratic activism by time to public school fee removal
Source: Baldwin 2025c.
Note: Figure displays the average level of criticism (on a 0–2 scale) of the country's liberal democratic institutions in pastoral letters by Catholic bishops' conferences in countries with Catholic public primary schools and in countries without Catholic public primary schools in the years before and after the removal of school fees in public primary schools in their country. Data is plotted in three-year periods.

schools is indicated by the solid line. The average for the seven countries with Catholic public primary schools is indicated by the dashed line. Prior to the introduction of universal primary education policies in each country, both sets of churches criticize the country's democratic institutions at similar levels and appear to be following parallel trends. But after the introduction of universal primary education policies, criticism by churches with public primary schools, which are newly dependent on capitation grants from the state, drops dramatically and, going forward, remains lower than their counterpart churches without public primary schools.

Are there interpretations of these effects that are consistent with other theoretical frameworks? In Table 5.4, I consider the differential effect of fee removal on alternative outcomes to consider the plausibility of other possible interpretations.

One alternative explanation is that fee removal in countries with Catholic public schools reduces the need for church criticism of educational and social policy, rather than specifically reducing their political criticism. If political criticism is simply a by-product of pastoral letters produced primarily for other purposes (including criticism of education policy), and increased government support for church schools creates less need for these types of missives, it could be driving the effect. Another possible interpretation may be that fee removal tends to happen immediately after elections, and there is less need for political commentary in those years (although this does not explain why this effect would be

TABLE 5.4 *Effect of fee removal on other outcomes*

	(1)	(2)	(3)	(4)	(5)
	Pastoral letter	Political pastoral letter	Liberal democracy	GDP per capita	Catholic president
Fee removal × public	−0.085 (0.126)	−0.089 (0.100)	0.031 (0.067)	128.5 (114.8)	0.001 (0.276)
Fee removal	−0.056 (0.102)	−0.022 (0.116)	0.058 (0.051)	−74.2 (76.3)	−0.018 (0.180)
N	499	499	486	469	497
Country effects	FEs	FEs	FEs	FEs	FEs
Year effects	FEs	FEs	FEs	FEs	FEs

$^+p < 0.10$, $^*p < 0.05$, and $^{**}p < 0.01$; coefficients are from OLS regression models; standard errors are clustered at the country level in parentheses.

different across countries with and without public Catholic primary schools). In models 1 and 2 of Table 5.4, I cast doubt on this interpretation by showing that the interaction between fee removal and the existence of Catholic public primary schools is not significantly associated with fewer pastoral letters in general or even fewer letters that discuss political institutions; it is only associated with fewer pastoral letters that criticize political institutions.

An alternative interpretation is that fee removal occurs in more democratic countries so there are simply fewer problems with democratic institutions in those countries, leading to fewer critical letters (although this logic also doesn't explain why this effect would be different across countries with and without public Catholic primary schools). But model 3 of Table 5.4 shows that the interaction between fee removal and Catholic public primary schools is not significantly associated with higher levels of liberal democracy, so the results aren't due to there being fewer democratic problems to criticize in these contexts.

A further possibility is that fee removal is associated with higher state fiscal capacity, perhaps particularly in places where church schools are classified as public insofar, as this implies greater state capacity to oversee them and greater fiscal capacity to support them. Higher state capacity may create less need to criticize the government or make being critical more dangerous if the government has greater capacity to respond to such criticism with repression. In model 4, I show that this is unlikely to be the case because the interaction term is not associated with significantly higher GDP per capita, which can be considered a proxy for state fiscal capacity.

Still another explanation is that intergroup competition for power and resources drives both funding transfers and church criticism of government. Perhaps Catholic presidents are particularly likely to push forward policies that increase government funding for Catholic schools and particularly unlikely to be criticized by the Catholic bishops. In model 5, I show that the interaction effect isn't associated with having a Catholic president, indicating that Catholic presidents aren't more or less likely to implement policies that give increased state funding to Catholic schools.

The results in Table 5.4 give confidence that the measured effect of school fee removal on church criticism of liberal democratic institutions is not spurious. The negative effect of school fee removal on the likelihood of the Catholic Church criticizing the country's liberal democratic institutions in countries with public Catholic primary schools is consistent with my theoretical claim that fiscal dependence on the state depresses church activism. But it is worth further considering whether school fee removal could reduce church activism through a different mechanism.

As discussed above, fee removal policies did not differentially influence the proportion of the population attending Catholic schools in the two sets of countries, but it may have changed the types of students attending these schools. Is it possible that Catholic churches whose educational systems begin to serve poorer students could become less engaged in prodemocratic activism? Theoretically, it isn't clear why this should be the case, especially with democracy promising the empowerment of poor citizens.[15] Indeed, Chapter 4 shows no relationship between the socioeconomic composition of churches and church democratic advocacy. This type of change would also take time to manifest, inconsistent with the immediate decline in democratic activism observed in Figure 5.2. Instead, I view as much more plausible that school fee removal depresses Catholic democratic activism by increasing dependence on state subsidies. This increased dependence makes Catholic churches more concerned about the possibility of the state cutting funding to their schools in response to any prodemocratic activism.[16]

Indeed, my interviews with church leaders suggest that they understand the strings that the government can use to harm their schools and social service wings more generally. Governments can "put threats on" that they will not fund church-run schools and clinics, and they can "forget" to allocate funding to the church-run social sector.[17] As a result, churches are unlikely to criticize the financial sponsor of their schools. Although church-run schools increase church exposure to autocratic risk and thereby augment church incentive to support democratic institutions, the positive effects of church schools on prodemocratic activism are mitigated when these schools are fiscally dependent on the state.

*****

[15] Acemoglu and Robinson 2006; Stasavage 2005.
[16] A slightly different interpretation would be that the church reduces criticism of the state because they are happy with the increased state subsidies for their school (which reduce the burden on parents to pay school fees) rather than worried about the risks to their schools of state removal of support. In some ways, this is simply the flip side of fiscal dependence. However, the decrease in criticism is not larger in countries with greater versus smaller increases in state financing for primary education after the adoption of these policies, suggesting that concerns about the potential removal of funding versus satisfaction with funding increases are most important (results not shown).
[17] Interview with leader of Tanzanian Christian social service provision group, May 2018; Interview with Tanzanian Catholic religious leader, March 2019. See also interview with Ghanaian Methodist educationalist, May 2021.

The evidence in Chapters 4 and 5 points to the complex effects of church education systems on church incentives to advocate for liberal democratic institutions. As Chapter 4 demonstrates, churches with larger education systems are more likely to engage in activism, other things being equal. In this chapter, I show that education-providing churches drop their level of criticism of liberal democratic institutions when they become more dependent on the state for financing. Both autocratic risk exposure and dependence on state financing contribute to levels of church advocacy for liberal democracy.

Next, Part III further considers the consequences of church advocacy for liberal democracy, moving from mesolevel analysis to within-country analysis in Ghana, Tanzania, and Zambia. In all three countries, some churches have provided significant education at certain times, but with considerably higher funding for church schools in Ghana, as shown in Chapter 4 and Figure 4.1. Chapter 6 demonstrates the breadth of the coalition that churches in Tanzania and Zambia have been able to mobilize in support of democracy, including international actors in the Zambian case. In contrast, Chapter 7 shows that churches typically have had to rely on the openings provided by liberal democratic institutions to mobilize domestic pressure in support of their educational interests, sometimes against the wishes of international donors, drawing on evidence from Ghana and Zambia. In this way, the next section of the book explains why churches may need to protect liberal democratic institutions to guarantee their educational interests: Churches can mobilize wide cross-national coalitions in defense of liberal democracy and, in turn, depend on liberal democratic institutions to empower a smaller group of domestic actors to advocate for church-affiliated schools.

PART III

TESTING UNDERLYING ASSUMPTIONS

6

Church Activism and Support for Liberal Democratic Institutions

Evidence from Zambia and Tanzania

Thus far, this book has provided theory and evidence on the contexts in which churches are likely to engage in activism for liberal democracy. This activism only makes sense if churches have some probability of influencing the strength of liberal democratic institutions in their countries. Yet the power of churches to influence democratic institutions is not obvious. Indeed, a core argument of this book is that churches that lack committed partisan allies can best advance their educational policy interests when liberal democratic institutions provide openings. But what levers do they have to promote liberal democracy when these openings are few and possibly closing?

This chapter begins by demonstrating how churches have the potential to organize wide constituencies, including political elites, international actors, and citizens, in support of liberal democratic institutions. In contrast, Chapter 7 shows how churches cannot mobilize a similarly wide coalition in support of their educational interests. Instead, they rely on a smaller group of key allies to take advantage of policy openings created by liberal democratic institutions. Together, these explain why churches need to defend liberal democratic institutions to achieve their educational policy interests.

More specifically, this chapter shows that churches have a positive probability of influencing the strength of liberal democratic institutions in their countries and demonstrates how they accomplish it. I begin by describing the critical role that churches can play in advancing liberal democratic institutions by providing credible information and coordinating mechanisms that subsequently organize political elites, citizens, and international actors in defense of those institutions. I then draw on evidence from Zambia and Tanzania between 2017 and 2021 to highlight the potential and limits of church democratic activism during spells of democratic backsliding, with emphasis on the ability of churches to change public opinion and to affect citizens' willingness to defend liberal democratic institutions. These are countries in which some churches provide a significant portion of the education, especially at the secondary level. In particular, the Catholic Church in both countries, the Lutheran Church in Tanzania, and some mainline Protestant churches in Zambia all have some autocratic risk exposure because of their investments in education. Drawing on interviews, survey data, and endorsement experiments, I demonstrate that churches in Zambia have been effective in issuing coordinated pro-democracy statements that have changed public opinion and in creating conditions for broad constituencies to coordinate in defense of democratic institutions. In contrast, I demonstrate that churches in Tanzania have been much less effective in issuing coordinated pro-democracy statements and that, even if they had been more effective, they have more limited ability to move public opinion in favor of institutional changes due to deeper religious cleavages.

HOW CHURCHES MOBILIZE SUPPORT FOR LIBERAL DEMOCRACY: CHANGING OPINIONS AND COORDINATING BEHAVIOR OF DIVERSE CONSTITUENTS

How can church activism for liberal democracy advance a country's liberal democratic institutions? As Chapter 2 elaborates, church advocacy is particularly effective insofar as it informs and coordinates action by a broad coalition, including some political elites, key international actors, and diverse citizens, that has an interest in supporting liberal democracy. Members of all three groups are interested in preserving their power vis-à-vis the ruler. I view most citizens, most opposition politicians, and even most ruling-party backbenchers as having an interest in defending liberal democratic institutions that give them opportunities for political influence.[1] If these actors don't always act on this interest, it is due to countervailing pressures.

Political elites, international actors, and citizens also have the capacity to take action against rulers in support of liberal democratic institutions. For example, political elites can vote against legislation that removes

---

[1] For evidence on the strong popular demand for liberal democratic institutions in Africa, see Gyimah-Boadi, Logan, and Sanny 2021.

legislative or judicial checks on rulers, and international donors can freeze aid until democratic reforms are adopted. In countries experiencing democratic backsliding, citizens may play a particularly important role because they can vote against antidemocratic politicians in elections.[2] But these groups also face information and coordination problems when acting against antidemocratic rulers.

The information problem is that antidemocratic changes are often bundled in the sense that these actions accomplish multiple things or occur simultaneously with other changes. As a result, the government can give these changes alternative frames; for example, the ban of opposition rallies can be justified as mitigating public health or security risks, and constitutional changes that centralize power in the president can be described as necessary to increase government efficiency. In addition, citizens, political elites, and international donors may face coordination problems when organizing in support of democratic institutions. These actors often appreciate that positive changes in liberal democratic institutions are unlikely to be achieved unless diverse groups coordinate their actions. If they do not expect such coordination to happen, individuals may not judge it worthwhile to act in support of liberal democratic values.

Under some circumstances, churches may be well-positioned to inform and coordinate citizen action. First, churches are often considered credible sources of information about autocratic acts. Statements from ruling party and opposition party politicians are generally noncredible because it is difficult to assess whether the statements are true or self-serving. In contrast, churches can provide credible information about such acts, especially in cases in which they are not allied with political parties and in which they have a material interest in liberal democracy over autocracy. Insofar as churches with large educational systems are at greater risk under autocracy versus democracy, their interests are in making clear the true risk to liberal democracy of an action, and the statements of these churches may be particularly credible.

Second, as broadly trusted and prominent institutions, churches can potentially coordinate separate groups in support of pro-democracy actions, including diverse citizens, political elites, and international actors. Importantly, within countries, churches may be able to coordinate citizens across denominational lines in support of democracy. If churches have broad credibility on political issues within their country, they may be able to motivate individuals belonging to different churches

---

[2] Bermeo 2016; Svolik 2019.

to act.[3] In addition, interchurch coordinating bodies can help to organize citizens across denominations. In highly religious Christian-majority societies, churches are likely to have unique coordinating capacity due to their prominence.

Thus, churches have the potential to positively affect the level of liberal democratic institutions in their countries by mobilizing a diverse group of citizens, political elites, and international actors to act in their defense. Importantly, this is a much wider coalition than the one they can mobilize around their preferred educational policies. In the latter endeavor, they are typically more dependent on a small number of political elites to advance their policy interests, as I demonstrate in Chapter 7. In this chapter, I empirically examine the potential and limits of church democratic activism in mobilizing diverse actors, with particular attention to how citizens are affected by church statements in defense of liberal democracy. Citizens often play key roles in advancing liberal democratic institutions by protesting in favor of them or by voting against antidemocratic politicians.

THE ROLE OF THE CHURCH IN MOBILIZING SUPPORT FOR LIBERAL DEMOCRACY IN ZAMBIA

The first case that I consider is Zambia, where, since the country's transition to multiparty democracy in the early 1990s, churches have often spoken out in defense of liberal democratic institutions. My research on this case draws on a wide variety of sources, including original interviews, tailored survey questions, and survey experiments. I show that churches in Zambia have been able to mobilize wide constituencies in support of liberal democratic institutions, that they have broad credibility on issues related to democracy, and that they are able to mobilize citizens across church denominations to punish antidemocratic actions by politicians.

Church Mobilization of Diverse Prodemocratic Constituencies

Since the reintroduction of multiparty democracy in Zambia in 1991, there have been numerous incidents in which elected presidents have

---

[3] Weber provides an example of the broad credibility of the Catholic Church in the Democratic Republic of the Congo on issues of democracy, with a Protestant informant explaining that "while the Protestant Église du Christ au Congo (ECC) had religious legitimacy for him, he followed CENCO [the Catholic Episcopal Conference] on political issues." See Weber 2020, 63.

threatened to eliminate checks on their power through attacks on liberal democratic institutions. These attacks were particularly strong at the end of President Frederick Chiluba's second term in 2001, when Chiluba seemed poised to initiate constitutional changes that would permit him to seek a third term, and during the rule of President Edgar Lungu from 2015 to 2021, as Lungu sought to consolidate his power following the death of President Michael Sata in office. In both instances, Zambian churches took coordinated positions that allowed them to mobilize a diverse group, including citizens, political elites, and international actors, in support of liberal democracy.

The term-limit clash began in February 2001 when Chiluba indicated his openness to changing the constitution to allow him to serve more than two terms in office, if it were the will of the majority of citizens.[4] In response, the Zambian churches worked closely with disaffected politicians to organize opposition to this third-term bid. A key confidante of the Catholic bishops organized a meeting of religious leaders (including the Zambia Episcopal Conference [ZEC], representing the Catholic Church; the Christian Council of Zambia [CCZ], representing mainline Protestant churches; and the Evangelical Fellowship of Zambia [EFZ], representing many evangelical churches) and secular non-governmental organizations (NGOs) (in particular, the Law Association of Zambia and the Non-Governmental Organization Co-ordinating Committee [NGOCC]) at the Oasis restaurant in Lusaka to draft a collective response to the third-term bid.[5] The Catholic Church took the lead, with disaffected ruling party politicians playing a key role behind the scenes. As one politician recalls, "I worked closely with the Catholic Church, raised money for them to facilitate meetings such as the one that led to the formation of the Oasis Forum because we knew that the church had the capacity to get people together ..."[6] Ultimately, support from all three church groups, collectively known as the church mother bodies, was crucial in setting up the forum, with a Catholic activist from the forum recalling, "It was the churches that invited the other organizations."[7]

---

[4] *Agence France-Presse*, "Chiluba to abide by majority decision on third term: Zambian press," February 12, 2001.
[5] Mark Chona is reported to have coordinated the meeting as a confidant of the Catholic bishops, and the churches are noted to be the first organizations to join the initiative. See Gould 2006, 933, 935.
[6] Sishuwa 2020, 476.
[7] Interview with Joe Komakoma, cited in Gould 2006, 935.

The so-called Oasis Declaration, which called on Chiluba to "exercise statesmanship" by respecting the constitution and not contesting the 2001 elections, was read in churches across Zambia on Sunday, February 25.[8] Addressed also to members of parliament, the declaration stated, "This generation of leaders and especially those that wield the legislative power in the National Assembly are called upon to avert setting a precedent which will undermine our Constitutional Order, Peace and Security of the nation."[9] The signers of the declaration, the ZEC, the CCZ, the EFZ, the Law Association of Zambia, and the NGOCC, became known as the Oasis Forum. Over the next three months, the Oasis Forum provided public education in support of term limits, organized peaceful demonstrations against a third term, and coordinated with anti-third-term politicians inside the Movement for Multiparty Democracy. It organized countrywide street protests on March 9, with citizens encouraged to wear green ribbons to show their opposition to the third-term bid.[10]

The protests demonstrated strong popular opposition to Chiluba's third-term bid, ultimately paving the way for political elites and international actors to act against it. With the ruling party's convention approaching, on April 26, eight of Zambia's largest donors released a statement expressing their wish that Chiluba would step down at the end of his current term.[11] More protests, led by politicians opposed to the third-term bid and students, occurred after Chiluba managed to ban enough opponents from his party's convention to secure his renomination on April 30.[12] On May 3, parliamentarians introduced a legislative motion to impeach him, and it became evident that his administration did not have the two-thirds support of parliament necessary for a constitutional amendment that would allow him a third term.[13] The following day, Chiluba changed his stance and promised not to seek another

---

[8] Anthony Kunda, "Zambian Churches and Lawyers Oppose Presidential Plan for Third Term," *Christianity Today*, March 1, 2001, www.christianitytoday.com/2001/03/zambian-churches-and-lawyers-oppose-presidential-plan-for-t/.

[9] *The Post*, "Oasis Declaration: Civil Society Rejects Third Term," March 23, 2001, https://allafrica.com/stories/200103230186.html.

[10] *Agence France-Presse*, "Zambians Stage Protest against Chiluba's Third Term Bid," March 9, 2001. The Oasis Forum advertised these protests in independent newspapers.

[11] Joe Kaunda, "Diplomatic Missions Oppose President Chiluba's Third Term," *The Post*, April 27, 2001, https://allafrica.com/stories/200104270094.html; *COMTEX*, "Western Donors Urge Chiluba to Bow Out," April 28, 2001.

[12] *Agence France-Presse*, "Zambia's Chiluba vows no amendment for third term," May 6, 2001.

[13] Sishuwa 2020, 481.

term.[14] Ultimately, the churches' work through the Oasis Declaration and the Oasis Forum enabled them to coordinate action not only among their individual churches but also among a wider group of actors opposed to removing term limits from the constitution.

The second period of crisis for liberal democratic institutions in Zambia began about ten years later and occurred under the rule of the Patriotic Front (PF). In 2011, Michael Sata, the party's founder, was elected as the country's first Catholic president. At the time, many observers wondered if the Catholic Church would continue its tradition of speaking out. But even though some priests became known as PF partisans, the Catholic bishops continued to speak out in defense of liberal democracy, criticizing Sata's selective use of the Public Order Act to oppress political opposition and his attacks on parliamentary power.[15]

Following Sata's death in office in 2014, Edgar Lungu became president following a power struggle within the PF. A member of the United Church of Zambia for much of his life (a mainline Protestant church), Lungu tried to undercut the importance of statements from the church mother bodies by currying favor directly with some individual Pentecostal churches. His administration established a Ministry of National Guidance and Religious Affairs in 2016 that handed out money to particular churches at politically useful moments.[16] It tried to establish new church mother bodies (in addition to the existing three) to dilute the influence of the country's long-established churches.[17] The regime also sought to drive wedges within the existing church groups, seeking to undermine their ability to speak with one voice. Senior church members report being offered bribes – and knowing some who had accepted them – in return for ending their criticism of the regime's antidemocratic practices.[18] Still, the ZEC (renamed the Zambia Conference of Catholic Bishops [ZCCB] in 2016), the CCZ, and the EFZ managed to take a strong collective stance at moments of great threat to the country's liberal democratic institutions.

---

[14] Henry Cauvin, "Zambia's President Abandons Re-Election Bid," *New York Times*, May 5, 2001, www.nytimes.com/2001/05/05/world/zambia-s-president-abandons-re-election-bid.html.

[15] Catholic Bishops of Zambia, "A Pastoral Statement of Catholic Bishops: Act Justly and Walk Humbly with Your God," January 28, 2013.

[16] Interview with Zambian Anglican religious leader, April 2022.

[17] Ibid.

[18] Interview with Zambian Anglican religious leader, April 2022; Interview with Zambian Catholic religious leader, April 2022.

One of these moments was the jailing of the main opposition leader for four months beginning in April 2017. On April 8, Lungu's motorcade came upon United Party for National Development (UPND) leader Hakainde Hichilema's motorcade en route to a traditional ceremony in the country's Western province. Per video from the event, the president's motorcade overtook Hichilema's without the opposition leader's convoy pulling over to the side of the road.[19] Subsequently, on April 10, the police arrested Hichilema, throwing him in jail and charging him with treason.

In the following weeks, the CCZ, quickly followed by the ZCCB, spoke out against the imprisonment of Hichilema. When no action was taken, in June 2017, the original three church mother bodies issued a joint statement signed by the leaders of all three groups, which included the board chairperson of the EFZ, supporting the release of Hichilema from jail.

At that point, there was considerable pressure on the church mother bodies to break from their common position. Minor political and religious leaders were brought together for a press conference to speak against the mother bodies' statement. At this event, the outgoing board vice chair of the EFZ board tried to distance the entire organization from the joint statement.[20]

And yet overall, the church mother bodies were remarkably effective in maintaining a common front by purging those who were too far ahead of the group's joint statement and those who were too far behind it. The EFZ board vice chair was replaced by someone who was "working properly" for its stated goals.[21] Around the same time, a CCZ leader who was viewed as lacking sufficient independence from the regime served for only a few months.[22] And Catholic Archbishop Telesphore Mpundu, who drafted a statement calling the country a dictatorship in all but name, resigned his position in January 2018, indicating in a subsequent interview that he had been encouraged to do so because he had found his own public positions to be much stronger than those his fellow bishops were willing to take.[23]

---

[19] *BBC*, "Zambia Police Charge Hichilema over Motorcade Clash," April 12, 2017, www.bbc.com/news/world-africa-39577230.

[20] *Lusaka Times*, "EFZ Distances Itself from Statement Issued by Church Mother Bodies," June 17, 2017, www.lusakatimes.com/2017/06/17/efz-distances-statement-issued-church-mother-bodies/.

[21] Interview with Zambian Anglican religious leader, April 2022.

[22] Ibid.

[23] Archbishop Telesphore Mpundu, interview by Martin Kalungu-Banda, ZAMBITION Series, November 2021.

The activities of the three church mother bodies also helped draw international attention to the imprisonment of the opposition leader. In July 2017, the Catholic bishops began mediating talks between Lungu and Hichilema, with a delegation headed by the archbishop shuttling back and forth between State House and Mukobeko Maximum Security Prison.[24] The following month, the secretary general of the Commonwealth of Nations visited Zambia to start her own mediation efforts, meeting with the Catholic bishops, Lungu, and Hichilema.[25] As a senior Catholic leader involved in the efforts reflects, "We were very happy the Commonwealth team immediately came after reading what was happening … With the British Commonwealth involved, there is the possibility of squeezing the finances."[26] Four days after the secretary general concluded her visit, the administration released Hichilema from jail.[27] As in 2001, activism by the three church mother bodies helped coordinate other actors in defense of liberal democratic institutions.

Another critical period for Zambia's liberal democratic institutions was when the Lungu administration sought to pass Bill 10. The bill proposed to resolve ambiguities in the country's constitution by increasing the power of the presidency over the legislative branch and the judiciary. But the bill was long and included many noncontentious and even prodemocratic reforms, making it possible for the ruling party to frame it in a prodemocratic cloak. As one church leader who subsequently campaigned against the bill put it, "If I said 98 percent of this wine is fine but 2 percent is poison, would you drink that wine?"[28]

In response, academics, secular NGOs, and religious organizations campaigned against aspects of the bill, emphasizing their nondemocratic implications.[29] All three church mother bodies criticized the centralization

---

[24] Rebecca Mushota, "Analyst Tips Catholic Bishops," *Times of Zambia*, July 19, 2017, www.times.co.zm/?p=96972.

[25] *Commonwealth*, "Secretary-General meets Zambian president and opposition leader," August 7, 2017, https://thecommonwealth.org/news/secretary-general-meets-zambian-president-and-opposition-leader.

[26] Interview with Zambian Catholic religious leader, April 2022.

[27] Sishuwa Sishuwa, "The Real Reasons HH Was Released from Jail," *Lusaka Times*, September 20, 2017, www.lusakatimes.com/2017/09/20/real-reasons-hh-released-jail/.

[28] Interview with Zambian Anglican religious leader, April 2022.

[29] Nic Cheeseman, "Lungu Erodes Zambia's Democracy," *Mail and Guardian*, September 9, 2019, https://mg.co.za/article/2019-09-06-00-lunga-erodes-zambias-democracy/; Paul Samasumo, "Zambian Bishops Renew Calls for Withdrawal of Divisive Bill No. 10," *Vatican News*, June 16, 2020, www.vaticannews.va/en/africa/news/2020-06/zambian-bishops-renew-calls-for-the-withdrawal-of-divisive-bill.html; Ndulo 2020; Sishuwa Sishuwa, "This Is How Lungu Is Planning to Rig Zambia's

of presidential power. And the groups, through the Christian Churches Monitoring Group (CCMG), engaged in a coordinated advocacy campaign. In particular, the CCMG made presentations to parliamentary committees. Together with other NGOs, it gathered telephone numbers and messaged all ruling party MPs, encouraging them to vote against the bill. It also mobilized citizens to contact their members of parliament to say that they opposed the bill.[30] In the end, on October 29, 2020, the bill narrowly failed to win the two-thirds majority of the legislature needed for passage.[31]

These successes highlight the importance of coordination among the Zambian church mother bodies in drawing attention to democratic challenges in the country and mobilizing the behavior of a wide range of actors. Over time, the three groups developed a considerable reservoir of trust and well-established communication protocols to protect against attempts to divide them.[32] As one high-positioned church leader explains, the three groups always communicate and coordinate with one another before meeting with the president's office. For example, in one case, they had each been given separate appointments (one hour apart) at State House but showed up together at the first scheduled meeting, much to the surprise of the delegation receiving them.[33] The groups also have well-established contacts in the embassies of key donors.[34] In this way, they can coordinate the actions of political elites and key international actors, as the discussion in this section highlights. Their statements also have considerable influence over Zambian citizens, who themselves can play an important role in defending liberal democratic institutions during periods of democratic backsliding, as I demonstrate next.

Church Credibility in Zambia

The history of Zambian churches standing together for democracy has translated into broad political credibility for churches on issues of

---

2021 General Election," *Mail and Guardian*, September 25, 2020, https://mg.co.za/africa/2020-09-25-this-is-how-lungu-is-planning-to-rig-zambias-2021-general-election/.

[30] Interview with Zambian Anglican religious church leader, April 2022.

[31] *Lusaka Times*, "PF Makes Tabling of Bill 10 in 2021 an Election Issue," November 17, 2020, www.lusakatimes.com/2020/11/17/pf-makes-tabling-of-bill-10-in-2021-an-election-issue/.

[32] Interview with Zambian Catholic religious leader, April 2022; Interview with Zambian Anglican religious leader, April 2022.

[33] Interview with Zambian Catholic religious leader, April 2022.

[34] Interview with Zambian Anglican religious leader, April 2022.

democracy in that country. To examine the democratic reputation of churches, I collected data on whether citizens viewed various political and social organizations to be in favor of, against, or to have no position on democracy in the run-up to the 2021 Zambian elections. This data was collected between June and July 2021 as part of the Zambian Election Panel Survey.[35] The sample was not designed to be nationally representative but rather to survey two distinct regions: the capital region, Lusaka, and the rural eastern regions of Eastern and Muchinga provinces. This sample is ethnically and religiously diverse, with slight underrepresentation of Catholics compared to the national average (21 percent versus 30 percent) and slight overrepresentation of United Church of Zambia (10 percent versus 7 percent) and Seventh Day Adventists (16 percent versus 9 percent). It contains a mix of areas considered PF strongholds and so-called swing districts, but not the historical regional strongholds of the UPND in southern and western Zambia. As a result, the sample is more favorable to the PF than a nationally representative sample would be. In total, 1,615 people were sampled.

Respondents were asked about the democratic position of the ruling party (PF), the major opposition party (UPND), the Catholic Church, the EFZ, and the Zambian Congress of Trade Unions (ZCTU). The Catholic Church is widely considered the most politically active of the three church mother bodies, the EFZ is usually considered the least politically active of them, and the ZCTU is a nonreligious example of an NGO. The ZCTU is a useful baseline against which to compare opinions about the churches because it is often credited with propelling the transition to multiparty democracy in Zambia.[36]

The responses to the questions are presented in Table 6.1.[37] The top row shows the results across all respondents in the sample. Sixty-three percent view the PF as having prodemocratic positions compared to 22 percent who view it as having antidemocratic positions. The rest of the respondents state either that the party had no position on democracy or that they

---

[35] The Zambian Election Panel Survey was a collaborative research project with support from the Governance and Local Development Institute at the University of Gothenburg, the Swedish Research Council, and the University of Cape Town.
[36] The specific question wording was, "For each of the following groups, I would like to know: Do you consider them to be in favor of democratic government, against democratic government or not to have a position on democracy?"
[37] The statistics in Table 8.2 come from the round of the survey conducted in June and July 2021, except for the statistics for the EFZ, which were collected in the subsequent wave of the survey, conducted in July and August 2021.

TABLE 6.1 *Percentage of respondents reporting the organization to be in favor of or against democratic government*

	Perceptions of PF Position on Democratic Government		Perceptions of UPND Position on Democratic Government		Perceptions of Catholic Church Position on Democratic Government		Perceptions of EFZ Position on Democratic Government		Perceptions of ZCTU Position on Democratic Government	
	In favor	Against	In favor	Against	In favor	Against	In favor	Against	In favor	Against
All respondents	62.6	21.5	55.1	20.3	68.5	5.2	55.2	4.5	57.6	4.8
PF respondent	83.6	8.7	45.3	32.8	73.9	4.2	52.3	5.0	62.4	4.5
UPND respondents	43.4	46.5	79.6	9.2	74.4	5.2	56.7	5.4	59.6	4.5
Other partisanship respondents	56.3	16.1	47.2	16.4	59.5	6.2	56.8	3.4	51.7	5.2
Catholic respondents	64.9	21.9	55.6	20.9	79.8	4.3	59.1	3.6	61.6	3.6
Mainline Protestant respondents	65.1	21.7	57.7	21.3	67.8	5.4	53.8	4.3	60.0	5.0
Evangelical/Pentecostal respondents	64.4	22.1	55.8	19.9	69.1	5.9	55.7	4.6	56.1	6.0

Note: The table presents the percentage of respondents in each category stating that a particular organization is in favor or against democratic government. Respondents could also indicate that the organization did not have a position or that they did not know or refused to answer.

don't know. The comparable statistics for the major opposition party, the UPND, are 55 percent and 20 percent, respectively, with these numbers likely reflecting the sample's overrepresentation of historic PF strongholds. But the organization that is most consistently viewed as taking prodemocratic positions is the Catholic Church, with 69 percent of respondents viewing it as in favor of democratic government and 5 percent perceiving the Church as against it. By comparison, 55 percent of respondents view the EFZ as in favor of democratic government and 5 percent perceive it as against it and 58 percent of respondents view the ZCTU as in favor of democratic government and 5 percent consider it as against it.

The table also breaks down respondents by partisanship and religion. Unsurprisingly, the majority of partisans say that their own party is strongly committed to democratic government, and they are more suspicious of the other party's democratic commitments. This points to the difficulty for parties in coordinating broad societal mobilization against antidemocratic acts. In contrast, large majorities of PF and UPND supporters believe that the Catholic Church is in favor of democratic government (74 percent of both parties' supporters), indicating its wider credibility in labeling acts as antidemocratic. In line with its less prominent role in previous campaigns for democracy, the EFZ is less consistently identified as prodemocratic, although a majority of respondents in all subgroups identify it that way (52 percent of PF supporters, 57 percent of UPND supporters, and 57 percent of respondents not affiliated with either the PF or the UPND). For the ZCTU, 62 percent of PF supporters and 60 percent of UPND supporters believe the union is in favor of democratic government.

Even if the Catholic Church is viewed as prodemocratic by both ends of the political spectrum, citizens' perspectives on the church may be colored by their own religious affiliation. As a result, the last three rows in the table break down the sample by Catholics, mainline Protestants, and evangelical/Pentecostal Protestants. Although Catholics are more likely to say the Catholic Church is in favor of democracy, with fully 80 percent of Catholics reporting this view, a substantial majority of mainline and evangelical/Pentecostal Protestants (68 and 69 percent, respectively) also say that the Catholic Church is in favor of democracy. For Catholic and non-Catholic respondents alike, the Catholic Church is the organization most consistently viewed as having a prodemocratic stance. Majorities of Catholics, mainline Protestants, and Pentecostal Protestants also say that the EFZ is in favor of democratic government. These responses suggest that Zambian churches – and the Catholic Church in particular – play a unique role in providing public information that is widely credible about the democratic implications of particular events.

The Effect of Church Statements on Zambians' Assessment of Their Country's Democracy

In this section, I consider the ability of churches to frame actions as non-democratic, drawing on evidence from one of the most fraught periods of the Lungu presidency: the jailing of the main opposition candidate on treason charges. As discussed above, the police arrested Hichilema during an evening raid on his home in April 2017 and charged him with treason two days later for failing to yield to the president on a road and thereby endangering his life.

Although the severity of the charges suggests the ruling party was using the event as an opportunity to quash political opposition – if Hichilema had been found guilty of treason, he would have been ineligible to run in future elections – the police justified the arrest on security grounds in a way that may have been convincing for some citizens. Specifically, the statement from the Inspector General of Police read:

> It has been established that the opposition leader disobeyed police orders to give way to the Presidential motorcade on Limulunga road in an attempt to put the life of the Republican President in danger ... I wish to reiterate that the actions by the opposition leader were unreasonable, reckless and criminal. Therefore, members of the public are being warned that as police we are not going to watch such kind of behaviour by any person irrespective of their status or political affiliation. We shall ensure that all those that would want to cause unnecessary anarchy are arrested and prosecuted.[38]

The arrest happened right before Easter, but it seems that the churches did not seriously take up the issue until after Easter Sunday. The first church mother body to issue a statement was the CCZ. On Monday, April 17, it issued a press release that was carried in many news outlets, shared on social media, and planned for dissemination through all member churches down to the parish level.[39] The statement was clear on the undemocratic implications of the arrest:

> The Council of Churches in Zambia is very troubled and disturbed at the unfolding lawlessness, impunity and shear madness of the decisions being made

---

[38] *Lusaka Times*, "Zambia Police Finally Charge HH, Five Others with Treason," April 12, 2017, www.lusakatimes.com/2017/04/12/police-finally-charge-hh-five-others-treason/.

[39] Interview with Zambian mainline Protestant church leader, April 2022.

in this country i.e., the police, the political bureau and the entire political leadership ... This country does not belong to the ruling party the Patriotic Front ... The militarization of civil policy is frightening. To think that law, order and peace can only be enforced by guns and machetes is an affront to democracy and justice and an offense to humanity.[40]

The ZCCB followed suit with a statement released on Sunday, April 23. Issued by the conference's president, Archbishop Mpundu, after consultation with the other bishops, the strongly worded statement clearly warned Zambians about the implications of the arrest:

Our country is now all, except in designation, a dictatorship and if it is not yet, then we are not far from it. Our political leaders in the ruling party often issue intimidating statements that frighten people and make us fear for the immediate and future. This must be stopped and reversed henceforth.[41]

The statement from the CCZ and the letter from the ZCCB potentially provided new frames to allow their members to reinterpret Hichilema's arrest. In contrast to the security and rule-of-law frame employed by the police, the church statements emphasized the antidemocratic aspects of the action. The EFZ did not issue any statements on the political implications of the arrest during this period; its executive director merely urged UPND supporters to be patient while the legal system ran its course.[42]

The arrest of Hichilema, the press statement from the CCZ, and the statement from the ZCCB all occurred while a major survey research organization, Afrobarometer, was conducting a public opinion survey in Zambia that included a question about the extent to which respondents viewed their country as a democracy.[43] This timing provides an opportunity to assess the effects of the treason charge itself compared to statements from church leaders in influencing citizens' assessments of the quality of democracy in Zambia.

---

[40] In 2003, the Christian Council of Zambia was renamed the Council of Churches in Zambia, keeping the same acronym (CCZ). *Lusaka Times*, "Council of Churches tells off President Lungu, Zambia does not belong to the PF," April 19, 2017, www.lusakatimes.com/2017/04/19/council-churches-tells-off-president-lungu-zambia-not-belong-pf/.

[41] Zambia Conference of Catholic Bishops, "If You Want Justice Work for Peace: Statement on the Current Political Situation in Zambia," *Caritas Zambia*, April 23, 2017, www.caritaszambia.org/press/press-releases/if-you-want-peace-work-for-justice-paul-vi-zambia-conference-of-catholic-bishops; Interview with Zambian Catholic church leader, April 2022.

[42] *Lusaka Times*, "Three Church Mother Bodies Praise Lungu for Not Interfering in HH's Case," April 18, 2017, www.lusakatimes.com/2017/04/18/three-church-mother-bodies-praise-lungu-not-interfering-hhs-case/.

[43] *Afrobarometer* 2025.

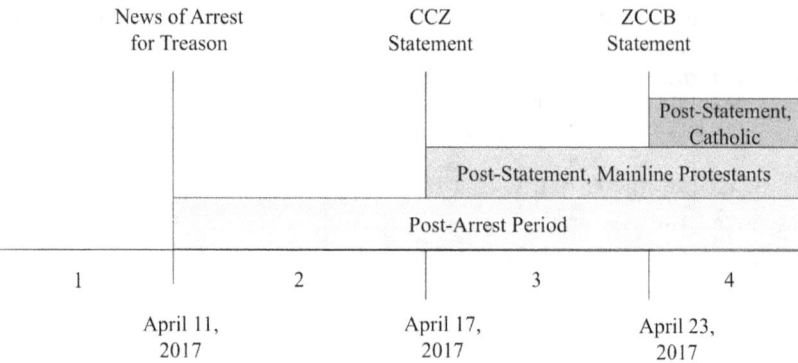

FIGURE 6.1 Timeline of opposition leader's arrest and church statements in Zambia

Figure 6.1 provides a timeline of the news of the opposition leader's arrest, the treason charge against him, and the subsequent church statements.[44] Mainline Protestants received antidemocratic frames earlier than Catholics, and evangelical Protestants did not receive any antidemocratic frames during this period. I expect the largest effects on members of the church (or church group) who made a statement providing an antidemocratic frame to the arrest. I assume these respondents are more likely to be exposed to a new frame when it comes from their own church and more likely to put weight on frames provided by their own church.

Given my expectation that the largest effects of the church statements will be on their own church members, I am able to parse the effects of church antidemocratic frames from other temporal effects and changes in the composition of survey respondents over time. This is important because there are reasons to think that respondents interviewed earlier in the survey process may be systematically different from those interviewed later.[45] If there are spillover effects of these frames across denominations, which the evidence on church credibility in the previous section suggests there may be, it should depress the estimated effects.

---

[44] For both the news of the arrest and the CCZ press statement, I coded exposure starting the day after the news and the press statement release because of the news cycle. For the Catholic statement, I coded exposure as starting on the Sunday itself because the time stamps on surveys indicate that all respondents would have responded after church services. This was the last full day of Afrobarometer surveying. An additional four respondents were interviewed on the Monday afterward, and two respondents were interviewed on the Tuesday afterward.

[45] For example, some survey firms start their survey teams in more difficult locations, hoping to keep up morale for enumerators throughout the survey.

I consider the effect of the church statements on citizens' assessments of the quality of democracy in the country and their expressed willingness to vote for the PF in the next election. To measure assessment of democratic quality, I used a question that asked respondents the extent to which they think Zambia is a democracy, with responses coded on a 0–3 scale (0 indicating not a democracy, 1 indicating a democracy with major problems, 2 indicating a democracy with minor problems, and 3 indicating a full democracy). The most common response was democracy with minor problems (33 percent of respondents), followed by democracy with major problems (28 percent of respondents). To measure electoral support for the PF, I created a dichotomous variable with 1 indicating the respondent said they planned to vote for the PF and 0 indicating they planned to vote for any other party.[46] I estimate the effects of church statements on these outcomes through an OLS model with denominational fixed effects (for Catholics and mainline Protestants, with other Christians as the omitted category); region fixed effects; and time-period fixed effects for the periods indicated in Figure 6.1 (with the pre-arrest period as the omitted category).[47] Standard errors are clustered by members of the same denomination surveyed on the same date. The results of this regression are presented in Table 6.2. In addition to reporting the estimated effects of church statements on members' beliefs about the extent of democracy, the table also reports the period fixed effects because they are relevant for assessing the extent of cross-denominational spillovers.

The results show a strong and statistically significant negative effect of church statements on church members' beliefs about the extent to which Zambia is a democracy. The statements reduced assessments of democracy by more than one-quarter of a point on the 3-point scale. This indicates the power of churches to frame particular governmental acts as nondemocratic in a way that convinces citizens. This power is all the more important because, considering time-period effects on their own, there is no evidence that citizens negatively updated their beliefs about Zambia's democratic credentials following news of the arrest itself.

---

[46] Respondents who said they would not vote (8 percent of the sample), refused to answer this question (12 percent of the sample), or did not know who they would vote for (6 percent of the sample) are excluded.

[47] I drop the small number of respondents (twenty-five) who do not identify as Christian. A small number of respondents (four) belong to the Coptic and Orthodox church, which belongs to the CCZ, so they are coded with mainline Protestant churches; the results are robust to dropping them.

TABLE 6.2 *Effect of church statements on assessments of democracy*

	(1)	(2)
	Extent of democracy (0–3)	Vote for PF (0/1)
Statement from own church body	−0.283*	−0.058
	(0.132)	(0.061)
Postarrest period	0.070	−0.104
	(0.271)	(0.067)
Post-CCZ statement period	−0.139	−0.212*
	(0.289)	(0.079)
Post-Catholic letter period	0.308	0.075
	(0.326)	(0.100)
N	1131	873
Denomination FEs	Yes	Yes
Region FEs	Yes	Yes

†$p < 0.10$, *$p < 0.05$, and **$p < 0.01$; coefficients are from OLS regression models; standard errors are clustered by denomination survey date in parentheses.

Interestingly, the coefficient on the postarrest period is positive but small and estimated with considerable error.

In the period following the CCZ statement, there is suggestive evidence of interdenominational spillovers because of it. In the third period, all respondents – regardless of religious denomination – had lower assessments of the quality of democracy in their country. The effect is not statistically significant compared to the pre-arrest period, which is captured by the coefficient reported in the table, but it is statistically significant at the 90 percent confidence level compared to the postarrest period (coefficient = −0.210 and se = 0.108). Because no other major civil society organization released a statement around the same time, these results imply the broad political credibility of churches beyond their own denominations in Zambia.[48]

[48] A number of foreign groups criticized the arrest, but the timing of the statements is distinct from the CCZ statement. For example, former Nigerian President Olusegun Obasanjo, the United States, and the European Union immediately criticized the arrest. *Zambian Watchdog*, "Obasanjo condemns harassment, arrest of HH," April 11, 2017; Embassy of the United States of America, *United States Remains Concerned Over Heightened Political Tensions*, April 13, 2017; *Lusaka Times*, "HH's arrest has increased political tension in Zambia," April 14, 2017. The EFF in South Africa released a statement that was reported on April 21, 2017. *Cape Times*, EFF Deplore Arrest, April 21, 2017. The only international statement that was released somewhat close to the timing of the CCZ statement was one from Raila Odinga, leader of the opposition in Kenya, but I find it implausible that it could be driving the effect, given the much earlier statement from Obasanjo. *Lusaka Times*, "Zambia's politics, arrest of HH worry former Kenyan Prime Minister Odinga," April 19, 2017.

In contrast, we see an apparent rebound in perceptions of Zambia's democratic credentials in the fourth period, although this effect must be interpreted with some caution, given the small number of respondents interviewed after the Catholic statement was released (the Afrobarometer survey all but wrapped up that Sunday). This time-period effect captures trends among evangelical Christians, who were the only Christians unexposed to an antidemocratic frame from their church at that point, and it is broadly consistent with Gwyneth McClendon and Rachel Riedl's observation that Pentecostal sermons generate increased optimism and political efficacy for a day or two among attendees.[49]

The church statements are also associated with slightly decreased expressed support for the PF among church members, although the effect is estimated with considerable error and is not statistically significant. The limited effect may be due to the large apparent spillover effects from the CCZ statement. Calculating the difference in support for the PF in the periods immediately before and after the CCZ statement (coefficient = −0.108 and se = 0.044), respondents across churches were 11 percentage points less likely to say they would vote for the PF in the period following the CCZ statement, an effect that is statistically significant at the 95 percent confidence level.

These results suggest that Zambian church statements can be effective in changing the assessments and political opinions of people within and outside their churches. The details of these statements probably disseminate further within the church that released the statement, leading to larger cognitive effects on church members' assessments of democracy, but the statements in and of themselves may have broad political impact, reducing expressed support for the ruling party even among nonchurch members.

The Effect of Church Statements on Zambians' Willingness to Punish Antidemocratic Politicians

For further validation of the effects of church activism on Zambians' willingness to punish antidemocratic politicians, I provide evidence from an original survey experiment. The experiment has an innovative design in that it combines an endorsement experiment and a conjoint candidate attribute experiment to assess whether citizens place greater weight on democratic positions following a pro-democracy statement from different social organizations. Specifically, the study draws on the campaign

---

[49] McClendon and Riedl 2015; McClendon and Riedl 2019.

against Bill 10 conducted by secular NGOs and religious organizations to assess whether church statements are particularly effective in reducing support for antidemocratic candidates. This survey experiment was conducted as part of a phone survey in Zambia in December 2020 and January 2021, the period after Bill 10's legislative defeat, but the issue could still be considered topical insofar as the government suggested it may revive the bill again in the future.[50]

The conjoint experiment aspect of the design builds on work by Matthew Graham and Milan Svolik, who use conjoint candidate attribute experiments to examine how much citizens value democratic institutions by comparing support levels for candidates who do or do not take antidemocratic positions.[51] Conjoint candidate attribute experiments ask respondents to choose candidates with different positions on multiple dimensions, which forces respondents to make trade-offs. As a result, they reduce demand effects that make it difficult to interpret standard survey questions about democratic attitudes, and they approximate an actual political behavior: voting for a particular candidate (over others). In my design, I asked respondents to state their level of support for one candidate with a randomly generated attribute profile, rather than asking them to choose between two candidates, which would have been cognitively taxing in a phone survey.

In particular, respondents were asked to consider the following statement, with the independently randomized attributes indicated in parentheses and prefaced by the attribute name in bold:

Parliamentary and presidential elections will be held next year in Zambia, and are already being discussed. But for now, I want you to consider a hypothetical situation. Please imagine the following candidate is running for parliament in your constituency. Imagine this candidate is a man who was born in this area (**local**: and currently lives here/currently lives elsewhere), is a (**religiosity**: practicing/devout) Christian, and is affiliated with the (**party**: Patriotic Front (PF)/United Party for National Development (UPND)) party. In response to the challenges (**Covid**: faced by constituents/faced by constituents, including those posed by the extraordinary Covid-19 pandemic), (**competency**: he has promised to improve the socioeconomic situation but has not released a detailed plan/he has provided a detailed plan to improve the socioeconomic situation based on expert recommendations). He has also said future Zambian presidents should (**democracy**: request more briefings from permanent secretaries of government ministries/

[50] *Lusaka Times*, "PF Makes Tabling of Bill 10 in 2021 an Election Issue," November 17, 2020, www.lusakatimes.com/2020/11/17/pf-makes-tabling-of-bill-10-in-2021-an-election-issue/.
[51] Graham and Svolik 2020.

request government ministries adjust their working hours/<u>have the power to remove judges who disagree with their positions</u>/<u>have the power to determine who is allowed to stand for parliament</u>).

Regarding the democracy attribute, the first two positions are considered democratically neutral (based on theoretical expectations and question testing), while the two underlined positions are considered antidemocratic. The antidemocratic arms provide clear information, and as such, credible information is probably not the main constraint to punishing these candidates.[52] Instead, the main constraint is designed to be crosspressures related to the candidate's partisanship, competency, and local connections.

Following the vignette, respondents were asked how likely they would be to vote for the candidate on a 4-point scale (not at all likely, not very likely, somewhat likely, or very likely). For the purposes of the analysis below, I dichotomize the results between supportive (very and somewhat likely) and unsupportive respondents (not very likely and not at all likely), although the results are similar using the 4-point scale.

The innovation of the design is that it overlays an endorsement experiment on top of the conjoint experiment to assess the extent to which Zambian churches can motivate respondents to place greater weight on candidate's democratic positions when assessing them. The endorsement experiment randomized whether respondents were informed of church or secular opposition to the centralization of power in advance of the conjoint candidate attribute experiment, with each arm assigned with equal probability.[53] In particular, respondents were told:

> I would like to provide some information on proposed constitutional changes currently being discussed in Zambia. Some politicians support constitutional changes that would increase the power of future presidents. (**Endorser:** Zambia's three church mother bodies, including the Zambia Conference of Catholic Bishops, the CCZ, and the EFZ/Zambian NGOs, including the Law Association of Zambia and the Chapter One Foundation) have opposed proposals that would increase the power of future presidents, saying that these proposals undermine democracy.

Note that both endorsements are true endorsements in the sense that all the actors had publicly stated these positions. Following the measurement

---

[52] Consistent with this, the endorsement experiment did not change citizens' assessments of whether a particular position is antidemocratic (results not included in the chapter).

[53] The experiment also included a pure control, but as the pure control did not receive the information that some politicians support constitutional changes that would increase the power of future presidents, it may have changed perceptions of the challenger supporting antidemocratic changes and so is not analyzed here.

of outcomes, respondents were asked if they had heard anything about the proposed constitutional changes in advance of the survey. Many of them had (44 percent), but only a small fraction of all respondents reported they had heard about it via an NGO (1 percent) or church group or church media (1 percent), consistent with church organizations and NGOs aiming their outreach on Bill 10 mainly at legislators.

I use the endorsement experiments to test whether religious endorsements can encourage citizens to weigh more negatively the antidemocratic position compared to endorsements from secular organizations. I show the effects of each arm of the endorsement experiment by estimating the average marginal component effects (AMCE) via OLS regressions, running separate models for each arm of the endorsement experiment. In total, 567 respondents are in the religious endorsement condition and 541 respondents are in the secular endorsement condition.

Figure 6.2 shows the AMCEs for each arm of the conjoint candidate experiment by the two arms of the endorsement experiment. The

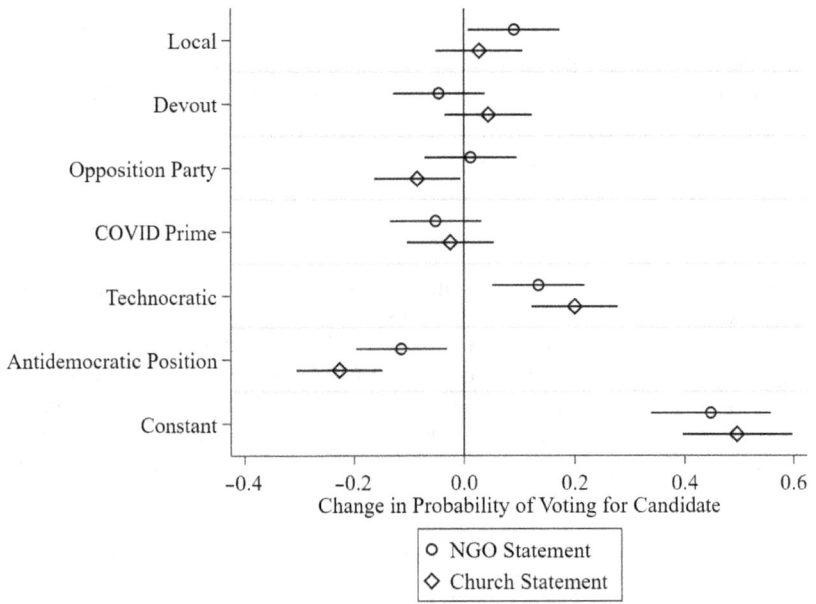

FIGURE 6.2 Average marginal component effects on likelihood of voting for candidate by endorsement condition
Note: Figure displays the average marginal component effects for each attribute by whether the respondent received the religious or secular NGO endorsement condition.

results show that receiving a church endorsement versus one from an NGO makes little difference in the weight that respondents place on most candidate attributes. Respondents are not significantly more or less likely to support local, devout, or competent candidates after a church endorsement, and they are significantly less likely to support opposition candidates (as compared to when they receive an NGO endorsement). Although at first glance this seems to suggest church endorsements create a pro-incumbency bias, below I demonstrate that the results are more consistent with NGO endorsements generating an anti-incumbency bias. Last and most important, although respondents punish antidemocratic positions in both treatment arms, church statements significantly increase the percentage that antidemocratic positions are punished compared to statements from secular NGO organizations. Respondents are 11 percentage points less likely to support an antidemocratic candidate in the NGO condition but 23 percentage points less likely to support an antidemocratic candidate in the church condition, a difference that is statistically significant at the 95 percent confidence level. Thus, church advocacy for liberal democratic institutions is likely to be particularly important in encouraging citizens to vote against antidemocratic politicians.

Figure 6.3 examines whether the effect of religious versus secular endorsements varies across the three major religious groups in Zambia – Catholics, mainline Protestants, and evangelical/Pentecostal Protestants. The power of this analysis is weakened by the relatively low proportion of Catholics in the sample, but the results are interesting because they suggest that church versus NGO endorsements are most effective for mainline and evangelical Protestants, with no observed differences for Catholics. Even though the Catholic bishops are generally recognized as the most politically active of the church mother bodies, the effects of collective endorsements are larger for Zambian Protestants, suggesting that churches have wide political credibility in the country.

Table 6.3 returns to the main findings of Figure 6.2 and considers how expressed levels of support for candidates vary based on endorsement condition, the candidate's partisanship, and the candidate's expressed support for antidemocratic actions. These patterns suggest that rather than viewing religious endorsements as creating bias in favor of the incumbent, it may be fairer to view secular NGO endorsements as creating bias in favor of the opposition. In the experiment, democratically neutral candidates can expect to receive the support of close to 60 percent of citizens in three of the four conditions. But when candidates have received a secular NGO endorsement *and* they belong to the PF, they

TABLE 6.3 *Support for candidates by endorsement conditions and candidate's political attributes*

	NGO statement		Religious statement	
	PF candidate	UPND candidate	PF candidate	UPND candidate
Neutral candidate	0.45	0.57	0.60	0.56
	(0.04)	(0.04)	(0.04)	(0.04)
Antidemocratic candidate	0.45	0.36	0.41	0.27
	(0.04)	(0.04)	(0.04)	(0.04)

Note: The table reports the proportion of respondents who support candidates with different partisanship and different positions on democratic institutions under the NGO endorsement condition and the religious endorsement condition; standard errors are in parentheses.

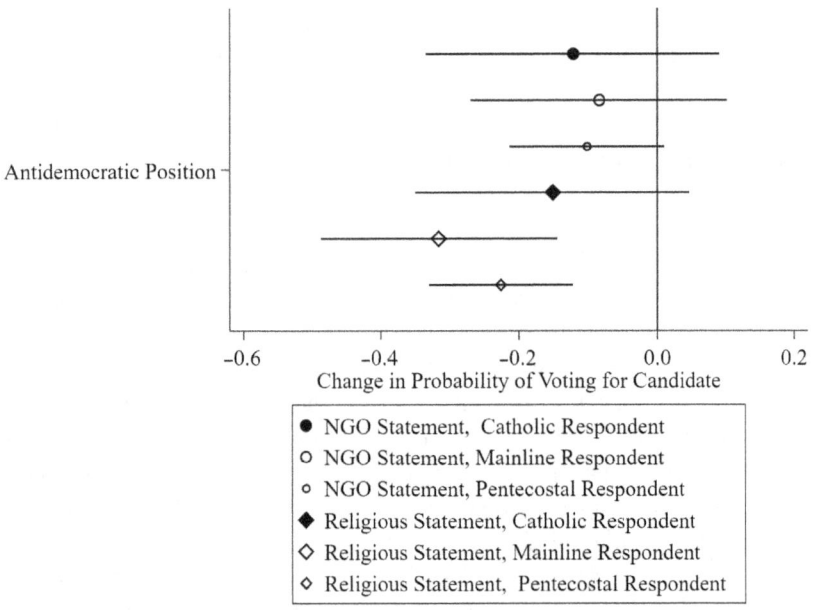

FIGURE 6.3 Average marginal component effect of antidemocratic position by endorsement condition and respondent religion
Note: Figure displays the average marginal component effect of the candidate taking an antidemocratic position by whether the respondent received the religious or secular NGO endorsement condition and the respondent's religion.

receive the support of only 45 percent of citizens. In fact, after a secular NGO endorsement, there is no difference in support for antidemocratic versus neutral PF candidates. In contrast, after a religious endorsement, antidemocratic candidates from both parties lose support as compared to neutral candidates, and although UPND candidates are punished slightly more, the difference in punishment across parties is much smaller following a church versus a secular NGO endorsement. This finding underscores the credibility of churches in encouraging the defense of liberal democratic institutions from diverse political threats.

The combination of evidence presented thus far demonstrates the political credibility of Zambian churches and the broad effect of their statements in support of democracy on citizens' assessments and behavioral intentions. Zambian churches frequently make coordinated statements in defense of liberal democracy, and these statements affect citizens' understanding of and willingness to punish antidemocratic candidates across religious and party lines. Churches that take lessons from the Zambian case are likely to take heart in their ability to affect positive change in liberal democratic institutions.

CHURCH POLITICAL CREDIBILITY AND CITIZENS' REACTIONS TO CHURCH ACTIVISM IN TANZANIA

The second case that I consider is Tanzania, where the ruling party's attack on liberal democratic institutions post-2015 has many parallels to the Zambian case. Nevertheless, drawing on interviews and experimental data, I show that churches in Tanzania lack the history and credibility of Zambian churches in engaging in collective democratic advocacy and that even if they had been better at acting in concert during this particular period, they would have been unlikely to coordinate citizens in support of institutional change.

Churches' Credibility and Coordination in Tanzania

I begin by providing qualitative evidence on the challenges Tanzanian churches face in projecting broad credibility on political issues. Tanzania is an extremely religiously heterogeneous country, especially the mainland, which is about one-third Protestant, one-third Catholic, and one-third Muslim. Most Protestant churches are organized under an umbrella organization, the Christian Council of Tanzania (CCT), and the bishops of the Catholic Church are organized at the national level as the Tanzania Episcopal Conference (TEC). The Muslim community has the state-recognized Supreme Council of Muslims (BAKWATA), although at least some portion of the Muslim community does not view it as a legitimately representative body. Overall, churches in Tanzania have a history of being less politically critical than in Zambia, but there have been historical moments of activism. For example, both the Catholic and Lutheran churches issued pastoral letters and statements in support of democracy in the run-up to the reintroduction of multiparty elections in 1995.[54]

In addition, the country has not experienced partisan turnover at the national level since independence. The Chama Cha Mapinduzi (CCM) ruled with minimal challenge to its dominant position in mainland Tanzania even after the immediate reintroduction of multiparty elections. Its first major electoral competition only emerged in 2010 when the opposition party, Chama cha Demokrasia na Maendeleo (CHADEMA), selected Wilbroad Slaa, a former Catholic priest and secretary general of the TEC, as its candidate. Slaa's anti-corruption message won significant support from numerous citizens and church leaders, but the ruling party was easily able to accuse church leaders of communalism in their support for the former priest over the CCM's Muslim candidate, Jakaya Kikwete.

This context makes it very difficult for Tanzanian churches to speak credibly on democratic issues to citizens across partisan and religious lines. As one religious leader puts it, you are assumed to be pro-opposition "if you are speaking about non-adherence to democratic principles ..."[55] In addition, many church leaders mention the challenges of engaging in advocacy without appearing to have religious prejudice, given the significant non-Christian population in Tanzania.[56]

I contrast the ability of churches to coordinate and to speak credibly on democratic issues in Zambia and Tanzania by comparing their responses to the attacks on opposition leaders in each country in 2017. A parallel to Hichilema's April 2017 arrest in Zambia occurred in September 2017 in Tanzania: the CHADEMA parliamentary whip, Tundu Lissu, barely survived an assassination attempt in which he was hit by sixteen bullets. This assassination attempt represents the most prominent attack in a wider repression of the country's political opposition throughout 2017.

---

[54] Catholic Bishops of Tanzania, *Good Conscience, Vision of our Nation*, November 21, 1993; Evangelical Lutheran Church of Tanzania, *Bagamoyo Statement*, March 1994. The greater tradition of activism within churches in Zambia is not only my own observation; it was explicitly noted by some religious leaders in Tanzania. Interview with Tanzanian Lutheran religious leader, May 2018; Interview with Tanzanian Catholic religious leader, May 2018.

[55] Interview with Tanzanian leader of Christian social service provision group, May 2018.

[56] Interview with Tanzanian leader of Christian social service provision group, May 2018; Interview with Tanzanian Catholic religious leader, May 2018.

Church Political Credibility in Tanzania 147

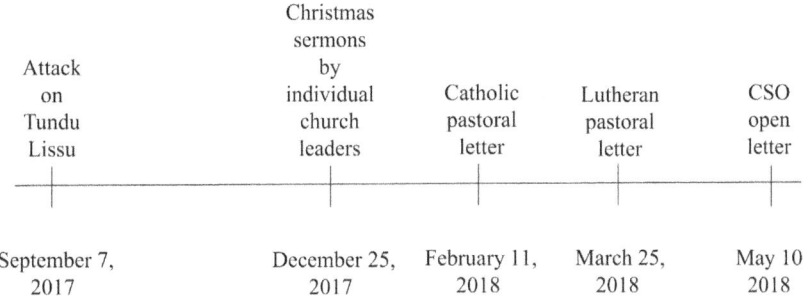

FIGURE 6.4 Timeline of opposition leader assassination attempt and church activism in Tanzania

In contrast to the Zambian case, it took churches in Tanzania a great deal of time to speak out against this repression, and they did not manage to coordinate their actions, as Figure 6.4 illustrates. During Christmas sermons in December 2017, several individual leaders spoke out against the erosion of political rights, but they spoke as individuals rather than on behalf of their church or church council. At the Lutheran Cathedral in Moshi, Bishop Fredrick Shoo, the presiding bishop of the Evangelical Lutheran Church of Tanzania, said that Tanzanians were living in fear of "saying the wrong things … There is a group of people whose duty is to instill fear in people who speak the truth. This is wrong. Jesus was born to enable us to live in truth and not in fear."[57] In Morogoro, the Catholic bishop of Morogoro, Telesphore Mkude, also alluded to the recent attacks on citizens' rights in his Christmas sermon.[58] In Dar es Salaam, the founder and leader of the Full Gospel Bible Fellowship Church, Zachary Kakobe, made perhaps the strongest criticism of the government in his Christmas address, accusing the government of "quietly turning the country into a one-state rule by systematically banning political activity."[59] But it took several months more before any of the churches in Tanzania took church-level stances in defense of democratic rights. And even at that point, there was limited coordination across churches.

---

[57] *The Citizen*, "Clerics warn against rights suppression in Christmas sermons," December 26, 2017.
[58] Ibid.
[59] Fumbuka Ng'wanakilala, "Tanzania threatens to de-register churches who rap president from pulpit," *Reuters*, December 29, 2017, www.reuters.com/article/world/tanzania-threatens-to-de-register-churches-who-rap-president-from-pulpit-idUSKBN1EN0WZ/.

The Catholic Church, through the TEC, was the first Tanzanian church to issue a church-wide statement. It issued a pastoral letter to mark the beginning of Lent. Signed by all thirty-four Catholic bishops in Tanzania, the letter noted that the suspension of political activities in the country was contrary to "the right of every citizen" and in "violation of the Constitution and national laws."[60] Six weeks later, the Lutheran Church released an Easter letter that was even more critical, explicitly calling out the "abduction, torture, disappearance of people, attempted assassination of political leaders" and the "shrinking space for the freedom of expression, freedom of assembly and freedom of information."[61] Both letters were powerful statements in support of democratic rights. The text of key passages is presented in Table 6.4. The statements were disseminated via church media, including church-owned radio stations and newspapers, and they were read in churches across the country during Sunday services.[62] They predated similar statements from secular civil society groups.[63]

But cracks in the united front of the two churches quickly emerged, significantly more so than in the Zambian case. After the release of the Catholic Lenten letters, Tanzania's only cardinal, who was also the archbishop of Dar es Salaam, was rumored to have disassociated himself from it.[64] In the case of the Lutheran Church, three Lutheran bishops – apparently under political pressure from local government administrators – did not read the Easter letter in their dioceses.[65] This caused turmoil and division within the Lutheran Church as the

---

[60] Tanzania Episcopal Conference, "Lenten Letter," February 11, 2018.
[61] Evangelical Lutheran Church of Tanzania, "Our Nation, Our Peace," March 25, 2018.
[62] Interview with Tanzanian leader of Christian advocacy group, May 2018.
[63] On May 10, 2018, sixty-five secular civil society groups from around the world signed an open letter to President John Magufuli voicing concern over the protection of human rights in Tanzania.
[64] Interview with Tanzanian Catholic religious leader, May 2018. See also, *The East African*, "Lutheran Church in Tanzania Accused of Playing Politics," June 9, 2018, www.theeastafrican.co.ke/tea/news/east-africa/lutheran-church-in-tanzania-accused-of-playing-politics--1395742.
[65] One claim is that these bishops leaked the letters to the regional commissioners, and they told them not to read them. Interview with leader of international church group in Tanzania, May 2018. A broader interpretation was that bishops do not like to deliver critical messages directly to those in power. For example, one Lutheran church leader said, "We may give some instructions, for example, on Easter we gave a pastoral letter ... but in some parishes, we might have people who are so political going there so they don't want to read it." Interview with Tanzanian Lutheran religious leader, March 2019.

TABLE 6.4 *Key passages from pastoral letters issued during Easter season, 2018*

Church	Name and date	Passages on democracy
Tanzania Episcopal Conference (TEC)	"Lenten Letter," February 11, 2018	"Politically, our country follows a multiparty democratic system ... However, political activities still continue to be prevented using statutory instruments. It means that the activities of political parties, such as public meetings, protests, conferences and even internal meetings, which is the right of every citizen, has ceased until another election. Legally, this is a violation of the Constitution and the laws of the country." "Also some media have been closed or suspended for a while, thus reducing the scope of freedom of access to information, comments and expression. The ban on the media has gone hand-in-hand with curtailing the independence of the judiciary and the Parliament through the abolition of the rights of parliamentarians and not giving public hearings ..."
Evangelical Lutheran Church of Tanzania (ELCT)	"Our Nation, Our Peace," March 25, 2018	"Contrary to the laws, procedures and our national values; we are now witnessing events that are contrary to the principles and values of our nation. Some of these events are: I. Fear based on actual events such as abduction, torture, disappearance of people, attempted assassination of political leaders, threats, false accusations, and misuse of the law enforcement agents against the people. II. The shrinking space for the freedom of expression, freedom of assembly and freedom of information. In this regard, there is a fear that even freedom of worship is beginning to shrink. III. Shrinking of the independence of Parliament, the judiciary, and the Electoral Commission. Furthermore, undermining of the Local Government Authorities which contradicts the devolution concepts. IV. Unfavourable environment that do not support the right and freedom to vote and to be voted for in various elections. All by-elections have been dominated by killings, brutality, violence, trickery, and threats ..."

offending bishops were subsequently sanctioned by and isolated from the rest of the council.⁶⁶

In addition, there was limited coordination across churches in Tanzania. One elder in the Lutheran Church was critical of the lack of coordination with the Catholic Church prior to the release of the Easter letter: "But they didn't play it strategic. What they should have done is spea[k] to the Catholics first so they would come out in support. Of course, individual pastors did, but not all."⁶⁷ In addition, other churches in Tanzania did not engage in significant activism against the democratic crackdown. The Protestant umbrella organization, the CCT, did not make a statement, nor did any other major Protestant church. Many other church leaders apparently agreed with the sentiment shared by one Anglican Church leader: "I have been struggling very hard to tell religious leaders not to politicize religion ..."⁶⁸

The government subsequently used considerable coercion to try to force the churches, especially the Lutheran Church, to retract its criticism. According to social media reports, which were subsequently picked up by private newspapers and opposition MPs, the government sent letters to the Lutheran Church in May 2018 demanding that it retract its Easter letter and warning of legal and financial sanctions on the church. In the aftermath of the letters, the government allegedly used bribes and threats against senior Catholic and Lutheran religious leaders, offering land and threatening travel bans or legal action if they did not walk back their criticism.⁶⁹ One interviewee summarizes the variety of coercive methods as such: "They have told them they are drug dealers, they are not paying tax, they are not citizens."⁷⁰ At least one bishop was questioned by authorities about his citizenship, and some church leaders sought to leave the country following threats.⁷¹

---

⁶⁶ *The Citizen*, "ELCT Bishop Apologizes for Failure to Deliver Easter Message," April 29, 2018, www.thecitizen.co.tz/tanzania/news/national/elct-bishop-apologises-for-failure-to-deliver-easter-message--2633588. As a result of the punishment, one of the errant bishops subsequently issued an apology and a statement in support of the Easter letter.
⁶⁷ Interview with Tanzanian former officer of the Lutheran church, May 2018.
⁶⁸ Interview with Tanzanian Anglican religious leader, May 2018.
⁶⁹ Interview with Tanzanian officer of the Lutheran church, May 2018; Interview with leader of international church group in Tanzania, April 2019.
⁷⁰ Interview with Tanzanian leader of Christian advocacy group, May 2018.
⁷¹ Interview with leader of international church group in Tanzania, April 2019; Interview with leader of international church group in Tanzania, May 2018.

Church leaders were also explicitly threatened with the elimination of funding for their social services.[72] Although churches in Tanzania receive almost no state funding for their education systems, which are focused exclusively on the secondary level, their hospitals and health clinics are much more dependent on it, and because churches value continuing these activities, I anticipate that these threats would also have had quieting effects.

Under sustained attacks from ruling authorities, that the Lutheran Church did not retract its letter is an achievement. The presiding bishop, Archbishop Shoo, stood firm in his support for the church's letter throughout this period, despite an apparent ultimatum from the Ministry of Home Affairs.[73] In the end, the Home Affairs minister was forced to disavow the existence of any letters presenting the Lutheran Church with an ultimatum, and he subsequently fired the civil servant whose signature appeared on the letter circulating on social media.[74]

But neither the Catholic nor the Lutheran churches managed to sustain their activism over time. As one Catholic priest expresses it, "The fact that a Bishop is willing to disassociate himself ... It shows the leadership is no longer united. The TEC Bishops conference is not united, so they won't make statements. They don't have the guts."[75] The Tanzanian churches were not able to sustain coordinated action even within their individual denominations.

The Effect of Church Statements on Citizens' Support for Legal Change in Tanzania

As the discussion above indicates, Tanzanian churches have had greater difficulty coordinating within and across churches in support of democratic issues than churches in Zambia. In the absence of interdenominational and interreligious coordination, is it likely that the statements

---

[72] Interview with Tanzanian Lutheran religious leader, March 2019.
[73] *The Citizen*, "ELCT Head: Our Easter Message Was Calculated, Deliberate," June 11, 2018, www.thecitizen.co.tz/tanzania/news/national/-elct-head-our-easter-message-was-calculated-deliberate-2640732.
[74] *The Citizen*, "'Not Ours': Government disowns letter to Lutheran Church," June 10, 2018, www.thecitizen.co.tz/tanzania/news/national/-not-ours-government-disowns-letter-to-lutheran-church-2640162; *The Citizen*, "Home Affairs Minister suspends register over disavowed letter to Lutheran Church," June 8, 2018, www.thecitizen.co.tz/tanzania/news/national/home-affairs-minister-suspends-registrar-over-disavowed-letter-to-lutheran-church-2640186.
[75] Interview with Tanzanian Catholic religious leader, May 2018.

they did issue affected public opinion? And if the churches had been more successful in issuing joint statements, could they have informed and coordinated the public in support of democratic institutions?

I consider these questions using evidence from an endorsement experiment conducted as part of a household survey with 2,400 respondents across 120 communities in five regions of mainland Tanzania (Kilimanjaro, Mbeya, Morogoro, Tabora, and Tanga). The sample was specifically constructed to be religiously and politically diverse: 30 percent of respondents were Muslim, 27 percent were Catholic, and 33 percent were Protestant, and the sample included regions considered government strongholds (Tabora and Tanga); regions considered strongholds of the main opposition party, CHADEMA (Kilimanjaro); and regions that were more politically divided (Mbeya and Morogoro). The survey was administered between late June and early September 2018.

The endorsement design is like the one employed in Zambia except that it considered whether endorsements from religious actors could encourage citizens to support candidates campaigning on promises to make legal changes that would protect workers' rights. It was necessary to make this shift because religious actors in Tanzania have not coordinated in making pro-democracy statements, and to assess whether they would have had more influence had they managed to coordinate, I wanted to include an experimental arm with a unified statement but without introducing deception. In addition, given the crackdown on churches that had issued prodemocratic statements in early 2018, these statements were considered too sensitive to include in the survey. Instead, I built the endorsement experiment around statements from religious actors in favor of legal changes to protect workers' rights. In 2017, all three major religious groups – the TEC, the BAKWATA, and the CCT – had issued a publication recommending that foreign companies working in Tanzania employ more Tanzanian staff.[76]

The second difference from the Zambian design is that I included treatment conditions in which only one of the peak religious associations in Tanzania (TEC, BAKWATA, or CCT) was explicitly identified in

---

[76] This recommendation was made as part of the 2017 publication *The One Billion Dollar Question Revisited: How Much Is Tanzania Losing in Potential Tax Revenues*, jointly published by the Tanzania Episcopal Conference (TEC), the National Muslim Council of Tanzania (BAKWATA), and the Christian Council of Tanzania (CCT), and funded by Norwegian Church Aid.

the endorsement, as well as a treatment condition akin to the one used in Zambia in which all the major religious actors were named. Doing so allowed me to assess the public opinion effects of individual church endorsements (akin to what unfolded in early 2018 in Tanzania) as well as the public opinion effects of coordinated endorsements (providing some insight into what may have happened in a counterfactual world where greater coordination was attained in Tanzania). The Tanzanian endorsement experiment also included a nonreligious condition in which respondents were told only that "NGOs in Tanzania and other organizations" had proposed the legal change.

The third difference is the design of the conjoint candidate attribute experiment. Because the survey was administered in person, it was feasible to ask respondents to choose between two different candidates. One of the two candidates supported the legal change and the other lobbied for local development. In this way, the trade-off between supporting the legal change advocated by religious actors and parochial preferences was forced in this design, and if religious cues prime parochial preferences, it is possible that their endorsements could have adverse effects. The other dimensions on which the respondents varied were the religion that their name signaled (which was held constant within pairs) and their stated religiosity. Unlike in the Zambian case, I did not explicitly manipulate partisanship due to the greater political sensitivity of opposition support in Tanzania.

The eight possible pairs of candidates that respondents could have been asked to choose between are indicated in Table 6.5. For example,

TABLE 6.5 *Candidate pair conditions in the Tanzanian survey*

Christian pairs		Muslim pairs	
Unspecified religiosity, local development	Unspecified religiosity, legal change	Unspecified religiosity, local development	Unspecified religiosity, legal change
High religiosity, local development	Unspecified religiosity, legal change	High religiosity, local development	Unspecified religiosity, legal change
Unspecified religiosity, local development	High religiosity, legal change	Unspecified religiosity, local development	High religiosity, legal change
High religiosity, local development	High religiosity, legal change	High religiosity, local development	High religiosity, legal change

under the third Christian pairing, respondents would be told, "James is a man who promises to promote the interests of this region by bringing development projects that will hire more local people. Emmanuel is a deeply religious man who promises to change Tanzania's policies so that foreign companies are required to employ more local staff." Respondents were subsequently asked to choose which of the two candidates they would support. In the analysis below, I consider respondent support for the candidate running on a platform promising legal changes to support workers' rights as the outcome of interest.

Do religious endorsements increase support for the candidate proposing legal changes to advance workers' rights in Tanzania? Figure 6.5 presents the average levels of support for the policy candidate by endorsement condition first across the entire sample and then by the country's three main religious subgroups, Catholics, Protestants, and Muslims. For each sample, I can compare the effect of the secular NGO endorsement to an in-group endorsement, an out-group endorsement, and a collective religious endorsement, with the last treatment most directly paralleling the Zambian experiment.

Figure 6.5(a) shows that across the entire sample, there is no evidence that religious endorsements – individual or collective – change support for the policy candidate compared to the secular NGO endorsement. But Figure 6.5(b–d) shows that the aggregate results hide more complex effects of religious endorsements when broken down by religious subgroup. Compared to the secular NGO endorsement, Catholics (Figure 6.5(b)) do not significantly increase support for the policy candidate when they hear either a collective religious endorsement or a Catholic endorsement. Protestants (Figure 6.5(c)) increase support for the policy candidate when they hear a collective religious endorsement, but not when they hear an endorsement from the CCT only. Muslims (Figure 6.5(d)) reduce support for the policy candidate when they hear a collective religious endorsement, an endorsement from BAKWATA only, or an endorsement from the Catholic bishops only. Expressed in reverse, Muslims increase support for the local public goods candidate following any of these three endorsements.

These results suggest that in the Tanzanian context, religious endorsements may not be able to induce increased support for liberal democratic institutions even when they are collectively coordinated. Even if Tanzanian religious actors had managed to unite in defense of democratic institutions in early 2018, they may not have been able to motivate citizens to place more weight on the defense of democracy as a result.

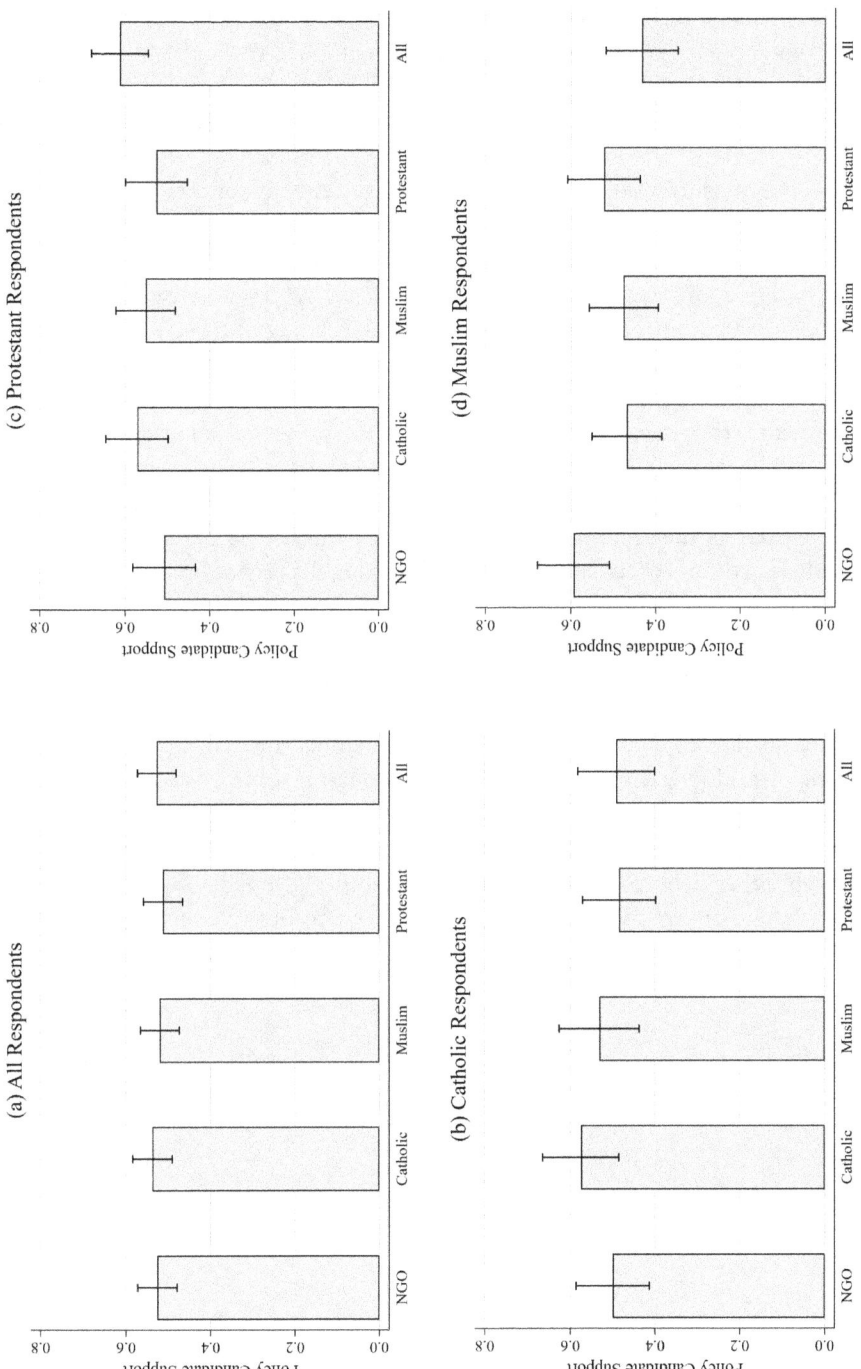

FIGURE 6.5 Levels of support for candidate proposing legal changes to workers' rights by endorsement conditions for (a) all respondents, (b) Catholic respondents, (c) Protestant respondents, (d) Muslim respondents

A key problem in the Tanzanian context is that religious endorsements can trigger parochialism, encouraging greater emphasis on local concerns versus national legal change.

*****

Church activism in favor of liberal democracy can sometimes be effective in mobilizing broad constituencies with leverage over rulers. This chapter focuses on the ability of churches to mobilize political elites, international actors, and especially voters to act in defense of liberal democratic institutions. As the first case study shows, Zambian churches have been effective in mobilizing broad constituencies in defense of liberal democracy. By issuing coordinated pro-democracy statements, they create conditions for citizens to act in defense of liberal democratic institutions. But the effectiveness of church activism in mobilizing citizens in support of liberal democracy is likely to vary by context, as the second case study demonstrates. Compared to their Zambian counterparts, churches in Tanzania have not managed to issue strongly coordinated pro-democracy statements, and even if they had, they probably have more limited ability to sway citizens' opinions in defense of political institutions due to deeper religious cleavages. Churches taking lessons from Tanzania are likely to be more pessimistic about their capacity to influence liberal democratic institutions than churches taking lessons from Zambia, although insofar as some of the difficulties in the Tanzanian case were due to lack of internal coordination, other churches may believe they can do better. Overall, it is likely that churches believe they have some probability of positively affecting liberal democratic institutions by reaching out to broad constituencies that have leverage over rulers.

7

Tracing Liberal Democracy's Influence on Educational Policy

Evidence from Zambia, Ghana, and Beyond

The central argument of this book is that churches with significant education systems are more likely to publicly advocate for liberal democratic institutions because those institutions protect their schools from higher levels of state control. In particular, liberal democratic institutions distribute policymaking influence in a way that often empowers individuals who work in the bureaucracy, parliament, or the judiciary and who are domestic policy advocates of churches to advance church educational interests. They also increase the ability of these advocates to protect church-state pacts through legal agreements and greater protections for freedom of expression. Churches can mobilize broad constituencies in support of liberal democratic institutions, as Chapter 6 demonstrates, and these liberal democratic institutions in turn create opportunities for their policy advocates to advance church education policy interests.

This chapter provides evidence on whether and how liberal democratic institutions help churches protect their educational interests. It begins by drawing on intertemporal evidence from different periods in Zambia and Ghana to demonstrate that elections and institutional checks distribute political power in ways that tend to favor church educational interests and that legally guaranteed church-state agreements help to secure the position of churches as managers of their own school systems. The chapter concludes with tests of these predictions using data from across all sub-Saharan African countries in which most schools were run by churches at independence.

I test the argument that liberal democratic institutions give churches policy influence because they offer wider opportunities for input into policymaking and policy implementation. In an autocracy, policymaking is the ruler's prerogative, and the ruler will take control of church schools if doing so is deemed in their interest. As a country's political institutions become more liberal democratic, rulers depend more on electoral majorities for support and multiple actors – presidents, legislatures, and judiciaries – have a say in the policymaking process. My claim is that well-established churches in sub-Saharan Africa can use these openings in the political process to advance their educational interests. Specifically, liberal democratic institutions create openings for individual bureaucrats, parliamentarians, and judges who share church policy interests to advance them. Furthermore, legal limits on the power of elected rulers under liberal democratic institutions prevent rulers from using state power to overstep agreements with churches that guarantee church educational roles and from suppressing public dialogue on educational policy. As a result, I expect churches to be better able to advance and protect their educational systems under liberal democratic institutions even if their church membership does not make up a majority of the electorate and even if they do not have closely aligned political parties to press their case.

In addition to empirically examining whether and how liberal democratic institutions benefit churches in education policymaking, I also provide evidence that churches can use these institutions to push back against pressure on governments from international donors to reduce the role of churches in education. In contrast to the evidence presented in Chapter 6, which shows that churches can ally themselves with powerful international actors in their campaigns for liberal democracy, here I show that churches often face opposition from key international powers, whether Marxist or capitalist in orientation, in defending religious education systems. Churches cannot typically mobilize the same broad coalitions in support of education policy that they can in defense of democracy. They need liberal democratic institutions first so that their domestic policy advocates in bureaucracies, parliaments, and judiciaries can advance their educational interests.

TRENDS IN LIBERAL DEMOCRACY AND POLICIES TOWARD CHURCH EDUCATION IN ZAMBIA AND GHANA

In this chapter, I analyze whether and how liberal democratic institutions have influenced the extent to which educational policymaking aligns with church interests across different episodes in Zambian and Ghanaian history.[1] The analysis combines within-country analysis of the correlation between policy outcomes and potential explanatory factors across time periods with process tracing of the policymaking process in different historic episodes. For each country, I draw on interviews with church leaders and educationalists, primary documents, and secondary sources to demonstrate how each component of liberal democracy – institutional checks, elections, and civil rights that can be defended in court – contributes to greater church autonomy over their schools in more democratic periods. I also rule out alternative explanations for the outcome, drawing on evidence on how they covary with education policy outcomes and process-tracing clues.

I consider government educational policy to be more favorable to church interests to the extent that it grants churches autonomy over school management (especially in selecting teachers) and provides more space for confessional religious education. In contrast, government policy is less favorable to church interests to the extent that it disempowers them from selecting and disciplining teachers or limits their ability to teach religion. In the extreme, these regulations take away the specific religious character of church-affiliated schools and in so doing, they are equivalent to full-scale nationalization of the schools. But in general, the autonomy of churches in running their schools is distinct from the mere number of church-affiliated schools. In fact, the worst outcome from the perspective of the church (and the best outcome from the perspective of the state) would be to have the church subsidize the costs of a large number of nominally church-affiliated schools in which the teachers and curriculum are controlled by the state. As such, this chapter focuses on changes in educational policy rather than changes in the number of church-affiliated schools.

Importantly, churches care most about the educational curriculum taught in schools versus the officially adopted educational policy, and in many time periods there are discrepancies between the two. As a result, my analysis considers not only the influence of churches on policymaking but also, to the extent that sources permit, their influence on policy implementation.

---

[1] The term "episode analysis" is from Capoccia and Ziblatt 2010, who say it "identifies the key political actors fighting over institutional change, highlights the terms of the debate and the full range of options that they perceived, reconstructs the extent of political and social support behind these options, and analyzes, as much as possible with the eyes of contemporaries, the political interactions that led to the institutional outcome." See Capoccia and Ziblatt 2010, 943.

I analyze the case of Zambia first, followed by the case of Ghana. These two countries are appropriate for the analysis, as both inherited a colonial education system under which churches provided a sizeable portion of education and both experienced significant variation in liberal democracy over time. In Zambia, the population is predominantly Christian (about 85 percent in 2015, with no sizeable religious minorities) and postindependence, the Catholic Church (about 30 percent) has been the only church with significant involvement in education (running about 20 percent of all schools at its peak in 1970). In contrast, in Ghana, there is a significant Muslim minority (about 20 percent of the population in 2015) and postindependence, the church-affiliated education sector has been consistently larger (more than 20 percent of all schools in many decades) and more diverse, involving both Catholic and mainline Protestant churches.[2]

To assess the effects of liberal democratic institutions on educational policy toward church schools, I begin by identifying different episodes of possible educational reform in each country. I define episodes by changes in the constitution or the presidency. In Zambia, there are seven distinct episodes from 1964, the year of independence, to 2020, described in Table 7.1. In Ghana, I consider twelve distinct episodes, beginning with the period of self-governance in 1952, through to 2020, described in Table 7.2. Of course, not every ruler instituted educational reforms, but the frequency with which they occurred is high in both countries, consistent with my claim about the perceived importance of the education system to economic and state-building goals.

For each episode, I consider the government's official policies and their implementation as they affect church autonomy in the management of church-affiliated schools and the content of religious education. Educational policies may either increase or decrease the autonomy of churches in these areas, which I distinguish in the table with plus and minus signs. In considering the level of implementation, I classify episodes into incidents of nonimplementation, partial implementation, full implementation, or extreme implementation, with the latter indicating instances of change that go beyond the letter of the policy. These policy proposals and the level of implementation, discussed at length further, are summarized in columns 1 to 4 of each table.

My hypothesis is that the country's level of liberal democracy allows churches greater autonomy in running schools. Column 5 summarizes

---

[2] Owusu-Ansah, Iddrisu, and Sey 2013.

TABLE 7.1 *Episodes of analysis in Zambia*

	(1) Effort at Church School Management Reform	(2) Outcome of Educational Management Reform	(3) Effort at Religious/Moral Curricular Reform	(4) Outcome of Religious/Moral Curricular Reform	(5) Level of Liberal Democracy	(6) Government Ideology	(7) Economic Performance
Kenneth Kaunda, First Republic (1964–1972)	Proposal to increase government authority over management, teachers (1966, 1969)	Contested; extreme implementation, beyond letter of law (--)	Proposal to shift religious instruction from confessional to academic (1971–1973)	Accepted; implementation (–)	Weak (decreasing)	United National Independence Party: socialism	Good
Kenneth Kaunda, Second Republic (1973–1990)	Continued to increase government authority over management of teachers (per 1969 framework)	Extreme implementation; government takes over Catholic primary schools (1974) (---)	Effort to introduce Marxist political education (1975 onward)	Contested; partial implementation (-)	Extremely weak	United National Independence Party: socialism	Very poor
Frederick Chiluba (1991–2001)	Proposal to increase church authority over teachers (1993); return some schools to church management (1996)	Contested; partial implementation (+)			Moderate	Movement for Multiparty Democracy: free market; Christian appeals	Very poor

(continued)

TABLE 7.1 (continued)

	(1) Effort at Church School Management Reform	(2) Outcome of Educational Management Reform	(3) Effort at Religious/Moral Curricular Reform	(4) Outcome of Religious/Moral Curricular Reform	(5) Level of Liberal Democracy	(6) Government Ideology	(7) Economic Performance
Levy Mwanawasa (2002–2008)					Moderate	Movement for Multiparty Democracy: free market	Very good
Rupiah Banda (2009–2011)					Moderate	Movement for Multiparty Democracy: free market	Very good
Michael Sata (2012–2014)			Proposal to make religious educational optional (2013)	Contested; no implementation in church schools (0)	Moderate	Patriotic Front: economic nationalism; Catholic appeals	Good
Edgar Lungu (2015–2020)					Limited (decreasing)	Patriotic Front: economic nationalism	Very poor

Note: The coding of liberal democracy is based on V-DEM's library democracy index, with 0.05–0.15 = extremely weak, 0.15–0.25 = weak, 0.25–0.35 = limited, 0.35–0.45 = moderate, 0.45–0.55 = substantial, and 0.55+ = strong. The coding of economic performance is based on the World Bank's data on annual GDP per capita growth. Rounding economic growth to the nearest integer, −1 percent or less is very poor, 0–1 percent growth is good, and 4 percent or more is very good. In columns 2 and 4, − indicates partial implementation of a policy that disempowers the church, − − indicates implementation, and − − − indicates extreme implementation; 0 indicates nonimplementation, + indicates partial implementation, and ++ indicates implementation of policy that empowers the church.

TABLE 7.2 *Episodes of analysis in Ghana*

	(1) Effort at Church School Management Reform	(2) Outcome of Educational Management Reform	(3) Effort at Religious/ Moral Curricular Reform	(4) Outcome of Religious/ Moral Curricular Reform	(5) Level of Liberal Democracy	(6) Government Ideology	(7) Economic Performance
Kwame Nkrumah, self-government (1951–1956)	Proposal to nationalize many church schools (1951)	Partly implemented (-)			Weak	Convention People's Party: socialism	Very good
Kwame Nkrumah, First Republic (1957–1965)	Proposal to increase government control over management (1961)	Implemented (- -)			Weak (decreasing)	Convention People's Party: socialism	Poor
Joseph Ankrah, National Liberation Council (1966–1969)	Competing proposals to increase and decrease church autonomy in school management (1967)	Not implemented (0)			Extremely weak (increasing)	National Liberation Council: free market	Very poor

(*continued*)

TABLE 7.2 (continued)

	(1) Effort at Church School Management Reform	(2) Outcome of Educational Management Reform	(3) Effort at Religious/ Moral Curricular Reform	(4) Outcome of Religious/ Moral Curricular Reform	(5) Level of Liberal Democracy	(6) Government Ideology	(7) Economic Performance
Kofi Busia, Second Republic (1970–1971)					Limited	Progress Party: free market	Very good
Ignatius Acheampong, National Redemption Council/Supreme Military Council (1972–1978)	Proposal to have district government manage schools (1974, 1975, 1976)	Contested; partly implemented (−)			Extremely weak	National Redemption Council/Supreme Military Council: economic nationalism	Very poor
Hilla Limann, Third Republic (1979–1981)					Limited	Progress Party: economic nationalism	Very poor
Jerry Rawlings, Provisional National Defense Council (1982–1992)	Proposal to have district government manage schools (1987)	Contested; partly implemented (−)	Proposal to merge religious education with cultural studies (1987)	Partly implemented (−)	Extremely weak	Provisional National Defense Council: socialism	Poor (improving)
Jerry Rawlings, Fourth Republic (1993–2000)	Proposal to acknowledge role of educational units (1999)	Contested; partly implemented (+)	Proposal to return religious and moral education to curriculum (1995)	Implemented (++)	Substantial (increasing)	National Democratic Congress: economic nationalism	Good

President, Republic (term)	Proposal to return mission schools to religious bodies (2017)		Proposal to remove religious and moral education from curriculum		Church strength	Ruling party: ideology	Democracy rating
John Kufuor, Fourth Republic (2001–2008)			Proposal to remove religious and moral education from curriculum (2007)	Contested; not implemented (o)	Strong	New Patriotic Party: free market	Good
John Atta-Mills, Fourth Republic (2009–2012)					Strong	National Democratic Congress: economic nationalism	Very good
John Mahama, Fourth Republic (2013–2016)					Strong (decreasing)	National Democratic Congress: economic nationalism	Good
Nana Akufo-Addo, Fourth Republic (2017–2020)	Proposal to return mission schools to religious bodies (2017)	Terms contested; not implemented (o)	Proposal to remove religious and moral education from curriculum	Contested; not implemented (o)	Strong	New Patriotic Party: free market	Good

Note: The coding of liberal democracy is based on V-DEM's library democracy index, with 0.05–0.15 = extremely weak, 0.15–0.25 = weak, 0.25–0.35 = limited, 0.35–0.45 = moderate, 0.45–0.55 = substantial, and 0.55+ = strong. The coding of economic performance is based on the World Bank's data on annual GDP per capita growth. Rounding economic growth to the nearest integer, −1 percent or less is very poor, 0–1 percent growth is poor, 2–3 percent is good, and 4 percent or more is very good. The coding of Ghana's performance preindependence is based on Jerven 2014. In columns 2 and 4, − indicates partial implementation of a policy that disempowers the church, − − indicates implementation, and − − − indicates extreme implementation; o indicates nonimplementation, + indicates partial implementation, ++ indicates implementation of policy that empowers the church.

the country's level of liberal democracy during the episode. One potential alternative explanation has to do with the governing party's ideology. From this perspective, one would expect ruling parties with left leanings or whose support base is made up of religious groups without schools to initiate educational reforms that would impinge on church educational autonomy. Column 6 summarizes the regime's ideology. Because regimes have never officially been declared Marxist–Leninist in Zambia or Ghana, I distinguish between governments with socialist, economic nationalist, or free-market ideologies. I also note whether the ruling parties made appeals to particular religious groups in column 6.

Another potential alternative explanation is that economic crises force governments to pursue private–public partnerships with churches in the education sector. This explanation predicts increases in church autonomy over education following economic crises, regardless of the country's political institutions. Column 7 summarizes the country's economic performance during the episode.

A quick glance at the relationships between democratic, partisan, and economic variables and changes in the extent to which government policies guarantee church autonomy over education in Tables 7.1 and 7.2 suggests that the patterns are better explained by liberal democratic institutions than by economic variables. Church school autonomy is effectively reduced only in periods of weak or very weak liberal democracy and is only effectively increased in periods of moderate or strong liberal democracy. In contrast, church school autonomy may be increased or reduced in periods of good or bad economic performance. These relationships on their own do not allow me to fully parse the effect of government ideology from the effect of democratic institutions, as the two variables are highly correlated. Socialist governments, which are always weakly or very weakly democratic in these two countries, only change policy implementation in the direction of reducing church autonomy; free-market governments only change it in the direction of increasing church autonomy; and economic nationalist governments make both types of changes, indicating that the level of liberal democracy makes a difference within this ideological group, but limiting our ability to make broader claims.

In the remainder of the chapter, I employ within-episode process tracing to show how liberal democratic institutions matter in the periods described in Tables 7.1 and 7.2 to further rule out alternative explanations. First, I use process tracing to show how the different components of liberal democratic institutions promote church school autonomy. Electoral competition to select rulers can create an opportunity for churches to advance their educational interests when significant numbers of citizens value church-run schools; we can see evidence of this from campaign platforms that promise increased church control of schools. But institutional checks that broaden the opportunities for involvement in policymaking appear to be even more important. The legislature, executive, bureaucracy, and judiciary all have opportunities to contest policy proposals and policy implementation under liberal democracy, which gives well-positioned church advocates multiple opportunities to influence the policymaking process, even when the positions they support are not particularly salient for voters. In addition, the level of protection for civil liberties in society also affects the autonomy of church-run schools, especially if churches can use the legal system to ensure that governments respect church-state educational agreements.

LIBERAL DEMOCRACY AND EDUCATION POLICY TOWARD CHURCH SCHOOLS IN ZAMBIA

At independence, Zambia inherited an educational system in which the Catholic Church ran 20 percent of primary and secondary schools; Catholics made up a similar proportion of the overall population. Mainline Protestant churches turned over much of their educational systems to the state prior to independence, although they still ran a handful of secondary schools.[3] The country's first political leader, Kenneth Kaunda, led the United National Independence Party (UNIP). He initially had very friendly relations with church leaders, identifying himself as a "Christian humanist."[4] In a speech to parliament, his first minister of education clearly stated that the government would not take over schools from churches against their will.[5]

Yet Kaunda's government ultimately hoped to use the education system to advance his vision of Zambian humanism, which, although somewhat based on Christian teachings, also departed from the Catholic Church's ideas in important ways, especially in its emphasis on the importance of

---

[3] Carmody 2007, 544; Hinfelaar 2004, 256.
[4] Kaunda 1966, 39.
[5] Hon. John M. Mwanakatwe is quoted as saying, "My ministry welcomes the participation of these agencies in primary as well as secondary education and has made it clear that, although it will welcome taking over any primary schools which agencies might wish to give up, it is not going to force them to give the schools up." See Hinfelaar 2004, 207.

loyalty to UNIP.[6] As Table 7.1 shows, churches lost significant autonomy over their instruction in their schools under Kaunda's rule, especially as his administration became more autocratic, centralizing control over the independent media immediately after independence, squeezing civic space in the late 1960s, banning opposition parties in the early 1970s, and officially establishing a one-party state in December 1972.[7] In particular, confessional religious instruction was replaced with an ecumenical Christian syllabus beginning in 1971, the government interfered with the management of Catholic primary schools to the extent that the church withdrew from them in 1974, and the government introduced political education in scientific socialism into teacher training and curricular plans after 1976. In contrast, following the reintroduction of multiparty elections in 1991 (in which Kaunda's regime was ousted), the church regained significant autonomy over school instruction. Under the new Movement for Multiparty Democracy (MMD) government, churches regained considerable influence over the appointment of teachers, especially head teachers, in church-affiliated schools, and discussions about adding Marxist-inspired political education to the school curriculum ended.

In the following paragraphs, I consider the extent to which these changes in educational policy were the specific result of the country's degree of liberal democracy, drawing on key informant interviews, pastoral letters from Zambian churches, church newspapers, archival documents from the country's transition to multiparty democracy, and secondary sources. I argue that liberal democratic institutions create openings in the policymaking process that churches can use to their

---

[6] Kaunda was the son of a Presbyterian missionary. In the government's second pamphlet conceptualizing humanism, Kaunda individually thanks three people for helpful discussions in developing the philosophy: Dr. Krapf (German theologian who worked at the Mindolo Ecumenical Center in Kitwe, Zambia), Reverend James Oglethorpe (Zambian minister in Dutch Reformed Church), and Reverend Dr. Colin Morris (British Methodist minister, first head of United Church of Zambia). Kaunda 1974, vi.

[7] The government acquired *Central African Mail* (later the *Zambia Daily Mail*) and incorporated the Zambia Broadcasting Corporation into the Ministry of Information and Postal Services in 1965. As Macola 2010 documents, as the 1960s progressed, membership in the governing party, the United National Independence Party (UNIP), increasingly became necessary to all aspects of economic and associational life. In 1969, the government pushed through a referendum to allow them to make future changes to the constitution via the National Assembly, setting the stage for the legislative bill that made the country a one-party state three years later. The opposition United Progressive Party (UPP) was banned in February 1972. In December 1972, the National Assembly passed the bill making Zambia a one-party state. For more details, see Macola 2010, 104, 112–15, 138–39.

advantage that are not available in more autocratic periods and that they also provide legal protections for church-state agreements.

At independence, Zambia inherited a multiparty political system and it held its first competitive elections in 1968. But during the late 1960s and early 1970s, the UNIP administration became increasingly autocratic, cracking down on dissent within civil society and insisting on allegiance to the nation and party above all else, with the two becoming increasingly intertwined in popular discourse. This push culminated in the declaration of a one-party state in 1972.[8]

Initially, the churches were not opposed to Kaunda's public ideology of Zambian humanism or his desire to unite mission schools into the national school system, even though so doing gave the Ministry of Education significant power over teacher appointments and curriculum in their schools (via the Education Act of 1966).[9] Yet with time, party members in the bureaucracy intruded more and more on church school management and instruction – well beyond the role of the state specified under the law – but the churches had no mechanism for stopping this intrusion under the increasingly autocratic regime.[10] The Catholic Church particularly resented increasing interference by the Ministry of Education in the appointment and disciplining of teachers. A prominent Catholic educationalist notes that the interference sometimes went beyond the role specified for the state in the laws regulating church schools, but that there was little the church could do to force the government to act within the law due to the absence of any checks and balances on decision-making.[11]

Ultimately, the Catholic Church had so little autonomy over instruction in the primary schools it ostensibly managed and to which it devoted significant human resources that it decided to hand them over to the government. The church's education secretary general wrote to the government on July 31, 1973, indicating its intention to withdraw as a result of its decreased de facto autonomy in school management.[12] Although the

---

[8] In 1964, the UNIP government had also violently suppressed and then banned the Lumpa Church of Alice Lenshina, which had refused to accept the new government. See Macola 2010, 105.

[9] Zambia, National Assembly, *Education Act 28 of 1966*, September 2, 1966. See also Carmody 2007, 544.

[10] Carmody 2007, 544; Carmody 1999, 110; Carmody 2003a, 295; Hinfelaar 2004, 256.

[11] Interview with Zambian Catholic educationalist, June 2021. The 1969 Report, *Education in Transition: Report of the Administrative Working Party Appointed to Examine Certain Aspects of the Teaching Service*, had recommended *gradually* phasing out the role of churches in the appointment of teachers to church schools.

[12] Carmody 1999, 113; Hinfelaar 2004, 311.

decision was ostensibly voluntary, there was a high degree of coercion behind it. As the archbishop of Kasama emphasizes, "We were forced out of the schools. We never decided to pull out. Government made it impossible."[13] A Catholic educationalist points out that the church had little ability to oppose the state's phasing out of church management under what "had become a very dictatorial system under Kaunda – and a dangerous one."[14]

The ruling party also came into conflict with all the Catholic and mainline Protestant churches through its assertion of control over moral instruction in schools. At independence, all public schools in Zambia included class periods for confessional religious instruction, with pastors and priests from parish churches responsible for educating students belonging to their denomination during these periods.[15] In 1969, the government asked the Catholic and Protestant churches to come together to develop a common religious education syllabus to replace confessional approaches to religious education.[16] They subsequently did this, and the syllabi, which were adopted at the primary and junior secondary levels in 1971 and 1973, respectively, have generally been considered successful examples of ecumenical collaboration, transforming religious education from bible and catechesis instruction by church leaders into an academic subject taught by professional teachers.[17] But there was also a coercive threat behind the seemingly willing collaboration between churches, and many Catholic and evangelical Protestant leaders viewed the decision to give up confessional religious education in schools as a significant loss.[18]

---

[13] Archbishop interviewed by and quoted in Carmody 1999, 115. Carmody notes that although some missionaries had lost interest in school management years earlier, the Bishop Director of Education emphasized the importance of maintaining schools per the teachings of the second Vatican Council. Carmody 1999, 108. Hinfelaar describes a divide within the Catholic Church between the White Fathers, who were in favor of handing over schools, and the Jesuits and Capuchins, who were not. See Hinfelaar 2004, 258. Carmody 1999 reports that Kaunda himself claimed to regret the decision after he stepped down as president, saying in 1996, "I don't think it was the right decision." See Carmody 1999, 115.

[14] Interview with Zambia Catholic educationalist, June 2021.

[15] Carmody 2003b, 143.

[16] Ibid., 144–46.

[17] Ibid., 147–48. At the senior secondary level, the Cambridge Bible Knowledge Syllabus from the UK was used until the late 1970s, when it was replaced with two religious education syllabi developed specifically for the Zambian context, Syllabus 2044 (perceived as a more Catholic-take on religious instruction) and Syllabus 2046 (perceived as a more Protestant Bible-based religious instruction). See also Mwale, Chita, and Cheyeka 2014, 43–44.

[18] Carmody 2003b, 144.

As one Catholic educationalist recalls, "The bottom line was that the ministry said that either you get together and put a common syllabus or religious education will be taken off the syllabus."[19]

More explicit conflict between churches and the Kaunda government occurred later in the 1970s, as the party's official ideology, humanism, shifted more closely toward Marxist philosophy, reflecting the country's shift toward Eastern Bloc countries for foreign aid and the new vanguard status of the UNIP in the one-party state.[20] Scientific socialism began being discussed regularly in the daily newspapers, all of which were firmly under government control. The impression among Zambian church leaders at the time was that Kaunda and other UNIP leaders had adopted this stance due to pressure from their Soviet financers.[21]

In the mid-1970s, new education reforms appeared to leave religious education off the syllabus in schools while introducing political education as a new subject, including lessons painting churches as colonial collaborators and describing the virtues of scientific socialism.[22] The Catholic Church responded in August 1976 by issuing a pastoral letter pointing out the omission of religious education from the reforms while also calling on Catholic allies within policymaking circles to engage in "the process of syllabus making, through constructive criticism or the making of alternative proposals on points, which seem to need improvement."[23] While this letter indicated the church's hope that the policymaking process was still open enough to be responsive to advocacy efforts, its efforts were only partially successful. The government was forced to explicitly state that

---

[19] Interview with Zambia Catholic educationalist, June 2021. See also Hinfelaar 2004, 202–3.

[20] In 1974, Kaunda's second pamphlet on humanism pointed toward potential tensions between the party and churches over control of moral education, with Kaunda writing:

> Religion must continue to play an important role in our national life. We need religious leaders to give us guidelines. But moral and spiritual development must also be part and parcel of the Party and Government programme. Hence it is seriously proposed that the Party's programme include moral and spiritual teaching. This is obviously a bold and even controversial proposal but deserves to be seriously analyzed.

See Kaunda 1974, 119. See also Hinfelaar 2008, 137.

[21] In an interview, one Zambian Catholic Church leader reported that he had "talked to Kaunda himself on this. He was never convinced of Scientific Socialism, that was an ideology that was coming from others.... He was never a true believer: 'I was supportive because they were giving us a lot of help.'" Interview with Zambian Catholic Church leader and educationalist, June 2021. See also McKenna 1997, 191.

[22] Lungu 1986, 397. These were proposed in 1976. According to McKenna, the churches learned of the proposed political education syllabus as early as 1975. See McKenna 1997, 195.

[23] Zambia Episcopal Conference, "Letter to All Catholics," August 25, 1976.

there was no intention of leaving religion off the syllabus, but the issue of including scientific socialism on the curricula remained on the table.[24]

In December 1978, all heads of secondary schools and teacher-training colleges were told to send one teacher, who had to be a member of UNIP, to a six-month course on political education at a national training college.[25] In response, the Christian churches collectively contested the government's shift toward scientific socialism, including in school instruction. The Catholics (Zambia Episcopal Conference), mainline Protestants (Christian Council of Zambia), and evangelical Protestants (Evangelical Fellowship of Zambia) issued a joint pastoral letter in August 1979 entitled, "Marxism, Humanism and Christianity: A Letter from the Leaders of the Christian Churches in Zambia to All Their Members about Scientific Socialism." The letter warned Zambians that "if Zambia follows a Marxist-Leninist, Scientific Socialist path, then the freedoms enshrined in our constitution will be threatened," and it explicitly questioned the government about its plans to instruct adults and children in scientific socialism through reeducation training, school curricula, and youth organizations.[26]

Under this autocratic environment, the president was able to avoid giving a formal response to the joint letter for more than two years. Finally, Kaunda invited 200 church leaders to a workshop on scientific socialism on March 18 and 19, 1982.[27] From the design of the workshop, it appears Kaunda genuinely believed he would be able to change church leaders' views about scientific socialism.[28] But rather than assuaging church leaders, the workshop highlighted their collective opposition to the government's political education syllabus and brought the conflict

---

[24] Hinfelaar 2004, 314.
[25] McKenna 1997, 195.
[26] Zambia Episcopal Conference, Christian Council of Zambia, and Zambia Evangelical Fellowship, "Marxism, Humanism and Christianity: A Letter from the Leaders of the Christian Churches in Zambia to All Their Members about Scientific Socialism," August 1979.
[27] Hinfelaar 2008, 138; Lungu 1986, 399; McKenna 1997, 199.
[28] He gave two speeches, presented a paper, and attempted to personally answer church leaders' questions, assuring them the party had not officially adopted a Marxist ideology and that schools would continue to teach religion alongside political education. The text of Kaunda's speech stated "Scientific Socialism will be taught in all schools in future as part of political education.... It will not replace religious education, and the Party has no intention of interfering with the freedom of religious organizations and freedom of worship, which are guaranteed in the constitution." Kaunda, "'Humanism and Development', Presidential Address to Church leaders," Lusaka, Zambia, March 18–19, 1982, quoted in Lungu 1986, 399. See also McKenna 1997, 200–01.

between church and government educational priorities to a head. The United Church of Zambia issued an individual statement, followed by a joint statement from the Catholics, mainline Protestants, and evangelical Protestants, highlighting the problems with scientific socialism. Clergy wrote letters to newspapers and arranged special prayers to protest curricular change.[29] In response, a (government-controlled) newspaper wrote that "many people would not shed a tear if the Party and its Government scrapped religion off the syllabus of our schools."[30] In late 1982, Kaunda ultimately quashed the churches' ability to advocate against the instruction of scientific socialism in the schools by banning further discussion of it in the public sphere, effectively ending church-led advocacy against introducing this form of political education in pretertiary school.[31]

Because the Kaunda administration could effectively stifle the ability of church allies to advocate against his government's educational policy, his government didn't have to adjust its policies to the preferred position of the churches. The administration continued training teachers in scientific socialism throughout the 1980s over church objections, but it was never officially made a stand-alone, examinable subject in primary or secondary schools.[32] Although some scholars view this as a partial victory for

---

[29] United Church of Zambia General Synod Meeting, "A Paper Written to Inform Our Church Members about Scientific Socialism," April 19–27, 1982; Zambia Episcopal Conference, the Christian Council of Zambia, and the Zambia Evangelical Fellowship, "A Letter from the Leaders of the Church in Zambia to Their Members about the President's Seminar on Humanism and Development," May 11, 1982; *Daily Mail*, Comment, May 24, 1982.

[30] *Daily Mail*, Comment, May 24, 1982.

[31] Kelly 1991 writes that "The debate continued for some time, but ended later in the year when President Kaunda, recognizing the divisiveness it was arousing, banned all further discussion of the subject." See Kelly 1991, 114. Lungu writes that "The debate on scientific socialism practically ended in 1982 when President Kaunda banned open discussion on the subject." See Lungu 1986, 400. Neither author states exactly when discussion was banned, but a review of the subject in the biweekly Church-owned paper, the *National Mirror*, suggests it was in September 1982. Up until the September 24, 1982 issue, the paper mentioned Scientific Socialism once per issue on average; from that issue onward, it was not mentioned at all for the remainder of the year. This is approximately the same date on which UNIP acted to take over the board of the daily newspaper, the *Times of Zambia*; the previous editor-in-chief was terminated on September 27, 1982. See *National Mirror*, "Times Take-Over: Party Appoints Directors," September 24, 1982.

[32] Carmody describes an effort in 1984 to introduce a textbook on Scientific Socialism into Catholic secondary schools. See Carmody 2003a, 302. Kelly writes that

the political education course has continued in teacher training institutions, where it appears to be accepted more in a spirit of patient tolerance than of alarm. The political education syllabus is not mentioned in CDC reports, but a syllabus on moral and spiritual education has been approved and

churches, it also indicates the limited ability of churches to reverse policy under autocratic institutions through which the president could unilaterally quash policy debate and under which civil liberties were extremely weak. Until the end of the 1980s, churches remained concerned that primary and secondary students were going to be instructed in scientific socialism.[33]

In September 1990, after years of economic decline and political protest, the government was forced to return the country to a multiparty electoral system.[34] Zambian church leaders were in favor of holding a referendum on returning the country to a multiparty political system.[35] Some Catholic priests and church-affiliated media outlets gave significant support to the opposition movement, led by trade union leader Fredrick Chiluba, and Chiluba fully advertised his credentials as a devout bornagain Christian in contrast to Kaunda's presumed weaker Christian beliefs.[36] Also in 1990, a coalition of opposition groups came together, formed the MMD, and registered it as a political party with Chiluba as its leader. The MMD won the 1991 election by a landslide and Kaunda conceded defeat. Civil liberties improved and a new independent newspaper, the *Post*, was founded that same year.

has been introduced throughout the school system with a full range of specially prepared and available texts.

See Kelly 1991, 114. On the continued pressures within UNIP for Marxist political education in Zambia in the late 1980s, see also McKenna 1997, 206–07. Zambian humanism was taught as part of the religious education syllabus in junior secondary schools in the 1980s. See Carmody 2003b, 148.

[33] Lungu 1986 in particular describes it as a victory, but this may have been a premature declaration, as his study covers the period through 1984 only. In particular, in a joint letter issued by Catholic, mainline Protestant and Evangelical Protestants in February 1987, the churches again raised their objections with the country's approach to political education, saying "Genuine political education differs from indoctrination… [it] will hardly be possible if the core of the Party and of political educators is sent to communist countries only for training. As a consequence, most of them may find themselves teaching basically scientific socialism (i.e., Marxist – Leninism) with only a superficial skin of Zambian Humanism." Christian Council of Zambia, Evangelical Fellowship of Zambia and Zambia Episcopal Conference, "Christian Liberation, Justice and Development: The Churches' Concern for Human Development" February 1987. On the continued concerns about the reintroduction of Scientific Socialism on the syllabus in the late 1980s, see also Kelly 1991, 114 and Hinfelaar 2008, 139, footnote 59.

[34] Kaunda 1990.

[35] The referendum itself was never held, as continuing protests motivated Kaunda to make the constitutional change soon after the idea was raised. See Kaunda 1990. The Catholic Bishops' support for the referendum was stated in their pastoral letter. See Catholic Bishops of Zambia, "Economics, Politics and Justice," July 23, 1990.

[36] Hinfelaar 2008, 141.

The new government immediately opened discussions with the churches about giving them increased legal authority over running their schools and hospitals, a promise that had been included in its electoral manifesto.[37] On March 11, 1993, the parliament passed Statutory Instrument 43, which gave churches greater control over primary and secondary education in their schools. Specifically, the instrument established school-level management boards for each grant-aided school, chaired by individuals appointed by the church, with responsibility for appointing teachers, deciding the subjects to be instructed, and setting fees.[38] In addition, the government gave churches the option of taking over management of public primary schools that had been fully nationalized in the 1970s, which led the Catholic Church to reacquire some primary schools.[39] These developments were welcomed by church educationalists, who describe church schools as experiencing a revival in this period.[40] Simultaneously, the government embraced a broad Christian public ideology, with Chiluba declaring the country a "Christian nation" and the Ministry of Education removing humanism from school curricula.[41]

---

[37] Movement for Multiparty Democracy, *Movement for Multiparty Democracy Manifesto: The Hour Has Come*, 9. The initiation of discussions was already noted in the Catholic church's pastoral letter in March 1992, which mentioned possible changes in the system in which "Churches would have more say over the appointment of managers," that this was a "complex issue," but that "we are pleased that discussions are currently going between Government and Church officials regarding this question." See Catholic Bishops of Zambia, "The Future is Ours: Pastoral Letter by the Catholic Bishops of Zambia," March 16, 1992.

[38] It also legally recognized the role of church-appointed Education Secretaries "who shall be responsible for the day-to-day administration of the aided educational institution," indicated that "teaching staff shall preferably belong to the particular church that owns the aided educational institution," and noted that "there should be an equitable distribution of funds per capita to Church and government institutions." Statutory Instrument 43 of 1993. See also Carmody 2016, 634, and Gifford 1999, 189.

[39] "Bishops Call Attention to the Massive Advertising Campaign in the Media: No of Seminaries May Increase – Kasama Schools to be Taken Back," *Impact: The Newsletter of the Zambia Episcopal Conference*, 1996, 1. See also Hinfelaar 2004, 446–47.

[40] Interview with Zambian Catholic educationalist, June 2021. See also separate interview with Zambian Catholic educationalist, June 2021.

[41] Cheyeka 2006, 25; Phiri 2003, 407. The Catholic and mainline Protestant churches were ambivalent or even opposed to the declaration of Zambia as a Christian nation, although the statement was welcomed by many Evangelical churches. The leaders of the Catholic Church, the Christian Council of Zambia, and the Evangelical Fellowship of Zambia released a press statement on the declaration in January 1992 expressing approval with the broad sentiment of basing governance on Christian values but expressing their concern that "the Church and State should continue to remain separate." See Christian Council of Zambia, Evangelical Fellowship of Zambia, Zambia Episcopal Conference,

This de jure policy change was favorable to church school autonomy, but passage of the policy by the legislature did not guarantee its de facto implementation. Following the adoption of Statutory Instrument 43, the Ministry of Education continued to try to intervene in the management of grant-aided church schools as it had done prior to the new law. For example, in the late 1990s under the MMD government, the ministry still tried to ignore church school staffing recommendations.[42] As a Catholic educationalist who worked in Zambia in the 1990s describes, "The problem was initially the education inspectorate didn't understand the new law ... in practice it was a battle with the Minister of Education."[43] But because the policymaking process was more open during this period and there were greater legal protections for existing agreements, the church was able to advocate for its interests and, for the most part, ensure the new law was implemented. The same Catholic educationalist explicitly recognized the situation as improved from the Kaunda era because there were mechanisms for influencing the policy process: "Kaunda's government was very top down – it was all letters from the ministry ... Before the Chiluba era, the church had to move very carefully. Chiluba may have had his faults, but they were able to talk about his government openly."[44]

These behind-the-scenes battles to ensure churches had the educational autonomy promised by 1993's Statutory Instrument 43 continued after 2011, when the MMD government was defeated by a relatively new opposition party, the Patriotic Front (PF). The first president from the PF, Michael Sata, was also the country's first Catholic president, and he was elected with significant support from Catholic priests and Catholic voters in the country's north; he explicitly included a promise to treat the church as a full partner in education as part of his platform.[45] But under the PF government, church educationalists still needed to actively defend their autonomy in running church schools. For example, in 2013 the PF government proposed a curricular reform that made religious

---

"Press Statement on the Declaration of Zambia as a Christian Nation," January 16, 1992. In a pastoral letter in March 1992, the Catholic Bishops clarified another concern with the declaration – "that a Nation is not Christian by declaration but by deeds." Catholic Bishops of Zambia, "The Future is Ours: Pastoral Letter by the Catholic Bishops of Zambia," March 16, 1992. See also Kaunda and Hinfelaar 2020, 203.

[42] Carmody 2016, 15.
[43] Interview with Zambian Catholic educationalist, June 2021.
[44] Ibid.
[45] Patriotic Front, *2011–2016 Manifesto*. Kaunda and Hinfelaar 2020, 202–03.

education an elective subject in all senior secondary schools, including church-run schools. According to a Catholic educationalist, the impetus for this change came from donor countries whose promised support for education was contingent on this reform.[46] But the Catholic Church's education secretary was able to prevent implementation of the law in church-run schools by using his knowledge of Instrument 43 "to defend" against the encroachment and by escalating matters up the bureaucratic chain within the Ministry of Education.[47]

Given the trends in church educational autonomy in Zambia, what conclusions can be drawn about whether these changes were the result of the country's political institutions, economic expediencies, or government ideology? Economic motivations by themselves seem insufficient, as discussed earlier; Zambian governments have infringed on church autonomy in good economic times and in bad. Although churches may in theory have more bargaining power when the government needs to share costs with them, in practice, embattled governments often prove unwilling to give up their control over education. During Zambia's budget crisis in the 1980s, for example, some political leaders began to call for churches to play a greater role in financing schools.[48] But without being offered guarantees of greater autonomy in the management of their schools, the churches were not eager to take up this offer.[49]

---

[46] Interview with Zambian Catholic educationalist, August 2021; Zambia Ministry of Education, Science, Vocational Training and Early Education, *The Zambia Education Curriculum Framework*, 2013.

[47] Interview with Zambian Catholic educationalist, August 2021. Catholic Education Secretaries have played a particularly important role in defending church schools vis-à-vis the Ministry of Education, and they have often been delegated by Protestant church leaders to act on their behalf. See Gifford 1999, 188.

[48] President Kaunda called for a week of prayer on Zambia's economic crisis in November 1985, and in his closing remarks, he asked the churches for greater contributions to the economic welfare of the country. McKenna 1997, 207; Komakoma 2003, 140.

[49] The Catholic, mainline Protestant, and evangelical churches issued a joint pastoral letter in response to Kaunda's remarks, asking that church schools and hospitals be "given a fair share of our limited national resources," while noting that "under certain circumstances, and under conditions, which would have to be negotiated in each case, our Churches would be willing to undertake the running of more schools or health institutions." Christian Council of Zambia, Evangelical Fellowship of Zambia, and Zambia Episcopal Conference, "Christian Liberation, Justice and Development: The Churches' Concern for Human Development," February, 1987. Father Michael Kelly, the former Catholic education secretary and Dean of the University of Zambia's School of Education, wrote in a policy study that "In the formal education sector, the churches' willingness to expand their involvement would probably be fostered if they had a greater role in pupil and teacher selection, and in curriculum design." See Kelly 1991, 84.

It is harder to parse the effects of the government's ideology, the government's coalition of support, and the country's political institutions in instigating the changes, as they were all altered almost simultaneously in 1991. Did the MMD instigate educational policy that gave churches greater autonomy because it was in favor of free-market policies, because it was elected with the support of church activists, or because of the country's more liberal political institutions? The process tracing described earlier shows that the de facto autonomy of churches depended not only on the de jure policy on the books but also on the church's ability to press for the implementation of that policy according to the letter of the law. Regaining control of church schools required church contestation with the bureaucracy over the implementation of policy.

This type of contestation is more likely to be successful when the policymaking process is more open and there are legal mechanisms for guaranteeing agreements. The MMD campaigned on a pro-market platform that promised "the MMD is committed to letting voluntary agencies [churches] manage and run their schools with grants from the government," but the election of the MMD was not sufficient to ensure that churches would have autonomy over management.[50] Indeed, Zambian parties of relatively diverse ideological stripes have campaigned on promises to increase church autonomy, but once elected have often proposed or tried to implement policies that went against church interests. The PF campaigned on a populist ideology in 2011 but also included promises to treat churches as full partners in education as part of its platform. Once elected, the PF acted against church interests; under pressure from international donors, it proposed to remove religious education from senior secondary schools, including church-run schools.[51] It is only because church allies took advantage of openings in the policymaking process that the churches were able to avoid this coming to pass.

What components of liberal democracy appear important for securing church educational interests? Elections by themselves may advance church educational interests, as suggested by the fact that Zambian political parties of diverse ideologies have promised to increase church autonomy over schools in their election manifestos. But these have not been particularly prominent electoral promises; the MMD pledge came on

---

[50] Movement for Multiparty Democracy, *Movement for Multiparty Democracy Manifesto: The Hour Has Come*, 1991, 9.
[51] Zambia Ministry of Education, Science, Vocational Training and Early Education, *The Zambia Education Curriculum Framework*, 2013.

page nine of an eleven-page declaration, and the PF promise was similarly buried.[52] The specific components that distinguish liberal democracy from electoral democracy also appear important. Liberal democratic institutions have given Zambian churches opportunities for influencing the implementation of educational policy by opposing decisions handed down by the executive branch. In this way, they have been able to assert greater control over their schools since 1991 than they had been able to in the late 1960s and early 1970s.

Thus, the Zambian case illustrates how liberal democratic institutions help to protect church educational interests. During the one-party era, churches were not able to lobby effectively for their preferred educational policies due to the top-down nature of policymaking and limited civil liberties. Since the reintroduction of multiparty politics in the 1990s, churches have had significant success in defending their educational autonomy through openings in the policymaking process and greater civil liberties.

LIBERAL DEMOCRACY AND EDUCATION POLICY TOWARD CHURCH-RUN SCHOOLS IN GHANA

Ghana, the second case that I consider, provides considerably more changes than Zambia between democratic and autocratic rule over time, allowing clearer distinction between the effects of regime type, ideology, and economic performance. The Ghanaian case offers more diversity within the church educational sector, too, with both Catholic and Protestant churches maintaining schools into the postindependence period. It also demonstrates how church influence plays out in a religiously divided country, where Muslims make up 20 percent of the electorate and the nation.

Yet even when Christians are not the only significant voting bloc in the country, educational policy is better aligned with church interests during democratic periods. As Table 7.2 shows, de facto church autonomy over education decreased in the 1960s during the First Republic (under Kwame Nkrumah's increasingly autocratic regime), in the 1970s under the military governments (led by General Ignatius Acheampong), and in the 1980s during the rule of the Provisional National Defense Council (PNDC) under Jerry Rawlings. Rawlings' government also removed

---

[52] Movement for Multiparty Democracy, *Movement for Multiparty Democracy Manifesto: The Hour Has Come*, 1991, 9. Patriotic Front, *2011–2016 Manifesto*.

religious studies as a stand-alone subject in primary and junior secondary schools. In contrast, when democratic institutions were established in the 1990s, Rawlings oversaw a series of educational reforms that were very favorable to church interests, acknowledging the role of churches in managing their own schools and returning religious and moral education to the curriculum.

The correlations between educational policy and liberal democratic institutions in Table 7.2 are strongly suggestive of the importance of democracy in explaining church influence in Ghana. There is less support for alternative explanations that emphasize ideology or economic performance. Governments subscribing to socialist and free-market ideologies have proposed reducing church autonomy over educational management and reducing the time spent on religion in schools. Similarly, as noted earlier, governments have proposed reducing church educational autonomy in good economic times and in bad; if anything, they have had slightly more success in implementing these proposals in bad economic times, which runs counter to theoretical expectations.

In the following paragraphs, I focus on tracing the effects of certain features of liberal democracy on church influence, describing how elections, institutional checks, and the protection of civil liberties within society have contributed to greater church autonomy. The analysis draws on key informant interviews, pastoral letters and communiques from Ghanaian churches, legal documents, education policy reports, policy memos, and secondary sources.

I begin with the period of self-government in the 1950s, which allows me to examine how Nkrumah's educational policy changed with reductions in checks on his power and respect for civil liberties in the period immediately after independence. During the self-government period, a locally elected legislature, led by Nkrumah and his Convention People's Party (CPP), was charged with policymaking, but policy was subject to veto by the British administration. The CPP regime had a broadly African socialist ideology. Nkrumah himself identified as both "a non-denominational Christian and a Marxist socialist" and was convinced that the "the state must be secular."[53]

In 1951, the CPP put forward a new education plan, the Accelerated Development Plan for Education, which indicated that mission schools were expected to be handed over to the state. Protestant and Catholic Church leaders publicly contested the policy, issuing press statements

[53] Pobee 1988, 39, 41.

and newspaper articles articulating their reasons for keeping their schools under church control.[54] This resulted in a policy compromise with the government in which established schools continued under the old regulations and with generous public support, but any new primary school needed permission from the local educational authority to open.[55]

After independence in 1957, Nkrumah immediately moved to crackdown on civil liberties and political dissent. In 1958, his government passed the Preventative Detention Act, which made it possible to throw opponents into jail without trial. In 1960, he instituted the Young Pioneer movement, based on similar movements in Eastern Europe, to train young people "to live by the ideals of ... Dr Kwame Nkrumah" and to report others who held dissenting opinions.[56] The country's independent newspaper, the *Ashanti Pioneer*, was shut down in 1962. By the early 1960s, the government had clearly adopted a strategy of maintaining political power through elimination of dissent.

During the same period, the ruling party increased state control of church-affiliated schools. In 1959, denominational schools in the Volta Region were briefly taken over by the government in response to allegations that some teachers had an anti-government attitude.[57] The Education Act of 1961 made church schools subject to all government regulations. Government orders directed that Young Pioneers, initially intended as a voluntary group, be set up in all secondary schools over the objections of church leaders who opposed its deification of Nkrumah.[58]

---

[54] Christian Council of the Gold Coast, *Statement on Christian Education in Primary and Middle Schools*, 1951, quoted in Pobee 1988; Archbishop W. T. Porter, "Catholics and Revised Education Plan: An Authoritative Statement," *Gold Coast Observer*, September 7, 1951.

[55] Gold Coast Education Department, *Accelerated Development Plan for Education*, 1951. Item 6 and item 38 indicate that "In (the) future no new (primary) school opened by a denominational religious body or by a person or group of persons will be eligible for assistance from public funds unless prior approval (of the Local Authority concerned under powers delegated by the Central Government) has been obtained (from the Central Government)." Item 6 (regarding primary schools) continues, "It is expected that considerable numbers of educational unit schools will be handed over to Local Authorities." However, the opening statement does indicate no "disregard for moral training and religious education. For these, full opportunity will be given in all institutions supported by public funds." See also *Pro Mundi Vita*, "The Church in Ghana," 1975, 8.

[56] Pobee 1988, 132. The concerns about Young Pioneers being used to spy on their families are reported in Coe 2005, 65–68.

[57] *Pro Mundi Vita*, "The Church in Ghana," 1975, 9. See also Barrett 1982, 324.

[58] Osagyefo, an honorific term used for Kwame Nkrumah, means redeemer in the Akan language. Coe provides details on how particular pro-Nkrumah teachers were assigned to organize the Young Pioneers within schools. See Coe 2005, 68.

When church leaders tried to advocate against these policies, first in private and then in public, the ruling authorities simply silenced them: It deported an Anglican bishop for criticizing the Young Pioneers movement and the state-controlled media refused to publish the churches' press statements opposing the deportation.[59]

In February 1966, Nkrumah's government was ousted by a coup d'etat that replaced his autocratic one-party regime with an autocratic military one. Under the new pro-market rulers, churches had more opportunities to express their policy preferences but limited leverage to ensure the regime adopted them. The new National Liberation Council (NLC) Party immediately instigated a thirty-two–member committee, including multiple church leaders, to review the country's educational system. The Educational Review Committee's recommendations, submitted in August 1967, were favorable to church interests, including a critical role for the "church education units" – the churches' own educational bureaucracies – in managing public schools, and emphasizing the importance of confessional religious education. But a separate commission, the Mills Odoi Commission on the structure and remuneration of the public service, published a report the same year recommending nationalization of all denominational schools.[60]

Ultimately, there was a gap between the Educational Review Committee's pro-church recommendations and the policies the military rulers adopted. The government's white paper on education rejected the Education Review Committee's recommendations to make religious knowledge a compulsory examination subject.[61] In July 1968, the Ministry of Education issued a letter calling for the abolition of all church education units. If it had been implemented, it would have ended the role of churches in the management of their schools, but the ministry was ultimately forced to officially withdraw the letter, perhaps in part because

---

[59] The heads of the Christian churches in Ghana had written to the Minister of Education in April 1962, saying they found it impossible to support the movement. In early August 1962, the Anglican bishop of Accra spoke out publicly against it, leading to his deportation. Both the Anglican church and the heads of other churches provided press statements in support of the bishop to Ghana News Agency in early August 1962, but neither was published. See Pobee 1988, 55, 128, 131–35, 173–76.

[60] *Mills Odoi Commission Report*, 1967, 8–9, quoted in Ekuban 1977, 11–12.

[61] Republic of Ghana, *White Paper on the Report of the Education Review Committee*, Section 29, 1968. See Ekuban 1977, 10–12 and Bolaji 2018, 82 on the competing recommendations of the Education Review Committee (ERC) and the Mills Odei Commission (MOC).

the military rulers were worried about its consequences for their political allies in the upcoming 1969 election that would mark the transition back to civilian rule.⁶² Certainly, the Catholic bishops seem to have believed the expected electoral transition offered an opportunity to pressure the government, writing in an October 1968 pastoral letter to Catholics that they should vote for representatives who valued religious education in the upcoming election.⁶³

The next significant reduction in the influence of churches over education came in the early 1970s during Ghana's subsequent military dictatorship, led first by Ignatius Acheampong's National Redemption Council (NRC) and then by his Supreme Military Council (SMC). This administration established a new organization, Ghana Education Service, to unify the administration of all pre-tertiary education, and it passed a decree making mission schools directly answerable to the government's district education departments.⁶⁴ Although the administration was not able to completely disband church educational units, the military rulers further sidelined them, centralizing state control over church-affiliated schools.⁶⁵ During this period, church leaders were repeatedly frustrated by the efforts of some government bureaucrats to relieve church-appointed administrators from their functions in managing schools, with many of those bureaucrats maintaining in interviews at the time that the

---

⁶² Ministry of Education, "The Abolition and Absorption of Educational Units," Ref. No. PE 450/1, July 6, 1968, quoted in Ekuban 1977, 13.

⁶³ "At the time of elections, you will consider it your duty that your representatives will deem the religious and moral education of your children as being very important," Catholic Bishops of Ghana 1968, *Message from the Catholic Hierarchy of Ghana to All Christians on Civic Responsibilities*, October 6, 1968; Martin 1976, 59; Bolaji 2018, 82. The head of the new elected government, Kofi Busia, had been the head of the advisory committee to the National Liberation Council (NLC) and then the chair of its center for civic education. Ekuban describes "a measure of agreement ... on certain issues between the Educational Units and the Ministry of Education" during the period of the NLC government and the early period of the Progress Party Government. See Ekuban 1977, 14.

⁶⁴ In addition, the Evans-Anfom National Consultative Committee on Education Finance in 1975 recommended that the district council take over the functions of the Educational Units where necessary and possible. See Ekuban 1977, 19.

⁶⁵ In general, the 1970s were a period of weak implementation of proposed educational reforms. The ambitious reforms of the Dzobo committee, appointed in 1972 to review the country's educational system and recommending significant changes to the structure and content of education, were only piloted on a small scale during this decade. One suggestion of the Dzobo report was the introduction of the new subject of cultural studies, but no steps were taken to implement cultural studies as a curricular subject in the 1970s. See Coe 2005.

church education units had no legitimate role to play in the educational bureaucracy.[66]

The trends in educational policy toward religious schools and religious studies in the 1980s and 1990s provide an opportunity to examine how Rawlings ruled under varying degrees of liberal democratic constraint. Rawlings first came to power following a coup d'etat in 1979, a brief but bloody period in which numerous senior military members and former heads of state were executed. He turned over power to an elected civilian government in September 1979, but then led a military coup against this government on December 31, 1981. The subsequent period of military rule through the PNDC was highly centralized and brutal in its crackdown on dissent. All executive, legislative, judicial, and administrative power was vested in the PNDC. Alleged opponents of the ruling authorities regularly went missing. The PNDC instituted a system of local tribunals, initially called People's Defense Committees and Worker's Defense Committees, and then rebranded as Committees for the Defense of the Revolution, through which citizens could exact retribution by labeling others as enemies of the revolution.

In this environment, it was exceedingly difficult for the churches to prevent the state from increasing control over the management of their schools and advancing the PNDC's curricular agenda, which emphasized instruction in Ghanaian culture at the expense of religious studies. Rawlings abolished the governing council of the Ghana Education Service – a council that had included teachers and religious leaders – and centralized power under a secretary for education.[67] He appointed a twenty-member National Education Commission in 1984 to review the education system and to produce regular reports for the regime, some of which became the basis for the education reforms of 1987. But the commission had limited ability to consult relevant parties, hampered both by a lack of funds and the limited willingness of citizens to submit memoranda due to the ruling authorities' intolerance of political dissent.[68] In addition, the commission had limited authority within the administration. As its initial chair, Dr. Emmanuel Evans-Anfom writes in his autobiography, "I was really tired of the marginalization of the Commission and thought I was really wasting my time."[69]

[66] Interviews with officers of Ghana Education Service, quoted in Ekuban 1977, 17.
[67] Evans-Anfom 2003, 375.
[68] On the limited funds for travel, see Evans-Anfom 2003, 358. On the limited submissions, see Boakye 2019, 109.
[69] Evans-Anfom 2003, 358.

The 1987 education reforms had two components that ran against church interests. First, the reforms placed all schools under the responsibility of district governments, which meant that church educational units no longer managed church schools. Second, they removed religious education as an independent subject from the school curricula, replacing it with cultural studies, a new subject that focused on language, customs, music, and dance, with only limited attention to world religions. The cultural studies textbooks were developed by a nine-member Ministry of Education-appointed panel that was led by an expert on Islamic education in Ghana and included a representative of the Ahmadiyya education unit, but excluded representatives from any of the church education units.[70] The churches were deeply opposed to the removal of religious studies from the curriculum but lacked the necessary policy influence to preserve it.[71]

Indeed, the churches were on the defensive on multiple fronts by the late 1980s, as Rawlings eventually challenged their autonomy in their congregations, too. In 1989, his administration introduced PNDC Law 221, which would have given bureaucratic agencies the power to register churches and, possibly, to seize their assets. Ultimately, the churches managed to successfully oppose this law simply through noncompliance, indicating the great difficulty rulers have constraining church autonomy in their congregations as opposed to in their schools.

The 1992 democratic transition provides a unique opportunity to examine how the policies enacted by one leader change with democratization

---

[70] The Ahmadiyya movement is a global Islamic movement with a long history of involvement in formal education in Ghana. Curriculum Research and Development Division, *Cultural Studies for Junior Secondary Schools: Pupils' Book 1*, Accra: Adwinsa Publications Ltd., 1987; Curriculum Research and Development Division, *Cultural Studies for Junior Secondary Schools: Pupils' Book 2*, Accra: Adwinsa Publications Ltd., 1988; Curriculum Research and Development Division, *Cultural Studies for Junior Secondary Schools: Pupils' Book 3*, Accra: Adwinsa Publications Ltd., 1989.

[71] Ghana Catholic Bishops Conference, *Communique Issued by the Catholic Bishops of Ghana at the End of their Plenary Assembly in Wa*, 1991; Ghana Catholic Bishops Conference, *Communique by the Ghana Bishops' Conference and the Heads of the Member-Churches of the Christian Council*, 1993; Ghana Catholic Bishops Conference, *Communique Issued by the Catholic Bishops of Ghana at the End of their Plenary Assembly in Takoradi*, 1993; Ghana Catholic Bishops Conference, *Pastoral Letter on AIDS*, 1990; Ghana Catholic Bishops Conference, *Communique Issued by the Catholic Bishops of Ghana at the End of their Annual Conference in Tamale: July 7–11, 1987*, 1987; Ghana Catholic Bishops Conference, *Communique Issued by the Catholic Bishops of Ghana at the End of their Annual Conference Held in Cape Coast: July 2–6, 1990*, 1990. As Coe 2005 notes, teachers themselves may have been able to obstruct instruction in the new subject, especially if they had not yet received textbooks.

of political institutions. Rawlings reinvented himself as a democrat during Ghana's Fourth Republic, leading a newly branded party, the National Democratic Congress (NDC), to victory in the 1992 multiparty elections. Although the elections themselves had serious problems, which led the major opposition parties to boycott the parliamentary round, they created electoral pressures for the Rawlings government. In addition, the new constitution institutionalized checks and balances, including reestablishing the Ghana Education Service council, with representation for church education units.[72] Between 1992 and 1996, private newspapers and radio stations began to operate again in the country.

Almost immediately, Rawlings' government became more responsive to church educational interests. He instituted a new National Education Reform Review Committee in 1994 to review the 1987 educational reforms, and the government immediately accepted its recommendation to reintroduce religious studies as an independent subject in 1995.[73] The churches also lobbied for a clearer demarcation of the role of education units in managing church schools that would spell out their right to assign, promote, and discipline teachers in church-affiliated schools. This culminated in a ministerial directive issued by the Ministry of Education on October 18, 1999, that specifies that religious education units have the right to appoint teachers.[74] Implementation of this directive has been inconsistent, but church and Islamic educational units alike refer to it as established policy in asserting their autonomy from the state.[75]

Indeed, since 1992, there have been no instances in which the government of the day has successfully acted against church educational interests. Ghana has become an established two-party political system, with the NDC and the New Patriotic Party (NPP) rotating in and out of office. Ghanaian political parties, especially the NPP, have included

---

[72] Republic of Ghana, *Constitution of Ghana*, 1992, Article 190, 3. See also interview with Ghanaian Methodist religious leader, July 2021.
[73] Ghana Catholic Bishops Conference, *Communique of Plenary Assembly in Sunyani*, 1995. According to Coe 2005, it took a few more years for implementation in Eastern Region.
[74] Ekwow Spio-Garbrah, "The Right of Educational Units to Manage and Supervise Educational Institutions Established and Developed by their Respective Religious Bodies in Partnership with the Government," Letter Ref. DA257/261/05, 1999. The letter indicates that payment of teachers will occur through the District Director of Education but that "Unit Managers should be allowed to continue to post, transfer and discipline their teachers according to the laid down GES regulations, and keep District Directors duly informed."
[75] Bishop Matthew Gyamfi, "Church-State Education Partnership," Presentation at Miklin Hotel, October 9, 2012; Interview with Ghanaian scholar, June 2021.

promises to improve church-state educational partnerships in their election manifestos. For example, campaigning as the opposition party, the NPP promised a stronger educational partnership with religious bodies in its manifestos for the 2000, 2012, and 2016 elections.[76]

Nevertheless, there have been moments when governments have proposed removing religious studies from the curriculum as part of technocratic educational reforms, typically with considerable international encouragement and financial support.[77] For example, in September 2007, the Ministry of Education under President John Kufuor's NPP administration recommended removing religious and moral education from the basic school curriculum. This recommendation immediately led to criticism from all major religious groups in the country. By the end of November, the president's office was forced to respond, calling a meeting with the concerned parties to discuss the issue.[78] By March 2008, Kufuor had asked the ministry to reinstate religious and moral education in the primary school curriculum while also calling for a committee to discuss the partnership between the religious bodies and the government.[79] The next NPP administration, under Nana Akufo-Addo, made a similar proposal to remove religious education from the curriculum as part of a broader educational reform, only to eventually retreat under pressure from Christian and Muslim leaders.[80] In both cases, organized campaigns by religious organizations against the change forced the government to abandon its plans. Domestic support protected the status of religious studies on the curriculum from international pressures to eliminate it.

Which aspects of liberal democracy have proven most important in protecting church educational interests? Electoral accountability offers one mechanism; party platforms have at times mentioned the need to give churches greater autonomy over their schools. There are also explicit examples of churches trying to put church educational autonomy on the

---

[76] New Patriotic Party, "Agenda for Positive Change: Manifesto 2000 of the New Patriotic Party," August 1, 2000, 28; New Patriotic Party, "Transforming Lives, Transforming Ghana: Building a Free, Fair and Prosperous Society," 2012, 26; New Patriotic Party, "Change An Agenda for Jobs: Creating Prosperity and Equal Opportunity for All," 2016, 31.
[77] Interview with Ghanaian Methodist educationalist, May 2021; Interview with Ghanaian Catholic religious leader, August 2021.
[78] *Modern Ghana*, "Government Acts on Pastoral Letter," November 29, 2007, www.modernghana.com/news/148815/governmentt-acts-on-pastoral-letter.html.
[79] *Ghana News Agency*, "Kufuor asks Education Ministry to include RME in school curriculum," March 5, 2008, https://allafrica.com/stories/200803101555.html.
[80] Interview with Ghanaian activist for Islamic education, August 2021.

political agenda prior to an election, suggesting that churches believe their position is electorally popular.[81] As one national-level church leader puts it, "Those that are in politics, they won't ignore such a large vote bloc."[82]

In addition, greater checks and balances in the policymaking process offer opportunities for churches to advance their interests. The reinstatement of the Ghana Educational Service council as part of the 1992 constitution has been particularly important. As a former general secretary of the Christian Council of Ghana notes, "The principle is negotiations, even with the syllabus that is used. If the religious bodies find that there is something that they don't like, they will take it to the Ghana Educational Service council."[83]

Other church leaders describe more diverse points of access they can use to influence education policy through the liberal democratic institutions reestablished during the Fourth Republic, including the parliament, senior bureaucrats, and even the president.[84] The comments of a national leader of one church, which had only recently established a church educational unit, are particularly revealing on this point. He emphasizes that it was not productive to build church schools when the church was first establishing itself because it did not have allies in government to ensure the church would not lose control of the schools:

> The government may want to transfer someone who doesn't [belong] to your church to head your school. You have very little to say. You'd have to go and negotiate .... So you lose control of the schools except if you are smart enough you negotiate and ensure you have enough teachers from your church .... Now we think we can negotiate better. Thank God, the church is now well established, and we have church members in high positions in the country.[85]

In addition, the greater protection of civil liberties has likely reinforced church positions on education in several ways. First, churches have been able to use freedom of expression and freedom of mobilization

---

[81] The Catholic Bishops' representative concluded a presentation calling for a national conference on the partnership between Government and Faith-Based organizations by emphasizing, "This conference should take place before November this year so that it can form part of the political agenda for the 2012 Elections for the new Government of January 2013." See Damian Avevor, "Strengthening Church-State Partnership in Education," *Modern Ghana*, September 5, 2012, www.modernghana.com/news/415646/strengthening-church-state-partnership-in-education.html.

[82] Interview with Ghanaian Methodist religious leader, July 2021. See also interview with Ghanaian Methodist educationalist, May 2021.

[83] Interview with Ghanaian Methodist religious leader, July 2021.

[84] Interview with Ghanaian Catholic religious leader, August 2021.

[85] Interview with Ghanaian Pentecostal religious leader, September 2021.

to reinforce their policy influence. For example, the Catholic Church organized fora in all ten regions of Ghana to discuss the church-state educational relationship in the run-up to the 2012 elections.[86] The availability of legal rights provided new ways for churches to make claims for their autonomy. As one interviewee describes his interactions with the government, "We wouldn't even call it a lobbying effort, you can say a matter of exercising our rights."[87] In this way, civil liberties may protect church schools not only by reinforcing church policymaking influence but also by guaranteeing church-state agreements.

Together, the evidence from Zambia and Ghana demonstrates how liberal democratic institutions allow churches to promote their autonomy in managing schools and teaching religion. In addition, the evidence suggests that many high-ranking church leaders are aware of these benefits of liberal democracy. Church leaders have directly emphasized to governments the potential electoral costs of acting against their preferred educational positions. In interviews, they emphasize their ability to resolve problems through institutions created by liberal democratic constitutions. In addition, some church leaders appreciate the danger that weak protections of civil liberties will lead to totalitarian aspirations. As the well-known Ghanaian theologian John Pobee writes in his discussion of Nkrumah's conflict with churches over schools, "The issue was more than that of who called the tune; rather, it was a Marxist socialist philosophy versus liberal democracy .... In the totalitarian aspirations of Nkrumah the political arena encompassed all aspects of human life, education included. That is the root cause of the conflict over education."[88]

LIBERAL DEMOCRACY AND PATTERNS IN CHURCH EDUCATIONAL CONTROL IN SUB-SAHARAN AFRICA

Does liberal democracy advance and protect church educational interests in sub-Saharan Africa more broadly? This section considers the relationship between liberal democracy and church educational control in the

---

[86] Ghana Catholic Bishops' Conference, *Communique Issued by the Ghana Catholic Bishops' Conference at the End of their Annual Plenary Assembly Held at Koforidua in the Eastern Region of Ghana*, November 2–9, 2012.

[87] Interview with Ghanaian Catholic religious leader, August 2021; Interview with Ghanaian Methodist religious leader, July 2021; Interview with Ghanaian Pentecostal church leader, September 2021.

[88] Pobee 1988, 92. A number of Ghanaian church leaders recommended that I read this book, suggesting this interpretation is widely known and accepted by senior church leaders.

twenty-five countries in sub-Saharan Africa in which missions provided the majority of education at independence and that have significant Christian populations: Angola, Botswana, Burundi, Cameroon, the Democratic Republic of the Congo, Equatorial Guinea, Gabon, Ghana, Guinea-Bissau, Kenya, Lesotho, Liberia, Malawi, Madagascar, Mozambique, Namibia, Nigeria, the Republic of the Congo, Rwanda, South Africa, Tanzania, Togo, Uganda, Zambia, and Zimbabwe. These countries include former British, Belgian, German, Portuguese, and Spanish colonies, as well as two colonies that had been in French Equatorial Africa.[89] To analyze the settings under which churches secure greater educational autonomy, I constructed timelines of educational and curricular reforms from independence until 2018, focusing on church management of schools and Christian religious content in the curricula. These timelines were drawn from primary and secondary sources.[90] The timelines and the data set that I constructed from them use country years as the unit of analysis because the educational policy proposals that I reviewed were usually intended to apply to all church schools in the country.[91]

From the timelines, I coded each instance of a policy that would, if implemented, increase or decrease church control over either teacher management or the curriculum. As emphasized earlier, churches and states in sub-Saharan Africa are in conflict over two key issues: the appointment and management of teaching staff and the prominence of Christian religious education in the curriculum. On school management, policies that increase the ability of the state bureaucracy to supervise schools, including appointing management boards and teachers, restrict church autonomy, while policies that increase the authority of churches to appoint management bodies and teachers increase it. On religious instruction, policies that reduce the educational focus on Christian religious education are considered to reduce church autonomy, whether by eliminating the subject or by merging it with other types of religious or moral education. In contrast, policies that increase the educational focus

---

[89] For Liberia and South Africa, I begin the analysis in 1950, rather than at independence. Education in Sierra Leone was also mission dominated, but it is excluded because no church makes up more than 5 percent of the population in the country.

[90] For more details on the data set, see Appendix B. These timelines were created with the assistance of three research assistants. I am also grateful to Nicole Garnett for sharing research on Ghana, Kenya, Nigeria, Tanzania, South Africa, and Uganda.

[91] In one case in which legal instruments were church specific, the government of Burundi signed conventions with individual churches in 1990 and 1991 but, even in this case, conventions were quickly offered to all the major church actors with historical interests in education.

on specifically Christian religious education, for example, by making it a stand-alone subject, are considered to increase church influence.[92]

I consulted multiple sources to assess whether a policy was implemented. If I found any indication that a policy proposal was even partly implemented, the policy is coded as being implemented.[93] In the cross-national coding, I used a dichotomous coding of policy events that increased or contracted church autonomy; I did not consider subtler variation in the extent to which policies expanded or reduced church autonomy over teacher management or moral curriculum, which is difficult to code consistently across countries and time periods. I separately coded instances of changes in autonomy over teacher management and moral curriculum in each year, and the most significant policy reforms simultaneously change both.

Figure 7.1 plots the education policy events that increased or decreased church autonomy over education in each of the twenty-five countries in the analysis. This figure demonstrates two key points. First, struggles over control of the education sector were particularly prominent in the period after each country's independence and churches almost always conceded some control at that point. Second, control of the education sector was by no means settled during the period immediately after independence. Churches and states continue to contest control over teachers and religious and moral education curricula through the present day, with churches experiencing both gains and losses in their autonomy over schools through the decades.

I also consider the extent to which churches are better able to advance and protect their policy interests in education when liberal democratic

---

[92] Another common development in the postcolonial period has been the replacement of Christian religious instruction with Christian religious education, with the latter in theory being a more academic approach to the study of Christianity. In the cross-national data, I do not code the replacement of Christian religious instruction with a formalized Christian religious education syllabus as a loss of church influence due to challenges in determining whether these types of subtle curricular changes actually alter the way teachers teach Christianity.

[93] In some cases, policies are retracted before implementation and are coded as nonimplementation; in other cases, policies are retracted after implementation and are coded as a policy change in the opposite direction. In a few cases, governments pass a series of policies expanding or restricting church school autonomy (the state-level edicts nationalizing schools in Nigeria in the 1970s; the series of laws expanding the government's control over teachers in mission schools in Kenya in the 1960s). In these cases, I coded the policy change as happening during the year of the most important law (in the case of federal states, I coded the first one). In the case of curricular change, I coded changes as occurring in the first year they were implemented.

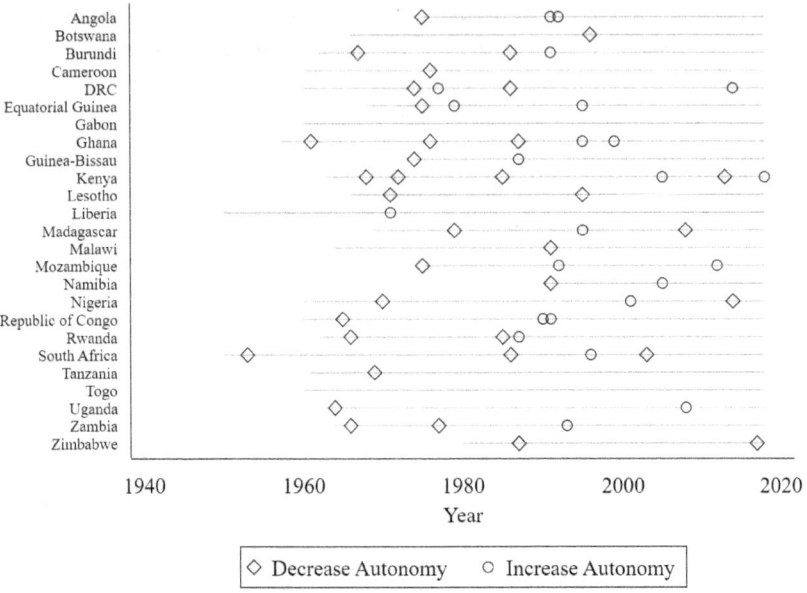

FIGURE 7.1 Timeline of events expanding and contracting church educational control
Source: Baldwin 2025d.
Note: Figure indicates changes in policy that expand or decrease church control of schools across countries in Africa in which churches provided a majority of education at independence.

institutions are stronger in these twenty-five countries. I conceptualize liberal democracy as the extent to which a country's political institutions incorporate checks on the power of leaders through elections, institutional constraints, and guarantees of civil liberties. Countries with elected and unelected leaders can incorporate some liberal checks and balances. As a result, I conceive of liberal democracy as a dimension against which all countries can be measured, operationalized using the V-DEM project's liberal democracy index. This measure has a theoretical maximum of one and a theoretical minimum of zero.[94]

---

[94] The V-DEM liberal democracy measure is an index composed of eight mid-level indices: freedom of expression and alternative sources of information index, freedom of association index, share of population with suffrage, clean elections index, elected officials index, judicial constraints on the executive index, legislative constraints on the executive index, and equality before the law/individual liberties index. The last index is made up of ten variables, one of which is freedom of religion. Freedom of religion is a distinct concept from church control of education – indeed, in many instances,

I am interested in examining the correlation within each country between the levels of liberal democracy each year and the likelihood of policy changes that either increase or decrease church control of education. I do this by running OLS regressions with country fixed effects in which the outcomes are binary variables indicating the onset of a policy change to increase (or decrease) church control; standard errors are clustered by leader. Because of temporal trends in both liberal democracy and educational policy over time, all models include decade fixed effects and an indicator for the ten-year period after each country's independence. In some models, I include additional variables that could potentially confound the relationship between liberal democracy and policy toward church-affiliated schools. Specifically, I consider the potentially confounding effect of regimes that have officially declared Marxist–Leninism to be their state ideology (presumed to be less liberal democratic and more opposed to the church) and the country's GDP per capita (insofar as modernization theory predicts that economic growth increases levels of liberal democracy and secularization).[95]

Table 7.3 presents the findings on the relationship between liberal democratic institutions and changes in church control of schools. The results suggest that liberal democratic institutions do generally help churches advance their preferred policy positions. Model 1 shows that higher levels of liberal democracy are associated with a greater likelihood of a change in policy to increase church control of schools, even when controlling for the fact that churches were particularly unlikely to have their power increased in the decade immediately after independence, with the relationship statistically significant at the 95 percent confidence level.

---

church control of education could be said to decrease freedom of religion. However, to avoid concerns that this variable could be driving results, I have created a slight variant of the V-DEM liberal democracy measure that includes seven of the mid-level indices but excludes the equality before the law/individual liberties index. These results are provided in Appendix C.

[95] Although many postindependence regimes in sub-Saharan Africa have included self-identified Marxists in senior leadership roles, a much smaller number officially declared Marxist–Leninism to be their official ideology. I coded Marxist–Leninist regimes as beginning at the moment of such a declaration and as ending when the regime overturns this declaration (or is overthrown by another regime). I follow the coding in Young 1982, combined with country-specific analysis of the date Marxism was abandoned in each of Young's cases. In addition to the cases discussed in Young 1982, Burkina Faso adopted Marxism–Leninism as its official ideology in 1983. Many of Africa's Marxist–Leninist states are outside the scope of this analysis because of relatively limited mission contributions to religion and/or the education sector in colonial period (i.e., Benin, Ethiopia, and Somalia).

TABLE 7.3 *Relationship between liberal democracy and policy changes to church educational control*

	(1) Increase Church Control of Education	(2) Increase Church Control of Education	(3) Increase Church Management	(4) Increase Christian Education	(5) Decrease Church Control of Education	(6) Decrease Church Control of Education
Liberal democracy index	0.09* (0.04)	0.10* (0.05)	0.08* (0.04)	0.05* (0.02)	0.01 (0.04)	0.01 (0.04)
Postindependence decade	−0.03** (0.01)	−0.03** (0.01)	−0.02* (0.01)	−0.03* (0.01)	0.07** (0.03)	0.08** (0.03)
Marxist state		0.00 (0.02)	0.01 (0.01)	0.01 (0.02)		0.00 (0.03)
Log GDP per capita		−0.01[+] (0.01)	−0.01* (0.01)	−0.01 (0.01)		0.01[+] (0.01)
Country FEs	Yes	Yes	Yes	Yes	Yes	Yes
Decade FEs	Yes	Yes	Yes	Yes	Yes	Yes
N	1,363	1,313	1,313	1,313	1,318	1,268
Sample	All years	All years	All years	All years	All years with church schools	All years with church schools

[+] $p < 0.10$, * $p < 0.05$, ** $p < 0.01$; coefficients with standard errors clustered by leader in parentheses

Model 2 shows that these results are robust to additionally controlling for whether regimes are officially Marxist, with the relationship between liberal democracy and pro-church policy changes remaining statistically significant at the 95 percent confidence level. Indeed, Marxism itself does not appear to change church control of schools. This finding may seem surprising from some theoretical perspectives, but, as I argue, church-state educational conflict is pervasive in sub-Saharan Africa, with regimes of all ideological stripes having educational goals that are distinct from church educational goals.[96] Model 2 also shows that the results are robust to controlling for the country's level of economic development, with the coefficient on GDP per capita suggesting that countries at higher levels of development are less likely to give power to churches, consistent with modernization theory.

Models 3 and 4 separately consider the likelihood of changes that increase the power of the church over school management versus changes that increase the prominence of Christian religious education on syllabi. The first type of change is consistent with the view that the state should have limited power in liberal democratic systems, but the second type sits in tension with freedom of religion in that it privileges one belief system over others. Interestingly, liberal democratic institutions appear helpful in pushing through both types of changes; the coefficient on liberal democracy score is positive and statistically significant at the 95 percent confidence levels in all models.

Models 5 and 6 consider whether liberal democratic institutions also help churches avoid the implementation of policy changes that decrease their control of church schools. For these models, the sample is restricted to country years in which church schools existed because it is difficult to conceive of legislation further reducing the power of churches over schools when they have been completely nationalized. Counter to the evidence from Zambia and Ghana, I find little evidence that liberal democratic institutions protect churches from negative policy changes across the wider sample. This may be partly due to the difficulty of coding

---

[96] In understanding the null result on Marxism, it is important to note that many countries that eventually adopted Marxist–Leninism as their official ideology lacked significant histories of mission schools (as in Ethiopia, Somalia, and even Benin, which failed to meet the threshold for inclusion in this analysis) or had nationalized, church-affiliated schools in advance of making such a declaration (as in Angola, Congo-Brazzaville, and Mozambique). In addition, it is important to note the many educational conflicts that churches have had with regimes explicitly espousing capitalist economic ideologies, including Cameroon, Kenya, and Nigeria.

nonimplementation of anti-church policies in the wider sample, introducing noise into this measure. Still, taking the results at face value, the main factor explaining policy changes that decrease the influence of the church is whether a country is within its first decade of independence. In the broader sample, the main benefit of liberal democratic institutions is that they can help churches gain new educational powers, including ones lost in the immediate postindependence period, not that they can prevent loss of influence.

Substantively, how much difference do liberal democratic institutions make in helping churches advance their educational policy interests? Across the sample, in any given year there is a low likelihood of a policy being implemented that increases the power of churches over schools – only a 1.8 percent chance on average. The median country in the sample experienced a 0.28-point change in its liberal democracy score during this period. Taking the coefficient on liberal democracy in model 2 as the baseline, this means the median country was 2.5 percentage points (or greater than 100 percent) more likely to implement a policy that increased the educational power of churches in its most liberal democratic year as compared to in its least liberal democratic one.

This evidence shows a strong association between liberal democracy and policy changes that increase the power of churches over schools. Furthermore, the descriptive relationship between liberal democratic institutions and education policy changes is highly relevant in evaluating my theory. The correlation between liberal democracy and expanded church school autonomy within countries is the empirical relationship observed firsthand by church leaders, and it likely informs their choices. If they observe a positive relationship between liberal democratic institutions and church school autonomy, they are likely to infer benefits from this type of regime.

*****

This chapter demonstrates that churches with significant educational systems have good reasons to support liberal democracy – it is associated with improvements in their control over their educational activities. Drawing on process-tracing evidence from Zambia and Ghana and a cross-country regional comparison, the chapter shows that churches are more likely to augment their power over church-affiliated schools in periods in which liberal democratic institutions in their country are strong. Furthermore, the evidence shows that churches can use liberal democratic institutions to mobilize domestic support for their schools against international pressure to reduce their educational influence. Together with Chapter 6, which shows the broad coalitions churches can sometimes mobilize in support of liberal democracy, including some international actors, it explains why churches need to speak out in defense of liberal democracy to secure educational policy influence. Next, Part IV, the last part of the book, considers the effects of church-run schools for democratic citizenship and the implications of the argument more broadly for democracy around the world.

PART IV

EXTENSIONS AND IMPLICATIONS

8

Church School Legacies for Citizenship

Evidence from Zambia and Tanzania

The central task of this book is to show how variation in church-affiliated school systems provides different incentives for church leaders to speak out in defense of liberal democracy. But church schools have the potential to influence democracy through another channel as well – the education of the next generation. If church schools sometimes have an indirect positive effect on citizens' support for democracy via the activism of church leaders, how is that weighed against their more direct effects on the political values and engagement of their former students? This chapter considers whether church-run schools have distinctive effects on former students' political attitudes and if so, whether there is a trade-off between church schools' positive effect on prodemocratic activism mobilized by church leaders and the effects the schools have on the political attitudes of their former students.

Specifically, this chapter tests how church-run schools compare to their state-run counterparts in fostering political attitudes toward inclusive national identities, political engagement, and gender equality. It focuses on these three attitudes because they are recognized as critical to underpinning a healthy democracy and because some existing theoretical frameworks suggest that state-run schools may play a special role in promoting them. I begin by outlining these theories and then examine original research from Zambia and Tanzania that tests the hypotheses by looking at the long-term consequences of church- versus state-run schools on former students' political attitudes. In Zambia, I causally identify the effects of Catholic schooling by measuring variation in attitudes of birth-year cohorts educated around the 1974 transfer of Catholic primary schools to the state, complementing the quantitative analysis with life history interviews of fifteen former Catholic school attendees. In Tanzania, I rely on an original survey of respondents about their parents' life histories to understand the varied trajectories of an earlier generation of citizens who attended Catholic, Protestant, or state-run schools.

The evidence suggests that church-run schools do not generally foster antidemocratic attitudes. I find no proof that church schools harm the development of broad national identities or that they depress political engagement. In fact, Catholic education in Zambia and Protestant education in Tanzania increase women's political engagement, with one important exception. Even as Catholic education generates engaged female citizens in Zambia, it also generates less progressive views on gender equality among men and women. To the extent that there is a trade-off between the effect of church schools on democratic advocacy mobilized by church leaders and their effects on citizens' attitudes, it occurs in the domain of gender equality.

THEORIZING THE SPECIAL ROLE OF STATE-RUN VERSUS CHURCH-RUN SCHOOLS ON FORMER STUDENTS' CITIZENSHIP

Many politicians and policymakers view state-run public schools as uniquely positioned to foster democratic citizenship, with church-run schools hypothesized to perform significantly worse in inculcating national identity and political engagement.[1] But there is little existing empirical scholarship on whether that is the case, especially outside the American context.[2] Although scholars have conducted significant research on the educational inequalities fostered by mission-centered colonial school systems in sub-Saharan Africa, there has been much less work on the political identities and values fostered specifically by church-run schools.[3] To the extent that scholars have studied whether religious schools have distinctive effects on political attitudes, the focus has largely been on Islamic schools and madrasas.[4]

Still, existing scholarship and policy debates point to at least three democratically relevant attitudes that could be fostered differently

---

[1] Banana 1982; Nyerere 1967.
[2] On Catholic schools and democratic education in the United States, see Bryk, Lee, and Holland 1993.
[3] Bauer, Platas, and Weinstein 2022; De Haas and Frankema 2018; King 2013; Pierskalla, Juan, and Montgomery 2017; Platas 2014.
[4] Bleck 2015; Sirin, Ryce, and Mir 2009.

in church- versus state-run schools, as I elaborate later. The first is national identity. Political theorists have long emphasized the benefits of a common national identity for democracy insofar as it clarifies who the people are and gives legitimacy to their collective decisions.[5] The second is political interest and engagement. Political scientists widely recognize the importance of an informed and engaged citizenry to the operation of democracy, even though there are debates about how much citizens need to know to make democracy work.[6] The third is attitudes toward gender equality. Democracy is diminished in circumstances in which half the society is not able to express autonomous political views.[7]

Regarding the first attitude, how might church- and state-run schools foster distinct levels of national identity? One hypothesis is that church-run schools foster parochial identities that create intolerance and societal conflict in religiously diverse societies.[8] A second, weaker form of this hypothesis is that even if church-run schools do not explicitly foster intolerance, they are less effective than state-run schools in generating new national identities. The classic literature on nationalism describes mass public education as playing a critical and unique role in inculcating national identity through exposure to common language and common historical frames.[9] Both the strong and weak forms of the hypothesis suggest reasons that church-run schools may foster weaker attachments to national identity than state-run schools.

On the second attitude, there is a vast literature demonstrating that education generally increases political engagement, but it pays little empirical attention to whether church-run schools are distinctive.[10] Some scholars hypothesize that religious teachings' emphasis on otherworldly matters could reduce their students' engagement in politics.[11] Others hypothesize that the emphasis on deference to authority in Christian

---

[5] Linz and Stepan 1996; Rustow 1970.
[6] Dahl 1971; Lupia and McCubbins 1998.
[7] Paxton 2000; Teele 2018.
[8] One particularly common claim from American policymakers after the 9/11 attacks was that madrasa education promoted Islamic militancy. For a careful review of the lack of evidence for this particular claim in Pakistan, see Fair 2008. For an assessment of the role of church-controlled education system in fostering conflict in Rwanda, see King 2013.
[9] Weber 1976. See also Darden and Grzymala-Busse 2006; Darden and Mylonas 2016; Gellner 1983; Hobsbawm 1990; Miguel 2004.
[10] Almond and Verba 1963; Croke et al. 2016; Sondheimer and Green 2010.
[11] Campbell 2004.

teaching could inhibit democratic participation.[12] Scholars who study nonstate service provision emphasize a different potential mechanism through which church-run schools may lead to disengagement: Insofar as church-run schools are viewed as being outside the state, they may not provide graduates with the same motivation to engage with the state to improve the quality of public services as do state-run schools.[13] Still others hypothesize that teachers in state-run schools may place more emphasis on curriculum that imparts knowledge about the country's political system (as part of the nation-building efforts described earlier), potentially giving their graduates an informational advantage in engaging with the country's political system.[14] These hypotheses suggest that graduates of church-run schools may have lower political engagement compared to graduates of state-run schools.

On the third attitude, church-run schools may impart more conservative gender ideologies than state-run schools. Religious groups, including churches, have long traditions of regulating procreation and inheritance rules as a means of defining and protecting group membership.[15] From this perspective, church-run schools may be expected to teach more conservative gender norms than state-run schools. This particularly may be the case when compared to state-run schools in countries with socialist leanings, as in Zambia and Tanzania postindependence.[16]

Nevertheless, against these hypotheses, it is plausible that church-run schools do not have significantly different effects compared to other schools, especially in the post–World War II period in which their teaching standards and curricular content have been subject to considerable state regulation. Furthermore, church educationalists often emphasize the value of their schools' common collective identity and attention to moral discipline in serving their graduates, including in the public sphere.[17] As a result, it is plausible that church-run schools could have salutary effects on values and attitudes relevant to good citizenship.

This chapter tests these hypotheses by drawing on research comparing the experiences of students in church- versus state-run schools in Zambia and Tanzania. Importantly, this research employs a distinct

---

[12] Cliffe 1971, 63; Rink 2018.
[13] MacLean 2011.
[14] Bleck 2015 notes that public schools are often polling stations, providing students and their families an advantage in knowing where to vote.
[15] Htun and Weldon 2005; Htun and Weldon 2018; Lazarev 2023; Tunón 2017.
[16] Engels 1942.
[17] Bryk, Lee, and Holland 1993.

counterfactual from existing studies of the legacies of mission education that have focused on comparing locations with mission education to locations without any education, thereby estimating an effect that bundles the effects of education per se and the effects of education by church groups.[18] My hypotheses and research design focus on the effects of attendance at different types of schools, parsing the effects of churches running schools from the effects of schools themselves.

THE CASE OF ZAMBIA: LEVERAGING THE TRANSFER OF CATHOLIC PRIMARY SCHOOLS TO THE STATE

In Zambia, my research design takes advantage of the 1974 transfer of Catholic primary schools to the government to estimate the effects of Catholic education on former students' political attitudes. Because this transfer was not simultaneous with other educational reforms, it allows me to estimate the distinct effects of church management of schools on student outcomes and attitudes by drawing on quantitative and qualitative evidence.

In Zambia, as elsewhere in sub-Saharan Africa, primary schools were a central part of the Catholic Church's strategy for accessing and evangelizing the population. This strategy was encouraged by the British colonial administration, which, after 1925, both provided funds for schools and threatened mission societies with reallocation of their schools to other missionary groups if they did not provide sufficient quality schools.[19] Three Catholic missionary societies operated in Zambia: the White Fathers in the north, the Jesuits in the south, and the Capuchins in the west. By the late colonial period, Catholic schools were spread across Zambia, with concentration in the White Father's area in the north of the country. The goal of the Catholic Church in Zambia in the 1940s and 1950s was "Catholic schools for Catholic children, where there were sufficient Catholic children,"[20] even if this goal could not always be realized due to the colonial administration's reluctance to support multiple schools in small communities.

Protestant churches handed over their mission schools entirely to the government at independence in 1964. But even as the Ministry of

---

[18] Gallego and Woodberry 2010; Lankina and Getachew 2012; Lankina and Getachew 2013; Wantchekon, Klašnja, and Novta 2015.
[19] Carmody indicates that the governor warned the White Fathers of this possibility in 1925. See Carmody 2002, 785.
[20] Carmody 2002, 794–97.

Education increased its control over the content of education and the appointment of teachers postindependence, the Catholic Church continued to play an important part in the management of its schools, running about 20 percent of the total number of primary schools in Zambia until 1974 (644 in 1967 and 733 in 1973).[21]

I focus on understanding the effects of Catholic primary schools during the relatively brief postindependence period before they were handed over to the Zambian government (1965–1973). During this period, these schools were grant aided, which meant that the state determined the subjects and syllabi of the schools' secular education and paid the teachers' salaries. The Ministry of Education and the Catholic education secretariat in theory shared responsibility for appointing and sanctioning teachers. Students did not pay tuition fees to attend these schools following the abolition of such fees in 1965, and students were not supposed to be denied admission based on religious affiliation.

These schools managed to maintain a distinctly Catholic character for three reasons: the Church's role in the selection and management of teachers assured almost all were Catholic, the content of the religious education was Catholic, and the specific school culture included Catholic worship along with extracurricular activities. These features were particularly attractive to Catholic students, who composed most of the student body in Catholic schools in most Zambian dioceses and about 60 percent of the student body in Catholic primary schools across the country as a whole.[22] For its part, the Catholic Church was expected to contribute to the upkeep of the infrastructure of the schools, which were often on church property. It also devoted significant religious personnel to managing the schools and teaching in them.

In mid-1973, the Catholic Church made the decision to hand over all its primary schools to the Zambian government at the end of the school year. As discussed in Chapter 7, the government had been exerting greater control over aspects of education in Catholic primary schools, often bypassing the Catholic education secretariat in key decisions, including teacher appointments. Under the impression that the Church would eventually be pushed out of the primary education sector altogether, the

---

[21] These figures are both from Hinfelaar 2004. At the point of its maximum contribution to the Zambian education system in 1945, the Catholic Church ran 33 percent of all primary schools. Carmody 2002, 790.

[22] Carmody 1999, 111.

Catholic bishops decided to withdraw from it.[23] The Catholic Church served the government with notice of its intent to withdraw in July 1973, and the handover occurred at the beginning of the next school year, in January 1974.[24] This handover provides an opportunity for estimating the effects of Catholic schools on student identities and values. Specifically, I can estimate these effects by examining how they change across cohorts of primary school completers who were denominationally Catholic and likely to have attended Catholic schools before the handover and all of whom attended state-run schools after it. I can parse Catholic school effects from any other birth-year cohort effects by comparing this change to the one experienced by non-Catholic (Protestant) primary school completers over the same period in a difference-in-difference design.

Specifically, among Catholic students, I am interested in the effects of the proportion of years spent in Catholic- versus state-run primary schools on their subsequent identities and values. During this period, primary school consisted of grades 1–7; students were supposed to enter the first grade at age seven.[25] As a result, Catholic children born in 1959 would likely have attended Catholic-run schools for all their primary education, while Catholic children born in 1966 or later would have attended state-run schools for all their primary education. For the birth cohorts born between 1960 and 1965, a fraction of their primary school years would be expected to be in Catholic- versus state-run schools, as indicated in Figure 8.1.

A substantial number of Catholics who attended primary school before 1974 also attended state-run schools, but unfortunately, my data sources do not permit me to know precisely which Catholic students attended Catholic schools. As a result, this analysis is akin to an intent-to-treat analysis. From the educational statistics available for 1965–1973, we can infer that 60 percent of Catholic primary school students attended Catholic schools during this period.[26] The other 40 percent of Catholic primary school students

---

[23] The education secretary general, Father O'Riordan, presented the bishops with three options at a meeting prior to the decision: "To resist this pernicious encroachment and insist upon their rights, or to hand over all the responsibility immediately, or to go along with the process of being eventually completely phased out of this area of service to the country," Hinfelaar 2004, 311.
[24] Hinfelaar 2004, 312. This matches information obtained from interviews with students who attended schools during this period, discussed in more detail later. Aspects of the handover process lasted the entire 1974 school year.
[25] The Zambian academic calendar begins in January. Primary school was shortened from eight to seven years in 1965.
[26] In this period, about 60 percent of students in Catholic schools in Zambia were Catholic. The Catholic Church operated about 20 percent of all primary schools (644 primary

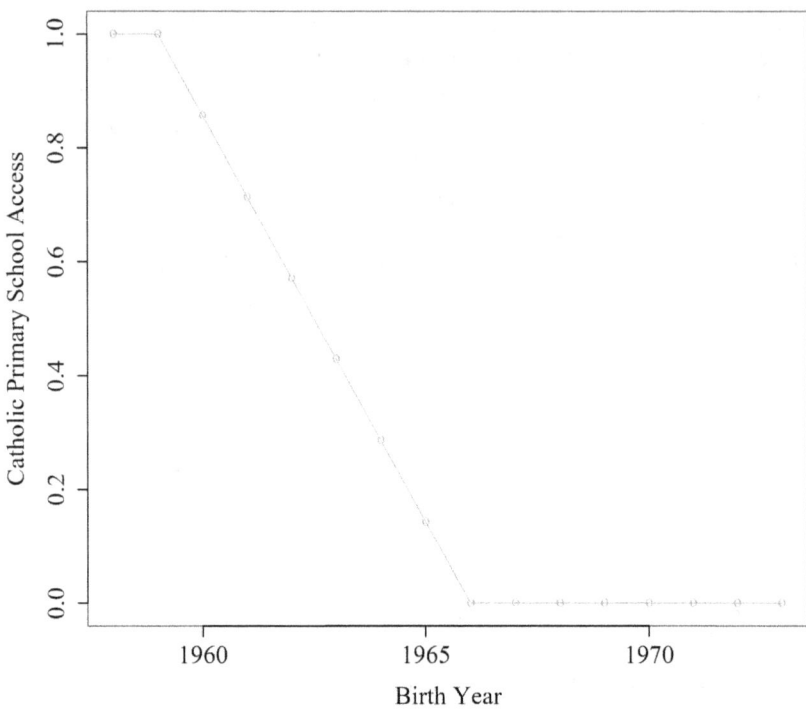

FIGURE 8.1 Catholic primary school access by birth year

would have been only minimally affected by the nationalization of Catholic schools, although almost simultaneously, Catholic priests lost their right of entry to non-Catholic schools to teach religion to Catholic students. Only 10 percent of non-Catholic students attended Catholic schools before 1974; the other 90 percent attended state-run schools.

The handover of Catholic primary schools in Zambia is a particularly useful case for estimating the effects of Catholic-run schools independent of other educational reforms because other educational policies influencing educational access and content in these schools did not change around the handover but remained constant. The similarities and differences in the educational environment pre- and post-handover are summarized in Table 8.1. Importantly, primary school fees were eliminated at

schools across all dioceses of the country in 1967; 733 in 1973), and Catholics made up 22 percent of the Zambian population. See Hinfelaar 2004, 256, 311; Carmody 2003a, 294; Zurlo and Johnson 2025. Insofar as Catholics and non-Catholics were equally represented in the school system, which the Afrobarometer data suggests is the case, this implies that about 40 percent of Catholics were attending non-Catholic schools.

TABLE 8.1 *Comparison of (former) Catholic primary schools, pre- and post-government handover*

	1965–1973	Post-1973
Proportion of primary-aged children in primary schools	76 percent	78 percent
Years of primary education	7 years	7 years
Language of primary education	English	English
Source of operational budget (teachers' salaries)	Government	Government
Source of capital budget	Government and Catholic Church	Government
Primary school fees	None[a]	None
Student selection and religion	Schools open to all; 60 percent Catholic student body	Schools open to all; little immediate change in the composition of schools
Secular education	Government curricula and testing standards	Government curricula and testing standards
Religious education	Catholic religious instruction, taught by Catholic clergy (with opt out clause)	Academic religious studies, taught by professional teachers
Teacher selection	Church and government both play roles in selecting and promoting teachers; most teachers Catholic; some teachers are foreigners; some teachers are priests, brothers, or nuns	Government selects and promotes teachers; some foreigner teachers; priests, brothers, and nuns removed from schools
Teacher discipline	Church and government both play roles in disciplining teachers	Government alone responsible for disciplining teachers
School management	Church and government oversee head teacher; subject to church and government inspections	Government oversees head teacher; subject to government inspections
Religious paraphernalia	Present	Removed

[a] At independence, some primary schools still had boarding facilities for the higher grades (that is, grades 5–7). These were phased out before the transfer of schools in 1974. Although students did not pay tuition fees, some students reported paying nominal boarding fees in the 1960s.

independence, and so few students were excluded from Catholic education based on their inability to pay. The probability of a primary school–aged child being able to attend school remained similar before and after the handover and was relatively high compared to other countries in sub-Saharan Africa at the time – three-quarters of Zambia's primary school–aged students attended school in the 1970s.[27] Catholic schools were required to teach the secular curriculum set by the Zambian government, including civics courses.[28] Furthermore, Catholic withdrawal from running primary schools had limited immediate effects on the financing of secular education in these schools because the teachers were already paid by the state before the transfer, and the church made only occasional investments in school infrastructural upkeep.

These particularities of the Zambian educational system mean that the analysis measures nonfinancial effects of transferring Catholic schools to the state. These changes involved religious education, teacher management and selection, school management, and the broader ethos of the school. Before the handover, students in Catholic schools were taught confessional religious instruction by Catholic clergy; after the handover, they were taught religious education by professional teachers using an ecumenical syllabus developed through a partnership between Catholic and Protestant church leaders.[29] The selection and discipline of teachers also changed. Almost all the 2,500 teachers in Catholic primary schools prior to the handover were Catholic; most were lay Catholics and a handful were foreign missionaries. Some teachers and many more school administrators were nuns, brothers, or priests. Although after the handover teacher reassignment between schools would take several years to unfold, the removal of church management affected teacher discipline immediately. In particular, former teachers describe how Catholic administrators had fired teachers for polygyny and alcohol abuse but that after the handover, government administrators turned a blind eye toward these behaviors.[30]

---

[27] Kelly 1991 notes that the net primary enrollment rate remained stagnant at about 78 percent between 1975 and 1985. This is only a slight increase from 1972 (the only data available from UNESCO for the pre-1974 period), when net primary enrollment was 76 percent.

[28] Schools were mandated to teach the principles of Zambian Humanism from the late 1960s onward as the country's national ideology, although formal instruction on humanism seems to have come mainly at the secondary level. Interview with former student at transferred school, December 2021. See also Kaunda 1968, 24.

[29] Carmody 2003b.

[30] Carmody conducted interviews with teachers at this time, which indicate many male teachers supported the change in administration as a result, while female teachers

Such differences in teacher management, alongside broader changes to the ethos of the school, including the removal of religious paraphernalia and significant shifts in student extracurricular activities, were the most pronounced changes around the handover.

Thus, the handover in Zambia provides an excellent case for identifying the effects of changes in school management distinct from other changes in school structure or financing. It could also be considered a hard case for identifying whether there is a distinctive Catholic school effect insofar as Catholic school management practices and curricula were considerably constrained by the state before the handover. In practice, the scope of government regulation of Catholic schools in Zambia prior to 1974 is quite similar to the scope of government regulation imposed in other cases in sub-Saharan Africa, where Catholic schools are generally highly regulated (discussed in Chapter 7), and as such, it is a representative case.

A COHORT-BASED STUDY OF CATHOLIC EDUCATION'S EFFECTS ON POLITICAL IDENTITY, ENGAGEMENT, AND GENDER

I am interested in the effects of access to Catholic primary education on citizen's national identification, political engagement, and gender attitudes. To measure these, I rely on public opinion surveys administered by Afrobarometer between 2003 and 2017, when the cohorts of young people immediately affected by the handover of schools were between thirty-two and fifty-nine years old.[31] I examine the effects of Catholic primary education on citizens' political attributes by examining whether the degree of access to Catholic education (the proportion of their primary school years in which Catholics ran primary schools), illustrated in Figure 8.1, has particular effects on subsequent characteristics for

---

opposed it. For example, a former male teacher, manager of schools, and district education officer said, "Teachers welcomed [the government takeover] because of indiscipline. Under [the Catholic] agency, teachers were expected to keep families well – one wife and good behavior. When the handover came, a teacher could be drunk early in the morning or could absent himself. Those were the people who welcomed the handover of the schools." In contrast, a female teacher indicated, "most of us women liked the [missionary] rules very much because they were safeguarding our homes. They were good rules because our husbands were afraid of losing their jobs if they went for other women." Both are quoted in Carmody 1999, 112.

[31] An Afrobarometer survey was also conducted in Zambia in 1999, but it did not ask respondents' religion, which is crucial for this analysis.

Catholics who completed primary school. To rule out the possibility of a concurrent historical event influencing the results, I employ a difference-in-difference design that compares cohort effects for Catholics and non-Catholics, as the latter group should have been only minimally affected by the school handover.[32]

Specifically, I estimate the effect of Catholic school attendance by analyzing the interaction between Catholic school access, coded as indicated in Figure 8.1, and whether respondents are Catholic, with the models also including each of these variables. In all models, I control for the respondents' birth year, which is constrained to have a constant linear effect before and after the cohort cutoff corresponding to the primary school handover. I include survey fixed effects (to account for time-varying shocks, including changes in the party and leader in power) and region fixed effects (to account for differences across Zambian regions, which are politically salient identities).[33] The standard errors are clustered at the religion-birth year cohort level, which is the level at which the treatment of interest is assigned, to account for possible correlation in the attitudes of people born in the same year and belonging to the same religion. I run the model separately for women and men, given the hypothesized possibility of effects on gender attitudes.

The main specification that I present focuses on people born between 1958 and 1973, with eight birth cohorts at least partially exposed to Catholic education and eight birth cohorts exposed to state education only. I do not include earlier birth cohorts due to the significant changes in education at independence, including the handover of Protestant mission schools and the removal of school fees. In Appendix D, I show that the results are similar if I include fewer or additional cohorts of students who attended state-run primary schools. I also show that the results are largely robust to an alternative specification that considers whether students attended most of their primary schooling in Catholic- or state-run schools.

The measure of national identity is coded using a question from the Afrobarometer survey that asks, "Let us suppose that you had to choose between being a Zambian and being a (ethnic group). Which of the following statements best expresses your feelings?" Respondents

---

[32] Respondents who partially completed primary school are not included in the analysis, due to the difficulty of determining precisely how much access to Catholic school they would have had.

[33] On the significance of regional identities in Zambia, see Posner 2003; Posner 2005.

could give one of five possible answers: I feel only (ethnic group), I feel more (ethnic group) than Zambian, I feel equally Zambian and (ethnic group), I feel more Zambian than (ethnic group), or I feel only Zambian. I turn these ordered statements into a 1–5 scale, with higher numbers indicating higher national identification. This question was included in the Afrobarometer survey rounds conducted in Zambia in 2005, 2009, 2012, and 2014.

I measure political engagement using the respondents' reported interest in public affairs (defined as politics and government). The political interest variable is measured on a four-point scale (not at all interested, not very interested, somewhat interested, and very interested), and was included in five of the Afrobarometer survey rounds in the analysis (2003, 2005, 2009, 2012, and 2014).

I measure attitudes toward women's political empowerment by averaging two questions that asked respondents to choose between a progressive and a conservative statement on women's rights and then to state how strongly they agreed with that statement. The first question asked respondents to choose how much they agreed with the statements "Men make better political leaders than women, and should be elected rather than women" or "Women should have the same chance of being elected to political office as men." The second asked how much they agreed with the statements "Women have always been subject to traditional laws and customs, and should remain so" or "In our country, women should have equal rights and receive the same treatment as men do." Each response is coded on a 1–4 scale, with 1 indicating strong agreement with the conservative statement, 2 indicating weak agreement with the conservative statement, 3 indicating weak agreement with the progressive statement, and 4 indicating strong agreement with the progressive statement. The first question was included in four Afrobarometer survey rounds (2005, 2012, 2014, and 2017), and the second was included in three Afrobarometer survey rounds (2003, 2005, and 2012).

In addition to these political attitudes, I also measure respondents' educational attainment (whether they completed secondary school); their economic well-being in adulthood (an index averaging the frequency with which they reported going without food, water, cooking fuel, or a cash income, measured on a 0–4 scale where 0 is never and 4 is always); and their attendance at religious services, excluding weddings and funerals (measured on a 1–6 scale, where 1 is never and 6 is more than once a week).

CATHOLIC-RUN PRIMARY SCHOOLS AS BASTIONS OF PAROCHIALISM OR EMPOWERMENT?

In advance of considering the effects of Catholic-run primary schools on former students' political attitudes, it is important to first consider whether these schools have effects on conversion and primary school completion of men and women. Both types of effects are plausible, but they would complicate the comparison in the main analysis insofar as they suggest selection effects into the sample. In models 1 and 3 of Table 8.2, I examine whether respondents in birth cohorts who could have attended Catholic school are more likely to identify as Catholic (as opposed to another religion or denomination) as adults. I find no evidence of that, suggesting that Catholic schools were not particularly effective instruments of conversion in the postindependence period. This finding also suggests that in the absence of a measure of childhood religious affiliation, we can use adult religious affiliation without introducing bias into the analysis. Models 2 and 4 of Table 8.2 consider the effects of Catholic

TABLE 8.2 *Effects of Catholic schools on conversion and primary school completion*

	Men		Women	
	Catholic (0/1) (1)	Finished primary (0/1) (2)	Catholic (0/1) (3)	Finished primary (0/1) (4)
Catholic school attendance (access × Catholic)		0.11 (0.08)		−0.06 (0.10)
Catholic school access	−0.10 (0.45)	0.06 (0.09)	0.13 (0.45)	−0.00 (0.12)
Catholic		0.03 (0.03)		0.02 (0.04)
N	730	918	555	864
Birth-year trend	Yes	Yes	Yes	Yes
Survey round FEs	Yes	Yes	Yes	Yes
Region FEs	Yes	Yes	Yes	Yes
Years included	1958–1973	1958–1973	1958–1973	1958–1973
Sample	Male primary completers	All men	Female primary completers	All women

$^{+}p < 0.10$, $^{*}p < 0.05$, $^{**}p < 0.01$; coefficients with standard errors clustered by religion-year of birth in parentheses.

schools on primary school completion, using the main specification that interacts Catholic school access with Catholicism (access × Catholic) as a proxy for Catholic school attendance but without excluding respondents based on primary school completion. I find no evidence that Catholic men or women were differentially likely to complete primary school in Catholic versus state schools.

Table 8.3 considers the effects of Catholic versus state schools on men's socioeconomic outcomes, religiosity, and political attitudes. Overall, the results suggest that Catholic management of primary schools made little difference to their male students. These schools did not improve their socioeconomic trajectories, did not increase their religious attendance, did not change how much they identify with the nation-state, and did not influence their interest in politics. The only substantively large effect is to reduce men's support for women's rights – a 0.56-point reduction on a four-point scale that is statistically significant at the 90 percent confidence level. To the extent that Catholic schools make a difference, it is on gender attitudes.

Table 8.4 considers the effects of Catholic schools on women's socioeconomic outcomes, religiosity, and political attitudes. In contrast to the men's results above, Catholic school attendance makes a much larger difference on women's socioeconomic trajectories, religiosity, and political attitudes, but with a complex pattern of effects. Models 1 and 2 show that Catholic primary school attendance improves women's socioeconomic trajectories, making Catholic women more likely to finish secondary school (by 0.22 percentage points, statistically significant at the 90 percent confidence level) and less likely to experience scarcity as an adult (by 0.37 points on the five-point scale, statistically significant at the 95 percent confidence level) if they attend Catholic primary school. Model 3 shows that women who attend Catholic primary school also attend church more frequently as adults; the 0.44-point increase (statistically significant at the 90 percent confidence level) is substantial considering that there isn't much room for upward movement on the religiosity scale: Average church attendance for Catholic women attending only state-run primary schools is already 5.1 out of 6.

Models 4–6 of Table 8.4 consider whether Catholic school attendance affects women's political attitudes later in life. Model 4 shows that Catholic education makes little difference to national identification; female Catholic school attendees are not more or less likely to identify with the Zambian nation versus their ethnic group as compared to Catholic women who do not attend Catholic schools. But models 5

TABLE 8.3 *Effects of Catholic school attendance on socioeconomic status and political attitudes – men*

	Finished secondary (0/1) (1)	Scarcity index (0–4) (2)	Religiosity (1–6) (3)	National identity (1–5) (4)	Interest in politics (0–3) (5)	Women's rights (1–4) (6)
Catholic school attendance (access × Catholic)	−0.13 (0.13)	−0.10 (0.16)	0.18 (0.24)	0.26 (0.23)	0.01 (0.18)	−0.56[+] (0.31)
Catholic school access	−0.12 (0.12)	0.12 (0.18)	−0.34 (0.31)	−0.15 (0.25)	0.47** (0.16)	−0.49 (0.29)
Catholic	0.06 (0.05)	−0.06 (0.07)	0.26** (0.09)	−0.03 (0.08)	0.12 (0.10)	0.26[+] (0.13)
N	730	730	363	544	649	612
Birth-year trend	Yes	Yes	Yes	Yes	Yes	Yes
Survey round FEs	Yes	Yes	Yes	Yes	Yes	Yes
Region FEs	Yes	Yes	Yes	Yes	Yes	Yes
Years included	1958–1973	1958–1973	1958–1973	1958–1973	1958–1973	1958–1973
Sample	Male primary completers	Male primary completers	Male primary completers	Male primary completers	Male primary completers	Male primary completers

[+] $p < 0.10$, * $p < 0.05$, ** $p < 0.01$; coefficients with standard errors clustered by religion-year of birth in parentheses.

TABLE 8.4 *Effects of Catholic school attendance on socioeconomic status and political attitudes – women*

	Finished secondary (0/1) (1)	Scarcity index (0–4) (2)	Religiosity (1–6) (3)	National identity (1–5) (4)	Interest in politics (0–3) (5)	Women's rights (1–4) (6)
Catholic school attendance (access × Catholic)	0.22⁺ (0.12)	−0.36* (0.15)	0.44⁺ (0.25)	−0.07 (0.31)	0.59⁺ (0.34)	−0.58⁺ (0.30)
Catholic school access	0.13 (0.12)	0.30⁺ (0.15)	−0.15 (0.33)	0.33 (0.36)	−0.16 (0.31)	−0.23 (0.23)
Catholic	−0.03 (0.05)	0.11 (0.06)	−0.14 (0.12)	0.02 (0.10)	−0.06 (0.11)	0.06 (0.11)
N	555	555	302	401	497	470
Birth-year trend	Yes	Yes	Yes	Yes	Yes	Yes
Survey round FEs	Yes	Yes	Yes	Yes	Yes	Yes
Region FEs	Yes	Yes	Yes	Yes	Yes	Yes
Years included	1958–1973	1958–1973	1958–1973	1958–1973	1958–1973	1958–1973
Sample	Female primary completers	Female primary completers	Female primary completers	Female primary completers	Female primary completers	Female primary completers

⁺ $p < 0.10$, * $p < 0.05$, ** $p < 0.01$; coefficients with standard errors clustered by religion-year of birth in parentheses.

and 6 indicate that Catholic education has distinct effects on women's interest in politics and their attitudes toward women's rights. Catholic school attendance generates substantively higher levels of political interest (0.59 points higher on a four-point scale, statistically significant at the 90 percent confidence level) and substantively lower levels of support for gender equality (0.58 points lower on a four-point scale, statistically significant at the 90 percent confidence level) among Catholic women; Catholic women who attend Catholic primary school are more politically engaged and less supportive of progressive gender views than Catholic women who do not. Indeed, the pernicious effect of Catholic primary school education on attitudes toward women's rights is the only consistent effect observed across males and females.

How can we make sense of Catholic primary school's dual political effects – encouraging greater political interest among women but also fostering greater support for traditional gender roles? In fact, this pattern of religious institutions fostering highly engaged, socially conservative women is fairly common, with examples outside sub-Saharan Africa ranging from early twentieth-century France to contemporary Colombia.[34] As the evidence from Zambia suggests, Catholic schools may make women better educated, financially more secure, and more politically engaged while simultaneously making them more religious and less likely to overturn gender hierarchies.

Overall, the results from Zambia provide only limited evidence that Catholic-run schools are harmful for democratic citizenship. These schools do not depress national identity and they foster higher political engagement among former female students, but they simultaneously promote conventional gender roles among men and women. Insofar as women should have the same rights and opportunities as men for their views to be expressed in a democracy, this effect is harmful.

REMEMBERING CATHOLIC PRIMARY SCHOOLS: EVIDENCE FROM ORAL HISTORIES WITH FORMER STUDENTS

To further understand the effects of Catholic schools on political attitudes in Zambia, I draw on oral histories conducted with thirteen women and two men who attended primary schools that transitioned from Catholic-run to state-run in the 1970s. This is a snowball sample,

---

[34] Sarkar 2023; Teele 2018.

with initial interviewees contacted through personal networks. A female Zambian researcher conducted the oral histories.[35] The gender sample is intentionally skewed toward women, given that the analysis above demonstrates larger effects on them. These histories focused on respondents' educational experiences at these schools, which were attended either just before, just after, or during the transfer. Former students' recollections of their school days suggest that Zambian Catholic schools were both relatively tolerant of religious diversity and relatively effective in promoting identification with the new nation of Zambia, which aligns with the findings from the birth-year cohort study. The oral histories also suggest several mechanisms through which Catholic-run schools may have promoted women's political engagement without fostering more progressive gender attitudes.

All the interviewees remembered the schools as being religiously diverse, with students of all religious denominations in attendance. Interviewees differed in their recollections of how accommodating the schools were of the religious practices of students belonging to different denominations. Most remembered school mass being mandatory for all students. But one woman, a Jehovah's Witness, recalls that she had not needed to attend mass or to sing the national anthem at her Catholic school in Lusaka. Her teachers "were flexible and accommodating, though sometimes it wasn't easy, they would chase us for not wanting to participate in some activities," and students from other religious denominations were permitted to form their own religious groups at the school.[36] Another woman, a Methodist who attended a different Catholic school in Lusaka, emphasizes that she and her non-Catholic friends had to participate in the schools' religious services, but were "happy" to do so. "For me, I loved the way they used to pray and conduct their prayers …. I used to like the way the nuns looked …. When I got home, I would wear my head scarf like that."[37] Another woman recalls efforts to persuade students to become full members of the Catholic Church at her rural school in Zambia's Western Province, although many students held out.[38]

The interviewees also describe receiving basic civics lessons in Catholic primary schools in the postindependence period. These lessons covered the independence movement in Zambia, the leaders of the new government,

---

[35] I am grateful to my incredible research assistant, Sepo Lemba, for her assistance in identifying potential interviewees and conducting these interviews.
[36] Interview with female former student, November 2021.
[37] Interview with female former student, December 2021.
[38] Ibid.

and the importance of having a national registration card.[39] At the primary level, students learned little about the country's new philosophy of Zambian humanism, but they were exposed to the basic symbols of the new nation, including singing the national anthem every morning.[40] This is consistent with what students attending state-run schools report and complements the finding that Catholic-run primary schools were generally no worse than state-run primary schools in inculcating a common Zambian identity.[41]

The interviews also suggest several plausible mechanisms through which Catholic schools may have generated female political engagement. First, Catholic-run schools focused on providing a holistic education, including extracurricular activities such as sewing, music, arts, and sports.[42] Although most Catholic primary schools in Zambia were coed, the extracurricular activities were often gender segregated.[43] They frequently involved activities congruent with conservative gender roles, but may have helped girls develop self-confidence, social networks, and skills to engage in the public sphere nonetheless.[44] For example, one woman who attended a transferred Catholic school in the mid-1970s emphasizes the loss of extracurricular activities as the biggest change. "We no longer had music, we no longer had sewing. It just became school."[45] When one considers that the alternative to these extracurricular activities was often doing household chores at home, these activities may have been important in developing girls' sense of efficacy.[46] Another woman recalls being instructed in all aspects of life at her Catholic primary school, including aspects related to the public sphere: "When you are going for a job interview, how you should dress and that you should not sit before you are told to sit …. No cancellation, no late coming …. Up to today, that's what I do when I have an appointment …."[47]

---

[39] Interview with female former students, December 2021; December 2021; February 2022; February 2022; interview with male former student, April 2022.
[40] Interview with female former student, November 2021; February 2022.
[41] Interview with female former student, February 2022.
[42] Interview with female former students, December 2022; February 2022; April 2022.
[43] Interview with Zambian Catholic religious leader, April 2022.
[44] On the importance of extra-curricular activities for student learning in the American context, see Mehta and Fine 2019.
[45] Interview with female former student, December 2022.
[46] One interviewee reflected on the difficulty of managing chores at home and studying. Interview with female former student, February 2022.
[47] Interview with female former student, February 2022.

Second, the Catholic-run schools may have fostered a commitment to and self-confidence in one's ability to affect the common good through traditional gender roles. Female teachers were often remembered as role models of commitment to public service. The interviewees consistently reflected on the kindness of the female teachers with whom they had formed warm relationships. One woman remembers how she and her sister never had money for lunch: "There was one of the teachers, she was single and very nice to us ... she would invite us with my sister to go to her place at lunch time to go and eat."[48] Another woman, who otherwise walked two hours to get to school, remembers a teacher who "would give me a lift to school."[49] Another fondly recalls attending her teacher's Christian wedding.[50] These female role models did not defy gender roles, but they inspired their female students with their commitment to service. In contrast, interviewees consistently suggested that teachers showed less commitment to their vocations after the handover. As one church leader and educationalist explains, "With the government taking over, things started going down, of course. Dedication to work was not so much .... It's just the thing of looking at nothing is serious if it is government. So, there was just laxity."[51]

These interviews suggest how Catholic schools both inspired women's public engagement and fostered a commitment to traditional gender roles. Extracurricular activities fostered empowerment within traditional spheres and female role models encouraged political engagement without challenging gender hierarchies. As a result, Catholic primary schools in Zambia have a complicated legacy for gender equality.

CHURCH VERSUS GOVERNMENT SCHOOLS AND POLITICAL CITIZENSHIP IN TANZANIA

What are the effects of Catholic and Protestant church-run schools in a more religiously divided context in which church-run schools may foster more divisive identities? To consider this, I supplement the Zambian analysis with evidence from Tanzania. The advantage of this case is its religious diversity – with mainland Tanzania approximately equally divided between Catholics, Protestants, and Muslims – as well as its long history

---

[48] Interview with female former student, December 2022.
[49] Interview with female former student, February 2022.
[50] Interview with female former student, December 2022.
[51] Interview with Zambian Catholic educationalist, May 2022.

of Catholic-, Protestant-, and state-run schools. Although the country's educational history does not provide the same opportunities for identifying the effect of schools that are available in the Zambian context, I am able to assess how Catholic and Protestant education compares to state education in influencing political attitudes using data from an original survey that collected information on the past generation's educational experiences as well as on their adult children's recollections of their parents' lives and political engagement. I begin by providing background on mission schools in Tanzania before describing the research design and results.

In Tanzania, all mission schools were nationalized in 1970 as part of broader educational reforms, and so it is impossible to use a cohort-based study to isolate the effects of confessional schools independent of the effects of other educational reforms. But in contrast to the Zambian case, Tanzania has a long history of the colonial government financing both church- and state-run schools, and there is variation within birth-year cohorts in the types of schools that were attended from the 1920s up until 1970.

In Tanzania, the role of missionaries in providing education was complemented by state-run schools early in the colonial period due to the country's large Muslim population. Under the German colonial administration's education policy, state- and mission-run schools were promoted and subsidized. The British administration that took over the mandate after World War I organized schools for Africans into three categories: those run by the central government, those run by missions, and those run by local native administrations, with the latter two categories subsidized by grants-in-aid from the government and subject to government curricula and regulations as a condition for receiving those grants.[52] I consider schools run by the central government and those run by local native administrations to be state (government) schools.

How did education in government schools and mission schools differ? In Table 8.5, I focus on differences during the period of the British mandate (1925–1961). This is because only a handful of respondents in the survey were old enough to have parents who had been educated during

---

[52] The percentage of education at mission schools is often inflated by the high number of students at bush schools, which did not meet government standards for receiving aid and which provided very little formal education. For example, in 1930 it was estimated that 5,500 African students attended central government schools and about 90,000 attended mission schools. Sayers 1930, 381. However, Thompson notes that the government was providing over 48 percent of the schools of the standard required for aided status in 1931. Thompson 1976, 57.

TABLE 8.5 *Comparison of mission and government schools in colonial Tanzania*

	Mission schools	Government schools
Primary school language of instruction	Swahili	Swahili
Source of budget	40–75 percent government-funded; remainder from school fees and other church funds	Entirely government-funded (central government and native authorities), except for school fees
Primary school fees	Government set; minimal at primary level, greater at secondary	Government set; minimal at primary level, greater at secondary
Teacher selection and religion	Church and government both play roles in selecting and promoting teachers; some instruction by clergy, brothers, or nuns	Government selects and promotes teachers
Student selection and religion	Schools open to all; 20 percent Muslim student body	Schools open to all; at least 50 percent Muslim student body
Secular education	Government curricula and testing standards; 54 percent pass rate on school exit exam (1929–1933)	Government curricula and testing standards; 41 percent pass rate on school exit exam (1929–1933)
Religious education	Confessional religious instruction (with opt out clause and right of entry for other religions)	All religions have right of entry to provide confessional religious instruction to their students
School management	Church and government oversee head teacher; subject to church and government inspections	Government oversees head teacher; subject to government inspections

the period of German rule in mainland Tanzania.[53] After independence, the differences between the two sets of schools became smaller.

From 1925 onward, the British administration gave grants-in-aid to mission schools provided that they hired qualified teachers and followed

---

[53] The British were formally mandated to take over the territory in 1922 but began their new education policy three years later.

the government's set curriculum for secular subjects.[54] As a result, there were many similarities in the secular education provided in both sets of schools, including the language of instruction, which at the primary-school level was required to be Swahili rather than vernacular.[55] The limited evidence that exists on the quality of secular education in the two sets of schools, for example, the pass rate on centralized exams, suggests that the schools were fairly comparable in quality, although mission school students achieved a higher pass rate.[56] During this period, state and mission schools charged only nominal fees.[57]

Religious instruction was prominent in mission schools, but it was required to be held during either the first or last period of the school day so that students could not be compelled to attend. In state-run schools, religious leaders had right of entry to instruct students of their faith.[58] Muslim students were present in mission schools in significant numbers (composing 22 percent of students in Catholic schools in 1961), but made up a larger proportion of students in state schools, where they were a majority in the late colonial period.[59]

After independence in 1961, the government exerted further control over mission schools, decreasing their autonomy in appointing, promoting, and dismissing teachers while paying 100 percent of teacher salaries.[60] Nevertheless, for the next decade, two-thirds of schools continued to be administered by the TEC and the CCT.[61] With Tanzania's fully socialist turn in 1967, the role of mission churches in the country's education system became less tenable. The Education Act of 1969, passed in December 1970, fully nationalized mission schools while also introducing several other educational reforms.

[54] Iliffe 1979, 338; Sayers 1930, 377; Thompson 1976, 67.
[55] Iliffe 1979, 339.
[56] For example, between 1929 and 1933, 41 percent of Government School Candidates and 54 percent of Mission School Candidates passed the Central School Leaving Certificate exam. Thompson 1976, 63.
[57] Thompson 1976, 62–63, 93–96, 101.
[58] Thompson 1976, 43.
[59] Morrison 1976, 67, footnote 29. According to Thompson 1976, 22 percent of students in Catholic schools were Muslim, 104. Many sources report on the bias toward Muslim students in mission schools. See also Interview with elder, March 2017.
[60] Thompson 1976, 105. The Education Ordinance of 1961 also strengthened the right of religious minorities in school, emphasizing not only that they could not be compelled to attend religious instruction, but that the schools had a positive obligation to try to procure religious instruction in their preferred faith. Bahendwa 1990, 175; Cliffe 1971, 61; Thompson 1976, 103–104.
[61] Cliffe 1971, 61; Morrison 1976, 131.

A SURVEY OF ADULT CHILDREN ABOUT THEIR PARENT'S LIFE HISTORIES

Due to the bundled nature of the Tanzanian reforms, I cannot use a cohort approach to identify the effects of church schools in that context. In addition, at the time of my research in Tanzania – fifty years after the reform – it was not possible to directly measure the attitudes of significant numbers of students who attended church- and state-run schools in the pre-1970 period. Instead, I consider whether education in a church or state school subsequently influences political attitudes by drawing on a household survey in which respondents were asked about a parent's experience in school and their recollections of their parents' lives and political engagement.

To conduct this analysis, I draw on data from an original survey of 120 villages conducted in five regions of Tanzania in the summer of 2018. These regions, Kilimanjaro, Mbeya, Morogoro, Tabora, and Tanga, were selected for having the highest density of both Protestant and Catholic mission stations in the colonial period. Proximity to mission stations is an important determinant of access to church-run schools, and this sampling strategy permits me to examine the effects of both Protestant- and Catholic-run schools. Within each region, I compiled data on all existing mission stations and their level of activity over time and selected forty non-mission localities that were otherwise similarly situated to the high-activity mission stations.[62] Within each selected locality, one community was randomly selected for the survey, and twenty households in that community were surveyed in person.[63] The gender of the respondents was alternated so that an equal number of men and women in each

---

[62] Specifically, the selected non-mission communities were required to have approximately the same historic population density, distance to colonial roads, exposure to tsetse flies, and elevation as the active mission stations, to fall in the same contemporary administrative district as the active mission stations, but to have at least a five-kilometer buffer from any colonial mission station. I thank Jan Pierskalla for sharing the historical data for Tanganyika territory. For more details, see Pierskalla, Juan, and Montgomery 2017. In the (typical) case that more than one locality met the criteria for a match, the match was randomly selected from among the eligible communities.

[63] Enumerators visited the community one week in advance of surveying to map the community and sampled twenty households, contacting every nth household so that even sampling was achieved throughout the sub-locality. Within the contacted households, either an adult male or an adult female was randomly selected and invited to participate in an in-person household survey in one week's time. In a handful of cases where the selected community was too small to achieve a sample of twenty households, the nearest community was also included in the sampling frame for the household survey.

community were sampled. All communication and surveys were done in Swahili.

Each survey respondent was asked questions about one parent's childhood (mother or father), as well as their household during their own childhood and their current household. Questions included the selected parent's years of education, whether that parent attended a faith-based school, their family's wealth during their childhood, their parents' marriage, their religious attendance as a child, and their parents' level of political engagement. This method relies on respondents being knowledgeable about their parents' educational experiences and backgrounds instead of asking the older generation directly about these traits, given that a substantial portion of that generation is deceased.[64] The trade-off is that doing so limits my sample to respondents who have significant knowledge of their parents' life histories. Only 20 percent of respondents were not aware of whether their parents went to school or the type of school that they attended.

To assess the effects of attending church- versus state-run schools, I further narrow my sample to parents who attended school between 1925 and 1970, the period in which the state provided significant funding to both sets of schools. To distinguish the effect of church-run schools versus Christianity more generally, and due to the small number of Muslim students in church-run schools, I limit my sample in the analysis to Christian families.[65] The sample breaks down to 296 fathers and 239 mothers, with fewer mothers due to the higher proportion of mothers without any education and the slightly lower age of mothers on average. Among fathers, 21 percent attended Catholic school, 14 percent attended Protestant school, and 65 percent attended state school. Among mothers, 20 percent attended Catholic school, 21 percent attended Protestant school, and 59 percent attended state school. In this sample, two-thirds of the parents who attended Protestant schools attended Lutheran schools. Fully 93 percent of parents attended primary school only. Thus, the analysis parallels the Zambian one in that the estimated effect largely captures the difference between church-run versus state-run primary education.

---

[64] Given life expectancy averages, more than 75 percent of the older generation was expected to be deceased.

[65] I measure this through the religion in which the parents raised their children. Ideally, I would know the religion in which the parents were raised as children, but this was judged too difficult to assess.

THE EFFECTS OF TANZANIAN CATHOLIC- AND PROTESTANT-RUN CHURCH SCHOOLS

I assess the effects of Catholic and Protestant church schools by comparing parental attitudes among parents of the same sex, age, denomination (Catholic or Protestant), and ethnic group, but who attended different types of schools. Specifically, I run an OLS regression model that separately estimates the effects of a parent attending a Catholic or Protestant school as compared to a state school. The models also control for the parent's age, denomination, and ethnic group. I do not account for the length of time the parent attended school because, as the results in Table 8.6, model 1 demonstrate, this did not significantly vary across schools. On average, mothers who attended school did so for five years, and fathers who attended school did so for six years.

I begin by considering the effects of a parent attending church-run schools on the parent's years of education, the parent's household wealth in adulthood (a standardized index), and the parent's religiosity in adulthood (proxied by the frequency with which the respondent reported attending religious service as a child on a 1–7 scale, with 1 equal to never and 7 equal to more than once a week). I then consider the effects of church-run schools on the three social and political outcomes relevant for the quality of democracy: national identity, political engagement, and gender equality.

Because I cannot directly assess the parents' attitudes, I asked the respondent to report on parental or family behaviors closely related to these concepts. I measure national identification by whether the respondent reported speaking Swahili at home.[66] In this context, the use of Swahili in the home is a good measure of nationalism given President Nyerere's explicit embrace of Swahili as the national language and a key component of Tanzanian nationalism. In addition, the adoption of Swahili by Christian families may also capture a degree of interreligious tolerance, given the associations of the language with Arab influences and Muslim culture.[67] I measure parental political engagement by asking, "How active in politics would you say your parents were when you were a child?" with responses measured on a 1–4 scale, with 1 indicating not at all and 4 indicating very. I measure gender equality through whether

---

[66] This question measures whether the respondent speaks Swahili at home as an adult, not a child, but these two tendencies should be strongly correlated.
[67] Eastman 1971; Robinson 2024.

TABLE 8.6 *Effects of father's religious school attendance on socioeconomic, religious, linguistic, and political outcomes (Christians only)*

	Years of education (1–16) (1)	Household wealth (as adult, Std. index) (2)	Children's religious attendance (as children) (1–7) (3)	Children speak Swahili in adult home (0/1) (4)	Household political activity (as adult) (1–4) (5)	Polygynous marriage (0/1) (6)
Catholic school	0.20	0.09	−0.07	0.10	0.74**	0.01
	(0.46)	(0.05)	(0.18)	(0.09)	(0.23)	(0.08)
Protestant school	0.10	0.04	0.30	0.06	0.03	−0.09
	(0.45)	(0.07)	(0.24)	(0.09)	(0.28)	(0.09)
Catholic	0.38	0.01	0.08	−0.00	−0.07	−0.20*
	(0.54)	(0.06)	(0.22)	(0.10)	(0.28)	(0.09)
Lutheran	0.49	0.10+	0.02	−0.04	0.23	−0.20*
	(0.46)	(0.06)	(0.26)	(0.09)	(0.29)	(0.09)
Age (logged)	−4.55**	−0.05	−0.05	0.11	0.13	−0.22
	(0.95)	(0.12)	(0.53)	(0.23)	(0.62)	(0.20)
N	296	290	294	296	262	296
Ethnic group FEs	Yes	Yes	Yes	Yes	Yes	Yes

+ $p < 0.10$, * $p < 0.05$, ** $p < 0.01$; coefficients with robust standard errors in parentheses.

the parents' relationship was polygamous. In Tanzania, polygyny is legal and common, even among practicing Christians (one-third of Christian families in this sample).

Table 8.6 considers the effects of fathers attending Catholic- or Protestant-run schools as compared to state-run schools. Models 1 and 2 show that the type of school attended does not influence fathers' educational attainment or their household wealth. Models 3 and 4 show that neither Catholic nor Protestant education of fathers appears to influence the respondent's religious attendance during childhood or their national identification as adults, proxied by whether they speak Swahili at home. Model 5 shows that fathers who attended Catholic schools are reported to be part of more politically active couples as adults. Catholic school attendance is associated with a 0.74 increase on a 1–4 scale, which is statistically significant at the 99 percent confidence level. No similar effect is observed for fathers who attended Protestant schools. Last, model 6 shows that neither Catholic nor Protestant education affects fathers' polygyny.

Table 8.7 considers the effects of mothers attending Catholic- or Protestant-run schools as compared to state-run schools. Models 1 and 2 show that the type of school attended by mothers does not influence their educational attainment or their household's wealth. Model 3 considers the effects of mothers' Catholic or Protestant schooling on their children's childhood religious attendance, finding that only Protestant schooling significantly increases religious attendance (0.57 points on a seven-point scale, statistically significant at the 95 percent confidence level). Models 4–6 then consider the effects of Catholic and Protestant schools on political attitudes. Across these three models, mothers' attendance at Catholic schools makes little difference, but their attendance at Protestant schools has strong positive effects on the family's national identification, political engagement, and marriage patterns. Mothers who attended Protestant school increase national identification insofar as their children are more likely to speak Swahili at home (0.17 percentage points, statistically significant at the 90 percent confidence level); they themselves are part of more politically engaged households as adults (0.66 points on the four-point scale, statistically significant at 95 percent confidence level), and they themselves are less likely to be part of polygynous marriages (0.22 percentage points, statistically significant at the 95 percent confidence level).

One potential concern with the analysis in Tanzania is that distinct types of families may select into different types of schools. But the distinct patterns of effects across genders and Catholic versus Protestant

TABLE 8.7 *Effects of mother's religious school attendance on socioeconomic, religious, linguistic, and political outcomes (Christians only)*

	Years of education (1–16) (1)	Household wealth (as adult, Std. index) (2)	Children's religious attendance (as children) (1–7) (3)	Children speak Swahili in adult home (0/1) (4)	Household political activity (as adult) (1–4) (5)	Polygynous marriage (0/1) (6)
Catholic school	−0.02	0.01	−0.25	0.01	−0.33	−0.03
	(0.43)	(0.07)	(0.33)	(0.11)	(0.27)	(0.11)
Protestant school	0.13	0.06	0.57*	0.17+	0.66*	−0.22*
	(0.33)	(0.06)	(0.23)	(0.10)	(0.27)	(0.09)
Catholic	−0.54	−0.05	0.76*	0.10	0.31	−0.26*
	(0.44)	(0.09)	(0.30)	(0.13)	(0.37)	(0.12)
Lutheran	0.01	0.00	0.20	0.12	0.09	−0.19+
	(0.35)	(0.07)	(0.33)	(0.11)	(0.27)	(0.11)
Age (logged)	−6.34**	−0.18	−0.26	−0.25	−0.84	0.25
	(1.01)	(0.17)	(0.79)	(0.25)	(0.71)	(0.26)
N	239	236	236	239	215	238
Ethnic group FEs	Yes	Yes	Yes	Yes	Yes	Yes

+ $p < 0.10$, * $p < 0.05$, ** $p < 0.01$; coefficients with robust standard errors in parentheses.

schools suggest that these effects cannot be explained by simple selection stories. For example, if more religious families send their children to religious schools, both father's and mother's attendance at either Catholic or Protestant schools should be associated with increased family religiosity, but the results show only the mother's attendance at Protestant schools increases religiosity. The findings in Table 8.7 are also broadly consistent with the positive measured effects of proximity to Protestant versus Catholic missions on female empowerment in sub-Saharan Africa in studies of mission legacies.[68] But the evidence in Table 8.7 goes further, isolating the effects of church-run education from the effects of any education and showing that Protestant education may have particular benefits for women not only vis-à-vis Catholic education but also vis-à-vis state-run schools.

In the Tanzanian context, there is limited evidence that church-run schools have long-term effects on their students' attitudes that harm democracy. There is little difference between Catholic-run schools and state-run schools in the types of political attitudes they foster. It is Protestant – mostly Lutheran – schools that have distinctive effects on their female students, and the effects are in the direction of increasing national identification, political engagement, and commitment to women's rights. In this context, Protestant schools reinforce, rather than diminish, democratic citizenship.

* * * * *

That churches foster different values than state-run schools is both an implication of my theoretical framework and a potential trade-off that must be weighed against any benefits of church-run schools on church leaders' democratic activism. The fact that church-run schools foster distinct values is precisely what makes them so valuable to churches. But if these values are less compatible with democracy than those promoted by state schools, the direct consequences of their teachings must be weighed against any positive effects they have on leaders' democratic advocacy.

The evidence in this chapter shows that church-run schools do foster distinctive values, especially among female former students. Women who attend Catholic schools in Zambia and Protestant schools in Tanzania are more religious as adults than those who attend state-run schools, underscoring the benefits of church-run schools in securing future generations of church members. But in neither Zambia nor Tanzania do

---

[68] Nunn 2014; Pierskalla, Juan, and Montgomery 2017; Woodberry 2012.

church-run schools have generally pernicious effects on democratically relevant attitudes. In fact, in Tanzania, women's attendance at Protestant schools has positive effects on national identification, political engagement, and gender equality. In Zambia, the effects of Catholic education are more complex; they increase women's engagement but also reduce women's and men's commitment to women's rights. If there is a trade-off for democracy between church schools' effects on leaders' activism and former students' attitudes, it is in the domain of gender equality.

9

Reconsidering Churches, Education, and Democracy in the Contemporary World

In the early twenty-first century, Christian political movements often seem to herald authoritarianism rather than liberal democracy. In the United States, evangelical voters provide core support for the authoritarian white nationalist movement.[1] Radical right-wing parties in Europe simultaneously embrace religious nativism and attack liberal democracy.[2] And yet, church leaders are also among liberal democracy's strongest defenders in countries in sub-Saharan Africa. As this book shows, in contexts in which the historic investments of churches have high risk of state regulation, churches may depend on liberal democratic institutions to protect their activities from state control, incentivizing church leaders to engage in democratic activism.

How is it that Christianity is linked to both democratic and antidemocratic movements around the world? Does my theory travel beyond the cases of churches and educational systems in sub-Saharan Africa considered in this book? This chapter clarifies the types of religious politics my framework explains and how it can be applied beyond schools, beyond sub-Saharan Africa, and even, potentially, beyond churches. I conclude by discussing the implications of church activism for the liberal democratic values of tolerance and equality.

REVISITING THE ARGUMENT

With this book, I aim to bring churches into the comparative study of democratization, providing a theoretical framework for thinking about

[1] Gorski 2020.
[2] Minkenberg 2021.

the circumstances under which they are prominent advocates for liberal democracy. In doing so, my argument directly challenges earlier scholarship that emphasizes the antidemocratic consequences of political engagement by religious actors due to their dogmatic beliefs. I argue that religious actors' concern with protecting spaces for teaching their beliefs can provide motivation to speak out in defense of liberal democratic institutions.

But religious actors are not equally at risk when liberal democracy is weak. How they are affected depends on the modes in which they have invested for disseminating their worldviews. In this book, I show that churches in sub-Saharan Africa that have large investments in their educational empires have greater autocratic risk exposure than those that do not, and therefore they have greater incentives to speak out in support of liberal democracy. I also show that this incentive is mitigated when the churches are heavily dependent on state transfers for maintaining their educational empires.

In other words, churches are contingent democrats. Liberal democracy protects church education systems from overregulation by unchecked autocrats, and as a result, churches with investments in education have incentives to stand up for liberal democracy, especially when their schools are maintained through school fees rather than state transfers.

The book also demonstrates that churches choose to defend liberal democracy to maintain their policy influence in contexts in which wider coalitions can be mobilized in defense of it than can be mobilized in defense of church-run schools. Since the late twentieth and early twenty-first centuries, churches have been effective in mobilizing wide coalitions of political elites, citizens, and international actors in defense of liberal democratic institutions even in contexts in which civic space is shrinking. In contrast, the coalition willing to mobilize in support of changes to educational policy that would increase the influence of the church is often much narrower. Indeed, many Western donors have explicitly pressured governments in sub-Saharan Africa to reduce church influence over education in recent decades. As a result, churches have fewer levers for directly mobilizing against attempts to reduce their policy influence than they do for mobilizing in support of liberal democratic institutions. This book explains why liberal democracy is necessary to guarantee church policy influence.

INSTITUTIONAL VERSUS COALITIONAL GUARANTEES OF CHURCH INTERESTS

My research emphasizes the benefits of liberal democracy in enabling institutional guarantees of church educational interests; liberal democratic institutions create openings through which churches can influence policymaking in their favor. In contexts in which churches do not have credible partisan allies to represent their interests, liberal democracy is an attractive way to guarantee church policy interests. For historical reasons, churches generally lack strong partisan allies in sub-Saharan Africa, which makes relying on liberal democratic institutions a valuable strategy for protecting themselves from state regulation that goes against their educational interests.

But what about contexts in which churches have well-established coalitional partners? In settings where churches have aligned with political parties that they expect will defend their educational interests, their attitudes toward liberal democracy will be contingent on whether liberal democratic institutions maximize or minimize the power of their preferred party. These alliances explain why the Catholic Church was among the primary opponents of liberal democracy in nineteenth-century Europe and Latin America, where liberal democratic institutions promised to increase the power of anticlerical liberal politicians.[3] It also explains the limited concern about liberal democratic institutions among evangelical voters in the United States, who have aligned with the Republican Party to advance their policy interests since the 1970s.[4]

In contexts in which the party system presents churches with potential coalition partners, is it always a better option for churches to throw their support behind these parties, especially at the expense of liberal democratic institutions? This is an important question for future research, but there are reasons to think that even when the coalitional option is available, it may not always be strictly preferable. As Stathis Kalyvas emphasizes, even in contexts in which political parties are founded to represent religious interests, their need to maximize votes from the electorate makes them inherently unreliable in representing the interests of religious leaders.[5] And as Anna Grzymala-Busse shows, churches can lose moral legitimacy when they ally themselves with specific political parties, and so they prefer less visible institutional channels of exerting political influence where available. Importantly, although Grzymala-Busse tends to emphasize the backroom character of churches' direct institutional access in the democratic advanced economies that she studies, many of

---

[3] For a nuanced discussion of church positions vis-à-vis liberal politics in nineteenth-century Europe, see Gould 1999. On the Latin American cases, see Gill 1998.
[4] Balmer 2007; Grzymala-Busse 2015; Putnam and Campbell 2012.
[5] Kalyvas 1996.

the channels she mentions, including legislative consultation and parliamentary commissions, do not exist in countries that do not have some degree of checks on the power of the ruler. Indeed, she notes that churches experienced an increase in influence following democratization in her two postcommunist cases.[6] This finding suggests that churches that want to maintain institutional access have an interest in protecting liberal democratic institutions to ensure that power does not become too centralized in the presidency.

BREADTH OF SUPPORT FOR LIBERAL DEMOCRACY VERSUS CHURCH POLICY INTERESTS

Importantly, this book emphasizes that churches support liberal democratic institutions to secure their policy interests. The value of this strategy hinges on churches expecting some probability of success in advancing liberal democratic institutions, even in increasingly autocratic contexts. Historically, churches have at times mobilized wide coalitions, including political elites, citizens, and international actors, in support of liberal democratic institutions. But key international actors have been generally much less supportive of church educational interests in the early twenty-first century, and so churches depend on the domestic policy openings provided by liberal democratic institutions to secure those interests. The breadth of international and domestic support that can be mobilized for liberal democratic institutions versus specific church policy interests is therefore a scope condition of my predictions.

The breadth of the coalitions that churches can mobilize in support of liberal democracy versus their policy interests is likely to vary cross-nationally and over time. For example, Thad Dunning shows that Western donors only became willing to condition their aid based on the quality of democratic institutions in Africa after the Soviet threat declined in the late 1980s.[7] Christopher Anderson, Damien Bol, and Aurelia Ananda draw on World Values Survey data from 1994 to 2020 to demonstrate popular support for democracy around the world, with particularly high levels of support for it in sub-Saharan Africa.[8] Their research suggests that for the past forty years, churches in sub-Saharan Africa have been

---

[6] Grzymala-Busse 2015.
[7] Dunning 2004.
[8] Anderson, Bol, and Ananda 2021.

operating in a context in which they can mobilize particularly wide coalitions in support of liberal democratic institutions.

Future research should consider how shifts in the international environment and in domestic public opinion alter church tactics in advocating for liberal democratic institutions. The theoretical framework I outline suggests that churches should become less vocal in advocating for liberal democracy in contexts in which they have low expectation of mobilizing international and domestic support for their cause. Conversely, in contexts in which religious actors have significant international support for their direct policy interests and they can reliably mobilize citizens behind those interests, they may not need to defend liberal democratic institutions to maintain policy influence.

CHURCH INTERESTS VERSUS POLITICIZED CHRISTIAN IDENTITIES

I focus on the circumstances under which church leaders defend liberal democracy to secure their own policy influence and emphasize liberal democratic institutions as an alternative to coalitional partnerships with religious parties as a way to guarantee their interests. But the politicization of religion is not always the result of coalitional partnerships pursued by church leaders and is not always in the best interest of their churches. There is a difference between political leaders embracing religious rhetoric as a means of shoring up their own political support and church leaders embracing political parties as a means of advancing their interests.

In particular, the rise of radical right-wing parties in Europe espousing Christian nationalist ideologies in the last few decades cannot be primarily understood as a consequence of church strategy. Instead, it is the result of populist leaders legitimizing themselves by claiming to represent "the people," defined in opposition to social out-groups and elites.[9] In particular, radical-right parties in Europe have adopted Islamophobic stances, seeking to define "the people" according to Christian culture more than Christian faith.[10] The linkage of Christianity and antiliberal democratic parties in Europe is a result of politicians' strategy of othering Islamic immigrants more than it is a result of church leaders' seeking political influence by linking themselves to antidemocratic political forces.

---

[9] Mudde 2017.
[10] Minkenberg 2021, 100. See Kulska 2023 on Orban's invention of a Catholic identity in Hungary.

The reaction of church leadership to Christian nationalist parties that have embraced antidemocratic positions is another important topic for future research. On the one hand, churches could conceivably try to attach themselves to these new coalitional partners as a means of advancing their policy interests. On the other hand, radical-right political parties are likely to be unreliable advocates of church interests, and so church leaders may hesitate to embrace them, even if they have widespread popularity among church followers. Joanna Kulska's comparison of Catholic bishops' reactions to Christian nationalism in Hungary and Poland under Viktor Orbán and Jaroslaw Kaczynski, respectively, suggests both reactions are possible.[11] The Catholic bishops in Hungary have generally accepted the privileges offered to the Church by Orbán without expressing opposition to democratic backsliding, while the Catholic bishops in Poland eventually issued multiple public warnings about Kaczynski's attacks on the judiciary, the press, and the country's liberal democratic institutions, and sought to distance themselves from his right-wing Christian nationalist movement.[12] The reasons for these divergent choices require more detailed examination, but it is noteworthy that in Poland, the Catholic Church raises a higher proportion of its finances from congregations than it does in Hungary.[13] Consistent with my theoretical framework, state financing correlates with depressed democratic activism.

BEYOND EDUCATION

This book focuses on education as the primary example of a church investment that is highly subject to the state's regulatory power. In the contemporary world, states have many regulatory tools for increasing their control of church-run schools and multiple motivations for doing so insofar as their economic, social, and political goals for education are distinct from the goals of churches. The stakes of state versus church control would seem particularly important in this arena due to the importance of schools in disseminating ideas. As an empirical matter, the education sector is the key point of interface between church and state in many settings, including contemporary sub-Saharan Africa. In emphasizing the political implications of church school systems, my research helps

---

[11] Kulska 2023.
[12] Meyer, Resende, and Hennig 2021.
[13] See Enyedi and O'Mahony 2004 for details on the Catholic Church in Hungary. On the Catholic Church in Poland, see *Radio Poland*, "Compromise Reached over Poland's Church Funding," 2013.

to renew focus on the political consequences of education, which are "regrettably understudied in comparative politics."[14]

Nevertheless, education is not the only church investment over which states have both regulatory power and distinct motivations. The strongest parallel is between church-run education and church-run health care provision. Church and state leaders have frequently clashed over the regulation of church-operated hospitals in sub-Saharan Africa and beyond due to differences in beliefs about standards of care, including hot-button moral issues like abortion, but also issues of pastoral care. Indeed, the evidence in Chapter 4 suggests that church hospitals may create similar incentives for church leaders to advocate for liberal democracy.

The state may also want to expropriate other church assets, including properties and income-generating businesses. Future research should consider whether these investments incentivize liberal democratic activism. But these activities are sources of church income more than they are modes of disseminating church views, and as a result, churches may trade them off against other resources and benefits more easily than they give up control of their education and health care systems. In this way, business investments would be expected to generate lower democratic activism than investments in core activities for disseminating beliefs.

In emphasizing the autocratic risk exposure created by church-run education, this book offers a new lens for studying nonstate service provision.[15] The existing literature considers the implications of nonstate service provision for how citizens evaluate different political parties, candidates, and the government more generally.[16] I focus instead on how service provision by nonstate actors affects their regime preferences: churches with educational investments care more about political institutions because their activities are more exposed to autocratic risk.[17]

BEYOND SUB-SAHARAN AFRICA

The geographic focus of this book is sub-Saharan Africa, where numerous churches have advocated for liberal democracy. The relationship between autocratic risk and democratic advocacy is likely to be particularly

---

[14] Gift and Wibbels 2014. For notable exceptions, see Bleck 2015; Darden and Grzymala-Busse 2006; King 2013; and Paglayan 2021.
[15] See Cammett and MacLean 2011; MacLean and Cammett 2014.
[16] Brass 2016; MacLean 2010; Thachil 2014.
[17] On the relationship between patterns of service provision by nonstate actors and their political goals, see also Cammett 2014.

important on this continent insofar as there are no coalitional options. Due to historical legacies, I have been able to neatly capture church autocratic risk exposure and fiscal dependence on the state by homing in on the church education sector.

A global study would require alternative empirical measures of autocratic risk exposure and dependence on state subsidies. Globally, churches engage in a wide array of activities that states can regulate, including providing formal education, running medical services, forming unions, and organizing cooperatives. In addition, outside sub-Saharan Africa, churches receive more diverse financing from the state, including transfers for general activities. This diversity complicates measurement of the book's key theoretical concepts. Nevertheless, with careful operationalization, my theoretical framework could be applied beyond sub-Saharan Africa.

For example, consider the degree of activism by the Catholic Church for democracy during periods of military dictatorship in the late twentieth century in Latin America's Southern Cone, as studied by Benjamin Goldfrank and Nick Rowell.[18] The Church in Chile is well-known for its high levels of antiauthoritarian activism against Pinochet. In Uruguay, the Church engaged in consistent denunciation of the military's violence toward its political opponents. In contrast, the Catholic Church in Brazil was late in collectively criticizing the military dictatorship's abuse of power, even though individual church leaders spoke out early on. And in Argentina, the Church did not speak out at all against the military junta.

This variation is well-explained by the book's theoretical framework. In all four countries, the Catholic Church is engaged in considerable provision of social services and education (although the size of the Catholic school system in Brazil lags behind the other three countries on a per capita basis, suggesting somewhat lower autocratic risk exposure).[19] In addition, the Argentinian and Brazilian churches receive much higher state subsidies to support social services and, as a result of the quasi-reestablishment of the Church in Argentina in the 1930s, to support dioceses' activities in Argentina as well.[20] As in sub-Saharan Africa, churches in Latin America with higher autocratic risk exposure and lower reliance on state subsidies are most likely to defend democratic institutions.

Similarly, consider a comparison of the Philippines and Timor-Leste (East Timor), the only two majority Christian countries in East Asia.

---

[18] Goldfrank and Rowell 2012.
[19] Data from Catholic Church, *Annuarium Statisticum Ecclesiae*, 1973.
[20] Goldfrank and Rowell 2012, 34.

The majority of each country's population is Catholic, and there are large networks of private Catholic schools in each, creating autocratic risk exposure with low fiscal dependence on the state.[21] Catholic institutions in both countries suffered under autocratic rule in the late twentieth century – the Philippines was under military dictatorship and East Timor was under Indonesian occupation – including attacks on schools and church personnel. Consistent with expectations, the Catholic bishops played important roles in opposing autocratic rule during this period, with Filipino Cardinal Jaime Sin credited with starting the People's Power Revolution that overthrew Ferdinand Marcos' dictatorship and East Timorese Bishop Carlos Belo winning the Nobel Peace Prize for his role in denouncing the Indonesian occupation.[22]

But there have been dramatic differences in the levels of church activism in defense of liberal democracy in the twenty-first century in these two countries. In particular, following East Timor's independence in 2002 and the election of President Jose Ramos-Horta in 2007, the Catholic Church became a major recipient of funding from the state and correspondingly has become less critical of the government.[23] In contrast, in the Philippines, the Catholic Church has continued its public campaign in defense of liberal democratic checks on the presidency and the need to respect civil liberties, especially during President Rodrigo Duterte's war on drugs.[24] Consistent with my theoretical framework, both churches still have high levels of autocratic risk, but in East Timor, the incentive to speak out in defense of liberal democracy has been tempered by increased dependence on state subsidies.

These examples suggest my framework can be employed beyond sub-Saharan Africa. With contextual knowledge of the modes of disseminating church views, church financing, and the state's regulatory power, the theory can potentially be widely applied.

BEYOND CHURCHES

To reiterate, the focus of this book is on churches' autocratic risk exposure and how it incentivizes them to engage in activism for liberal

---

[21] Gutiérrez 2007.
[22] Bautista 2020.
[23] Guterres 2008. McGregor, Skeaff, and Bevan 2012 provide multiple quotes suggesting citizens in East Timor attribute the Catholic Church's relative silence to its increased financial support from the state.
[24] Brooke et al. 2023; Thompson 2016.

democracy. An important scope condition is that the theory applies to well-established churches that have formal leadership institutions beyond the individual who founded the church. In this way, the argument applies to Catholic, mainline Protestant, and older Pentecostal churches, but not to many new, neo-Pentecostal churches. Would the argument also extend to other religious groups or even to other social institutions, including ethnic groups?

Certainly, Christian churches are not the only religious groups in sub-Saharan Africa with large investments in education. Islamic education is also common in many countries on the continent, and states have also made efforts to regulate it. Ahmadiyyah communities established schools incorporating religious and secular subjects in Ghana and Sierra Leone in the 1920s and 1930s in partnership with the British colonial administration. Since the 1980s, the Ghanaian and Malian governments have made efforts to formalize relationships with Islamic schools, including paying the salaries of teachers instructing secular subjects in these schools in Ghana.[25] Further research is needed on this important but understudied subject. Pioneering interviews with Islamic educationalists suggest they share the concerns of church leaders about state overregulation of their schools.[26] Whether these concerns generate advocacy for liberal democratic checks on state power is not clear, as this type of activism would seem less likely in highly decentralized religious communities, including most Muslim communities in sub-Saharan Africa.

Additionally, ethnolinguistic groups may also have an incentive to defend liberal democratic checks on the power of rulers in their efforts to defend educational investments from state control. It is noteworthy that, in contrast to recent trends in surrounding regions, far-right populist parties have not gained a foothold in Belgium's French-speaking minority region.[27] More generally, Jan Rovny shows that mobilized ethnolinguistic minorities increase support for constitutional liberals in Eastern Europe.[28] Thus, church groups may not be the only ones with an incentive to check the regulatory power of the state. Other groups that have interests affected by state control of schools may also have incentives to protect liberal democratic institutions.

---

[25] Bleck 2015; Owusu-Ansah, Iddrisu, and Sey 2013.
[26] Owusu-Ansah, Iddrisu, and Sey 2013.
[27] Jonge 2021.
[28] Rovny 2023.

CHURCH SCHOOLS AND DEMOCRATIC SOCIETY

My work demonstrates how variation in church school systems provides different incentives for church leaders to speak out in defense of liberal democracy. Although liberal democratic institutions can be criticized on numerous grounds, I strongly believe they provide a better form of government than autocracy. As a result, insofar as church activism in support of democratic institutions is sometimes successful, I view it as a normatively good thing.

If church schools can have an indirect positive effect on liberal democracy via the activism of church leaders, how is that weighed against the values they impart on their students? Specifically, are these values in accord with tolerance and equality? In Chapter 8, I explicitly consider the legacy of church-run schools on the attitudes of former students in Zambia and Tanzania. The results suggest that church-run schools did not promote ethnic intolerance. Former students were equally or more likely to identify with the nation and to speak the national language as compared to students who attended fully state-run schools. Church-run schools also fostered equally or more politically engaged citizens. Interestingly, there was one significant exception to the general pattern of null or benign effects: Catholic schools in Zambia fostered more conservative gender attitudes among former students. Thus, to the extent that church-run schools teach values that push against democratic values, it is in the domain of gender. This is an important limitation, especially insofar as the rights of LGBTQ citizens are poorly protected and politically charged in many countries on the continent.[29]

In addition to the implications of church-run schools for student attitudes, these school systems may have implications for educational inequality. Even in countries where students cannot be denied admission to church-run schools based on their religion and where religious freedom is formally tolerated in these schools, the emphasis that church-run schools place on adherence to their own religious practices can create barriers and discomfort for students from different faiths.[30] This is clearly a major obstacle to interreligious equality. Returning to the book's central claim, I demonstrate that churches are most likely to speak out in defense of democratic institutions when they run schools that are funded primarily by parents. These schools are also likely to

---

[29] Grossman 2015.
[30] Platas 2014; Platas 2023.

create more socioeconomic inequality insofar as poorer students cannot afford to attend them. Liberal democratic institutions and equality of citizens are both important dimensions of democracy, and church-run educational systems may have opposing effects on each dimension.

On a more optimistic note, it is important to recognize that liberal democratic institutions have value in and of themselves. Churches that engage in activism for liberal democracy may not be advocates for all disadvantaged groups in society, but the liberal democratic institutions for which they do advocate have the potential to be used by diverse groups seeking protection from autocratic abuses. When churches seek institutional guarantees via liberal democratic institutions, it opens opportunities for other groups to find proponents who can protect their rights through these same institutions.

Appendices

APPENDIX A: LIST OF INTERVIEWS

The open-ended interviews were conducted in English by the author unless otherwise indicated, with two exceptions: the interviews with Zambian school attendees in the 1970s were conducted by a female Zambian research assistant in English and local Zambian languages, and the interviews with Tanzanian residents in former mission station communities were conducted with translation by a female Tanzanian research assistant in Swahili. All interviews were conducted in person unless the interview explicitly indicates that it was by a videoconferencing platform below. The interviews were open-ended and conversational, with questions tailored to each respondent based on their expertise and experience as uncovered by my background research on each respondent.

TABLE A.1 *List of interviews*

	List of interviews
Interviews with religious leaders in Zambia	Interview with Catholic educationalist, Zoom, June 2021
	Interview with Catholic educationalist, Zoom, June 2021
	Interview with Catholic religious leader, Zoom, April 2022
	Interview with Anglican religious leader, Zoom, April 2022
	Interview with Catholic religious leader, April 2022

(*continued*)

TABLE A.1 *(continued)*

	List of interviews
Interviews with former Catholic school attendees in Zambia	Interview with female former student, November 2021 Interview with male former student, November 2021 Interview with female former student, November 2021 Interview with female former student, November 2021 Interview with female former student, December 2021 Interview with female former student, December 2021 Interview with female former student, December 2021 Interview with female former student, December 2021 Interview with female former student, December 2021 Interview with male former student, December 2021 Interview with female former student, February 2022 Interview with female former student, February 2022 Interview with female former student, February 2022 Interview with female former student, February 2022 Interview with female former student, February 2022 Interview with female former student, March 2022 Interview with female former student, March 2022 Interview with male former student, April 2022 Interview with female former student, April 2022
Interviews with religious leaders in Ghana	Interview with Methodist educationalist, Zoom, May 2021 Interview with Methodist religious leader, Zoom, July 2021 Interview with Catholic religious leader, Zoom, August 2021 Interview with Catholic religious leader, Zoom, August 2021 Interview with Pentecostal religious leader, Zoom, September 2021 Interview with Pentecostal religious leader, Zoom, September 2021
Interviews with other key informants on Ghana	Interview with Ghanaian scholar expert on cultural education, Zoom, June 2021 Interview with Ghanaian scholar; expert on Islam, Zoom, June 2021 Interview with Ghanaian scholar; expert on Islamic education in Ghana, Zoom, August 2021 Interview with Ghanaian activist for Islamic education, Zoom, August 2021
Interviews with religious leaders in Tanzania	Interview with Lutheran religious leader, March 2017. Interview with Anglican religious leader, March 2017 Interview with Anglican hospital administrator, March 2017 Interview with Lutheran religious leader, March 2017. Interview with leader of Christian advocacy group, May 2018 Interview with coordinator of religious advocacy group, May 2018 Interview with leader of Christian social service provision group, May 2018

TABLE A.I (*continued*)

	List of interviews
	Interview with officer at Muslim advocacy group, May 2018
	Interview with leader of international church group, May 2018
	Interview with leader of international church group, May 2018
	Interview with officer of international church group, May 2018
	Interview with officer of Lutheran church, May 2018
	Interview with former officer of Lutheran church, May 2018
	Interview with officer of Lutheran church, May 2018
	Interview with former officer of Lutheran church, May 2018
	Interview with Anglican religious leader, May 2018
	Interview with Catholic religious leader, May 2018
	Interview with Catholic religious leader, March 2019
	Interview with Catholic religious leader, March 2019
	Interview with Lutheran religious leader, March 2019
	Interview with Lutheran religious leader, March 2019
	Interview with Lutheran religious leader, March 2019
	Interview with Catholic religious leader, March 2019
	Interview with Catholic religious leader, March 2019
	Interview with Lutheran religious leader, March 2019
	Interview with Lutheran religious leader, March 2019
	Interview with Lutheran religious leader, March 2019
	Interview with Lutheran religious leader, March 2019
	Interview with Lutheran religious leader, March 2019
	Interview with Catholic religious leader, March 2019
	Interview with leader of international church group, Skype, April 2019
Interviews with residents in former mission station communities in Tanzania	Interview with former village chairperson, March 2017
	Interview with elder, March 2017
	Interview with mission station caretaker, March 2017
	Interview with subdivision chairman, March 2017
	Interview with former village chairman, March 2017
	Interview with village chairperson, March 2017
	Interview with elder, March 2017
	Interview with grandson of first African pastor at Lutheran mission, May 2018
Interviews with other key informants in Tanzania	Interview with Tanzanian scholar; expert on social services, March 2017
	Interview with international donor, May 2018
	Interview with Tanzanian scholar; expert on religion, May 2018
	Interview with Tanzanian scholar; expert on religion, March 2019

APPENDIX B: DATA SETS

TABLE B.1 *Summary statistics for country-level data set on church and union democratic activism (1988–1998 and 2009–2018)*

Variable	Definition	Source	Mean	SD	Min	Max
Church democratic activism, 1988–1998	Whether the country had any significantly sized church (>5 percent of population) engage in activism in support of liberal democratic institutions in the decade.	Bratton and van de Walle 1992, Toft, Philpott, and Shah 2011.	0.586	0.501	0	1
Union democratic activism, 1988–1998	Whether the country had any trade unions engage in activism in support of liberal democratic institutions in the decade.	Bratton and van de Walle 1992, Haggard and Kaufman 2017.	0.552	0.506	0	1
Church democratic activism, 2009–2018	Whether the country had any significantly sized church (>5 percent of population) or church council engage in activism in support of liberal democratic institutions in the decade.	*Factiva News Archive* (2009–2018), supplemented by country-specific sources.	0.706	0.462	0	1
Union democratic activism, 2009–2018	Whether the country had any trade union federation associated with the International Trade Union Confederation engage in activism in support of liberal democratic institutions in the decade.	*Factiva News Archive* (2009–2018), supplemented by country-specific sources.	0.500	0.508	0	1
Church elections activism	Whether the country had any significantly sized church engage in activism in support of free and fair elections in the decade.	*Factiva News Archive* (2009–2018), supplemented by country-specific sources.	0.588	0.500	0	1

Church institutional checks activism	Whether the country had any significantly sized church engage in activism in support of institutional checks on the executive ruler in the decade.	*Factiva News Archive* (2009–2018), supplemented by country-specific sources.	0.324	0.475	0	1
Church rights of opposition activism	Whether the country had any significantly sized church engage in activism in support of the civil rights of opponents of the executive in the decade.	*Factiva News Archive* (2009–2018), supplemented by country-specific sources.	0.441	0.504	0	1

Note: Countries included in data set are: Angola, Benin, Botswana, Burkina Faso, Burundi, Cameroon, the Central African Republic, Chad, Cote D'Ivoire, the Democratic Republic of the Congo, Ethiopia, Equatorial Guinea, Eritrea, Gabon, Ghana, Guinea-Bissau, Kenya, Lesotho, Liberia, Madagascar, Malawi, Mozambique, Namibia, Nigeria, the Republic of the Congo, Rwanda, Senegal, South Africa, South Sudan, Tanzania, Togo, Uganda, Zambia, and Zimbabwe.

TABLE B.2 *Summary statistics for church-level democratic activism data set (2009–2018)*

Variable	Definition	Source	Mean	SD	Min	Max
Democratic activism	Degree to which church engages in activism in support of liberal democratic institutions in a particular year (0 = no activism, 1 = activism for aspect of liberal democracy without using language of democratic legitimacy, 2 = activism for aspect of liberal democracy using the language of democratic legitimacy).	*Factiva News Archive* (2009–2018), supplemented by country-specific sources.	0.109	0.367	0	2
Church education provision	Measure approximates the logged proportion of students attending church-affiliated primary schools plus the logged proportion of students attending church-affiliated secondary schools in 2008. For each level of education, 0 = None (less than 1 percent of all students), 1 = A little (1–2.5 percent of all students), 2 = Some (2.5–7.5 percent of all students), 3 = Significant (7.5–20 percent of all students), and 4 = A lot (more than 20 percent of all students), with these cutoffs designated to be approximately equal on the log scale. The variable has been rescaled to fall between 0 and 1 for comparability with other measures.	Data on Catholic enrollments is a three-year average (2007–2009) from Annuarium Statisticum Ecclesiae. Data on Protestant enrollments is from country-specific sources and often fails to provide specific numbers, necessitating a noncontinuous approach to coding this data. Data on total number of primary and secondary school students in the country is from the World Bank's Education Statistics (SE.PRM.ENRL; SE.SEC.ENRL).	0.357	0.335	0	1

State financing church education	Measure captures the amount of state funding that a church receives for its primary and secondary education combined. The amount of state funding is estimated by multiplying the five-point church education provision measure with a four-point measure of state funding for church schools, where 0 = no state transfers, 1 = some state transfers (less than 50 percent of operating expenses), 2 = significant state transfers (more than 50 percent of operating expenses, but also charge fees) and 3 = mainly state transfer (mainly dependent on state funds, do not charge fees). The amount of funding provided at the primary and secondary level are summed in the measure. The variable has been rescaled to fall between 0 and 1 for comparability with other measures.	Country-specific sources.	0.221	0.280	0	1
Catholic	Whether the church is Catholic.	Based on denomination reported in the World Christian Database.	0.396	0.489	0	1
Mainline Protestant	Whether the church belongs to a Mainline Protestant denomination (versus Pentecostal Protestant or Independent church)	Based on denomination reported in the World Christian Database.	0.321	0.467	0	1
Co-denominational president (Narrow)	Whether the country's president belongs to the church in a given year.	Country-specific sources.	0.243	0.429	0	1
Co-denominational president (Wide)	Whether the country's president belongs to the same denominational family as the church in a given year.	Country-specific sources.	0.303	0.460	0	1

(continued)

TABLE B.2 (*continued*)

Variable	Definition	Source	Mean	SD	Min	Max
Co-ethnic president	Whether the country's president belongs to the same ethnic group as the churches' plurality group.	Afrobarometer survey data (mainly 7th round) and Kristen Harkness' Ethnic Stacking Data Set.	0.423	0.494	0	1
Economic advantage (church members)	Three-point scale measuring whether the percentage of church members who graduated from secondary school is 15 percent higher than (+1), within +/−15 percent of (0), or 15 percent lower (−1) than the percentage of citizens in the country who graduated.	Afrobarometer survey data (mainly 7th round, with other rounds used if country was excluded from the 7th round sample).	0.157	0.697	−1	1
Civil society capacity	The strength and overall viability of the country's civil society sector, averaging across 7 dimensions: the legal environment, organizational capacity, financial viability, advocacy, service provision, infrastructure, and public image of the sector. Each dimension ranges from 1 to 7, with 1 indicating the strongest score.	FHI 360's Civil Society Organization Sustainability Index.	4.717	0.577	3.60	5.80
Size church	Proportion of the country's population belonging to the church in 2015.	World Christian Database.	0.188	0.160	0.050	0.710
Size church squared	Squared proportion of the country's population belonging to the church in 2015.	World Christian Database.	0.061	0.102	0.003	0.504
Activist Catholic missionaries	Whether there were Jesuit or Capuchian mission stations – both Catholic orders known for their social activism – operating in the 1920s within the country's present-day boundaries.	Bernard Arens' (1925) *Manuel Des Missions Catholiques*.	0.050	0.218	0	1
Church bank or insurance company	Whether the church ran a bank or insurance company between 2009 and 2018.	Country-specific sources.	0.174	0.379	0	1

Church hospital provision	Measure captures the proportion of hospitals run by the church between 2009 and 2018, with 0 = None, 1 = A little (1–2.5 percent of all hospitals), 2 = Some (2.5–7.5 percent of all hospitals), 3 = Significant (7.5–20 percent of all hospitals), and 4 = A lot (more than 20 percent of all hospitals). The variable has been rescaled to fall between 0 and 1 for comparability with other measures.	Annuarium Statisticum Ecclesiae, WHO Health Infrastructure Data (2010, 2013), and country-specific sources.	0.441	0.361	0	1
Democratic activism (1988–1998)	Whether the church engaged in minor (1) or major (2) democratic activism between 1988 and 1998.	Bratton and van de Walle 1992; Toft, Philpott, and Shah 2011; country-specific sources.	0.587	0.819	0	2
Church education provision independence	Measure approximates the logged proportion of students attending church-affiliated primary schools plus the logged proportion of students attending church-affiliated secondary schools in the first year after the country's independence for which data is available (or first year after 1950 for Liberia and South Africa). For each level of education, 0 = None (less than 1 percent of all students), 1 = A little (1–2.5 percent of all students), 2 = Some (2.5–7.5 percent of all students), 3 = Significant (7.5–20 percent of all students), and 4 = A lot (more than 20 percent of all students), with these cutoffs designated to be approximately equal on the log scale. The variable has been rescaled to fall between 0 and 1 for comparability with other measures.	Annuarium Statisticum Ecclesiae (1973), World Christian Encyclopedia (1982), and country-specific sources.	0.441	0.368	0	1
Autocratic exposure index independence	Average of Church Education Provision Independence and Church Hospital Provision 1970, with the latter measured on the same scale as Church Hospital Provision using data from the 1970s.	Annuarium Statisticum Ecclesiae (1973), World Christian Encyclopedia (1982), and country-specific sources.	0.329	0.265	0	0.938

(continued)

TABLE B.2 (*continued*)

Variable	Definition	Source	Mean	SD	Min	Max
Size church 1970	Proportion of the country's population belonging to the church in 1970.	World Christian Database.	0.134	0.157	0	0.756
Muslim population 2015	Proportion of the country's population that was Muslim in 2015.	World Christian Database.	0.132	0.181	0	0.910
Former British colony	Dichotomous variable indicating whether the country was mainly colonized by the British.	Historical sources.	0.440	0.497	0	1

Note: Churches included in data set are: Assemblies of God in Angola, Catholic Church in Angola, Catholic Church in Benin, Eglise du Christianisme Celeste du Benin, Catholic Church in Botswana, Assemblies of God in Burkina Faso, Catholic Church in Burkina Faso, Anglican Church in Burundi, Catholic Church in Burundi, La Communauté des Eglises de Pentecôte du Burundi, Catholic Church in Cameroon, Eglise Evangélique du Cameroon, Catholic Church in the Central African Republic, Eglise Evangélique des Frères, Catholic Church in Chad, Catholic Church in Cote D'Ivoire, Eglise Evangelique des Assemblées de Dieu en Côte d'Ivoire, Catholic Church in the Democratic Republic of the Congo, Church of Christ on Earth thru Prophet Simon Kimbangu in the Democratic Republic of the Congo, Église du Christ au Congo, Catholic Church in Equatorial Guinea, Eritrean Orthodox Tewahedo Church, Ethiopian Orthodox Church, Evangelical Church Mekane Yesus in Ethiopia, World of Life Evangelical Church in Ethiopia, Catholic Church in Gabon, Eglise Evangélique de Gabon, Eglise de Banzine (Bwiti) in Gabon, Assemblies of God in Ghana, Catholic Church in Ghana, Church of the Pentecost in Ghana, Catholic Church in Guinea-Bissau, Africa Inland Church in Kenya, Anglican Church of Kenya, Catholic Church in Kenya, Anglican Church in Lesotho, Catholic Church in Lesotho, Lesotho Evangelical Church, Catholic Church in Liberia, Catholic Church in Madagascar, Eglise Luthérienne Malgache (Lutheran) in Madagascar, Eglise du Jésus-Christ à Madagascar, Assemblies of God in Malawi, Catholic Church in Malawi, Church of Central Africa Presbyterian in Malawi, Catholic Church in Mozambique, Catholic Church in Namibia, Evangelical Lutheran Church in Namibia (Lutheran), Evangelical Lutheran Church in the Republic of Namibia (Lutheran), Anglican Church in Nigeria, Catholic Church in Nigeria, Catholic Church in the Republic of Congo, Eglise Evangelique du Congo, Anglican Church in Rwanda, Catholic Church in Rwanda, Seventh Day Adventist Church in Rwanda, Catholic Church in Senegal, Anglican Church in South Africa, Catholic Church in South Africa, Zion Christian Church South Africa, Anglican Church in South Sudan, Catholic Church in South Sudan, Presbyterian Church of the Sudan in South Sudan, Anglican Church in Tanzania, Catholic Church in Tanzania, Evangelical Lutheran Church in Tanzania (Lutheran), Assemblies of God in Togo, Catholic Church in Togo, Eglise Evangelique du Togo, Anglican Church of Uganda, Catholic Church in Uganda, Catholic Church in Zambia, New Apostolic Church in Zambia, Seventh Day Adventist Church in Zambia, United Church of Zambia, African Apostolic Church of Johan Maranke in Zimbabwe, Assemblies of God in Zimbabwe, Catholic Church in Zimbabwe, Seventh Day Adventist Church in Zimbabwe, Zion Apostolic Churches in Zimbabwe, and Zion Christian Church Zimbabwe.

TABLE B.3 *Summary statistics for Catholic democratic activism data set (1980–2018)*

Variable	Definition	Source	Mean	SD	Min	Max
Critical pastoral letter	Whether or not the country's episcopal conference issued any pastoral letters in a given year that offered strong criticism of how the country's political institutions allocate power, the country's elections, and/or the rights of the political opposition and civil society, including the media.	Catholic pastoral letters; media coverage of Catholic pastoral letters.	0.105	0.306	0	1
Degree of criticism	The degree of criticism of how the country's political institutions allocate power, elections in the country, and/or the rights of the political opposition and civil society, including the media, in any pastoral letters issued by the country's episcopal conference in a given year, with 0 = none, 1 = mild, and 2 = strong.	Catholic pastoral letters; media coverage of Catholic pastoral letters.	0.256	0.633	0	2
Any pastoral letter	Whether or not the country's episcopal conference issued any pastoral letters in a given year.	Catholic pastoral letters; media coverage of Catholic pastoral letters.	0.424	0.495	0	1
Political pastoral letter	Whether or not the country's episcopal conference issued any pastoral letters that discussed the country's political institutions in a given year.	Catholic pastoral letters; media coverage of Catholic pastoral letters.	0.229	0.420	0	1
Public	Whether country classified Catholic primary schools as public schools prior to fee-removal policy.	Country-specific sources.	0.531	0.500	0	1

(continued)

TABLE B.3 (*continued*)

Variable	Definition	Source	Mean	SD	Min	Max
Fee removal	Whether country had policy of eliminating primary school fees in given year.	Harding and Stasavage 2014; country-specific sources.	0.452	0.498	0	1
Proportion of primary school students in Catholic schools	Proportion of primary school students attending Catholic schools in a given year.	Data on Catholic school enrollments from Annuarium Statisticum Ecclesiae. Data on total number of primary and secondary school students in the country is from the World Bank's Education Statistics (SE.PRM.ENRL; SE.SEC.ENRL).	0.212	0.177	0	0.792
Liberal democracy index	The extent to which the ideal of liberal democracy is realized within a country in a given year.	Varieties of Democracy (VDEM) Liberal Democracy Index (v2x_libdem)	0.247	0.146	0.038	0.660
GDP/capita	Country's gross domestic product divided by its population in a given year.	World Bank GDP per capita in constant US dollars (2015).	719.7	382.4	164.5	1831.0
Catholic president	Whether the country had a Catholic president in a given year.	Country-specific sources.	0.400	0.490	0	1

Note: Countries included in data set are: Burundi, Cameroon, Ghana, Kenya, Lesotho, Liberia, Malawi, Mozambique, Rwanda, Tanzania, Togo, Uganda, and Zambia.

TABLE B.4 *Summary statistics for church educational control data set (independence–2018)*

Variable	Definition	Source	Mean	SD	Min	Max
Increase church control of education	Whether the country passed (and implemented) a policy that increased church control over either teacher management or the curriculum in church schools in a given year.	Country-specific sources.	0.018	0.131	0	1
Increase church management	Whether the country passed (and implemented) a policy that increased church control over teacher management in a given year.	Country-specific sources.	0.014	0.117	0	1
Increase Christian education	Whether the country passed (and implemented) a policy that increased church control over the curriculum in church schools in a given year.	Country-specific sources.	0.008	0.089	0	1
Decrease church control of education	Whether the country passed (and implemented) a policy that decreased church control over either teacher management or the curriculum in church schools in a given year.	Country-specific sources.	0.027	0.162	0	1
Liberal democracy index	The extent to which the ideal of liberal democracy is realized within a country in a given year.	Varieties of Democracy (VDEM) Liberal Democracy Index (v2x_libdem).	0.206	0.162	0.003	0.683
Postindependence decade	Whether a year fell within the first decade following independence.	Country-specific sources.	0.168	0.374	0	1
Marxist state	Whether Marxist–Leninism was the official state ideology in a given year.	Young 1982; country-specific sources.	0.073	0.259	0	1
Log GDP/capita	Log of country's gross domestic product divided by its population in a given year.	Varieties of Democracy (VDEM) GDP per capita measure (e_midppc).	7.617	0.863	4.898	10.750

Note: Countries included in data set are: Angola, Botswana, Burundi, Cameroon, the Democratic Republic of the Congo, Equatorial Guinea, Gabon, Ghana, Guinea-Bissau, Kenya, Lesotho, Liberia, Madagascar, Malawi, Mozambique, Namibia, Nigeria, the Republic of the Congo, Rwanda, South Africa, Tanzania, Togo, Uganda, Zambia, and Zimbabwe.

TABLE B.5 *Variables in Zambia opinion survey data set (summary statistics for birth years 1958–1973)*

Variable	Definition	Source	Mean	SD	Min	Max
Catholic school attendance (access × Catholic)	Proportion of respondent's primary school years before Catholic primary schools nationalized in 1974 × Catholic respondent.	Zambian Afrobarometer Surveys (Round 2–Round 7)	0.053	0.188	0	1
Catholic school access	Proportion of respondent's primary school years before Catholic primary schools nationalized in 1974.	Zambian Afrobarometer Surveys (Round 2–Round 7)	0.222	0.335	0	1
Catholic	"What is your religion, if any?" 1 = Catholic, 0 = Any other response.	Zambian Afrobarometer Surveys (Round 2–Round 7)	0.231	0.421	0	1
Finished primary	"What is the highest level of education you have completed?" 1 = Primary school completed or higher; 0 = Less than primary school completed.	Zambian Afrobarometer Surveys (Round 2–Round 7)	0.721	0.449	0	1
Finished secondary	"What is the highest level of education you have completed?" 1 = Secondary school completed or higher; 0 = Less than secondary school completed.	Zambian Afrobarometer Surveys (Round 2–Round 7)	0.284	0.451	0	1
Scarcity index	Index constructed from questions asking "Over the past year, how often, if ever, have you or anyone in your family gone without … enough food to eat, enough clean water for home use, enough fuel to cook your food, a cash income." 0 = Never, 1 = Just once or twice, 2 = Several times, 3 = Many times, 4 = Always. Index averages across the four components.	Zambian Afrobarometer Surveys (Round 2–Round 7)	1.354	0.776	0	4
Religiosity	"Excluding weddings and funerals, how often do you attend religious services?" 1 = Never, 2 = About once a year or less, 3 = About once every several months, 4 = About once a month, 5 = About once a week, 6 = More than once a week.	Zambian Afrobarometer Surveys (Round 2–3)	5.021	1.160	1	6

National identity	"Let us suppose that you had to choose between being a Zambian and being a (ethnic group). Which of the following statements best expresses your feelings?" 5 = I feel only Zambian, 4 = I feel more Zambian than (ethnic group), 3 = I feel equally Zambian and (ethnic group), 2 = I feel more (ethnic group) than Zambian, 1 = I feel only (ethnic group).	Zambian Afrobarometer Surveys (Rounds 3–Round 7)	3.412	1.061	1	5
Interest in politics	"How interested would you say you are in public affairs, you know, in politics and government?" 3 = Very interested, 2 = Somewhat interested, 1 = Not very interested, 0 = Not at all interested.	Zambian Afrobarometer Surveys (Round 2–Round 6)	1.591	1.088	0	3
Women's rights	Index constructed by averaging responses to two questions about women's rights: "Let's talk for a moment about the kind of society we would like to have in this country. Which of the following statements is closest to your view? Choose Statement A or Statement B. Do you agree or agree very strongly?... (A) In our country, women should have equal rights and receive the same treatment as men do vs. (B) Women have always been subject to traditional laws and customs, and should remain so. (A) Women should have the same chance of being elected to political office as men vs. (B) Men make better political leaders than women, and should be elected rather than women." 4 = Agree very strongly with A, 3 = Agree with A, 2 = Agree with B, 1 = Agree very strongly with B.	Zambian Afrobarometer Surveys (Round 2, 3, 5, 6, 7)	2.996	1.100	1	4
Female	Whether respondent is female based on enumerator coding.	Zambian Afrobarometer Surveys (Round 2–Round 7)	0.485	0.500	0	1
Birth year	Based on respondent's reported age and year of survey.	Zambian Afrobarometer Surveys (Round 2–Round 7)	1967	4.547	1958	1973

TABLE B.6 *Variables in Tanzania household survey data set (summary statistics for Christian families in sample)*

Variable	Definition	Source	Mean	SD	Min	Max
Catholic school	Did any of the schools your (mother/father) attended have a religious affiliation? If so, with what church or other religious group was it affiliated? 1 = Catholic, 0 = Other religious affiliation or no religious affiliation.	Author's original survey in Tanzania, 2018.	0.202	0.402	0	1
Protestant school	Did any of the schools your (mother/father) attended have a religious affiliation? If so, with what church or other religious group was it affiliated? 1 = Protestant, 0 = Other religious affiliation or no religious affiliation.	Author's original survey in Tanzania, 2018.	0.172	0.378	0	1
Catholic	"In what religion were you raised as a child, if any?" 1 = Catholic, Other responses = 0.	Author's original survey in Tanzania, 2018.	0.436	0.496	0	1
Lutheran	"In what religion were you raised as a child, if any?" 1 = Lutheran, Other responses = 0.	Author's original survey in Tanzania, 2018.	0.308	0.462	0	1
Age (logged)	Calculated from "What is the year of your "mother/father's birth?"	Author's original survey in Tanzania, 2018.	4.302	0.155	4.025	4.605
Years of education	"What is the highest year of education your (mother/father) completed?"	Author's original survey in Tanzania, 2018.	5.436	2.261	1	16
Household wealth (as adult)	Measure of household wealth based on EquityTool's weighting of responses to the following questions: "Now I would like to know about your family's home and assets when you were a child. Could you tell me whether you regularly had the following items? ... Television, Iron. What was the main material of the floor of your main dwelling as a child? What was the main material of the exterior walls of your dwelling as a child? What was the main material of the roof of your dwelling as a child? What was the main source of energy for lighting in the household?"	Author's original survey in Tanzania, 2018.	−0.100	0.311	−0.609	0.913

Children's religious attendance	"As a child, how frequently did you attend religious services or prayers?" 1 = Never, 2 = Seldom, 3 = A few times a year, 4 = About monthly, 5 = Almost every week, 6 = Every week, 7 = More than once a week.	Author's original survey in Tanzania, 2018.	5.675	1.117	1	7
Children speak Swahili at home	"What language do you most often speak in your home?" 1 = Swahili, 0 = All other responses.	Author's original survey in Tanzania, 2018.	0.535	0.499	0	1
Political activity (as adult)	"How active in politics would you say your parents were when you were a child?" 1 = Not at all, 2 = A little, 3 = Somewhat, 4 = Very.	Author's original survey in Tanzania, 2018.	2.050	1.246	1	4
Polygamous marriage	"Did your father have more than one wife?" 1 = Yes, 0 = No.	Author's original survey in Tanzania, 2018.	0.322	0.468	0	1

APPENDIX C: ADDITIONAL TABLE, CHAPTER 7

TABLE C.1 *Relationship between liberal democratic checks index and policy changes to church educational control*

	(1) Increase church control of education	(2) Increase church control of education	(3) Increase church management	(4) Increase Christian education	(5) Decrease church control of education	(6) Decrease church control of education
Liberal democratic checks index	0.09*	0.09*	0.08*	0.04+	0.01	0.01
	(0.04)	(0.04)	(0.04)	(0.02)	(0.04)	(0.04)
Postindependence decade	−0.03**	−0.03**	−0.02*	−0.03*	0.07**	0.08**
	(0.01)	(0.01)	(0.01)	(0.01)	(0.03)	(0.03)
Marxist state		0.00	0.01	0.01		0.00
		(0.02)	(0.01)	(0.02)		(0.03)
Log GDP per capita		−0.01+	−0.01*	−0.01		0.01+
		(0.01)	(0.01)	(0.01)		(0.01)
Country FEs	Yes	Yes	Yes	Yes	Yes	Yes
Decade FEs	Yes	Yes	Yes	Yes	Yes	Yes
N	1,363	1,313	1,313	1,313	1,318	1,268
Sample	All years	All years	All years	All years	All years with church schools	All years with church schools

Notes: Table presents coefficients with standard errors clustered by leader in parentheses. This table uses a slightly modified version of V-DEM's liberal democratic index that excludes the mid-level index measuring equality before the law/individual liberty insofar as this index contains a measure of religious freedom. The construction of the alternative measure follows the methods described in the V-DEM Codebook v10, except that v2xcl_rol is excluded from the v2x_liberal index, thereby giving more weight to the other two sub-indices of this index, legislative constraints and judicial constraints.

+ $p < 0.10$, * $p < 0.05$, ** $p < 0.01$.

APPENDIX D: ADDITIONAL TABLES, CHAPTER 8

TABLE D.1 *Effects of Catholic schools on conversion and primary school completion (1958–1976 birth years)*

	Men		Women	
	Catholic (0/1) (1)	Finished primary (0/1) (2)	Catholic (0/1) (3)	Finished primary (0/1) (4)
Catholic school attendance (access × Catholic)		0.13 (0.08)		−0.02 (0.10)
Catholic school access	−0.13 (0.34)	−0.01 (0.07)	0.14 (0.35)	−0.04 (0.10)
Catholic		0.01 (0.03)		−0.01 (0.03)
N	962	1,210	755	1,150
Birth year trend	Yes	Yes	Yes	Yes
Survey round FEs	Yes	Yes	Yes	Yes
Region FEs	Yes	Yes	Yes	Yes
Years included	1958–1976	1958–1976	1958–1976	1958–1976
Sample	Male primary completers	All men	Female primary completers	All women

Notes: Table presents coefficients with standard errors clustered by religion-year of birth in parentheses.
$^{+}p < 0.10$, $^{*}p < 0.05$, $^{**}p < 0.01$.

TABLE D.2 *Effects of Catholic school attendance on socioeconomic status and political attitudes – men (1958–1976 birth years)*

	Finished secondary (0/1) (1)	Scarcity index (0–4) (2)	Religiosity (1–6) (3)	National identity (1–5) (4)	Interest in politics (0–3) (5)	Women's rights (1–4) (6)
Catholic school attendance (access × Catholic)	−0.07 (0.12)	−0.19 (0.17)	0.15 (0.26)	0.07 (0.24)	0.12 (0.18)	−0.32 (0.32)
Catholic school access	−0.06 (0.10)	0.17 (0.14)	−0.25 (0.27)	−0.02 (0.17)	0.25⁺ (0.15)	−0.26 (0.23)
Catholic	0.03 (0.04)	−0.01 (0.06)	0.29** (0.09)	0.08 (0.11)	0.07 (0.09)	0.10 (0.12)
N	962	962	473	726	865	790
Birth year trend	Yes	Yes	Yes	Yes	Yes	Yes
Survey round FEs	Yes	Yes	Yes	Yes	Yes	Yes
Region FEs	Yes	Yes	Yes	Yes	Yes	Yes
Years included	1958–1976	1958–1976	1958–1976	1958–1976	1958–1976	1958–1976
Sample	Male primary completers	Male primary completers	Male primary completers	Male primary completers	Male primary completers	Male primary completers

Notes: Table presents coefficients with standard errors clustered by religion-year of birth in parentheses.
⁺$p < 0.10$, *$p < 0.05$, **$p < 0.01$.

TABLE D.3 *Effects of Catholic school attendance on socioeconomic status and political attitudes – women (1958–1976 birth years)*

	Finished secondary (0/1) (1)	Scarcity index (0–4) (2)	Religiosity (1–6) (3)	National identity (1–5) (4)	Interest in politics (0–3) (5)	Women's rights (1–4) (6)
Catholic school attendance (access × Catholic)	0.17 (0.11)	−0.29+ (0.15)	0.46+ (0.23)	−0.20 (0.28)	0.43 (0.33)	−0.63* (0.27)
Catholic school access	0.04 (0.10)	0.07 (0.15)	−0.20 (0.24)	0.37 (0.29)	−0.25 (0.27)	−0.19 (0.18)
Catholic	−0.00 (0.04)	0.06 (0.07)	−0.16 (0.10)	0.13 (0.08)	0.07 (0.08)	0.10 (0.09)
N	755	755	414	545	677	647
Birth year trend	Yes	Yes	Yes	Yes	Yes	Yes
Survey round FEs	Yes	Yes	Yes	Yes	Yes	Yes
Region FEs	Yes	Yes	Yes	Yes	Yes	Yes
Years included	1958–1976	1958–1976	1958–1976	1958–1976	1958–1976	1958–1976
Sample	Female primary completers	Female primary completers	Female primary completers	Female primary completers	Female primary completers	Female primary completers

Notes: Table presents coefficients with standard errors clustered by religion-year of birth in parentheses.
+ $p < 0.10$, * $p < 0.05$, ** $p < 0.01$.

TABLE D.4 *Catholic schools, conversion, and primary school completion – dichotomous measure of access*

	Men		Women	
	Catholic (0/1) (1)	Finished primary (0/1) (2)	Catholic (0/1) (3)	Finished primary (0/1) (4)
Catholic school attendance Di (Di access × Catholic)		0.07 (0.06)		−0.07 (0.08)
Catholic school Di access	−0.12 (0.25)	−0.00 (0.05)	0.03 (0.25)	0.01 (0.06)
Catholic		0.04 (0.03)		0.02 (0.04)
N	730	918	555	864
Birth year trend	Yes	Yes	Yes	Yes
Survey round FEs	Yes	Yes	Yes	Yes
Region FEs	Yes	Yes	Yes	Yes
Years included	1958–1973	1958–1973	1958–1973	1958–1973
Sample	Male primary completers	All men	Female primary completers	All women

Notes: Table presents coefficients with standard errors clustered by religion-year of birth in parentheses.
$^+p < 0.10$, $^*p < 0.05$, $^{**}p < 0.01$.

TABLE D.5 *Effects of Catholic school attendance on socioeconomic status and political attitudes – men – dichotomous measure of access*

	Finished secondary (0/1) (1)	Scarcity index (0–4) (2)	Religiosity (1–6) (3)	National identity (1–5) (4)	Interest in politics (0–3) (5)	Women's rights (1–4) (6)
Catholic school attendance Di	−0.08	−0.08	0.26	0.06	0.02	−0.56*
	(0.11)	(0.15)	(0.18)	(0.20)	(0.13)	(0.24)
(Di access × Catholic)	−0.05	0.05	−0.35+	−0.10	0.22*	−0.13
	(0.08)	(0.11)	(0.18)	(0.15)	(0.09)	(0.17)
Catholic school Di access	0.05	−0.07	0.24*	0.01	0.12	0.24+
	(0.05)	(0.07)	(0.09)	(0.09)	(0.09)	(0.12)
N	730	730	363	544	649	612
Birth year trend	Yes	Yes	Yes	Yes	Yes	Yes
Survey round FEs	Yes	Yes	Yes	Yes	Yes	Yes
Region FEs	Yes	Yes	Yes	Yes	Yes	Yes
Years included	1958–1973	1958–1973	1958–1973	1958–1973	1958–1973	1958–1973
Sample	Male primary completers	Male primary completers	Male primary completers	Male primary completers	Male primary completers	Male primary completers

Notes: Table presents coefficients with standard errors clustered by religion-year of birth in parentheses.
+ $p < 0.10$, * $p < 0.05$, ** $p < 0.01$.

TABLE D.6 *Effects of Catholic school attendance on socioeconomic status and political attitudes – women – dichotomous measure of access*

	Finished secondary (0/1) (1)	Scarcity index (0–4) (2)	Religiosity (1–6) (3)	National identity (1–5) (4)	Interest in politics (0–3) (5)	Women's rights (1–4) (6)
Catholic school Di attendance (Di access × Catholic)	0.18+ (0.10)	−0.13 (0.12)	0.39+ (0.20)	−0.23 (0.22)	0.30 (0.24)	−0.30 (0.28)
Catholic school Di access	0.04 (0.06)	−0.20 (0.11)	−0.24 (0.17)	0.07 (0.17)	−0.03 (0.17)	−0.01 (0.12)
Catholic	−0.02 (0.05)	0.06 (0.07)	−0.12 (0.11)	0.05 (0.10)	0.01 (0.12)	−0.01 (0.11)
N	555	555	302	401	497	470
Birth year trend	Yes	Yes	Yes	Yes	Yes	Yes
Survey round FEs	Yes	Yes	Yes	Yes	Yes	Yes
Region FEs	Yes	Yes	Yes	Yes	Yes	Yes
Years included	1958–1973	1958–1973	1958–1973	1958–1973	1958–1973	1958–1973
Sample	Female primary completers	Female primary completers	Female primary completers	Female primary completers	Female primary completers	Female primary completers

Notes: Table presents coefficients with standard errors clustered by religion-year of birth in parentheses.
+ $p < 0.10$, * $p < 0.05$, ** $p < 0.01$.

Bibliography

Acemoglu, Daron, and James A. Robinson. 2006. *Economic Origins of Dictatorship and Democracy*. Cambridge University Press.
Afrobarometer. 2025. Benin, Botswana, Burkina Faso, Burundi, Cameroon, Cote D'Ivoire, Ethiopia, Gabon, Ghana, Kenya, Lesotho, Liberia, Madagascar, Malawi, Mozambique, Namibia, Nigeria, Senegal, South Africa, Tanzania, Togo, Uganda, Zambia and Zimbabwe, Rounds 2–7. Available at www.afrobarometer.org.
Almond, Gabriel A., and Sidney Verba. 1963. *The Civic Culture: Political Attitudes and Democracy in Five Nations*. Princeton University Press.
Anderson, Christopher J., Damien Bol, and Aurelia Ananda. 2021. "Humanity's Attitudes about Democracy and Political Leaders: Patterns and Trends." *Public Opinion Quarterly* 85, no. 4: 957–86.
Ansell, Ben, and Johannes Lindvall. 2013. "The Political Origins of Primary Education Systems: Ideology, Institutions, and Interdenominational Conflict in an Era of Nation-Building." *American Political Science Review* 107, no. 3: 505–22.
  2020. *Inward Conquest: The Political Origins of Modern Public Services*. Cambridge University Press.
Ansell, Ben, and David Samuels. 2014. *Inequality and Democratization: An Elite-Competition Approach*. Cambridge University Press.
Arens, Bernard. 1925. *Manuel Des Missions Catholiques*. H. Bomans.
Arriola, Leonardo R. 2013. *Multi-Ethnic Coalitions in Africa: Business Financing of Opposition Election Campaigns*. Cambridge University Press.
Baggott Carter, Erin, and Brett Carter. 2023. *Propaganda in Autocracies: Institutions, Information, and the Politics of Belief*. Cambridge University Press.
Bahendwa, L. Festo. 1990. *Christian Religious Education in the Lutheran Dioceses of North-Western Tanzania*. Finnish Society for Missiology and Ecumenics.
Baldwin, Kate. 2025a. Country-Level Data Set on Church and Union Democratic Activism, 2009–2018.
  2025b. Church-Level Democratic Activism Data Set, 2009–2018.

2025c. Catholic Democratic Activism Data Set, 1980–2018.
2025d. Church Education Control Data Set, Independence–2018.
Balmer, Randall. 2007. *Thy Kingdom Come: How the Religious Right Distorts Faith and Threatens America*. Basic Books.
Banana, Canaan. 1982. *The Theology of Promise: The Dynamics of Self-Reliance*. College Press.
Barrett, David B. 1982. *World Christian Encyclopedia: A Comparative Study of Churches and Religions in the Modern World, AD 1900–2000*. Oxford University Press.
Bauer, Vincent, Melina Platas, and Jeremy M. Weinstein. 2022. "Legacies of Islamic Rule in Africa: Colonial Responses and Contemporary Development." *World Development* 152: 105750.
Bautista, Julius. 2020. "Catholic Democratization: Religious Networks and Political Agency in the Philippines and Timor-Leste." *Sojourn: Journal of Social Issues in Southeast Asia* 35, no. 2: 310–42.
Bayart, Jean-François. 1989. "Les Églises Chrétiennes et La Politique Du Ventre: Le Partage Du Gâteau Ecclésial." *Politique Africaine* no. 35: 3–26.
Beach, Harlan P., Charles H. Fahs, and John Bartholomew. 1925. *World Missionary Atlas*. Institute of Social and Religions Research.
Becker, Bastian, and Carina Schmitt. 2023. "License to Educate: The Role of National Networks in Colonial Empires." *World Development* 169: 106286.
Bellin, Eva. 2000. "Contingent Democrats: Industrialists, Labor, and Democratization in Late-Developing Countries." *World Politics* 52, no. 2: 175–205.
Berman, Edward H. 1975. *African Reactions to Missionary Education*. Publications of the Center for Education in Africa. Teachers College Press, Teachers College, Columbia University.
Bermeo, Nancy. 2016. "On Democratic Backsliding." *Journal of Democracy* 27, no. 1: 5–19.
Bleck, Jaimie. 2015. *Education and Empowered Citizenship in Mali*. Johns Hopkins University Press.
Boakye, Paul A. 2019. "Explaining Education Reforms in Ghana: An Institutional and Ideational Perspective." PhD Dissertation, University of Saskatchewan.
Boix, Carles. 2003. *Democracy and Redistribution*. Cambridge University Press.
Bolaji, Mohammed H. A. 2018. "Secularism and State Neutrality: The 2015 Muslim Protest of Discrimination in the Public Schools in Ghana." *Journal of Religion in Africa* 48, no. 1/2: 65–104.
Bondo, Pedro F. M. 2015. "The History of Angolan Education 1930–1980: The Convergence of Colonialism, Religion, and Decree." PhD Dissertation, Kansas State University.
Botha, Christo. 2016. "The Church in Namibia: Political Handmaiden or a Force for Justice and Unity?" *Journal of Namibian Studies: History Politics Culture* 20: 7–36.
Brancati, Dawn. 2016. *Democracy Protests: Origins, Features, and Significance*. Cambridge University Press.
Brass, Jennifer N. 2016. *Allies or Adversaries: NGOs and the State in Africa*. Cambridge University Press.

Bratton, Michael. 2003. "Briefing: Islam, Democracy and Public Opinion in Africa." *African Affairs* 102, no. 408: 493–501.

Bratton, Michael, and Nicolas van de Walle. 1992. "Popular Protest and Political Reform in Africa." *Comparative Politics* 24, no. 4: 419–42.

Brooke, Steven, David Buckley, Clarissa David, and Ronald Mendoza. 2023. "Religious Protection from Populist Violence: The Catholic Church and the Philippine Drug War." *American Journal of Political Science* 67, no. 1: 205–20.

Brown, Godfrey N. 1964. "British Educational Policy in West and Central Africa." *The Journal of Modern African Studies* 2, no. 3: 365–77.

Bryk, Anthony S., Valerie E. Lee, and Peter B. Holland. 1993. *Catholic Schools and the Common Good*. Harvard University Press.

Burdick, John. 1994. "The Progressive Catholic Church in Latin America: Giving Voice or Listening to Voices?" *Latin American Research Review* 29, no. 1: 184–97.

Bush, Sarah Sunn. 2015. *The Taming of Democracy Assistance: Why Democracy Promotion Does Not Confront Dictators*. Cambridge University Press.

Cammett, Melani. 2014. *Compassionate Communalism: Welfare and Sectarianism in Lebanon*. Cornell University Press.

Cammett, Melani, and Lauren MacLean. 2011. "Introduction: The Political Consequences of Non-State Social Welfare in the Global South." *Studies in Comparative International Development* 46: 1–21.

Campbell, David E. 2004. "Acts of Faith: Churches and Political Engagement." *Political Behavior* 26, no. 2: 155–80.

Capoccia, Giovanni, and Daniel Ziblatt. 2010. "The Historical Turn in Democratization Studies: A New Research Agenda for Europe and Beyond." *Comparative Political Studies* 43, no. 8–9: 931–68.

Carmody, Brendan. 1999. *Education in Zambia: Catholic Perspectives*. Bookworld Publishers.

2002. "The Politics of Catholic Education in Zambia: 1891–1964." *Journal of Church and State* 44, no. 4: 775–804.

2003a. "The Politics of Catholic Education in Zambia: 1964–2001." *Paedagogica Historica* 39, no. 3: 286–303.

2003b. "Religious Education and Pluralism in Zambia." *Religious Education* 98, no. 2: 139–54.

2007. "Catholic Church and State Relations in Zambian Education: A Contemporary Analysis." In Gerald Grace and Joseph O'Keefe, eds. *International Handbook of Catholic Education: Challenges for School Systems in the 21st Century*. Springer Netherlands.

2016. "Catholic Education in Zambia: Mission Integrity and Politics." *History of Education* 45, no. 5: 621–37.

Carney, James J. 2020. "Benedicto Kiwanuka and Catholic Democracy in Uganda." *Journal of Religious History* 44, no. 2: 212–29.

Carothers, Thomas. 2020. "Rejuvenating Democracy Promotion." *Journal of Democracy* 31, no. 1: 114–23.

Chandra, Kanchan. 2005. "Ethnic Parties and Democratic Stability." *Perspectives on Politics* 3, no. 2: 235–52.

Cheyeka, Austin M. 2006. "The Role of Zambian Humanism in the Development of Plural Religious Education in Zambia, 1972 to 1990." *African Social Research* no. 52: 15–30.

Cliffe, Lionel. 1971. "Socialist Education in Tanzania." In Kenneth Prewitt, ed. *Education and Political Values: An East African Case Study* East African Publishing House.

Coe, Cati. 2005. *Dilemmas of Culture in African Schools: Youth, Nationalism, and the Transformation of Knowledge.* University of Chicago Press.

Cogneau, Denis, and Alexander Moradi. 2014. "Borders that Divide: Education and Religion in Ghana and Togo Since Colonial Times." *The Journal of Economic History* 74, no. 3: 694–729.

Collier, Ruth B. 1999. *Paths toward Democracy: The Working Class and Elites in Western Europe and South America.* Cambridge University Press. Available at: www.cambridge.org/core/books/paths-toward-democracy/F400362A7AAD35668949544EDAF9A23E, accessed May 18, 2024.

Cooper, Frederick. 2002. *Africa Since 1940: The Past of the Present.* Cambridge University Press.

Coppedge, Michael, Staffan Lindberg, Svend-Erik Skaaning, and Jan Teorell. 2016. "Measuring High Level Democratic Principles Using the V-Dem Data." *International Political Science Review* 37, no. 5: 580–93.

Croke, Kevin, Guy Grossman, Horacio A. Larreguy, and John Marshall. 2016. "Deliberate Disengagement: How Education Can Decrease Political Participation in Electoral Authoritarian Regimes." *American Political Science Review* 110, no. 3: 579–600.

Dahl, Robert A. 1971. *Polyarchy: Participation and Opposition.* Yale University Press.

Darden, Keith, and Anna Grzymala-Busse. 2006. "The Great Divide: Literacy, Nationalism, and the Communist Collapse." *World Politics* 59, no. 1: 83–115.

Darden, Keith, and Harris Mylonas. 2016. "Threats to Territorial Integrity, National Mass Schooling, and Linguistic Commonality." *Comparative Political Studies* 49, no. 11: 1446–79.

De Haas, Michiel, and Ewout Frankema. 2018. "Gender, Ethnicity, and Unequal Opportunity in Colonial Uganda: European Influences, African Realities, and the Pitfalls of Parish Register Data." *The Economic History Review* 71, no. 3: 965–94.

Dowd, Robert A. 2015. *Christianity, Islam and Liberal Democracy: Lessons from Sub-Saharan Africa.* Oxford University Press.

Dunning, Thad. 2004. "Conditioning the Effects of Aid: Cold War Politics, Donor Credibility, and Democracy in Africa." *International Organization* 58, no. 2: 409–23.

Eastman, Carol M. 1971. "Who Are the Waswahili?" *Africa* 41, no. 3: 228–36.

Eichengreen, Barry J. 1996. *Globalizing Capital: A History of the International Monetary System.* Princeton University Press.

Ekuban, Erasmus E. 1977. *The Role of the Educational Units in Education in Ghana: Its Implications for the Educational Administrator.* University of Cape Coast University of Cape Coast, Institute for Educational Planning and Administration.

Elischer, Sebastian. 2021. *Salafism and Political Order in Africa*. Cambridge University Press.
Engels, Friedrich. 1942. *The Origin of the Family, Private Property and the State*. Current Book Distributors.
Englund, Harri. 2000. "The Dead Hand of Human Rights: Contrasting Christianities in Post-Transition Malawi." *The Journal of Modern African Studies* 38, no. 4: 579–603.
Enyedi, Zsolt, and Joan O'Mahony. 2004. "Churches and the Consolidation of Democratic Culture: Difference and Convergence in the Czech Republic and Hungary." *Democratization* 11, no. 4 Routledge: 171–91.
Evans-Anfom, Emmanuel. 2003. *To the Thirsty Land: Autobiography of a Patriot*. Africa Christian Press.
Fair, Christine. 2008. "The Madrassah Challenge: Militancy and Religious Education in Pakistan (Review)." United States Institute of Peace.
Fegley, Randall. 1981. "The U.N. Human Rights Commission: The Equatorial Guinea Case." *Human Rights Quarterly* 3, no. 1: 34–47.
FHI 360. 2025. Civil Society Organization Sustainability Index. Available at: https://csosi.org/.
Fonkeng, George E. 2007. *The History of Education in Cameroon: 1884–2004*. The Edwin Mellen Press.
Fox, Jonathan. 2020. *Thou Shalt Have No Other Gods before Me: Why Governments Discriminate against Religious Minorities*. Cambridge University Press.
Frankema, Ewout H. P. 2012. "The Origins of Formal Education in Sub-Saharan Africa: Was British Rule More Benign?" *European Review of Economic History* 16, no. 4: 335–55.
Gabudisa, Busugutsala G. 1997. *Politiques Éducatives Au Congo-Zaïre: De Léopold II à Mobutu*. L'Harmattan.
Gallego, Francisco A., and Robert Woodberry. 2010. "Christian Missionaries and Education in Former African Colonies: How Competition Mattered." *Journal of African Economies* 19, no. 3: 294–329.
Galston, William A. 2020. "The Enduring Vulnerability of Liberal Democracy." *Journal of Democracy* 31, no. 3: Johns Hopkins University Press: 8–24.
Gardinier, David E. 1974. "Schooling in the States of Equatorial Africa." *Canadian Journal of African Studies* 8, no. 3: 517–38.
  1980. "The Impact of French Education on Africa, 1817–1960." *Proceedings of the Meeting of the French Colonial Historical Society* 5: 70–82.
Gellner, Ernest. 1983. *Nations and Nationalism*. Cornell University Press.
Gifford, Paul. 1995. *The Christian Churches and the Democratisation of Africa*. E.J. Brill.
  1999. *African Christianity Its Public Role in Uganda and Other African Countries*. Fountain Pub Ltd.
Gift, Thomas, and Erik Wibbels. 2014. "Reading, Writing, and the Regrettable Status of Education Research in Comparative Politics." *Annual Review of Political Science* 17, no. 2014 Annual Reviews: 291–312.
Gill, Anthony. 1998. *Rendering unto Caesar: The Catholic Church and the State in Latin America*. University of Chicago Press.

Goldfrank, Benjamin, and Nick Rowell. 2012. "Church, State, and Human Rights in Latin America." *Politics, Religion & Ideology* 13, no. 1 Routledge: 25–51.

Gorski, Philip S. 2020. *American Babylon: Christianity and Democracy before and after Trump*. Routledge.

Gould, Andrew. 1999. *Origins of Liberal Dominance: State, Church, and Party in Nineteenth-Century Europe*. University of Michigan Press.

Gould, Jeremy. 2006. "Strong Bar, Weak State? Lawyers, Liberalism and State Formation in Zambia." *Development and Change* 37, no. 4: 921–41.

Graham, Matthew H., and Milan Svolik. 2020. "Democracy in America? Partisanship, Polarization, and the Robustness of Support for Democracy in the United States." *American Political Science Review* 114, no. 2: 392–409.

Groop, Kim S. 2012. "The Church, the State and the Issue of National Reconciliation in Namibia." *Journal of Namibian Studies: History Politics Culture* 11: 63–82.

Grossman, Guy. 2015. "Renewalist Christianity and the Political Saliency of LGBTs: Theory and Evidence from Sub-Saharan Africa." *The Journal of Politics* 77, no. 2: 337–51.

Grzymala-Busse, Anna. 2015. *Nations under God: How Churches Use Moral Authority to Influence Policy*. Princeton University Press.

Grzymała-Busse, Anna M. 2023. *Sacred Foundations: The Religious and Medieval Roots of the European State*. Princeton University Press.

Guriev, Sergei, and Daniel Treisman. 2022. *Spin Dictators: The Changing Face of Tyranny in the 21st Century*. Princeton University Press.

Guterres, Jose C. 2008. "Timor-Leste: A Year of Democratic Elections." *Southeast Asian Affairs* JSTOR: 359–72.

Gutiérrez, Angelina L. V. 2007. "Catholic Schools in the Philippines: Beacons of Hope in Asia." In Gerald Grace and Joseph O'Keefe, eds. *International Handbook of Catholic Education* Springer Netherlands.

Gyimah-Boadi, E., Carolyn Logan, and Josephine Sanny. 2021. "Africans' Durable Demand for Democracy." *Journal of Democracy* 32, no. 3: Johns Hopkins University Press: 136–51.

Haggard, Stephan, and Robert R. Kaufman. 2017. *Dictators and Democrats: Masses, Elites, and Regime Change*. Princeton University Press.

2021. *Backsliding: Democratic Regress in the Contemporary World*. Cambridge University Press.

Hagopian, Frances. 2008. "Latin American Catholicism in an Age of Religious and Political Pluralism: A Framework for Analysis." *Comparative Politics* 40, no. 2: 149–68.

Harber, Clive. 1985. "Weapon of War: Political Education in Zimbabwe." *Journal of Curriculum Studies* 17, no. 2: 163–74.

Harding, Robin, and David Stasavage. 2014. "What Democracy Does (and Doesn't Do) for Basic Services: School Fees, School Inputs, and African Elections." *The Journal of Politics* 76, no. 1: 229–45.

Harkness, Kristen A. 2022. "The Ethnic Stacking in Africa Dataset: When Leaders Use Ascriptive Identity to Build Military Loyalty." *Conflict Management and Peace Science* 39, no. 5: 609–32.

Hastings, Adrian. 1979. *A History of African Christianity 1950–1975*. Cambridge University Press.
Haynes, Jeff. 2004. "Religion and Democratization in Africa." *Democratization* 11, no. 4: 66–89.
Hincks, Craig W. 2009. *Quest for Peace: An Ecumenical History of the Church in Lesotho*. Christian Council of Lesotho.
Hinfelaar, Hugo. 2004. *History of the Catholic Church in Zambia*. Bookworld Publishers.
Hinfelaar, Marja. 2008. "The Political Role of the Roman Catholic Church." In Jan-Bart Gewald, Marja Hinfelaar, and Giacomo Macola, eds. *One Zambia, Many Histories: Towards a History of Post-Colonial Zambia*. Brill.
Hobsbawm, Eric J. 1990. *Nations and Nationalism Since 1780: Programme, Myth, Reality*. Cambridge University Press.
Hoffman, Michael. 2021. *Faith in Numbers: Religion, Sectarianism, and Democracy*. Oxford University Press.
Hollenweger, Walter J. 1972. *The Pentecostals*. S.C.M. Press.
Hook, Sidney. 1940. *Reason, Social Myths and Democracy*. The John Day Company.
Htun, Mala, and S. Laurel Weldon. 2005. "What It Means to Study Gender and the State." *Politics & Gender* 1, no. 1: 157–66.
  2018. *The Logics of Gender Justice: State Action on Women's Rights Around the World*. Cambridge University Press.
Huntington, Samuel P. 1991. *The Third Wave: Democratization in the Late Twentieth Century*. University of Oklahoma Press.
Hyde, Susan D. 2011. *The Pseudo-Democrat's Dilemma: Why Election Observation Became an International Norm*. Cornell University Press.
Iannaccone, Laurence, Roger Finke, and Rodney Stark. 1997. "Deregulating Religion: The Economics of Church and State." *Economic Inquiry* 35, no. 2: 350–64.
Iliffe, John. 1979. *A Modern History of Tanganyika*. African Studies Cambridge University Press.
  1995. *Africans: The History of a Continent*. Cambridge University Press.
İşcan, Talan, Daniel Rosenblum, and Katie Tinker. 2015. "School Fees and Access to Primary Education: Assessing Four Decades of Policy in Sub-Saharan Africa." *Journal of African Economies* 24, no. 4: 559–92.
Jimenez, Emmanuel. 1987. *Pricing Policy in the Social Sectors: Cost Recovery for Education and Health in Developing Countries*. Johns Hopkins University Press.
Jonge, Léonie de. 2021. "The Curious Case of Belgium: Why Is There No Right-Wing Populism in Wallonia?" *Government and Opposition* 56, no. 4: 598–614.
Kalyvas, Stathis N. 1996. *The Rise of Christian Democracy in Europe*. Cornell University Press.
  2000. "Commitment Problems in Emerging Democracies: The Case of Religious Parties." *Comparative Politics* 32, no. 4: 379–98.
Kaunda, Chammah J., and Marja Hinfelaar. 2020. *Competing for Caesar: Religion and Politics in Post-Colonial Zambia*. Augsburg Fortress Publishers.

Kaunda, Kenneth D. 1966. *A Humanist in Africa; Letters to Colin M. Morris from Kenneth D. Kaunda*. Abingdon Press.
1968. *Humanism in Zambia and a Guide to Its Implementation*. Zambia Information Services.
1974. *Humanism in Zambia and a Guide to Its Implementation Part II*. Division of National Guidance.
1990. "Address by His Excellency the President Comrade Dr. Kenneth Kaunda at the Opening of the 25th National Council of the United National Independence Party (UNIP)." September 24.
Kelly, Michael J. 1991. *Education in a Declining Economy: The Case of Zambia, 1975–1985*. World Bank.
Khaketla, B. Makulo. 1971. *Lesotho, 1970: An African Coup under the Microscope*. C. Hurst.
King, Elisabeth. 2013. *From Classrooms to Conflict in Rwanda*. Cambridge University Press.
Knighton, Ben. 2015. "Uganda." In Thomas Riggs, ed. *Worldmark Encyclopedia of Religious Practices*. Gale.
Komakoma, Joe, ed. 2003. *The Social Teaching of the Catholic Bishops and Other Christian Leaders in Zambia: Major Pastoral Letters and Statements, 1953–2001*. Ndola Mission Press.
Koski, Alissa, Erin C. Strumpf, Jay S. Kaufman, John Frank, Jody Heymann, and Arijit Nandi. 2018. "The Impact of Eliminating Primary School Tuition Fees on Child Marriage in Sub-Saharan Africa: A Quasi-Experimental Evaluation of Policy Changes in 8 Countries." Edited by Beth Blue Swadener *PLOS ONE* 13, no. 5: e0197928.
Kramon, Eric, and Daniel N. Posner. 2016. "Ethnic Favoritism in Education in Kenya." *Quarterly Journal of Political Science* 11, no. 1: 1–58.
Kraus, Jon. 2007. *Trade Unions and the Coming of Democracy in Africa*. Springer. Available at: https://books.google.com/books?hl=en&lr=&id=NsOADAAAQBAJ&oi=fnd&pg=PP1&dq=info:foAGaZWtzOkJ:scholar.google.com&ots=liGl6Uk31f&sig=KDM6Syq3UPPw4o1-z1j_h_6VV2U, accessed November 14, 2024.
Kulska, Joanna. 2023. "The Sacralization of Politics? A Case Study of Hungary and Poland." *Religions* 14, no. 4 MDPI: 525.
Kuran, Timur. 1991. "Now Out of Never: The Element of Surprise in the East European Revolution of 1989." *World Politics* 44, no. 1: 7–48.
Laitin, David D. 1986. *Hegemony and Culture: Politics and Religious Change among the Yoruba*. University of Chicago Press.
Lankina, Tomila, and Lullit Getachew. 2012. "Mission or Empire, Word or Sword? The Human Capital Legacy in Postcolonial Democratic Development." *American Journal of Political Science* 56, no. 2: 465–83.
2013. "Competitive Religious Entrepreneurs: Christian Missionaries and Female Education in Colonial and Post-Colonial India." *British Journal of Political Science* 43, no. 1: 103–31.
Lazarev, Egor. 2023. *State-Building as Lawfare: Custom, Sharia, and State Law in Postwar Chechnya*. Cambridge University Press.

Lemarchand, René. 1996. *Burundi: Ethnic Conflict and Genocide.* Woodrow Wilson Center Press.
Levitsky, Steven, and Lucan Way. 2010. *Competitive Authoritarianism: Hybrid Regimes after the Cold War.* Cambridge University Press.
Linden, Ian. 1980. *The Catholic Church and the Struggle for Zimbabwe.* Longman.
Linz, Juan J., and Alfred Stepan. 1996. *Problems of Democratic Transition and Consolidation: Southern Europe, South America, and Post-Communist Europe.* Johns Hopkins University Press.
Lipset, Seymour M., and Stein Rokkan. 1967. *Party Systems and Voter Alignments: Cross-National Perspectives.* Free Press.
Little, Andrew T., and Anne Meng. 2024. "Measuring Democratic Backsliding." *PS: Political Science & Politics* 57, no. 2: 149–61.
Locke, John. 1689. *Two Treatises of Government.* Cambridge University Press.
Longman, Timothy. 2010. *Christianity and Genocide in Rwanda.* Cambridge University Press.
Lungu, Gatian F. 1986. "The Church, Labor and the Press in Zambia: The Role of Critical Observers in a One-Party State." *African Affairs* 85, no. 340: 385–410.
Lupia, Arthur, and Mathew D. McCubbins. 1998. *The Democratic Dilemma: Can Citizens Learn What They Need to Know?* Cambridge University Press.
Lwanga-Lunyiigo, Samwiri. 2015. *A History of the Democratic Party of Uganda: The First Thirty Years (1954–1984).* Fountain Publishers.
MacGaffey, Wyatt. 1990. "Religion, Class, and Social Pluralism in Zaire." *Canadian Journal of African Studies* 24, no. 2: 249–64.
MacLean, Lauren M. 2010. *Informal Institutions and Citizenship in Rural Africa: Risk and Reciprocity in Ghana and Côte d'Ivoire.* Cambridge University Press.
  2011. "State Retrenchment and the Exercise of Citizenship in Africa." *Comparative Political Studies* 44, no. 9: 1238–66.
MacLean, Lauren M., and Melani Cammett. 2014. *The Politics of Non-State Social Welfare.* Cornell University Press.
Macola, Giacomo. 2010. *Liberal Nationalism in Central Africa: A Biography of Harry Mwaanga Nkumbula.* Springer.
Manning, Patrick. 2014. "African Population, 1650–2000: Comparisons and Implications of New Estimates." In Emmanuel Akyeampong, Robert H. Bates, Nathan Nunn, and James A. Robinson, eds. *Africa's Development in Historical Perspective.* Cambridge University Press.
Martin, Charles A. 1976. "Significant Trends in the Development of Ghanaian Education." *Journal of Negro Education* 45: 46–60.
McCauley, John F. 2014. "The Political Mobilization of Ethnic and Religious Identities in Africa." *American Political Science Review* 108, no. 4: 801–16.
  2017. *The Logic of Ethnic and Religious Conflict in Africa.* Cambridge University Press.
McClendon, Gwyneth, and Rachel B. Riedl. 2015. "Religion as a Stimulant of Political Participation: Experimental Evidence from Nairobi, Kenya." *The Journal of Politics* 77, no. 4: 1045–57.

2019. *From Pews to Politics: Religious Sermons and Political Participation in Africa*. Cambridge University Press.

McGregor, Andrew, Laura Skeaff, and Marianne Bevan. 2012. "Overcoming Secularism? Catholic Development Geographies in Timor-Leste." *Third World Quarterly* 33, no. 6: 1129–46.

McKenna, Joseph. 1997. *Finding a Social Voice: The Church and Marxism in Africa*. Fordham University Press.

Mehrotra, Santosh, and Enrique Delamonica. 1998. "Household Costs and Public Expenditure on Primary Education in Five Low Income Countries: A Comparative Analysis." *International Journal of Educational Development* 1, no. 18: 41–61.

Mehta, Jal, and Sarah Fine. 2019. *In Search of Deeper Learning: The Quest to Remake the American High School*. Harvard University Press.

Meng, Anne, 2020. *Constraining Dictatorship*. Cambridge University Press.

Meyer Resende, Madalena, and Anja Hennig. 2021. "Polish Catholic Bishops, Nationalism and Liberal Democracy." *Religions* 12, no. 2 MDPI: 94.

Miguel, Edward. 2004. "Nation Building and Public Goods in Kenya versus Tanzania." *World Politics* 56: 327–62.

Mill, John S. 1859. *On Liberty*. J.W. Parker. Available at: https://orbis.library.yale.edu/vwebv/holdingsInfo?bibId=2532134.

Minkenberg, Michael. 2021. "The Radical Right in Europe: Cultural Shifts and Religious Nativism." In Jeffrey Haynes, ed. *The Routledge Handbook of Religion, Politics and Ideology* Routledge.

Montalvo, José G., and Marta Reynal-Querol. 2005. "Ethnic Polarization, Potential Conflict, and Civil Wars." *American Economic Review* 95, no. 3: 796–816.

Moroff, Anika. 2010. "Party Bans in Africa – An Empirical Overview." *Democratization* 17, no. 4: 618–41.

Morrison, David R. 1976. *Education and Politics in Africa: The Tanzanian Case*. McGill-Queen's University Press.

Mwale, Nelly, Joseph Chita, and Austin Cheyeka. 2014. "Accounting for the Shift Towards 'Multifaith' Religious Education in Zambia, 1964–2017." *Zambia Social Science Journal* 5, no. 2. 37–60.

Ndulo, Muna. 2020. "Bill 10, If Enacted, Will Install a Constitutional Dictatorship and Undermine Democracy in Zambia." *Southern African Journal of Policy and Development* 5, no. 1. 31–43.

N'Gambwa, Kitenge. 1997. "Regime Legitimation in Education in Zaire." PhD Dissertation, Columbia University.

North, Douglass C., and Barry R. Weingast. 1989. "Constitutions and Commitment: The Evolution of Institutions Governing Public Choice in Seventeenth-Century England." *The Journal of Economic History* 49, no. 4: 803–32.

Nunn, Nathan. 2014. "Gender and Missionary Influence in Colonial Africa." In Emmanuel Akyeampong, James Robinson, Nathan Nunn, and Robert H. Bates, eds. *Africa's Development in Historical Perspective* Cambridge University Press.

Nyerere, Julius K. 1967. "Education for Self-Reliance." *The Ecumenical Review* 19, no. 4: 382–403.

O'Donnell, Guillermo A., Philippe C. Schmitter, and Laurence Whitehead. 1986. *Transitions from Authoritarian Rule: Latin America*. Johns Hopkins University Press.
Oliver, Roland. 1952. *The Missionary Factor in East Africa*. Longmans, Green & Co.
Owusu-Ansah, David, Abdulai Iddrisu, and Mark Sey. 2013. *Islamic Learning, the State and the Challenges of Education in Ghana*. Africa World Press, Inc.
Paglayan, Agustina S. 2021. "The Non-Democratic Roots of Mass Education: Evidence from 200 Years." *American Political Science Review* 115, no. 1: 179–98.
Paxton, Pamela. 2000. "Women's Suffrage in the Measurement of Democracy: Problems of Operationalization." *Studies in Comparative International Development* 35, no. 3: 92–111.
Philpott, Daniel. 2004. "Christianity and Democracy: The Catholic Wave." *Journal of Democracy* 15, no. 2: 32–46.
Phiri, Isaac. 2001. *Proclaiming Political Pluralism Churches and Political Transitions in Africa*. Praeger.
Phiri, Isabel A. 2003. "President Frederick J. T. Chiluba of Zambia: The Christian Nation and Democracy." *Journal of Religion in Africa* 33, no. 4: 401–28.
Pierskalla, Jan, Alexander De Juan, and Max Montgomery. 2017. "The Territorial Expansion of the Colonial State: Evidence from German East Africa 1890–1909." *British Journal of Political Science* 49, no. 2: 711–37.
Pierson, Paul. 2000. "Increasing Returns, Path Dependence, and the Study of Politics." *American Political Science Review* 94, no. 2: 251–67.
Platas, Melina. 2014. "Muslim Education in Africa: Trends and Attitudes Toward Faith-Based Schools." *The Review of Faith & International Affairs* 12, no. 2: 38–50.
  2023. "In Africa, Religion Predicts Educational Mobility." Nature.
Plattner, Marc. 1999. "From Liberalism to Liberal Democracy." *Journal of Democracy* 10, no. 3: 121–34.
  2019. "Illiberal Democracy and the Struggle on the Right." *Journal of Democracy* 30, no. 1: 5–19.
Pobee, John S. 1988. *Kwame Nkrumah and the Church in Ghana 1949–1966: A Study in the Relationship Between the Socialist Government of Kwame Nkrumah, the First Prime Minister and First President of Ghana, and the Protestant Christian Churches in Ghana*. Asempa Publishers.
Posner, Daniel N. 2003. "The Colonial Origins of Ethnic Cleavages: The Case of Linguistic Divisions in Zambia." *Comparative Politics* 35, no. 2: 127–46.
  2005. *Institutions and Ethnic Politics in Africa*. Cambridge University Press.
Posner, Daniel N., and Daniel J. Young. 2007. "The Institutionalization of Political Power in Africa." *Journal of Democracy* 18, no. 3: 126–40.
Przeworski, Adam. 1991. *Democracy and the Market: Political and Economic Reforms in Eastern Europe and Latin America*. Cambridge University Press.
  1999. "Minimalist Conception of Democracy: A Defense." In Ian Shapiro and Casiano Hacker-Cordon, eds. *Democracy's Value* Cambridge University Press.
Putnam, Robert D., and David E. Campbell. 2012. *American Grace: How Religion Divides and Unites Us*. Simon & Schuster.

Rawls, John. 1993. *Political Liberalism*. John Dewey Essays in Philosophy; No. 4. Columbia University Press.

Rink, Anselm. 2018. "Do Protestant Missionaries Undermine Political Authority? Evidence from Peru." *Comparative Political Studies* 51, no. 4: 477–513.

Roberts, Margaret E. 2018. *Censored: Distraction and Diversion Inside China's Great Firewall*. Princeton University Press.

Robinson, Morgan. 2024. "History of the Standard Swahili Language." In David Robinson and Paul Tiyambe Zeleza, eds. *Oxford Research Encyclopedia of African History*. Oxford University Press.

Rosenfeld, Bryn. 2017. "Reevaluating the Middle-Class Protest Paradigm: A Case-Control Study of Democratic Protest Coalitions in Russia." *American Political Science Review* 111, no. 4: 637–52.

2021. *The Autocratic Middle Class: How State Dependency Reduces the Demand for Democracy*. Princeton University Press.

Rosenfeld, Bryn, and Jeremy Wallace. 2024. "Information Politics and Propaganda in Authoritarian Societies." *Annual Review of Political Science* 27, no. 2024: 263–81.

Ross, Kenneth R. 1995. "Not Catalyst but Ferment: The Distinctive Contribution of the Churches to Political Reform in Malawi 1992–93." In Paul Gifford, ed. *The Christian Churches and the Democratisation of Africa* E. J. Brill.

Rovny, Jan. 2023. "Antidote to Backsliding: Ethnic Politics and Democratic Resilience." *American Political Science Review* 117, no. 4: 1410–28.

Rueschemeyer, Dietrich, Evelyne H. Stephens, and John D. Stephens. 1992. *Capitalist Development and Democracy*. Polity Press.

Rustow, Dankwart A. 1970. "Transitions to Democracy: Toward a Dynamic Model." *Comparative Politics* 2, no. 3: 337–63.

Sabar-Friedman, Galia. 1997. "Church and State in Kenya, 1986–1992: The Churches' Involvement in the 'Game of Change.'" *African Affairs* 96, no. 382: 22–52.

Sanneh, Lamin O. 1996. *Piety and Power: Muslims and Christians in West Africa*. Orbis Books.

Sarkar, Radha. 2023. "Religion and the Politics of Gender." PhD Dissertation, Yale University.

Sayers, Gerald F., ed. 1930. *The Handbook of Tanganyika*. Macmillan and Company, Limited.

Schoffeleers, Matthew J. 1999. *In Search of Truth and Justice: Confrontations between Church and State in Malawi, 1960–1994*. Christian Literature Association in Malawi.

Silva, Teresa Cruz e. 2017. "Christian Missions and the State in 19th and 20th Century Angola and Mozambique." In *Oxford Research Encyclopedia of African History*. Oxford University Press.

Sirin, Selcuk R., Patrice Ryce, and Madeeha Mir. 2009. "How Teachers' Values Affect Their Evaluation of Children of Immigrants: Findings from Islamic and Public Schools." *Early Childhood Research Quarterly* 24, no. 4: 463–73.

Sishuwa, Sishuwa. 2020. "Surviving on Borrowed Power: Rethinking the Role of Civil Society in Zambia's Third Term Debate." *Journal of Southern African Studies* 46, no. 3: 471–90.

Slater, Dan. 2013. "Democratic Careening." *World Politics* 65, no. 4: 729–63.
Smith, Amy E. 2019. *Religion and Brazilian Democracy: Mobilizing the People of God*. Cambridge University Press.
Somé, Magloire. 2001. "Christian Base Communities in Burkina Faso: Between Church and Politics." Translated by Cecily Bennett. *Journal of Religion in Africa* 31, no. 3: 275–304.
Sondheimer, Rachel M., and Donald P. Green. 2010. "Using Experiments to Estimate the Effects of Education on Voter Turnout." *American Journal of Political Science* 54, no. 1: 174–89.
Sperber, Elizabeth, Gwyneth McClendon, and O'Brien Kaaba. 2024. "Comparing Religious and Secular Interventions to Increase Young Adult Political Participation: Evidence from WhatsApp-Based Civic Education Courses in Zambia." *American Journal of Political Science*.
Sperber, Elizabeth, and Paige Wietzel. 2024. "Delivering Democracy? Comparing Catholic Bishops' Advocacy for Democracy in Malawi and Zambia, 1987–2022." *Journal of Religion in Africa*.
Stamatov, Peter. 2010. "Activist Religion, Empire, and the Emergence of Modern Long-Distance Advocacy Networks." *American Sociological Review* 75, no. 4: 607–28.
Stambach, Amy. 2009. *Faith in Schools: Religion, Education, and American Evangelicals in East Africa*. Stanford University Press.
Stasavage, David. 2002. "Credible Commitment in Early Modern Europe: North and Weingast Revisited." *The Journal of Law, Economics, and Organization* 18, no. 1: 155–86.
  2005. "Democracy and Education Spending in Africa." *American Journal of Political Science* 49, no. 2: 343–58.
Stepan, Alfred. 2001. "The World's Religious Systems and Democracy: Crafting the 'Twin Tolerations.'" In *Arguing Comparative Politics*. Oxford University Press.
Streit, Karl. 1929. *Atlas Hierarchicus: Descriptio Geographica Et Statistica Sanctae Romanae Ecclesiae*. Typographia Bonifaciana.
Sundkler, Bengt, and Christopher Steed. 2000. *A History of the Church in Africa*. Cambridge University Press.
Sutton, Francis X. 1965. "Education and the Making of Modern Nations." In James Coleman, ed. *Education and Political Development* Princeton University Press.
Svolik, Milan. 2008. "Authoritarian Reversals and Democratic Consolidation." *American Political Science Review* 102, no. 2: 153–68.
  2019. "Polarization versus Democracy." *Journal of Democracy* 30, no. 3: 20–32.
Teele, Dawn L. 2018. *Forging the Franchise*. Princeton University Press.
Thachil, Tariq. 2014. *Elite Parties, Poor Voters: How Social Services Win Votes in India*. Cambridge University Press.
Thompson, Arthur R. 1976. "Historical Survey of the Role of the Churches in Education from Pre-Colonial Days to Post-Independence." In Allan Gottneid, ed. *Church and Education in Tanzania* East African Publishing House.
Thompson, Mark R. 2016. "The Early Duterte Presidency in the Philippines." *Journal of Current Southeast Asian Affairs* 35, no. 3 SAGE Publications Ltd.: 3–14.

Toft, Monica D., Daniel Philpott, and Timothy Samuel Shah. 2011. *God's Century: Resurgent Religion and Global Politics*. W. W. Norton & Company.

Trejo, Guillermo. 2012. *Popular Movements in Autocracies: Religion, Repression, and Indigenous Collective Action in Mexico*. Cambridge University Press.

Tunón, Guadalupe. 2017. "When the Church Votes Left: How Progressive Religion Hurts Gender Equality." *APSA Annual Meeting*. A Paper Presented at the 2017 Annual Meetings of the American Political Science Association in San Francisco, August–September 2017.

van de Walle, Nicolas. 2001. *African Economies and the Politics of Permanent Crisis, 1979–1999*. Cambridge University Press.

Wallace, Jeremy L. 2022. *Seeking Truth and Hiding Facts: Information, Ideology, and Authoritarianism in China*. Oxford University Press.

Wantchekon, Leonard, Marko Klašnja, and Natalija Novta. 2015. "Education and Human Capital Externalities: Evidence from Colonial Benin." *The Quarterly Journal of Economics* 130, no. 2: 703–57.

Warner, Carolyn M. 2000. *Confessions of an Interest Group*. Princeton University Press.

Weber, Max. 1976. *The Protestant Ethic and the Spirit of Capitalism*. Allen & Unwin.

Weber, Sam. 2020. "Church and State: On the Role of the Catholic Church in the 2018 Presidential Election in the DR Congo." MA Thesis, Yale University.

Weingast, Barry R. 1997. "The Political Foundations of Democracy and the Rule of Law." *American Political Science Review* 91, no. 2: 245–63.

Whitehead, Clive. 2007. "The Concept of British Education Policy in the Colonies 1850–1960." *Journal of Educational Administration and History* 39, no. 2: 161–73.

Widner, Jennifer. 1992. *The Rise of a Party-State in Kenya: From Harambee! To Nyayo!* University of California Press.

Wittenberg, Jason. 2006. *Crucibles of Political Loyalty: Church Institutions and Electoral Continuity in Hungary*. Cambridge University Press.

Woodberry, Robert D. 2012. "The Missionary Roots of Liberal Democracy." *American Political Science Review* 106, no. 2: 244–74.

World Bank. 2009. *Abolishing School Fees in Africa: Lessons from Ethiopia, Ghana, Kenya, Malawi and Mozambique*. Development Practice in Education World Bank: In collaboration with UNICEF. Available at: https://documents.worldbank.org/en/publication/documents-reports/documentdetail/780521468250868445/abolishing-school-fees-in-africa-lessons-from-ethiopia-ghana-kenya-malawi-and-mozambique.

World Health Organization. 2010. Health Infrastructure Data. Available at: https://apps.who.int/gho/data/view.main.30000.

2013. Health Infrastructure Data. Available at: https://apps.who.int/gho/data/view.main.30000.

Young, Crawford. 1982. *Ideology and Development in Africa*. Yale University Press.

Zakaria, Fareed. 1997. "The Rise of Illiberal Democracy." Foreign Affairs. Available at: www.foreignaffairs.com/world/rise-illiberal-democracy.

Zurlo, Gina, and Todd Johnson. 2025. World Christian Database. Available at: https://worldchristiandatabase.org/.

Index

Acheampong, Ignatius, 164, 183
activism, 5–7, 10–11, 13–14, 17, 21,
  23–24, 29, 34, 42–43, 74, 76–78, 80,
  86, 89–92, 97–98, 118, 248–50
 antiauthoritarian, 240
 Catholic, 114, 117, 125, 255
 church, 10–12, 18, 27, 42–44, 70–73,
   77–78, 86–87, 89, 98, 100, 116–17,
   121–22, 139, 156, 243
 democratic, 18–19, 21, 23–30, 34–35,
   37–38, 42–47, 70, 74, 76–83, 86–99,
   101, 117, 231–33, 238–39, 253
 human rights, 23
 liberal democratic, 6, 12, 14, 18,
   23, 25–26, 33, 35, 44–45, 69–73,
   118–22
 narrow, 80, 86
 political, 6, 9, 74, 91
 prodemocratic, 33–34, 40, 117, 201
 social, 85, 92, 98, 252
 strong, 86
 Tanzania, 145, 147
 Zambia, 4, 121, 129, 146, 232
advocacy, 3, 6, 10, 23, 26, 33, 73, 77–78,
  104, 146, 171, 242, 252
 Catholic, 111
 church, 6, 12, 14, 26, 33, 35–36, 77,
   100–1, 118, 122, 143
 church-led, 35, 173
 direct, 35
 intensive, 73
 for liberal democratic institutions, 5–6,
   11–12, 105, 108

Muslim, 247
 national-level, 22
Afrobarometer, 83, 88, 135, 139,
  211–13, 252
Ahmadiyya community, 185, 242
aid, 171
Akufo-Addo, Nana, 165, 187
Anglican church, 7, 55, 81, 150, 245–46
 leaders, 150, 182
Angola, 59, 68, 102, 190
Ansell, Ben, 66
anticlericalism, 47, 235
antidemocratic actions, 123–24, 133, 135,
  141, 143, 237
antidemocratic candidates, 140, 143, 145
antidemocratic politicians, 123–24,
  139, 143
archbishops, 50–51, 129, 148, 170
Atta-Mills, John, 165
autocracy, 6, 17, 21, 27, 34–36, 39, 111,
  123, 158, 168–69, 179, 241, 243
 abuses, 244
 illiberal, 39, 41
 transition, 23
autocratic environment, 172
autocratic exposure index independence,
  95, 253
autocratic risk, 18, 20–21, 24, 37, 41, 46,
  64, 76–77, 97, 100, 117, 239, 241
 exposure, 19–20, 29, 33–34, 37–38,
   43–44, 69–73, 85, 91, 94–99, 118,
   122, 234, 239–41
autocratization, 27

283

Index

autocrats, 4, 17, 29, 32, 34, 74, 98, 234
autonomy, 18–21, 32, 41, 47, 66, 100, 160–69, 176–78, 185–89, 191
   church, 14, 26, 38–41, 54, 159–67, 177–81, 185, 190–93, 238, 257
   church school, 21, 39, 76, 166, 176, 196
   educational, 22, 40, 166, 176–77, 179–80, 187, 190
   regulatory, 41

Belgian Congo, 48, 58
Belgium, 47–48, 57–58, 67, 102, 162, 190
bishops, 7–10, 48, 53, 101, 108–10, 128, 135, 145–51
   Catholic, 4, 8, 61, 75, 109, 113, 116, 125, 127, 129, 141, 143, 154, 183, 207, 238, 241
   Lutheran, 9, 148
budget, 34, 40, 68, 99–100, 223
   constraints, 40–41
   school, 40
   transfers, 53
bureaucracy, 18, 38–39, 157–58, 167, 169, 178, 190
   educational, 182, 184
bureaucrats, 37, 39, 69, 158, 183
Burkina Faso, 61, 63, 103
Burundi, 10, 49, 54, 59, 63, 68, 80, 106, 109, 190
   bishops, 7

Cameroon, French, 58–59, 63, 68, 106, 190
campaigns, 6, 52, 75, 82, 133, 139, 158
   coordinated advocacy, 130
   organized, 187
   platforms, 167
capacity, 19–20, 30, 33, 35–36, 53–54, 61, 77, 116, 125, 156
   fiscal, 116
   organizational, 21, 94, 98, 252
   regulatory, 46
   state, 116
Capuchins, 85, 92, 205, 252
Catholic church, 4–5, 7–9, 21, 26–27, 42, 44, 47–51, 54–55, 81–82, 84–85, 101, 105, 108, 111–12, 116–17, 125, 131–34, 167, 169, 171, 205–7, 240–41
   bishops, 4, 9–10, 43, 50, 108, 114, 147
   clergy, 10, 210–11
   German, 109
   leaders, 50, 170, 180, 247
   Malawi bishops, 111
   missionaries, 48, 205
   priests, 146, 151, 174, 176, 208
   Tanzania bishops, 148
   Zambia bishops, 4, 6, 9, 219
Catholic education, 169–71, 176–77, 202, 205, 210–12, 215–18, 231–32, 245
   formal, 55
   secretariat, 206
Catholic Episcopal Conference, 224
Catholic schools, 55, 61, 106–8, 112–13, 116–17, 205–11, 214–21, 226–27, 256, 263–68
   private, 241
   system, 240
Catholic wave, 97
the Central African Republic, 51, 68
centralization, 7, 17, 32, 123, 129, 141
Chiluba, Frederick, 9, 125–26, 161, 174–76
Christian base of support, 52
Christian church, 47, 172, 242
   education, 22, 55, 194, 257, 262
   mainline, 52
   missionaries, 47, 58–59
Christian Churches Monitoring Group (CCMG), 130
Christian Council
   Ghana, 188
   Tanganyika, 224
Christian Democratic Party, 49–51
Christian Democrats, 31, 49, 54
Christianity, 91, 172, 226, 233, 237
Christians, 15, 47–48, 56, 137–38, 140, 160, 179, 190–91, 229, 233
   evangelical, 139
church leaders, 6, 21–22, 30–31, 42–44, 48–49, 52–54, 69–75, 77, 89, 129–30, 146, 150, 170, 172, 181–83, 188–89, 196, 201–2, 231–33, 237–38, 242–43
   democratic activism, 89
   national, 188
church management, 161, 170, 194, 210, 257, 262
   schools, 190, 205
church newspapers, 168
church political engagement, 5, 44, 201–4, 211, 213, 218–22, 226–34
church-run education, 18–21, 24–29, 37, 44–46, 55, 64, 69, 76, 83–84, 91–99, 175–76, 239–40, 250–51, 253
church-run media, 18

Index

church-run schools, 20–21, 26–27, 38–41,
  54–55, 61–67, 73, 75–76, 98–104,
  112, 116–18, 158–60, 167, 177–78,
  181, 185–86, 195–204, 225–27,
  231–32, 243, 257
  finance, 40
  grant-aided, 176
  nationalized, 54, 96
  private, 67
  regulating, 169
  secondary, 84
church–state agreements, 39, 75, 157,
  169, 189
civil liberties, 77, 167, 174, 179–81, 189,
  192, 241
  limited, 179
  protection of, 180, 188
civil society, 10, 32, 74, 80, 89–90, 110,
  148, 169, 252, 255
  secular, 125, 129, 140, 143–45,
  148, 180
  strong, 84
  weak, 91
class, 4, 43–44
  industrial, 15
  lower, 14, 23
  middle, 14, 23
  ruling, 43, 74
clergy, 173, 223
coalitions, 22, 30, 118–21, 124, 174, 234,
  236–37
  broad, 37, 122, 158
  cross-national, 118
  explicit, 50
  government's, 178
  partners, 16, 24, 31–32, 39, 44–46, 54,
  69, 235
  political, 36, 44, 49
  religious, 24
Cold War, 7, 10
colonial administration, 22, 47–48, 58–59
  British, 59, 180, 205, 222–23, 242
  German, 222
  Portuguese, 58
colonial period, 47, 49–50, 57, 59, 67,
  92–93, 205, 222–25
colonies, 48, 57–58, 190
  British, 48, 57–59
  French, 57, 67, 102
  German, 58
  Portuguese, 47–48, 57, 67, 102, 190
  Spanish, 190

competition, 43, 74, 91
  religious, 23, 43, 90
confessional schools, 68, 222
  private, 68
conflict
  church-state, 37, 63–64, 101
  civil, 105
  class, 74
  direct, 64
  educational, 195
  intergroup, 73
  societal, 203
constitution, 4, 7–8, 36, 81–82, 109,
  125–27, 148, 160, 172, 186, 188
  amendment, 9, 126
  liberal democratic, 189
  reform, 8, 80, 123, 125, 141–42
coordination, 9, 36, 77, 122–23, 127,
  129–30, 145–47, 150, 152
  citizen, 123, 145
  internal, 156
  interreligious, 151
  problems, 36, 123
Cote D'Ivoire, 53, 68, 80
coup, 49, 80, 182, 184
  military, 184
curricular reforms, 64, 176, 190
curriculum, 38, 40, 62, 64, 159, 164–65,
  168–69, 172, 175, 180, 185, 187,
  190, 204, 257
  government, 209, 222–23
  primary school, 187

democracy
  defense of, 19, 29, 41, 118, 124, 155,
  158, 197–201, 234, 241
  electoral, 14, 31, 39, 179
  liberal, 3–7, 10–14, 16–18, 21–23,
  25–26, 28–37, 39–43, 75–78, 104,
  108, 121–24, 156, 158–67, 178–80,
  189, 192–97, 233–37
  multiparty, 124, 131, 168
  strong, 166
  weak, 166
democratic backsliding, 4, 35, 122–23,
  130, 238
democratic institutions, 9–10, 23, 27–30,
  35–37, 76–77, 79, 114–21, 123, 140
  liberal, 10, 19, 21–22, 26, 35, 77,
  121–22, 124, 157, 234, 236–37
  protecting, 4, 25, 73, 80, 122, 124, 129,
  145, 155, 234, 236, 243

the Democratic Republic of the Congo, 8–10, 20, 53, 58–59, 63–64, 68–69, 80, 190
democratization, 7, 14, 23, 27, 78, 87, 185, 233, 236
dictatorship, 3, 111, 128, 135
  military, 183, 240–41
dissent, 12, 17, 169, 181, 184
  political, 181, 184
donors, 32, 62, 101, 126, 130
  international, 103, 118, 123, 158, 177–78, 247
  Western, 234, 236

economy
  crisis, 100, 111, 166
  development, 105, 195
  growth, 62, 162, 165, 193
  performance, 161–63, 165–66, 179–80
education, 19–21, 37–38, 54–66, 68–69, 75, 83–84, 91–100, 122, 167, 175–80, 182–84, 186–90, 203, 205–6, 222, 225–26, 228–33, 238–40
  church-run, 21, 92, 94, 191–94, 257, 262
  civic, 9, 64
  confessional, 64, 159, 161, 168, 170, 182, 210, 223
  contemporary, 98
  formal, 19, 22, 38, 55–56, 86
  higher, 98
  Islamic, 22, 185, 242, 246
  missionary, 59
  moral, 64, 164–65, 180, 187, 190
  pre-tertiary, 183
  primary, 101–4, 207, 211, 218, 226
  Protestant, 55, 202, 222, 229, 231
  public, 9, 111, 126, 203
  religious, 64, 159–60, 170–71, 176–78, 182–83, 185, 187, 190–91, 195, 206, 210
  secondary, 66, 84, 105, 175, 251
  secular, 206, 210–11, 223
education policy, 26–27, 57, 115, 124, 157–60, 168, 173, 178–80, 184, 190–93, 196–97, 234
education systems, 20–21, 25–26, 37–40, 61–62, 64–66, 83–84, 94, 101, 117–18, 123, 157–58, 167, 205, 210
  colonial, 67, 160
  contemporary, 39
  formal, 19
  religious, 68, 158
  segregated, 61
elections, 4, 6–8, 11–12, 51, 75–77, 79–80, 109–10, 115, 126, 137, 149, 174, 178, 183, 186–89, 255
  fair, 12–13, 75
  legislative, 4
  multiparty, 10, 146, 168, 186
empire, 47, 57–59
Equatorial Guinea, 49, 53–54, 59, 68, 91, 190
Ethiopia, 53
Ethiopian Orthodox Church, 5, 15, 31, 47, 235
ethnicity, 73, 83, 88, 212–13, 215, 227, 242, 252, 259
Europe, 15, 44, 47, 233, 237
  contemporary, 31
evangelical churches, 9, 55–56, 83, 86–88, 125
  leaders, 56, 170
evangelical Protestants, 136, 143, 172–73
evangelization, 33, 38, 54, 61, 75, 205
experiment, 139, 143
  conjoint, 141–42
  survey, 124, 139–40
  Tanzania, 153

faith-based schools, 226
financial dependence, 29, 37, 84, 101–2, 104
financial support, 41, 53, 84, 102, 104, 187
financing, 19–21, 41, 67, 76, 101–3, 118, 210–11, 240
  church, 97
  education, 97, 111
  government, 108
  independent, 35
  international, 62
  operational, 18, 21
  schools, 101, 108, 177
  state, 19, 26, 34, 43, 69–70, 84, 97–99, 101, 112, 118, 238, 251
France, 47, 58
  early twentieth-century, 218
  Third Republic, 47
Francophone Africa, 58
freedom, 12, 16–17, 80, 148, 172, 188
  assembly, 148
  expression, 82, 148, 157
  religious, 14, 243, 262
  restricting media, 80
  worship, 149

Index

French administration, 58–59
French Equatorial Africa, 58, 190
French Togoland, 58
French West Africa, 58
funding, state, 34, 41, 46, 57, 98–99, 114, 116, 151, 251

Gabon, 58, 68, 80, 190
gender, 211–12, 215, 218, 220, 225, 229, 243
  conservative attitudes, 243
  equality, 14, 201–3, 218, 221, 232
  hierarchies, 218, 221
  roles, 218, 221
gender norms
  conservative, 28, 204, 220
  traditional, 218, 221
Germany, 47, 58, 223
Ghana, 25–27, 63–64, 68, 75, 118, 157–66, 179, 185–90, 195–96, 242, 246
  churches in, 180
  church-run schools, 179
  Convention People's Party (CPP), 163, 180
  Education Service, 183–84, 188
  Education Service Council, 186
  Fourth Republic, 186
  Ministry of Education, 182, 186–87
  National Democratic Congress (NDC), 164, 186
  National Liberation Council (NLC), 163, 182
  National Redemption Council (NRC), 164, 183
  New Patriotic Party (NPP), 165, 186–87
  Provisional National Defense Council, 164, 179, 184–85
  students, 59
  Supreme Military Council, 183
governance, 4, 6, 22, 29–30
government, 61, 79–80, 104, 111–14, 116–17, 147, 150, 158–78, 180–89, 205–7, 209, 221–24
  central, 104, 222–23
  efficiency, 123
  funding, 116
  independent, 49
  military, 179
  nationalist, 166
grants, 57, 104, 178, 206
  capitation, 104, 115
  in-aid, 57, 222–23

Grzymala-Busse, Anna, 44, 235
Guinea-Bissau, 59, 68, 80, 102, 190

health care, 18, 33, 94, 108, 151
  church-run, 94, 98, 239
  investments, 97
Hichilema, Hakainde, 128–29, 134–35, 146
hospitals, 85–86, 151, 175, 253
  church-operated, 94–95, 97, 239, 253
human rights, 5–6, 14, 23, 42
humanism, 171–72, 175
Hungary, 238

identity, 61, 166
  class, 88
  national, 39, 62, 201–3, 211–13, 215–18, 227–32, 259, 264–68
  political, 202
  religious, 43
  upper-class, 89
ideology, 166, 169–71, 175, 178–80, 237
  antireligious, 64, 204
  government, 166–67, 177
  national, 62
  populist, 178
  religious, 24
independence, 12, 48–51, 62–64, 67, 94–97, 149, 167–70, 180–81, 190–91, 193–96, 205, 210
inequality, 109
  education, 202, 243
  socioeconomic, 243
institutions, 12–14, 17, 32, 36–37, 56, 73, 86, 121, 123, 157–58, 189, 242
  access, 44, 235–36
  autocratic, 16, 37, 174
  change, 122, 145
  democratic, 13–14, 29, 42, 44
  liberal, 4, 154, 178
  liberal democratic, 3–6, 9–15, 23–29, 32–33, 35–41, 45–46, 69, 75, 110, 115–16, 118–25, 129–30, 143, 145, 155–58, 160–66, 191–96, 233–38, 242–44
  political, 7, 24, 32, 37, 76–78, 109–16, 155–58, 177–78, 186, 192, 255
  religious, 218
  social, 242
interest group, 44

investments, 18, 33–34, 38–39, 55, 61, 75–76, 98–99, 122, 210, 233–34, 239, 242
  business, 239
  education, 20, 24, 26, 59–61, 66, 69–70, 75, 239, 242
Islam, 22, 47, 246

Jakaya Kikwete, 146
Jesuits, 61, 85, 92, 205, 252
judiciary, 9, 12, 35, 39, 129, 149, 157–58, 167, 238
  autonomous, 3, 32
  captured, 12

Kabila, Joseph, 8
Kalyvas, Stathis, 44, 235
Kaunda, Kenneth, 161, 167–76
Kenya, 20, 59, 63, 69, 75, 80, 190
  clergy, 7
Kufuor, John, 165, 187

Latin America, 5, 31, 74, 91, 109, 235, 240
laws, 4–5, 30, 39, 63, 79–80, 135, 149, 161, 169, 177–78, 185
  democratic, 82
  electoral, 8
  illiberal, 36
  national, 148
  religious, 29
  traditional, 213, 259
leaders
  church-political, 88
  elected, 82
  evangelical, 15
  foreign, 16, 48
  founding, 22, 30
  institutional, 77
  Lutheran Church, 247
  Muslim, 187
  national, 188
  opposition, 3, 128, 136
  Pentecostal, 56
  Protestant, 7, 43, 180, 210
  religious, 9, 75, 125, 128, 146, 150, 184, 224, 235, 245–46
  ruling party, 9
  unelected, 192
leadership, 30, 80, 151
  foreign, 49
  political, 86, 135
  spiritual, 51

legal changes, 80, 82, 151–55
legal system, 39, 75, 135, 167
legislation, 35, 63, 122, 195
legislature, 3, 9, 39, 129–30, 158, 167, 176
  elected, 180
  independent, 32
  strong, 3
  weak, 12
Lesotho, 20, 49, 54, 59, 63, 68, 106, 190
Lesotho Catholic Bishops' Conference, 109
liberal democracy index, 192, 194, 256–57
Liberia, 59, 68, 106, 190, 253
lobbying, 35, 39, 69, 179
Lungu, Edgar, 3, 9, 125, 127–29, 134, 162
Lutheran church, 4–5, 9, 55, 81, 146, 148–51, 228–31, 246, 260

Madagascar, 51, 59, 63, 68, 80, 190
Madagascar, I Love Madagascar Party, 51
Magufuli, John, 9
Mahama, John, 165
Malawi, 7, 50–51, 54, 59, 68, 106, 110–12, 190
  Congress Liberation Party, 51
  Congress Party, 51
Marxism, 158, 161, 171–72, 189, 195
Marxism–Leninism, 166, 172, 193, 257
McClendon, Gwyneth, 139
media, 12, 80, 110, 149, 255
  censored, 12
  coverage, 255
  independent, 3, 7, 168
  social, 134, 151
  state-controlled, 182
missionaries, 17, 20, 47, 49, 55–59, 190, 210, 222
  Catholic, 59
  legacies, 231
  Protestant, 58, 225
Mkude, Telesphore, 147
mobilization, 17, 19, 21–22, 35–37, 41, 52, 118–21, 124–25, 130, 133, 155–58, 196–97, 234, 236–37
  church, 124
  democratic, 10
Mpundu, Telesphore, 128, 135
Muslim communities, 23, 47, 145, 152, 154, 179, 221, 242
Mwanawasa, Levy, 162

Namibia, 4, 59, 190
nationalism, 62, 203, 227
  economic, 162, 164–66
  Tanzanian, 227
  white, 233
newspapers, 78, 148, 171, 173
  national, 79
  private, 150, 186
  pro-government, 79
Nigeria, 58–59, 68, 190
Nkrumah, Kwame, 163, 179–82, 189
Nkurunziza, Pierre, 7
Nujoma, Sam, 5
Nyerere, Julius, 227

Oasis Declaration, 126–27
Oasis Forum, 9, 125–27
opposition, 8, 81, 125–26, 143, 150, 158, 172, 237
  nonviolent, 12
  political, 6, 11, 50, 81, 110, 122, 127, 134, 255
  public, 80
  secular, 141

parliament, 3, 73, 75, 126, 130, 140–41, 149, 157–58, 167, 175, 188
  commissions, 236
parliamentarians, 9, 36, 75, 126, 149, 158
parochialism, 153, 156, 214
parties, 24, 30–31, 39, 48–52, 54, 131–33, 137, 140, 145, 158, 171, 173–74, 186–87, 235
  nationalist, 54
  opposition, 3–4, 12, 80, 131–33, 152, 176, 186–87
  radical-right, 237–38
  religious, 51–52, 237
  ruling, 4, 10, 64, 122–23, 129, 131, 134–35, 139, 146, 166, 170, 181
pastoral letters, 27, 75, 101, 108–16, 135, 146–48, 150–51, 171–73, 176, 178, 182–83, 255
Pentecostal churches, 22, 30, 56, 127, 242
Poland, 6, 238
police, 3, 111, 128, 134–35
  anti-church, 196
policymaking, 25, 27, 32, 39, 44, 167–68, 171, 176, 178–80, 188
political attitudes, 28, 201–2, 205, 213–15, 218, 222, 225, 229, 231, 264–68

political elites, 35–37, 77, 121–26, 130, 156, 234, 236
politicians, 3, 7, 16, 30–31, 49–50, 52, 124–26, 141, 202, 237
  incumbent, 104
  liberal, 235
  opposition, 123
Portugal, 47
postindependence, 4, 45–49, 53, 61–62, 102, 160, 196, 202, 206, 214, 219
Presbyterian church, 7, 55
priests, 49, 127, 170, 210–11
Protestant churches, 9, 125, 145, 150, 154, 170, 202, 205, 221–22, 225, 227, 231
  mainline, 43, 49, 51, 53, 55–56, 86–89, 92, 98, 127, 133–34, 136–37, 170–73, 251
Protestant schools, 28, 212, 221, 226–32, 260
protests, 4, 7, 36, 61, 126, 149, 237
  peaceful, 12
  political, 174

radio stations, 3, 186
  church-owned, 148
Rawlings, Jerry, 164, 179–80, 184–86
reforms, 63–64, 104, 171, 177, 185, 191, 225
  democratic, 123, 129
  education, 62, 160–66, 171, 180, 184–87, 205, 208, 222, 224
regulations, 21, 30, 33–34, 38, 40, 46, 53–54, 94, 159, 181, 211, 222, 233, 235
regulatory power, 18–19, 31–32, 38–41, 75, 94, 98–99, 238–39, 241–42
regulatory tools, 18, 34, 38, 61, 238
religion, 23–24, 50–51, 91, 133, 150, 172, 209, 212, 214, 223, 247, 260
  freedom of, 195
  traditional, 47
religiosity, 140, 153, 215, 231, 258, 264–68
religious liberty, 5, 42
religious nativism, 233
the Republic of the Congo, 53, 58–59, 63, 68, 190
rights, 6, 8, 11–13, 79, 110, 147, 149, 152–53, 189, 218, 243–44, 255
  civil, 32, 159
  equal, 213, 259

rights (cont.)
  legal, 13, 189
  political, 29, 36, 109, 147
  women's, 213, 215–18, 231–32, 259, 264–68
  workers', 155
risk, 16–18, 33–34, 41, 75, 98–100, 123, 233
  institutional, 97
  regulatory, 86
  security, 123
Rwanda, 20, 63, 68, 84, 103, 106, 190

Sata, Michael, 125, 127, 162, 176
school fees, 40–41, 67, 76, 84, 101, 103–4, 107–8, 111–12, 206, 223, 251
  abolition, 102, 107–8, 206
  boarding, 211
  primary, 101, 103–4, 108, 113, 208–9, 223, 256
  public, 114
  removal, 101–8, 111–17, 212, 256
school systems, 40, 64, 86, 100, 157, 243
  national, 169
  public, 66–67, 112
schools
  church-affiliated, 201
  government, 221, 223
  Islamic, 22, 202, 242
  missionary, 20, 55–59, 62–63, 67, 102, 165, 169, 180, 183, 205, 222–24
  nationalized, 63, 94, 224
  parochial, 28
  primary, 28, 102–8, 111–16, 169, 175, 201, 205–12, 214–15, 218–21, 253, 255, 258
  private, 67, 102–4
  public, 28, 67, 101–5, 115, 170, 182, 202, 255
  religious, 100, 184, 202, 231
  secondary, 20, 64–65, 67, 89, 102, 104, 167, 172–73, 177–78, 180–81, 215, 250–52, 258
  state-run, 201–4, 207–8, 212, 214–15, 222–27, 231, 243
secularization, 15, 193
Senegal, 68
service provision, 24, 239, 252
  public, 182, 204, 221
  social, 86, 98
Shoo, Fredrick, 147, 151
Sierra Leone, 242

Slaa, Wilbroad, 146
social movements, 4, 49, 51, 168, 181
  antidemocratic, 233
  democratic, 14
  nationalist, 48, 50
  political, 233
  right-wing, 238
social services, 20, 31, 54, 108, 151, 240, 247
  church-provided, 18, 117
socialism, 64, 166–68, 171–74
socialist, 166, 180
South Africa, 64, 68, 80, 190, 253
South Korea, 6
South Sudan, 68, 80
state control, 157, 233, 242
subsidies, 19, 46, 57, 59, 100–1
  educational, 48, 58
  financial, 40
Swahili, 223, 226–27, 229, 245, 261
syllabi, 64, 170–73, 188, 195, 206
  ecumenical, 210

Talon, Patrice, 4
Tanzania, 9, 25–28, 51, 118–22, 145–48, 151–56, 201–2, 221–25, 228–32, 246–47, 260–61
  Chama cha Demokrasia na Maendeleo (CHADEMA), 146, 152
  Chama Cha Mapinduzi (CCM), 146
  Christian Council of, 145, 150, 152, 154
  churches in, 27, 122, 145–47, 150–51, 156
  Civic United Front, 51
  colonial, 223
  Evangelical Lutheran Church of, 82, 147, 149
  Lutheran church, 122
  post-independence, 204
  Tanzania Episcopal Conference (TEC), 145–48, 151–52
teachers, 38, 61, 63–64, 67, 159, 161, 172, 190–91, 204, 206, 210–11, 219, 221, 223
  appointment of, 38, 159, 168–69, 175, 206, 209, 223
  Catholic, 209
  disciplining of, 63, 159, 169, 186, 206, 209–10
  dismissal, 210, 224

salaries, 57, 67, 224, 242
training, 168, 173
training colleges, 172
theology, 15, 55, 85, 105
political, 21, 23, 42
threats, 9, 15–16, 127, 148–50
coercive, 170
political, 145
Timor-Leste, 240
Togo, 53, 58, 68, 80, 106, 112, 190
trade unions, 4, 10–11, 74, 133, 240
activism, 10–12
federations, 11

Uganda, 20, 50–53, 59, 63–64, 68, 103, 106, 190
Church of, 68
Democratic Party, 50–51
United States, 15, 233, 235

Varieties of Democracy (VDEM), 51, 162, 165, 192, 256–57, 262
Vatican, 47, 50, 58
Vatican II, 42
Vatican, Second Council, 5, 23, 55
violence, 4, 36, 149
institutional, 111
military, 240
state, 80
voters, 16, 156, 167
evangelical, 233, 235
voting, 9, 16, 35–36, 51, 122–24, 130, 137–41, 143, 149, 183

women, 202, 212–19, 221, 225, 231–32, 259, 263–68
conservative, 218
Worker's Defense Committees, 184
World Christian Database, 83, 85, 251–54
World War II, 48, 58–59, 231

Zambia, 25–26, 80, 118, 124–27, 129–30, 134–40, 145–47, 151–53, 158–73, 176–79, 205–6, 208–13, 215–22, 231–32, 259
budget crisis, 177
Catholic church, 205
Catholic schools, 220–21, 243
church leaders, 171, 174
churches in, 125, 130, 133, 139, 141, 145, 156, 168, 172
Conference of Catholic Bishops, 4, 127, 141
Congress of Trade Unions, 131–34
Council of Churches, 9, 125–28, 134–35, 138, 141, 172
Education Act, 169, 181, 224
Education Fellowship of, 9, 125–28, 131–35
Episcopal Conference, 172
Evangelical Fellowship of, 9, 125, 172
government, 28, 206, 210
Law Association of, 125–26, 141
major religious groups, 143
Ministry of Education, 175–77, 205–6
Movement for Multiparty Democracy (MMD), 126, 161–62, 168, 174–78
Patriotic Front (PF), 127, 131–40, 143, 162, 176–79
political parties, 178
Protestants, 143
United Church of, 127, 131, 173
United National Independence Party (UNIP), 161, 167–69, 171–72
United Party for National Development (UPND), 128, 131–33, 135, 140, 144
White Fathers, 205
Zambian Humanism, 167, 169, 220
Zimbabwe, 51, 59–61, 63, 68, 190
Zimbabwe African National Union-Patriotic Front, 51

Cambridge Studies in Comparative Politics

OTHER BOOKS IN THE SERIES (continued from page ii)

Isabel M. Perera, *The Welfare Workforce: Why Mental Health Care Varies Across Affluent Democracies*
Graeme Blair, Fotini Christia, and Jeremy M. Weinstein, *Crime, Insecurity, and Community Policing: Experiments on Building Trust*
Georgia Kernell, *Inside Parties: How Party Rules Shape Membership and Responsiveness*
Volha Charnysh, *Uprooted: How post-WWII Population Transfers Remade Europe*
Catherine Boone, *Inequality and Political Cleavage in Africa: Regionalism by Design*
Soledad Artiz Prillaman, *The Patriarchal Political Order: The Making and Unraveling of the Gendered Participation Gap in India*
Charlotte Cavaillé, *Fair Enough?: Support for Redistribution in the Age of Inequality*
Noah L. Nathan, *The Scarce State: Inequality and Political Power in the Hinterland*
Scott de Marchi and Michael Laver, *The Governance Cycle in Parliamentary Democracies: A Computational Social Science Approach*
Egor Lazarev, *State-Building as Lawfare: Custom, Sharia, and State Law in Postwar Chechnya*
Lorenza B. Fontana, *Recognition Politics: Indigenous Rights and Ethnic Conflict in the Andes*
Martha Wilfahrt, *Precolonial Legacies in Postcolonial Politics: Representation and Redistribution in Decentralized West Africa*
Sidney Tarrow, *Power in Movement: Social Movements and Contentious Politics*
Victor C. Shih, *Coalitions of the Weak: Elite Politics in China from Mao's Stratagem to the Rise of Xi*
Torben Iversen and Philipp Rehm, *Big Data and the Welfare State: How the Information Revolution Threatens Social Solidarity*
Eduardo Moncada, *Resisting Extortion: Victims, Criminals and States in Latin America*
Jacob S. Hacker, Alexander Hertel-Fernandez, Paul Pierson, and Kathleen Thelen, *The American Political Economy: Politics, Markets, and Power*
Lily Tsai, *When People want Punishment: Retributive Justice and the Puzzle of Authoritarian Popularity*
Kevin Mazur, *Revolution in Syria: Identity, Networks, and Repression*
Andreas Wiedemann, *Indebted Societies: Credit and Welfare in Rich Democracies*
Antje Ellerman, *The Comparative Politics of Immigration: Policy Choices in Germany, Canada, Switzerland, and the United States*
Michael Albertus, *Property without Rights: Origins and Consequences of the Property Rights Gap*
Ben W. Ansell and Johannes Lindvall, *Inward Conquest: The Political Origins of Modern Public Services*
Yanilda María González, *Authoritarian Police in Democracy: Contested Security in Latin America*
Robert H. Bates, *The Political Economy of Development: A Game Theoretic Approach*
Guillermo Trejo and Sandra Ley, *Votes, Drugs, and Violence: The Political Logic of Criminal Wars in Mexico*

Janet I. Lewis, *How Insurgency Begins: Rebel Group Formation in Uganda and Beyond*
David Szakonyi *Politics for Profit: Business, Elections, and Policymaking in Russia*
Mai Hassan, *Regime Threats and State Solutions: Bureaucratic Loyalty and Embeddedness in Kenya*
Daniel C. Mattingly, *The Art of Political Control in China*
Adam Michael Auerbach, *Demanding Development: The Politics of Public Goods Provision in India's Urban Slums*
Gwyneth H. McClendon and Rachel Beatty Riedl, *From Pews to Politics in Africa: Religious Sermons and Political Behavior*
David Rueda and Daniel Stegmueller, *Who Wants What? Redistribution Preferences in Comparative Perspective*
Yue Hou, *The Private Sector in Public Office: Selective Property Rights in China*
Thad Dunning et al., *Information, Accountability, and Cumulative Learning: Lessons from Metaketa I*
Ignacio Sánchez-Cuenca, *The Historical Roots of Political Violence: Revolutionary Terrorism in Affluent Countries*
G. Bingham Powell Jr., *Ideological Representation Achieved and Astray: Elections, Institutions, and the Breakdown of Ideological Congruence in Parliamentary Democracies*
Noah L. Nathan, *Electoral Politics and Africa's Urban Transition: Class and Ethnicity in Ghana*
S. Erdem Aytaç and Susan C. Stokes, *Why Bother? Rethinking Participation in Elections and Protests*
Deborah J. Yashar, *Homicidal Ecologies: Illicit Economies and Complicit States in Latin America*
Simeon Nichter, *Votes for Survival: Relational Clientelism in Latin America*
Santiago Anria, *When Movements Become Parties: The Bolivian MAS in Comparative Perspective*
Benjamin Lessing, *Making Peace in Drug Wars: Crackdowns and Cartels in Latin America*
Richard A. Nielsen, *Deadly Clerics: Blocked Ambition and the Paths to Jihad*
Kanchan Chandra, *Why Ethnic Parties Succeed: Patronage and Ethnic Head Counts in India*
Mary E. Gallagher, *Authoritarian Legality in China: Law, Workers, and the State*
Karen Jusko, *Who Speaks for the Poor? Electoral Geography, Party Entry, and Representation*
Alisha C. Holland, *Forbearance as Redistribution: The Politics of Informal Welfare in Latin America*
John D. Huber, *Exclusion by Elections: Inequality, Ethnic Identity, and Democracy*
Laia Balcells, *Rivalry and Revenge: The Politics of Violence during Civil War*
Daniel Ziblatt, *Conservative Parties and the Birth of Democracy*
Gretchen Helmke, *Institutions on the Edge: The Origins and Consequences of Inter-Branch Crises in Latin America*
Ana Arjona, *Rebelocracy: Social Order in the Colombian Civil War*
Rory Truex, *Making Autocracy Work: Representation and Responsiveness in Modern China*
Daniel Corstange, *The Price of a Vote in the Middle East: Clientelism and Communal Politics in Lebanon and Yemen*

Philipp Rehm, *Risk Inequality and Welfare States: Social Policy Preferences, Development, and Dynamics*
Prerna Singh, *How Solidarity Works for Welfare: Subnationalism and Social Development in India*
Alberto Diaz-Cayeros, Federico Estévez, and Beatriz Magaloni, *The Political Logic of Poverty Relief: Electoral Strategies and Social Policy in Mexico*
Sarah Zukerman Daly, *Organized Violence after Civil War: The Geography of Recruitment in Latin America*
Melanie Manion, *Information for Autocrats: Representation in Chinese Local Congresses*
Kate Baldwin, *The Paradox of Traditional Chiefs in Democratic Africa*
Michael Albertus, *Autocracy and Redistribution: The Politics of Land Reform*
Jesse Driscoll, *Warlords and Coalition Politics in Post-Soviet States*
Isabela Mares, *From Open Secrets to Secret Voting: Democratic Electoral Reforms and Voter Autonomy*
Carles Boix, *Political Order and Inequality: Their Foundations and their Consequences for Human Welfare*
Kenneth M. Roberts, *Changing Course in Latin America: Party Systems in the Neoliberal Era*
Yuhua Wang, *Tying the Autocrat's Hand: The Rise of the Rule of Law in China*
Ben W. Ansell and David J. Samuels, *Inequality and Democratization: An Elite-Competition Approach*
Kevin M. Morrison, *Nontaxation and Representation: The Fiscal Foundations of Political Stability*
Tariq Thachil, *Elite Parties, Poor Voters: How Social Services Win Votes in India*
Timothy Hellwig, *Globalization and Mass Politics: Retaining the Room to Maneuver*
Roger Schoenman, *Networks and Institutions in Europe's Emerging Markets*
Kathleen Thelen, *Varieties of Liberalization and the New Politics of Social Solidarity*
Catherine Boone, *Property and Political Order in Africa: Land Rights and the Structure of Politics*
Ken Kollman, *Perils of Centralization: Lessons from Church, State, and Corporation*
Michael Hechter, *Alien Rule*
Susan C. Stokes, Thad Dunning, Marcelo Nazareno, and Valeria Brusco, *Brokers, Voters, and Clientelism: The Puzzle of Distributive Politics*
Ben Ross Schneider, *Hierarchical Capitalism in Latin America: Business, Labor, and the Challenges of Equitable Development*
Richard M. Locke, *The Promise and Limits of Private Power: Promoting Labor Standards in a Global Economy*
Christopher Adolph, *Bankers, Bureaucrats, and Central Bank Politics: The Myth of Neutrality*
Stephen B. Kaplan, *Globalization and Austerity Politics in Latin America*
Edward L. Gibson, *Boundary Control: Subnational Authoritarianism in Federal Democracies*
Andreas Wimmer, *Waves of War: Nationalism, State Formation, and Ethnic Exclusion in the Modern World*
Leonardo R. Arriola, *Multi-Ethnic Coalitions in Africa: Business Financing of Opposition Election Campaigns*
Milan W. Svolik, *The Politics of Authoritarian Rule*

Guillermo Trejo, *Popular Movements in Autocracies: Religion, Repression, and Indigenous Collective Action in Mexico*
Cathie Jo Martin and Duane Swank, *The Political Construction of Business Interests: Coordination, Growth, and Equality*
Pablo Beramendi, *The Political Geography of Inequality: Regions and Redistribution*
Roger D. Petersen, *Western Intervention in the Balkans: The Strategic Use of Emotion in Conflict*
Jane R. Gingrich, *Making Markets in the Welfare State: The Politics of Varying Market Reforms*
Sidney Tarrow, *Power in Movement: Social Movements and Contentious Politics, Revised and Updated Third Edition*
Pepper D. Culpepper, *Quiet Politics and Business Power: Corporate Control in Europe and Japan*
Eric C. C. Chang, Mark Andreas Kayser, Drew A. Linzer, and Ronald Rogowski, *Electoral Systems and the Balance of Consumer-Producer Power*
Karen E. Ferree, *Framing the Race in South Africa: The Political Origins of Racial Census Elections*
Layna Mosley, *Labor Rights and Multinational Production*
Pauline Jones Luong and Erika Weinthal, *Oil is Not a Curse: Ownership Structure and Institutions in Soviet Successor States*
Dan Slater, *Ordering Power: Contentious Politics and Authoritarian Leviathans in Southeast Asia*
Sven Steinmo, *The Evolution of Modern States: Sweden, Japan, and the United States*
Stephen E. Hanson, *Post-Imperial Democracies: Ideology and Party Formation in Third Republic France, Weimar Germany, and Post-Soviet Russia*
Timothy Frye, *Building States and Markets After Communism: The Perils of Polarized Democracy*
Lauren M. MacLean, *Informal Institutions and Citizenship in Rural Africa: Risk and Reciprocity in Ghana and Côte d'Ivoire*
Ben W. Ansell, *From the Ballot to the Blackboard: The Redistributive Political Economy of Education*
Herbert Kitschelt, Kirk A. Hawkins, Juan Pablo Luna, Guillermo Rosas, and Elizabeth J. Zechmeister, *Latin American Party Systems*
James Mahoney, *Colonialism and Postcolonial Development: Spanish America in Comparative Perspective*
Monika Nalepa, *Skeletons in the Closet: Transitional Justice in Post-Communist Europe*
Orit Kedar, *Voting for Policy, Not Parties: How Voters Compensate for Power Sharing*
Maria Victoria Murillo, *Political Competition, Partisanship, and Policy Making in Latin American Public Utilities*
Henry Farrell, *The Political Economy of Trust: Institutions, Interests, and Inter-Firm Cooperation in Italy and Germany*
Andy Baker, *The Market and the Masses in Latin America: Policy Reform and Consumption in Liberalizing Economies*
Mark Hallerberg, Rolf Ranier Strauch, and Jürgen von Hagen, *Fiscal Governance in Europe*
Mark Irving Lichbach and Alan S. Zuckerman, eds., *Comparative Politics: Rationality, Culture, and Structure*, 2nd edition

John M. Carey, *Legislative Voting and Accountability*
Thad Dunning, *Crude Democracy: Natural Resource Wealth and Political Regimes*
Scott Gehlbach, *Representation through Taxation: Revenue, Politics, and Development in Postcommunist States*
Margarita Estevez-Abe, *Welfare and Capitalism in Postwar Japan: Party, Bureaucracy, and Business*
Henry E. Hale, *The Foundations of Ethnic Politics: Separatism of States and Nations in Eurasia and the World*
Bonnie M. Meguid, *Party Competition between Unequals: Strategies and Electoral Fortunes in Western Europe*
Austin Smith et al, *Selected Works of Michael Wallerstein*
Robert H. Bates, *When Things Fell Apart: State Failure in Late-Century Africa*
Lily L. Tsai, *Accountability without Democracy: How Solidary Groups Provide Public Goods in Rural China*
Aníbal Pérez-Liñán, *Presidential Impeachment and the New Political Instability in Latin America*
Daniel Treisman, *The Architecture of Government: Rethinking Political Decentralization*
Christian Davenport, *State Repression and the Domestic Democratic Peace*
Marc Howard Ross, *Cultural Contestation in Ethnic Conflict*
Anna Grzymala-Busse, *Rebuilding Leviathan: Party Competition and State Exploitation in Post-Communist Democracies*
José Antonio Cheibub, *Presidentialism, Parliamentarism, and Democracy*
Jeremy M. Weinstein, *Inside Rebellion: The Politics of Insurgent Violence*
Beatriz Magaloni, *Voting for Autocracy: Hegemonic Party Survival and its Demise in Mexico*
Alberto Diaz-Cayeros, *Federalism, Fiscal Authority, and Centralization in Latin America*
Julia Lynch, *Age in the Welfare State: The Origins of Social Spending on Pensioners, Workers, and Children*
Stathis Kalyvas, *The Logic of Violence in Civil War*
Regina Smyth, *Candidate Strategies and Electoral Competition in the Russian Federation: Democracy without Foundation*
Jason Wittenberg, *Crucibles of Political Loyalty: Church Institutions and Electoral Continuity in Hungary*
Isabela Mares, *Taxation, Wage Bargaining, and Unemployment*
Joshua Tucker, *Regional Economic Voting: Russia, Poland, Hungary, Slovakia and the Czech Republic, 1990–1999*
M. Steven Fish, *Democracy Derailed in Russia: The Failure of Open Politics*
Charles Tilly, *Trust and Rule*
Torben Iversen, *Capitalism, Democracy, and Welfare*
Gretchen Helmke, *Courts Under Constraints: Judges, Generals, and Presidents in Argentina*
Yoshiko Herrera, *Imagined Economies: The Sources of Russian Regionalism*
Michael Bratton, Robert Mattes, and E. Gyimah-Boadi, *Public Opinion, Democracy, and Market Reform in Africa*
Kathleen Thelen, *How Institutions Evolve: The Political Economy of Skills in Germany, Britain, the United States, and Japan*
Joseph Jupille, *Procedural Politics: Issues, Influence, and Institutional Choice in the European Union*

Stephen I. Wilkinson, *Votes and Violence: Electoral Competition and Ethnic Riots in India*
Daniele Caramani, *The Nationalization of Politics: The Formation of National Electorates and Party Systems in Europe*
Kanchan Chandra, *Why Ethnic Parties Succeed: Patronage and Ethnic Headcounts in India*
Catherine Boone, *Political Topographies of the African State: Territorial Authority and Institutional Change*
Junko Kato, *Regressive Taxation and the Welfare State*
Evan Lieberman, *Race and Regionalism in the Politics of Taxation in Brazil and South Africa*
Elisabeth J. Wood, *Insurgent Collective Action and Civil War in El Salvador*
Carles Boix, *Democracy and Redistribution*
Beverly Silver, *Forces of Labor: Workers' Movements and Globalization since 1870*
Lyle Scruggs, *Sustaining Abundance: Environmental Performance in Industrial Democracies*
Layna Mosley, *Global Capital and National Governments*
James Mahoney and Dietrich Rueschemeyer, eds., *Historical Analysis and the Social Sciences*
John D. Huber and Charles R. Shipan, *Deliberate Discretion? The Institutional Foundations of Bureaucratic Autonomy*
Roger D. Petersen, *Understanding Ethnic Violence: Fear, Hatred, and Resentment in Twentieth-Century Eastern Europe*
Lisa Baldez, *Why Women Protest? Women's Movements in Chile*
Fabrice E. Lehoucq and Ivan Molina, *Stuffing the Ballot Box: Fraud, Electoral Reform, and Democratization in Costa Rica*
Pauline Jones Luong, *Institutional Change and Political Continuity in Post-Soviet Central Asia*
Scott Morgenstern and Benito Nacif, eds., *Legislative Politics in Latin America*
Jefferey M. Sellers, *Governing from Below: Urban Regions and the Global Economy*
Anna Grzymala-Busse, *Redeeming the Communist Past: The Regeneration of Communist Parties in East Central Europe*
Robert F. Franzese, *Macroeconomic Policies of Developed Democracies*
Duane Swank, *Global Capital, Political Institutions, and Policy Change in Developed Welfare States*
Mark Beissinger, *Nationalist Mobilization and the Collapse of the Soviet State*
David C. Kang, *Crony Capitalism: Corruption and Capitalism in South Korea and the Philippines*
Amie Kreppel, *The European Parliament and the Supranational Party System*
Simona Piattoni, ed., *Clientelism, Interests, and Democratic Representation*
Joel S. Migdal, *State in Society: Studying How States and Societies Constitute One Another*
Nancy Bermeo, ed., *Unemployment in the New Europe*
Susan C. Stokes, *Mandates and Democracy: Neoliberalism by Surprise in Latin America*
Susan C. Stokes, ed., *Public Support for Market Reforms in New Democracies*
Richard Snyder, *Politics after Neoliberalism: Reregulation in Mexico*
Jeff Goodwin, *No Other Way Out: States and Revolutionary Movements*
Maria Victoria Murillo, *Labor Unions, Partisan Coalitions, and Market Reforms in Latin America*

Stefano Bartolini, *The Political Mobilization of the European Left, 1860–1980: The Class Cleavage*
Ton Notermans, *Money, Markets, and the State: Social Democratic Economic Policies since 1918*
Gerald Easter, *Reconstructing the State: Personal Networks and Elite Identity*
Ruth Berins Collier, *Paths toward Democracy: The Working Class and Elites in Western Europe and South America*
Wolfgang C. Müller and Kaare Strøm, *Policy, Office, or Votes?*
Herbert Kitschelt, Zdenka Mansfeldova, Radek Markowski, and Gabor Toka, *Post-Communist Party Systems*
Herbert Kitschelt, Peter Lange, Gary Marks, and John D. Stephens, eds., *Continuity and Change in Contemporary Capitalism*
Carles Boix, *Political Parties, Growth, and Equality: Conservative and Social Democratic Economic Strategies in the World Economy*
Sidney Tarrow, *Power in Movement: Social Movements and Contentious Politics, Revised and Updated Fourth Edition*
Geoffrey Garrett, *Partisan Politics in the Global Economy*
Anthony W. Marx, *Making Race, Making Nations: A Comparison of South Africa, the United States, and Brazil*
Michael Bratton and Nicolas van de Walle, *Democratic Experiments in Africa: Regime Transitions in Comparative Perspective*
J. Rogers Hollingsworth and Robert Boyer, eds., *Contemporary Capitalism: The Embeddedness of Institutions*
Miriam Golden, *Heroic Defeats: The Politics of Job Loss*
Robert O. Keohane and Helen B. Milner, eds., *Internationalization and Domestic Politics*
Frances Hagopian, *Traditional Politics and Regime Change in Brazil*
David Knoke, Franz Urban Pappi, Jeffrey Broadbent, and Yutaka Tsujinaka, eds., *Comparing Policy Networks*
Doug McAdam, John McCarthy, and Mayer Zald, eds., *Comparative Perspectives on Social Movements*
Donatella della Porta, *Social Movements, Political Violence, and the State*
Roberto Franzosi, *The Puzzle of Strikes: Class and State Strategies in Postwar Italy*
Ashutosh Varshney, *Democracy, Development, and the Countryside*
Marino Regini, *Uncertain Boundaries: The Social and Political Construction of European Economies*
Paul Pierson, *Dismantling the Welfare State? Reagan, Thatcher, and the Politics of Retrenchment*
Theda Skocpol, *Social Revolutions in the Modern World*
Joel S. Migdal, Atul Kohli, and Vivienne Shue, eds., *State Power and Social Forces: Domination and Transformation in the Third World*
Herbert Kitschelt, *The Transformation of European Social Democracy*
Thomas Janoski and Alexander M. Hicks, eds., *The Comparative Political Economy of the Welfare State*
Catherine Boone, *Merchant Capital and the Roots of State Power in Senegal, 1930–1985*
Sven Steinmo, Kathleen Thelen, and Frank Longstreth, eds., *Structuring Politics: Historical Institutionalism in Comparative Analysis*
David D. Laitin, *Language Repertoires and State Construction in Africa*

For EU product safety concerns, contact us at Calle de José Abascal, 56–1°,
28003 Madrid, Spain or eugpsr@cambridge.org.

www.ingramcontent.com/pod-product-compliance
Lightning Source LLC
LaVergne TN
LVHW011801060526
838200LV00053B/3646